For a generation, the history of the *ancien régime* has been written from the perspective of the *Annales* school, with its emphasis on long-term economic and cultural factors in shaping the development of early modern France. In this detailed study, Henry Heller challenges such a paradigm and assembles a huge range of information about technical innovation and ideas of improvement in sixteenth-century France. Emphasizing the role of state intervention in the economy, the development of science and technology, and recent research into early modern proto-industrialization, Heller counters notions of a France mired in an archaic, determinist *mentalité*. Despite the tides of religious fanaticism and seigneurial reaction, the period of the religious wars saw a surprising degree of economic, technological and scientific innovation, making possible the consolidation of capitalism in French society during the reign of Henri IV.

CAMBRIDGE STUDIES IN EARLY MODERN HISTORY

Labour, science and technology
in France, 1500–1620

CAMBRIDGE STUDIES IN EARLY MODERN HISTORY

Edited by Professor Sir John Elliott, University of Oxford, Professor Olwen Hufton, Harvard University, and Professor H.G. Koenigsberger

The idea of an 'early modern' period of European history from the fifteenth to the late eighteenth century is now widely accepted among historians. The purpose of Cambridge Studies in Early Modern History is to publish monographs and studies which illuminate the character of the period as a whole, and in particular focus attention on a dominant theme within it, the interplay of continuity and change as they are presented by the continuity of medieval ideas, political and social organization, and by the impact of new ideas, new methods and new demands on the traditional structure.

For a list of titles published in the series, please see end of book

Labour, science and technology in France, 1500–1620

HENRY HELLER

University of Manitoba

CAMBRIDGE
UNIVERSITY PRESS

Published by the Press Syndicate of the University of Cambridge
The Pitt Building, Trumpington Street, Cambridge CB2 1RP
40 West 20th Street, New York, NY 10011–4211, USA
10 Stamford Road, Oakleigh, Melbourne 3166, Australia

First published 1996

Printed in Great Britain at the University Press, Cambridge

A catalogue record for this book is available from the British Library

Library of Congress cataloguing in publication data

Heller, Henry.
Labour, science and technology in France / Henry Heller.
p.   cm. – (Cambridge studies in early modern history)
Includes bibliographical references and index.
ISBN 0 521 55031 9 (hc)
1. Technological innovations – Economic aspects – France – History – 16th
century.
2. Technology and state – France – History – 16th century.
3. Industrialization – France – History – 16th century.
4. Labour supply – France – History – 16th century.
5. France – Economic policy. 6. France – History – 16th century.
I. Title. II. Series.
HC280.T4H45 1996
338'.064'094409031 – dc20   95–6125   CIP

ISBN 0·521 55031 9 hardback

To my beloved parents
Dora and Irving

Contents

Illustrations

Preface

For many years the history of France in the *ancien régime* has been written from the perspective of the *Annales*. Particularly important to the conceptualization of this epoch have been the writings of Fernand Braudel and Emmanuel Le Roy Ladurie, who have emphasized the importance of the notion of *la longue durée* or of long-term economic and cultural factors in shaping the history of early modern France. The following work represents a critique of this perspective based on a renewed appreciation of the role of the state, on Marx's concept of primitive accumulation, and recent research on early modern proto-industrialization.

I am especially indebted to my colleague Mark Gabbert, who has helped me to think through some of the theoretical problems raised in the course of this investigation. I am grateful to James McConica and Gillian Lewis for permitting me to present some of the ideas in this book in their research seminar on early modern Europe at All Souls College, Oxford University, in 1992. I recall with pleasure the hospitality of Bob Scribner at Clare College, Cambridge, who allowed me to try out my ideas on his graduate students as well. I would also like to thank the librarians of the Bibliothèque Nationale and Bodleian and University of Manitoba libraries, without whose assistance this work would have been impossible. The editorial skill of Margaret Deith of the Cambridge University Press must be acknowledged. My scholarly efforts over the years have been generously supported by the Social Science and Humanities Research Council. The following manuscript has been written with the help of a research and study leave grant from that body.

Abbreviations

AN	Archives Nationales
BHR	*Bibliothèque d'humanisme et renaissance*
BHVP	Bibliothèque de l'histoire de la ville de Paris
BN	Bibliothèque Nationale
BSHPF	*Bulletin de la société de l'histoire du protestantisme français*
Bull. soc. hist. Paris	*Bulletin de la société de l'histoire de Paris*
Coll. Lamoignon	Collection Lamoignon
DBF	*Dictionnaire de biographie française*
DNB	*Dictionary of National Biography*
DSB	*Dictionary of Scientific Biography*
Haag	Eugène and Emile Haag, *La France protestante*
Herminjard	A.L. Herminjard, *Correspondence des réformateurs dans les pays de langue française*
Isambert, *Recueil général*	François André Isambert, *Recueil général des anciennes lois françaises*
Min. Cent.	Minutier Centrale
MSHP	*Mémoires de la sociéte de l'histoire de Paris*
Nouv. biog. univ. ed. Michaud	*Nouvelle biographie universelle*, ed. L.-G. Michaud
Recueil des poésies, ed. Montaiglon	*Recueil des poésies françoises des XVᵉ et XVIᵉ siècles*, ed. Anatole de Courde de Montaiglon
Reg. BVP	*Registres des délibérations du Bureau de la ville de Paris*, ed. François Bonnardot *et al.*

Introduction

Bernard Palissy is the hero of the final chapter of *The Conquest of Poverty: The Calvinist Revolt in Sixteenth Century France* which I published in 1986.[1] In that book I represented Palissy as an isolated figure who, while appalled by the tragedy of the onset of civil war, was nevertheless unique in his understanding of the economic and social problems which had helped to provoke the crisis. While retreating into a religious vision in the face of an increasingly uncertain future, Palissy nevertheless singled out the agrarian problem as a key to France's troubles. Under-investment in agriculture, responsible for the grain shortages and the high cost of food, was at the heart of the difficulties which were exacerbating the political and religious crisis into which France had fallen.

I portrayed Palissy as more or less a lone voice and saw his proposed remedy of an agrarian capitalism as utopian in the French context. As I depicted it, the ongoing strength of seigneurialism and the absorption of the middle class into the ranks of the notables of the expanding state, foreclosed the possibility of a capitalist breakthrough in agriculture and a resolution of France's economic problems.

At a certain level there continues to be a certain truth to this view of France in the *ancien régime*. However, in pursuing my research on the wars of religion, I began to have doubts as to whether Palissy was quite the isolated figure I had imagined him to have been. By the middle of the sixteenth century France was on the threshold of a deep crisis. Were there not perhaps other Frenchmen beside Palissy who perceived the need to improve the productivity of French agriculture?[2] Were there not possibly others, who, confronted by shrinking profit margins in industry, might have cast about for fresh answers? It seemed inconceivable that the monarchy, itself increasingly hard-pressed financially, would not have seen the need to promote economic innovation as a way out of its crisis.

These questions did not come to me out of a vacuum, I must hasten to add. Already in the 1970s I had been much affected by reading Charles Webster's *Great Instauration*, which demonstrated the close tie between English Puritanism,

---

[1]   Leiden.

[2]   See additional evidence of a concern with agricultural improvement in Heller, *Iron and Blood: Civil Wars in Sixteenth Century France* (Montreal, 1991), pp. 52–3.

the desire for social and economic improvement and the rising interest in Baconian science.[3] If seventeenth-century Calvinists in England had made these connections, was it not possible that similar ideas might have surfaced in France during its period of political and religious turmoil in the latter half of the sixteenth century? Likewise in that decade, I was influenced by Joan Thirsk's *Economic Policy and Projects*.[4] In that work Thirsk showed that the English government, in the face of the negative economic conjuncture of the later half of the sixteenth century, pursued a policy of economic protectionism, patents, monopolies and subsidies to stimulate the English economy. It was already well known that the government of Henri IV did likewise in the aftermath of the religious wars and growing English and Dutch economic success. It occurred to me that this kind of economic intervention might have begun even earlier in France and have its own history. It was with these questions in mind that I set off for a summer's research in 1989 into the Bibliothèque Nationale and Archives Nationales. On that first trip I was able to turn up a good deal of interesting material. But the highlight was certainly microfilm manuscript 63 of the Collection Lenain in the Archives Nationales. Among other things this manuscript contained a list of inventions patented by the crown during the wars of religion and in its immediate aftermath. This find revealed that the French crown during the reign of Charles IX, like the English government under Elizabeth, was, indeed, pursuing a policy of state-supported economic development in the face of the negative economic conjuncture of the late sixteenth century.

Most striking about the Lenain manuscript was the number of patents for new machines or processes in both agriculture and industry. Naturally, we connected this inventory of new patents with the mechanical inventions to be found in Jacques Besson's ground-breaking *Théâtre des machines*, a manuscript of which was presented to Charles IX in 1569. Besson's work was the first in a series of technological treatises published during the wars of religion. What was the reason for this notable interest in new inventions at this time? In part a concern with improvements in military technology could account for it. But, as a matter of fact, in Besson's work or in that of his nearest rival, Agostino Ramelli, military machines play an entirely secondary role. Most of the machines conceived by these two inventors were designed to do productive work.

My interest in Renaissance technology dates back to the days I sat in the history of science seminar of Henry Guerlac in graduate school at Cornell University. I remember the fascination I felt looking at the engravings of early modern machinery in the books I was then reading. What struck me at the time was the cleverness of these machines, which seemed to be the product of a creative impulse which was barely to be distinguished from the aesthetic inspiration of the

---

[3]   *The Great Instauration: Science, Medicine and Reform, 1626–1660* (London, 1975).
[4]   *Economic Policy and Projects: The Development of a Consumer Society in Early Modern England* (Oxford, 1978).

artists of the period. Both these marvellous machines and the idealized paintings of the Renaissance masters appeared to be inspired by a similar attempt to escape from the limitations of common existence. On the other hand, the specifically economic motivation behind the invention of such machinery, while it continued to fascinate, escaped me.

However, the economic interest in new machines in the context of the religious wars now seemed perfectly evident as I continued my archival research in subsequent trips to France. The introduction of machinery could be one way of cheapening the cost of labour and enhancing profitability. It was one possible path out of a situation of economic stagnation which characterized the second half of the sixteenth century. Whether such technological initiatives could lead to such an issue in the concrete circumstances of the French economy at this juncture is another matter. Indeed, I came to the realization that the reorganization of the workforce or forcing it to work longer or harder might serve as an alternative or complement to the introduction of new technology as a way of enhancing profitability. Nevertheless, the idea of linking up the history of technology and economic history after all these years was an enthralling one.

But this notion of enhancing the productivity of labour led me towards another aspect of the problem. If there was an increasing interest in new technology in this period, this somehow must have been related to the growing availability of labour which could work such machines. Looking at the engravings of Renaissance machinery in graduate school, I recall staring at the anonymous little men pictured at work around these machines, asking myself how one could ever get at the history of such obscure figures. Gradually, as I came to think more about the dispossession of the peasantry during the religious wars, I came to realize the probable connection between the rising interest in technology and the growing availability of wage labour.

For one of the striking things about the period of the religious wars is that, despite their destructiveness, the bourgeoisie actually seems to have become stronger rather than weaker as the conflict proceeded. How can this have been in the context of so much material destruction? As my research unfolded it occurred to me that, despite the devastation of the wars, it was not only the acquisition of land through the dispossession of the peasantry, but also the increasing availability of pools of exploitable labour which might help, among other factors, to explain the phenomenon of growing bourgeois strength. Underneath the apparent archaism of seigneurial reaction, the period of the religious wars was in fact a period of real capitalist advance.

In order to study the development of wage labour in the sixteenth century I determined to concentrate on its development in the city of Paris and the surrounding Ile-de-France. The Ile-de-France was the site of a major transfer of property out of the hands of subsistence peasants into the possession of an urban and rural bourgeoisie. The Parisian bourgeoisie was able to acquire a good deal of

3

this property and to extend the tentacles of its economic activity over not only the Paris region but over a large part of the rest of France as well. The economic history of this region in this period has been much advanced by the work of Bezard, Fourquin and, especially, Jacquart.[5] More to the point, the history of skilled labour could be illuminated by study of the hundreds of employment and apprenticeship contracts to be found in Coyecque's collection of Parisian notarial documents for the first part of the sixteenth century.[6] But more broadly the police ordonnances to be found in the Collection Dupré in the Bibliothèque Nationale and the Collection Lamoignon at the Archives de la Préfecture de Police could be of inestimable value in reconstructing the history of both the skilled and unskilled workforce in both Paris and the Ile-de-France.

The manuscript which has emerged begins with a study of the role of Parisian merchant capital in the French economy in the sixteenth century. It proceeds to an examination of the Parisian labour force in the same period. It then investigates both public and private responses to the mid-century economic crisis. In the course of doing so it explores the growing interest in technology and the emergence of a concern with a new empirical approach to scientific investigation in the reign of Charles IX. It next studies the period of the religious wars linking the upheavals of that period with a partial proletarianization of the rural population and a continuing preoccupation with new technology. Finally, it deals with the economic recovery of the reign of Henri IV, tying together the economic programme of the crown with the further development of a wage-earning population and the rising interest in science and technology.

Reinterpreting the period of the religious wars by viewing it as a period which was much more economically vibrant than had previously been thought seemed to be a major gain of this research. It appeared to me that my study of the development of capitalism within the tissues of the *ancien régime* of France also made a fascinating contrast with the more successful models of capitalist development characteristic of Holland and England. Finally, my work seemed to throw some light on the French background to the Scientific Revolution of the seventeenth century.

But as I proceeded with this work it seemed especially important to me that my findings overall were at variance with the model of French history that I had imbibed as a graduate student and young university teacher who had been awestruck by the achievements of Braudel and Le Roy Ladurie. What did my research – with its preoccupation with technology, science, state intervention,

---

5   Yvonne Bezard, *La vie rurale dans le sud de la région parisienne de 1450 à 1660* (Paris, 1929); Guy Fourquin, *Les campagnes de la région parisienne à la fin du moyen âge* (Paris, 1964); Jean Jacquart, *La crise rurale en Ile-de-France, 1550–1670* (Paris, 1974); Jacquart, *Paris et Ile-de-France au temps des paysans* (Paris, 1990). See now the work of Jacquart's student J.M. Moriceau, *Les fermiers de l'Ile-de-France, XVᵉ–XVIIIᵉ siècle* (Paris, 1994).

6   Ernest Coyecque, *Recueil d'actes notariés relatifs à l'histoire de Paris et de ses environs au XVIᵉ siècle*, 2 vols. (Paris, 1905).

proto-industrialization, proletarianization, and class conflict – have to do with their *longue durée?* The determinism of their approach seemed sharply at odds with the importance in my research of individual and collective volition.

At this point serendipity intervened. A friend of mine, Marie-Hélène Choisy, gave me a copy of a recent history of the *Annales* called *L'histoire en miettes* published by a young colleague of hers named François Dosse at the Lycée Jacques Prévert in Boulogne-Billiancourt.[7] This *tour de force* brilliantly revealed the conservative prejudices which lay behind the environmental and Malthusian determinism of these two historians. Dosse's work helped to give me the intellectual and moral force to carry through my work, turning the last chapter of this book into a challenge to their stagnationist view of the *ancien régime.*

[7]   *L'histoire en miettes. Des Annales à la 'nouvelle histoire'* (Paris, 1987). This work has since been translated into English under the somewhat misleading title *New History in France: The Triumph of the Annales,* tr. Peter V. Conroy Jr (Urbana, Chicago, 1994).

The expansion of Parisian merchant capital

Has there ever been an age more flourishing than our own in philosophy ... and new inventions necessary to the life of men?

Jacques Peletier du Mans, *L'arithemetique* (1549)

France in the sixteenth century was hardly a unified state, let alone a national market. Although the monarchy was more powerful than it had ever been, the balance of political power still lay with local elites. Likewise, the overwhelmingly largest part of trade and manufacture was locally consumed. Indeed, this ongoing political and economic localism helps to explain the striking vitality of small and medium-sized towns in France in the first part of the sixteenth century. In this period of the Renaissance, the monarchy was nevertheless more powerful than it had ever been. The expanding capacity of the state was facilitated by a surge of economic expansion which promoted a growing economic interdependence between different parts of the kingdom at the higher levels of trade and exchange. One of the two focal points of this economic expansion – second only to Lyons in importance – was Paris. Taking advantage of its strategic location between Mediterranean and Atlantic and its growing importance as the political capital of the kingdom, the growth of the capital was a reflection of the economic dynamism and political integration of sixteenth-century France as a whole.

Paris was by far the largest city in France in the sixteenth century. At mid-century its population stood at more than 250,000 – four times the size of its nearest rival among French cities.[1] The overwhelming majority of the inhabitants of the city were merchants, craftsmen, impoverished students and unskilled workers making up the bulk of producers and consumers. But the numerically smaller upper classes with their large disposable incomes exercised an inordinately large influence on the economic life of the city. For long intervals during the century the city served as the residence of the royal court. In addition to the Louvre palace the city contained the *hôtels* of some forty members of the high aristocracy or of princes of the Church. Hundreds and, at times, thousands of courtiers, nobles and their retinues were thus more or less permanently resident in the city, providing a pool of affluent consumption. The clergy's influence over

[1]   Philip Benedict, 'French Cities from the Sixteenth Century to the Revolution' in *Cities and Social Change in Early Modern France*, ed. Benedict (London, 1989), p. 9.

the city, likewise, was of the greatest importance. A guide to Paris published towards the close of the century listed some forty-eight colleges on the Left Bank and a total of 129 monasteries, convents, hospitals, churches and chapels scattered throughout the city.[2] This clerical establishment further enlarged the market of wealthy consumers.

Paris was increasingly assuming the role of a modern political capital becoming the focal point of the kingdom's expanding system of justice, administration and taxation. As such it was able to draw to itself a large portion of the rents and taxes collected from throughout the kingdom, a major portion of which was spent on consumption by the court, clergy and the expanding elite of officials and magistrates.[3] Such a throng of rich consumers made the city into an emporium of luxury consumption which favoured the growth of those crafts producing goods of high quality.

But the great size of the population provided an immense market for all types of food, clothing and furnishings. The merest journeyman ordinarily owned a feather bed made of good, sturdy oak set off by a canopy, tables, chairs, benches, pewterware, several linen shirts and at least one good robe made of wool for himself and his wife to wear on Sundays and holy days.[4] Among 141 corporations in 1586, the largest fourteen, each with 500 or more members, devoted themselves entirely to providing food or clothing to the population.[5]

A city the size of Paris required the importation of an immense amount of food and other commodities. At the time of the siege of the city by the army of Henri de Navarre towards the end of the sixteenth century, the dimensions of its commerce was described with admiration by Filipo Pigafetta:

Provisions of all kinds are brought to Paris from different regions by boats on the Seine which operate above and below the city. These vessels navigate not only on the Seine but on other rivers as well which are highly navigable and abound in fish. Beside these advantages Paris has that of being surrounded by the most fertile areas of France like Burgundy, Champagne, Brie, the duchy of Valois, the Vexin, Normandy, the region of Chartres, upper and lower Beauce and Hurepoix. By the rivers and principal roads these regions send fruits, foodstuffs and an infinitude of merchandise not even counting that which arrives by sea or land from more distant parts.[6]

---

[2] Enumeration in *Les cris de Paris qu'on crie journellement par les rues de ladicte ville avec ce, le contenue de la despense qui se faict par chacun jour* (Paris, 1584).

[3] Bertrand Gille, 'Fonctions économiques de Paris' in *Paris, fonctions d'une capitale*, ed. Guy Michaud (Paris, 1962), p. 128.

[4] See for example the death inventory of Thomasse Chemynede, wife of Jean Audiguet, journeyman tailor, 7 February 1533 (n. st.), AN Min. Cent. étude XIX, 65.

[5] Alfred Franklin, *Dictionnaire historique des arts, métiers et professions exercés dans Paris depuis le treizième siècle* (Paris, 1906; New York, 1968), p. 213.

[6] 'Relation du siège de Paris', ed. A. Dufour in *MSHP* 2 (1876), 39. On Parisian food imports see Ronda Larmour, 'The Grocers of Paris in the Sixteenth Century' (Columbia University, Ph.D. Dissertation, 1963), pp. 63–4.

Paris imported wheat and other grains, straw, hay, wood, charcoal, poultry, eggs, butter, fruits, vegetables, cheese, cattle and hides from the Ile-de-France. It drew to itself fish from Normandy, wine from Burgundy and Guyenne, silk from Tours and Lyons, paper from Champagne, Normandy and Auvergne, salt from Brouage, ironware from Champagne, Burgundy, Normandy, Berry and Nivernais and cloth from Amiens, Rouen, Beauvais, Reims and Meaux.

Paris did not merely import merchandise for its own use. On the contrary, it acted like a filter through which a large part of the goods produced in the centre and south of the kingdom passed on the way north to England, the Baltic and, above all, to Antwerp.[7] Parisian merchant capital, reinforced by the power of the municipal government, was deployed to capture the flow of these commodities and to channel them through the markets of Paris. The presence of the court and the growth of royal administration accentuated the process of economic centralization.

THE GROWTH OF MANUFACTURERS

The drapers were the most important merchants of the city. Their operations were national and even international in scope, involving the finishing of cloth from Amiens, Rouen, Beauvais, Reims and Meaux as well as its re-export to all the provinces of the kingdom and beyond. At the height of their activity, towards the middle of the sixteenth century, as many as 600,000 pieces of cloth were dyed and finished annually at Paris.[8] The fairs of Guibrey played an important role in disseminating Parisian cloth to the west of France. Lyons and Toulouse served a like role in furnishing the Mediterranean and Iberian market.[9] The Parisian wool cloth industry was important not only to the working population of the city but to the livelihood of the inhabitants of small towns in the Ile-de France. Indeed, the Parisian drapers claimed that their industry provided employment not only for the populace of Paris but for a large fraction of the population of such towns as Melun, Rozai-en-Brie and Meaux which were dependent upon them.[10]

The book trade was likewise an industry which was national and even international in scale. The paper manufacturers supplied the printers and book dealers from mills located in the Ile-de-France, Champagne, Normandy and the Auvergne. The paper manufacturer Pirette was in reality a great Parisian merchant

---

[7]   Emile Coornaert, 'Anvers et le commerce parisien au XVIe siècle', *Mededelingen van De Koninklijke Vlamse Academie voor Wetenschappen, Letteren en Schone Kunsten van Belgie* (Brussels, 1950), p. 3.

[8]   Gille, 'Fonctions économiques de Paris', p. 126.

[9]   Roger Gourmelon, 'L'industrie et le commerce des draps à Paris du XIIIe au XVIe siècles', *Ecole des Chartes, position des thèses*, 1950, pp. 61–3; Gourmelon, 'Etude sur le rayonnement commerciale des marchands drapiers parisiens au XVIe siècle', *Bulletin philologique et historique (jusqu'à 1610) du comité des travaux historiques et scientifiques* (1961), pp. 265–75; Jean-François Belhoste, 'La maison, la fabrique et la ville: l'industrie du drap fin en France: XV–XVIII siècle', *Histoire, économie et société* 13 (1994), 457–71.

[10]   Coll. Lamoignon, VI, fo. 362r.

grocer who traded in a large variety of merchandise which he imported and exported abroad. At the same time he owned several paper mills in the hinterlands in which he produced a wide assortment of paper in substantial quantities.[11] The firm of Guillaume Godard and Guillaume Merlin, which specialized in ecclesiastical literature, claimed to own thirteen or fourteen presses and to have 250 workers in its employ. The partners estimated that the firm required 100,000 sheets of paper per week to keep its presses in operation.[12] Its inventory totalled no less than 260,000 volumes.[13] Books printed in Paris especially found a market in northern France but through Lyons found an outlet in the Midi as well as in Italy and Spain.

The leading merchants of the city were keenly aware of the national and international scope of Parisian economic life. Among the most important merchants in the community were to be found Italians, Germans and Flemings. The development of the maritime commerce of Rouen was in good part due to the capital made available by Parisian merchants.[14] In 1535 a Parisian merchant Thomas Noël operated some fifteen ships sailing from Rouen which were active in the salt trade and in the export of wine and pastel from southwest France to England. In 1563 the largest single investor in the spice trade at Marseilles was a Parisian, Guillaume Bassereau. In the second half of the sixteenth century Parisian entrepreneurs like the Gobelins, Lelièvre, Lamy, Saly and Rouillé became deeply involved with the Antwerp market.[15]

The interests of these Parisian merchants were large and extensive enough to lead them to view matters of economic policy from a national perspective. Thus, they collectively remonstrated over the conclusion of the Anglo-French commercial treaty of 1564 which provided for increased English tariffs on French goods.[16] On this occasion, the king explained to the Parisians that the objective of the French negotiators had been not to prevent the English from increasing tariffs, which was out of the question, but to moderate them as much as possible. The raising of tariffs by the English was designed to offset a trade imbalance which was overwhelmingly in favour of the French. Analysis of commercial exchanges between the two countries in the middle of the sixteenth century reflects a decisive French superiority. French exports to England consisted of a total of sixty-eight items as against only twelve commodities exported to France from England. Eighty per cent of French exports were manufactured or

---

[11] Ibid., VI, fos. 507v.–508r. See Annie Parent, *Les métiers du livre à Paris au XVIᵉ siècle* (Geneva, 1974), p. 65.

[12] Coll. Lamoignon, IV, fo. 601r.

[13] Parent, *Les métiers du livre*, p. 211.

[14] Michel Mollat, 'Rouen avant-port de Paris à la fin du moyen âge', *Bulletin de la société d'études historiques, géographiques et scientifiques de la région parisienne* 71 (1951), 1–8; *Histoire de Rouen*, ed. Mollat (Toulouse, Privat, 1979), p. 153; Larmour, 'The Grocers of Paris', pp. 65–8.

[15] J.-P. Babelon, *Nouvelle histoire de Paris. Le XVIᵉ siècle* (Paris, 1986), pp. 321–33. See also Larmour, 'The Grocers of Paris', pp. 29–30, 39–42, 44, 46.

[16] *Reg. BVP* v, 463–4.

processed goods, including canvas, linen, buckram, woollens, ribbons, knitwear and says. England's sole manufactured export was its cloth.[17] The dominance of French commerce undoubtedly reflects the greater strength at this stage of the French economy.[18]

The year following the signing of this commercial agreement the leading merchants and notables of the city protested the establishment of a kingdom-wide monopoly on the export of pastel, an item crucial to the dyeing industry of the city. Such a monopoly would have as devastating an effect on the cloth industry, they warned, as had the previous monopoly on alum of 1543–8 which had been controlled by the Italians Del Bene and Sardini.[19] Notable in this document is the emphasis on the importance of industry in the economic life not simply of Paris but of the kingdom as a whole. According to this remonstrance, France was poor in precious metals. Its only real resources were its agriculture and its industries. According to this text, the methods of agriculture changed little in the course of time. Its practice was tied to a fixed location. It could cease altogether for a while without its techniques being lost. In contrast, the crafts, like the arts and sciences, were in a state of constant flux. They were portable and could easily move from one country to another. Hence the techniques of different crafts had to be practised and developed constantly or they might be lost or transported elsewhere. Industries like the manufacture of wool, canvas and tapestry demanded the work of a lifetime and like the other arts had to be carefully preserved and transmitted from one generation to the next. On the other hand, this remonstrance warned, through waste or bad policy these skills could be lost in a brief span of time.[20]

A remarkable feature of this complaint drawn up by these Parisian bourgeois is the knowledge it reflects of the complexities involved in the production of pastel, the cultivation of which was concentrated in the Lauragais, located hundreds of kilometres away. The production of pastel in this remote region was crucial to the cloth industry of the city. The awareness that the authors of this document had of the commercial activity, not only of Paris but of the whole kingdom, is similarly significant. Thus they note in passing that as a matter of fact there were only 600 merchants in the whole of France capable of carrying on overseas trade.[21] It seems that the merchants of Paris had a grasp of the entirety of the wholesale trade of the kingdom. Indeed, as our discussion has suggested, the merchant community of Paris had close ties with the merchants

---

[17] Ibid., v, 464–6. At this point English cloth exports to France were of minor significance consisting of little more than some Devonshire kerseys chiefly of the coarser type. See G.D. Ramsay, *The English Wool Industry* (London, 1982), p. 30.

[18] Prosper Boissonade, 'Le mouvement commercial entre la France et les Iles Britanniques au XVIe siècle', *Revue historique* 134 (1920), 193–225; 135 (1920), 1–27.

[19] Jean Delumeau, *L'alun de Rome, XVe–XIXe siècle* (Paris, 1962), pp. 211, 251.

[20] *Reg. BVP* v, 509.

[21] Ibid.

of the six or seven other major commercial centres of the kingdom – to the cloth merchants of Amiens, Rouen and Beauvais, to the wine and salt exporters of Bordeaux, to the pastel merchants of Toulouse, the silk merchants of Lyons and Tours and to the overseas traders of the port of Marseilles. In contact with merchants from the four corners of the kingdom, the resistance of the Parisian merchants to the threat of monopoly from the wealthy Italian merchants of Lyons is likewise notable.

Although it was in touch with these regional metropolitan centres, Paris made the towns of the Ile-de-France a direct part of its economic and political orbit. The Paris basin, like the Rhône-Saône valley, Languedoc and Guyenne, was unusual in the number of towns with a population close to or above a population of 5,000. These towns – Senlis, Compiègne, Mantes, Dreux, Etampes, Melun, Nemours, Meaux – were economic and political dependencies of the capital.[22] Etampes, Meaux and Melun played an especially sensitive role in ensuring the movement of grain to the capital.[23]

The outstanding characteristic of the cloth industry in sixteenth-century France was the dispersion of its operations. There continued to be regional urban centres. These larger provincial towns served as headquarters for the merchants who controlled the production and marketing of the cloth. In Picardy and Normandy the industry was to be found concentrated around Rouen, Beauvais, Montdidier and Vire. Champagne's cloth industry was centred around Reims, Troyes and Châlons. Bourges in Berry, Châtellerault, Niort and Parthenay in Poitou, and Beziers, Lodève, Saint-Pons, Carcassonne, Limoux and Montpellier in Languedoc, were the focal points of the industry in the rest of France.[24] While the major steps of manufacturing were carried out in the countryside, the merchants collected the product, saw to its finishing in the towns and brought it to market for sale. The reach of the cloth merchants of Paris who specialized in dyeing and finishing cloth was broader than that of their provincial counterparts. They bought up cloth which had been manufactured all over northern France including Picardy, Normandy, Ile-de-France and Champagne.

During the sixteenth century the putting-out system spread over large parts of the French countryside. The small towns and countryside of the Brie were critical to the cloth industry of Paris. Elsewhere in France the production of cloth in the countryside became a characteristic of major parts of Poitou, Picardy, Orléannais, Berry, Normandy, Languedoc and later of Beauce, Sologne and Gâtinais. Linen and canvas manufacturing was carried out by the peasantry in Brittany, Normandy

---

22 In sum there were thirty-three closed towns in the *prévôté* of Paris by the mid-sixteenth century. See BN MS Fr. 8081, fos. 959r.–960r.

23 Micheline Baulant and Jean Meuvret, *Prix des céréales et extraits de la mercuriale de Paris: 1520–1698* (Paris, 1960), I, 26 [bis].

24 *Histoire économique et sociale de la France*, ed. Fernand Braudel and Ernest Labrousse, Part I *De 1450 à 1660*, vol. I: *L'état et la ville*, ed. Pierre Chaunu and Richard Gascon (Paris, 1970), p. 251.

and lower Maine as well as in Anjou, Poitou, Lyonnais, Forez, Beaujolais and parts of Dauphiné.[25] Some 40,000 people in the Touraine were sustained by its silk industry.[26]

MILLS AND MANUFACTURING

The location of industry in the countryside was in part based on the availability there of cheap labour, but it also sprang from the access to water-power. It has been estimated that at the beginning of the sixteenth century there were some 60,000 water-mills and 12,000 windmills in France.[27] It is remarkable that three hundred years later at the beginning of the age of steam the number of such installations was almost the same, totalling some 66,000 water-mills and 10,000 windmills. The full significance of these figures emerges in the context of recent scholarship on the economic history of early modern Europe. According to E.L. Jones, the tendency today is to minimize the degree to which the Industrial Revolution represented a decisive break, to stress the importance of the period prior to the eighteenth century to the process of economic development and to emphasize continental European as against English development.[28] Such a perspective does not require us to abandon the contention, first advanced by J.U. Nef, that England acquired its lead in economic development over France in the course of the sixteenth century.[29] Indeed, the further research of Joan Thirsk appears to confirm this conclusion.[30] On the other hand, such a viewpoint, taken together with the estimates given above of the widespread use of wind and water power, does suggest that the extent of industrial development in sixteenth-century France has been understated.

In the late seventeenth century Vauban estimated that of the total number of mills in the kingdom five-sixths were grain mills.[31] That would mean that at least 10,000 mills were devoted to manufacture and industrial processing, being

[25]   Herman Kellenbenz, 'Industries rurales en Occident à la fin du moyen âge au XVIe siècle', *Annales: ESC* 18 (1963), 845–6. Jean Tanguy, *Le commerce du port de Nantes au milieu du XVIe siècle* (Paris, 1956), p. 29. Nicolas de Nicolay, *Description générale de la ville de Lyon et des anciennes provinces du Lyonnais et du Beaujolais*, ed. Victor Advielle (Lyons, 1881), p. 162.

[26]   L.A. Bosseboeuf, 'La fabrique des soieries de Tours', *Mémoires de la société archéologique de Tours* 41 (1900), 246–7. Henri Hauser, *Les débuts du capitalisme* (Paris, 1931), p. 192.

[27]   Robert Philippe, 'Les premiers moulins à vent', *Annales de Bretagne* 32 (1982), 100; Braudel, *L'identité de la France* (Paris, 1986), II, 130.

[28]   Eric Lionel Jones, *Growth Recurring: Economic Change in World History* (Oxford, 1988), pp. 11, 15, 17, 22–4, 54.

[29]   John Ulric Nef, *Industry and Government in France and England, 1540–1640* (Philadelphia, 1940), pp. 1–2.

[30]   Thirsk, *Economic Policy and Projects*.

[31]   Terry S. Reynolds, *Stronger Than A Hundred Men: A History of the Vertical Water Wheel* (Baltimore, 1983), p. 123. On grain mills see Steven Laurence Kaplan, *Provisioning Paris: Merchants and Millers in the Grain and Flour Trade During the Eighteenth Century* (Ithaca, 1984), pp. 221–37.

employed to full cloth, tan leather, make paper, bore pipe, crush ore, make gunpowder, saw wood, hammer iron, operate pumps and process oil. The mill made possible a massive increase in output and a considerable saving of labour. The harnessing of energy which such mills made possible was tremendous. As a focused source of power the mill promoted the concentration of workers at specific sites.[32] Rabelais celebrated the enormous saving in labour made possible by the windmill. He was especially struck by the utility of the canvas sails of the mills, 'by which heavy mill wheels are lightly turned to the great benefit of mankind. It astounds me that the practicality of such a process was hidden for so many centuries from the ancient philosophers considering the inestimable benefit it provides and the intolerable labours they had to perform in their mills through the lack of it.'[33] The sixteenth century was the age of sail not only by sea but in a manner of speaking also by land. Rabelais was here not only celebrating the power of the windmill but also the positive benefits of canvas manufacture which was an industry newly spreading through the countryside of Normandy and the west of France.

Most wind- and water-mills were found in the countryside. There were, to be sure, mills located in towns which were devoted to producing manufactures as well as processing grain into flour. In Paris, for example, there were fifty-five boat-mills on the river between the Ile-Notre-Dame and the Pont-aux-Meuniers. There was another mill under the Pont Notre Dame, two more under the Pont du Change and no less than thirteen under the Pont-aux-Meuniers.[34] The manufacturing faubourg of Saint-Marcel was particularly well served by water power. A survey, carried out at the beginning of the seventeenth century by the king's engineer, Jean Errard, revealed that the river Bièvre which ran through the faubourg had no less than twenty-six water-mills along its course.[35] On the right bank the faubourg Montmartre had at least thirty windmills.[36] Visiting the capital in the 1590s, Thomas Platter noted that the city in fact was surrounded by windmills.[37]

The windmill of the Gobelins is a striking Parisian example of the industrial use of wind power. The Gobelins, alongside the Canaye, were the most important dyers and among the richest and most powerful merchant families

[32] Reynolds, *Stronger Than A Hundred Men*, pp. 4–6.
[33] Quoted in Alexander Keller, 'Mathematical Technologies and the Growth of the Idea of Technical Progress in the Sixteenth Century' in *Science, Medicine and Society in the Renaissance: Essays to Honour Walter Pagel*, ed. Allen G. Debus (New York, 1972), I, 14.
[34] Jean Favier, *Paris au XVe siècle, 1380–1500* (Paris, 1974), pp. 28–9. See also Franklin, *Dictionnaire historique*, p. 487.
[35] BN MS Fr. 16744, fos. 289r.–290v. See Jean Capitan, 'Notules sur la Bièvre', *Bulletin de la Montagne Sainte-Geneviève et ses abords* 5 (1905–8), 245–61.
[36] Marcel Arpin, *Histoire de la meunerie et de la boulangerie depuis les temps préhistoriques jusqu'à l'année 1914* (Paris, 1948), I, 34–5.
[37] Thomas Platter, *Description de Paris*, tr. Louis Sieber (Nogent-le-Routrou, 1896), p. 48. On the design of windmills in the Paris region see Claude Rivals, *Le moulin à vent et le meunier dans la société traditionelle française* (Paris, 1987), pp. 127–42.

in the city.[38] Their windmill was located between the faubourgs Saint-Marcel and Saint-Jacques. Consulting the early maps of the city can help us to appreciate its importance. It is clearly visible on the map of Paris produced by Olivier Truschet and Germain Hayau in the mid-sixteenth century.[39] But it is in the map of Saint-Victor which dates from about the same time and which is attributed to J.-A. Du Cerceau that we achieve a sense of the enormous size of the mill.[40] The mill, in fact, is at the centre of a large factory made up of five or six buildings, the whole enterprise surrounded by a wall. This establishment, large as it is, we may parenthetically note, pales in significance compared to Toulouse's gigantic Bazacle mills, whose eighteen water-mills constituted the largest industrial enterprise in the kingdom. Not only were these mills used to mill grain but to manufacture paper, pulverize pastel, and full cloth. La Bazacle was not merely a private enterprise, it was an early example of a joint-stock company whose *eschaus* or issues were worth 300 *livres* in 1500 and had appreciated to 2,000 a hundred years later. The stock was mainly owned by the councillors of the Parlement of Toulouse and other notables of the region.[41]

The Paris map of Georges Braun dated 1530 indicates mills in the faubourgs of Saint-Marcel, Saint-Victor and near the porte Saint-Honoré.[42] The map of Truschet and Hayau confirms these locations, while noting further sites just to the west of the porte Saint-Denis as well as beyond Saint-Germain des Près. But it is in Mathieu Merian's map of 1615 that we see the city for the first time against the background of the landscape that lies beyond it. Looking eastward from an imaginary elevation to the west, we discern an eastern horizon beyond the walls of the city covered with the sails of innumerable windmills.[43] In other words, by far the greater part of milling necessary to the Parisian economy was carried on well outside the walls of the city.

Indeed, in the late middle ages mills, including water-mills, tended to be located more and more away from the towns. In fact, from the fourteenth century the construction of systems of moats and canals for military purposes around towns like Paris tended to favour stagnant as against flowing water. Such still water was suitable to industrial activities like tanning leather and dyeing cloth rather than to

[38] Jules Guiffrey, 'Les Gobelins, teinturiers en écarlate au faubourg Saint-Marcel', *MSHP* 31 (1904), 1–92.

[39] *Plan de Paris sous le règne de Henri II par Olivier Truschet et Germain Hayau*, ed. Jules Cousin, F. Hoffbauer, Louis Sieber (Paris, 1877).

[40] *Plan de Saint Victor attribué à J.-A. Du Cerceau, copié et engravé par Dheulland en 1756* (Paris, 1880). Cf. Belhoste, 'La maison, la fabrique et la ville', pp. 465–6.

[41] See Pierre Gérard, Germain Sicard and Brigitte Saulais, 'Les moulins de Toulouse' in *Technologies et cultures traditionelles: mission d'action culturelle en milieu scolaire* (Toulouse, 1980), pp. 49–60.

[42] Franklin, *Extrait des notices historiques et topographique sur les anciens plans de Paris. Notice extraite des études archéologiques sur les anciens plans de Paris* (Paris, 1851).

[43] *Plan de Paris sous Louis XIII, 1615*, ed. Mathieu Merian. *Extrait des études archéologiques sur les anciens plans de Paris*, ed. A. Bonnardet (Paris, 1880).

milling by water-power.[44] According to Paul-Jacques Malouin writing in the eighteenth century, there were more than 1,000 windmills as well as 3,000 water-mills in the *generalité* of Paris, most of which were located outside Paris.[45] The many tributaries of the Seine south of Paris were particularly favourable sites for water-mills. A document dated 1542 lists some twenty-one such mills along the course of the Essones.[46] Such mills were particularly numerous in the valley of the river Yvette including two at Chevreuse, six at Saint-Rémy and four at Cernay. The seigneur de Chevreuse alone had eleven.[47] By the sixteenth century many water-mills in the region were controlled by Parisian notables and merchants. Typical is a fulling mill on the river Vaulx near Essones owned by a *bonnetier*, Jean Arment, from the faubourg Saint-Marcel. Arment leased his mill to another *bonnetier*, Roch Bourgeois, who employed a journeyman to full *bonnets* and to transport them to and from his workshop in Paris.[48]

The proliferation of paper mills in the Paris region is particularly noteworthy. They were to be found at Villepreux, Senlis, Crépy, Saint-Cloud, Essonnes, Dreux and Etampes.[49] Such mills were designed to supply the nearly insatiable demand for paper coming from the book trade but also from the Parisian clergy, student body and the burgeoning state bureaucracy. Parisian capital played a considerable role in the development of paper manufacture at Troyes.[50] Another important source of supply was Ambert in the Auvergne. Prior to the wars of religion there were no less than ninety paper mills operating in Ambert and its region.[51]

FORGES AND MINES

The rural location of industry was also favoured by the dependency of industry on wood as a fuel. Hauling wood to meet the needs of large towns was a growing problem in the sixteenth century. It made more sense to locate industry in the forests. One such industry which grew rapidly during the century was iron

---

[44] Andre Guillermé, *The Age of Water: The Urban Environment in the North of France, A.D. 300–1800* (College Station, Texas, 1988), pp. 137–8, 140–1, 149.

[45] Arpin, *Histoire de la meunerie*, I, 33.

[46] AN K 955, no. 39.

[47] Bezard, *La vie rurale*, pp. 172–6.

[48] Coyecque, *Recueil d'actes notariés*, no. 4098.

[49] Henri Alibeux, *Les premières papeteries françaises* (Paris, 1926), p. 113; Georges Degaast and Germain Rigaud, *Les supports de la pensée* (Paris, 1942), p. 17.

[50] Coll. Lamoignon, VI, ffos. 507v–508r.

[51] Alibeux, *Les premières papeteries*, p. 150. In the 1930s Léon Rostaing published a fascinating account of labour relations in the mills of Ambert in the fifteenth and early sixteenth century based on family papers. According to Rostaing, the mills operated on the basis of almost total paternalistic control of the workers by the masters. The workers were ranked strictly according to age, sex, skill and seniority and were provided with clothing, lodgings and common meals. The work was done mainly at night. Unfortunately, the sources on which Rostaing's description was based have apparently been lost. See Rostaing, *La famille de Montgolfier, ses alliances, ses descendants* (Lyons, 1933), p. 7.

manufacturing. To quote Bertrand Gille, the historian of this industry: 'In the second half of the fifteenth century and at the beginning of the sixteenth century a marvellous economic recovery occurs in France which is sustained by the progress of technology.'[52] The forges of Berry, Nivernais, Champagne, Burgundy and Normandy were the most important to Paris. But all the traditional centres of iron production including Brittany, Vendée, Limousin, Périgord, Pyrénées, Forez and Dauphiné were involved in this surge in production. By the beginning of the sixteenth century Périgord and Limousin were covered with new iron forges. A memoir on the forges in the *generalité* of Perpignan in the eighteenth century noted that most dated from the fifteenth and sixteenth centuries. Dauphiné, with its excellent sources of water-power, saw a parallel growth.[53] But it is in lower Champagne that we can perhaps appreciate the dramatic nature of this industrial growth best. In the course of his study of the iron industry in Champagne, Marcel Bulard prepared a map of the forges in operation in the province in the sixteenth century.[54]

The proliferation of such enterprises in Champagne and elsewhere in France in the sixteenth century is astonishing. The majority of these forges were creations of the economic renaissance we have been discussing. Invariably they were sited on rivers which provided the water-power for the mills which operated the bellows and hammers used in the smelting and forging process. According to the papers of Chancellor Poyet dating from the early 1540s, there were some 460 iron forges and foundries in the kingdom, of which 400 had been created in the past fifty years.[55]

Attempts to control iron manufactures by seigneurial or gild restrictions collapsed in the course of the sixteenth century.[56] Capital, rather than labour, was the dominant element with respect to these enterprises, associated as they often were with mills, mines and forests over a dispersed terrain. The capital necessary to construct these forges or to the opening of mines was seldom provided by a single individual. Nobles, merchants and even workers together formed associations which pooled their resources to provide a sufficient supply of capital while

---

[52] Gille, *Les origines de la grande métallurgie en France* (Paris, 1947), p. 7. For the development of the iron industry in the proximity of Paris see Jean Boissière, 'La consommation parisienne de bois et les sidérurgies périphèriques: essai de mise en parallèle (milieu XV–milieu XIXe siècles)' in *Forges et forêts: recherches sur la consommation proto-industrielle de bois*, ed. Denis Woronoff (Paris, 1990), pp. 29–56.

[53] Ibid., pp. 7–8.

[54] Marcel Bulard, 'L'industrie de fer dans la Haut-Marne', *Annales de géographie* 13 (1904), 231. See also Serge Benoit, 'Les Hospitaliers et les débuts de la sidérurgie indirecte dans le Grand Prieuré de Champagne' in *Colloque: moines et métallurgie dans la France médiévale*, ed. Benoit and Denis Cailleaux (Paris, 1991), p. 222; Belhoste *et al.*, *La métallurgie normande: XII–XVIIe siècles – la révolution du haut fourneau* (Caen, 1991), pp. 77–80.

[55] Michel Devèze, *La vie de la forêt française au XVIe siècle* (Paris, 1961), II, 39–43. Pierre Léon estimates the number of forges in the kingdom at 1,000 in 1560. See 'Réflexions sur la sidérurgie française à l'époque ante–colbertienne (1500–1600)' in *Schwerpunkte der Eisengewinnung und Eisenverarbeitung in Europa: 1500–1650*, ed. Kellenbenz (Cologne, 1974), p. 116.

[56] Gille, *Les origines de la grande métallurgie*, pp. 25–7.

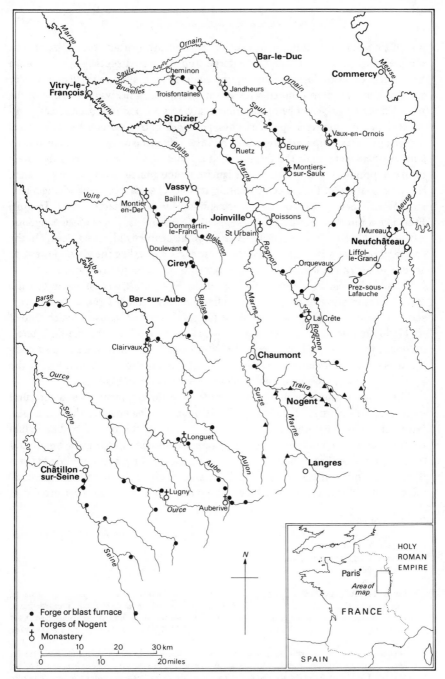

Map 1   Iron forges in sixteenth-century Champagne, Marcel Bulard, 'L'industrie de fer dans la Haut-Marne', *Annales de géographie* 13 (1904), 231.

minimizing risk.[57] In the last quarter of the fifteenth century these associations required a director at the site of the forge who was also a specialist. Born out of the milieu of iron-workers, this figure achieved a higher rank than ordinary workers and was often charged with recruiting labour. This was the origin of the so-called *maître des forges* who, out of necessity, was an engineer, accountant, jack-of-all-trades or universal specialist equipped with both theoretical and practical knowledge. The *maître des forges* assumed the role of boss over the often unruly and obstinate workers of the forge and, as a result of his special knowledge, took on the appearance of a wizard in the ignorant rural milieu in which he operated. By the beginning of the sixteenth century this novel social type embodying a new kind of economic power was given recognition by the monarchy itself. In 1516 Francis I confirmed the special privileges of the *maîtres des forges* of the kingdom. Attempts to cancel these privileges later on in the century did not succeed. On the contrary, one notes the tendency of the *maîtres des forges*, like the glass-blowers, to acquire or usurp noble titles in the late sixteenth and seventeenth centuries.[58]

These industrial sites were heavy consumers of wood. It was estimated that the annual consumption of wood at each of these places totalled some 4,000 cords, seriously jeopardizing the survival of the forests.[59] Another industry which tended to be located in the forests was glass-making, found in the Ile-de-France, Normandy, Picardy and Nivernais.[60] It is estimated that there were some 2,500–3,000 so-called gentlemen glass-blowers in the kingdom in the second half of the sixteenth century, most of whom employed several *valets* or assistants.[61]

The growing shortage of wood prompted the development of another rural industry, coal-mining, at Creusot, in the basin of Champagne, the Cevennes, Nivernais as well as around Saint-Etienne.[62] Indeed, the use of coal as a fuel became the basis of the ironware and firearms industries which grew up around St-Estienne as well as in the Nivernais and at Alais in the Cevennes.[63] At the end of the sixteenth century, Guy Coquille, whose family had interests in the coal-mines of the Nivernais, observed that the ironmasters of the region preferred coal

---

57 Ibid., pp. 28–9.
58 Ibid., pp. 162–3. On the social evolution of the *maître des forges* see Belhoste, *La métallurgie normande*, pp. 64, 146–52.
59 Devèze, *La vie de la fôret française*, II, 46.
60 Ibid., II, 48–50.
61 Ibid., II, 49.
62 Louis Trénard, 'Le charbon avant l'ère industrielle' in *Charbon et sciences humaines: actes du colloque organisé par la faculté des lettres de l'université de Lille en mai 1963*, ed. Trenard (Paris, 1963), p. 54; Anatole de Charmasse, 'Note sur l'exploitation de la houille au Creusot au XVIe siècle: 1510–11', *Mémoires de la société édueene* NS 12 (1883), 387–402; Devèze, *La vie de la fôret française*, I, 136–7.
63 Nicolay, *Description générale de la ville de Lyon*, p. 162; Paul Destray, 'Les houillières de La Machine au XVIe siècle', *Revue internationale du commerce et de l'industrie et de la banque* 15 (1914), 361–92; Guy Thuiller, *Georges Dufaud et les débuts du grand capitalisme dans la métallurgie en Nivernais au XIXe siècle* (Paris, 1959), pp. 122, 132; Achille Bardon, 'L'exploitation du bassin houillier d'Alais sous l'ancien régime', *Mémoires de l'Academie de Nîmes* 20 (1897), 147–8.

to charcoal because it supplied a hotter flame in the forge.[64] It is commonly supposed that the coal-mining that did develop during the sixteenth century was largely confined to the exploitation of surface deposits. However, Jean Du Choul, writing in 1555, noted the subsurface activities of coal-mine operators on the flanks of Mont Pilat. According to his account, the underground nature of the mines left the surface of the land undisturbed.[65] Likewise, underground shafts were sunk to exploit the coal seams in the region around Alais in the second half of the sixteenth century.[66] Such subterranean works suggest the investment of substantial amounts of capital in these enterprises.

From the mid-fifteenth century there was a rapid development of the mining industry overall in France.[67] Notable was the growth of mining in Nivernais, Dauphiné, Lyonnais, and the Pyrenees. The development of silver, gold, zinc, copper and other mines entailed the pooling of significant amounts of capital through associations formed along lines similar to those used to construct and operate forges. The operation of these mines required the use of what were for the times sophisticated machines like pumps, mine-shaft elevators, wooden tracking, water-driven hammers, bellows, kilns and furnaces.

The industrial hinterland of Paris, one notes in summary, included cloth manufacture in the Brie and, somewhat later, in Beauce, Hurepoix and Beauvais, glass manufacture in the forests of Ile-de-France, the production of millstones in the quarries of Brie, the fulling of cloth, hats and paper in the mills of Essones and Champagne, and further afield the production of iron and ironware in Nivernais, Champagne, Normandy and Burgundy. The influence of Parisian capital in cloth and paper manufacture is particularly notable.

It can be concluded from this review of the development of textile manufacturing, iron and glass manufacture and mining that, while towns saw a rise in their populations during the sixteenth century, the really significant economic improvements largely occurred in the rural areas. Towns like Paris remained the focal points of economic control and marketing but the most dramatic change occurred in the countryside with the spread of rural cloth manufacture as well as the development of mining and the use of wind and water-power to carry on all kinds of manufacturing.

IDEAS OF PROGRESS

The unprecedented prosperity enjoyed by the Parisian middle class in the first half of the sixteenth century is reflected in the attitude of the humanists who lived

---

[64] Coquille, *Histoire du pays et duché de Nivernais* (Paris, 1612), p. 353. See also Claude Longeon, 'La description du Mont Pilat par Jean Du Choul(1555)' in *Hommes et livres de la Renaissance* (Saint-Etienne, 1990), pp. 53–8.

[65] *Description du Mont Pilat*, tr. E. Muslant (Lyons, 1868), p. 21. The edition published at Lyons was republished the same year at Zurich in Conrad Gesner's *De raris et admirandis herbis*.

[66] Bardon, 'L'exploitation du bassin houiller d'Alais', pp. 148–9.

[67] Philippe-Jean Hesse, *La mine et les mineurs en France de 1300 à 1550* (Paris, 1973), p. 401.

in the city during the period. These intellectuals began to compare their own times favourably with Antiquity. Some began to adumbrate a rudimentary idea of progress. The hopefulness which these decades inspired is to be seen in Rabelais' description of flax or *Pantagruelion* at the close of Book III of his masterpiece. The details of his description Rabelais took from Pliny. His point of view, however, was completely different.[68] Pliny lamented humanity's audacity in daring to invent new things. He spoke of mankind's transformation and utilization of flax as violence done to its nature. In contrast, Rabelais praised the devising of new mechanical tools and regarded the ingenious uses of flax as a boon. As we have seen, he professed astonishment that the ancient philosophers knew nothing about these modern applications of flax. Looking to the future, Rabelais exclaimed: 'Who knows but that Pantagruel's children will discover some plant equally effectual? Who knows but that humans, by its means, may visit the source of hail, the forge where lightning is produced? Who knows but that they will invade the regions of the moon, intrude within the territories of the celestial signs?'[69]

Rabelais' work also reflected a growing appreciation of the practical activity of craftsmen. In Book I observation of the work of the craftsmen of Paris is an essential element of Gargantua's education. On rainy days, Panocrates takes Gargantua into the streets of Paris

to watch workmen forging metals or cutting pieces of ordinance – lapidaries, goldsmiths and cutters of precious stones in their ateliers, the alchemists in their laboratories, the coiners at the mint, the tapestry-workers, velvet workers and weavers at their looms, the watch-makers, looking-glass framers, printers, lutemakers, dyers and other such artisans in their workshops ... invariably investigating and learning the various inventions and industry of the trade.[70]

A sense of material change for the better is likewise evident in the Parisian printer and humanist Henri Estienne's *Introduction au traicte de la conformité des merveilles anciens avec les modernes*.[71] In this work Estienne contrasted the level of material comfort in the middle of the sixteenth century with that of a hundred years earlier. He noted that the houses of his day had all kinds of improved features which those of a century earlier lacked. He pointed out, especially, the far superior windows in contemporary buildings compared with those of a hundred years past. The furniture of a century earlier, according to Estienne, looked as if it were made by carpenters instead of furniture makers. The locks of modern times were incomparably superior to those of the past hundred years. Estienne observed that these differences were probably due to the much higher quality of the tools employed in his own time in comparison with those used in the previous century. If one tests the

[68] Alexander G. Keller, 'The Idea of Progress in Rabelais', *Publications of the Modern Language Association* 66 (1951), 237.
[69] Quoted in ibid.
[70] Ibid.
[71] [Antwerp (Lyons,) 1568].

armour of today, he claimed, one finds it to be half the weight of that manufactured in the past and even bullet-proof. The craftsmen of the present day, he asserted, are more efficient than those of the past. They can manufacture three swords out of the metal once used to make one.[72] According to Estienne, the manufactures of his time were of higher quality and more economically made than those made in the past.

A few years later Estienne visited the Frankfort fair. What he saw there emboldened him to compare the material achievements of his own age no longer with the medieval past but with Antiquity itself. Thus, he asserts that 'as some once called Rome an epitome of the world so it seems to me I speak truly if I say that the Frankfort Fair should be called ... an epitome of all the emporiums of the whole world'.[73] Above all it is the achievements of the craftsmen, especially in metals, which he praises to the point of claiming that they have gone beyond the achievements of Antiquity:

For, on the contrary, when I say this, I refer to those things in which this Fair deserves especial praise – to those products which are wrought in gold, silver, bronze, iron and other metals: I refer to vases of gold and silver engraved with such skill that in them it may be said that the workmanship surpasses the material, and even that the artists have triumphed over their art. Let Antiquity cease so much to admire the skill of Mentor, Mys, or Calamis. Let it cease so much to boast of the vases of Corinthian, or Lycian or Naxian workmanship. For the Frankfort Fair presents for inspection even greater wonders in that same class. And, indeed, not less honour is given by the workmen there to bronze, and even greater is given to iron. For iron is often deemed worthy of sculptures in the making of which even gold itself would elsewhere be honoured.[74]

The Parisian humanist Jacques Peletier du Mans was particularly concerned to make the case for the moderns with respect to his own speciality of mathematics. Thus, in the preface to *L'arithemetique*, a work of theory but also of practical application, he claimed that the science of mathematics had been reborn in his own age through the efforts of a large number of well-trained professors of mathematics. If he had the space he could fill his work with the names of countless men from Germany, Italy, Spain and France whom he would not hesitate to compare favourably to the Ancients in no matter what profession, including mathematics.[75] After a long fallow period following Antiquity, the present age was

[72] Ibid., pp. 437–8.
[73] *The Frankfort Book Fair. The Franco-fordiense Emporium*, ed. and tr. J.W. Thompson (New York, 1911; New York, 1968), p. 155.
[74] Ibid., pp. 160–1.
[75] *L'arithemetique* (Poitiers, 1549; Geneva, 1969), n.p. Peletier's contribution to the development of mathematics is discussed in Giovanna Cleon Cifoletti, 'Mathematics and Rhetoric: Peletier and Gosselin and the Making of the French Algebraic Tradition' (Princeton University, Ph.D. Dissertation, 1992), pp. 111–21. On mathematical education in France cf. Jean-Claude Margolin, 'L'enseignement de mathématiques en France (1540–70), Charles de Bovelles, Finé, Peletier, Ramus' in *French Renaissance Studies*, ed. Peter Sharrat (Edinburgh, 1976), pp. 109–55; Denise Hilliard and Emmanuel Poole, 'Oronce Finé et l'horloge planétaire de la Bibliothèque Sainte-Geneviève', *BHR* 33 (1971), 311–51.

bringing forth a harvest of invention and learning that was equal, or indeed, superior to any time in the past: 'Had there ever been an age more flourishing than our own in philosophy, poetry, painting, architecture and in new inventions of all things necessary to the life of men?'[76]

The Parisian magistrate Guillaume Budé was so struck by the advances of his age that it led him to elaborate a general theory of human progress based on Divine Providence:

I think that Divine Providence is an architect who arranges mortal affairs as follows: he prescribes and commands something new to be designed by his workers and artisans in art and nature in which they apply themselves to one and the same thing in each age, so that each age may be distinguished, and just as life may be more abundantly furnished from day to day, so also it may be from age to age ... Recent centuries have brought forth unheard of things, however, which Antiquity, however ingenious, never ... suspected ... I think that many other things ... which will be important in the future, have been set down in the deep secrets of nature, which must be brought to light each in its own time.[77]

The notion of going beyond the achievements of Antiquity appears to have had a particular appeal to those who were trying to elevate the status of their own craft. Nowhere do we find a more assertive kind of modernism than from those who worked with their hands. The Parisian surgeon Ambroise Paré had to carry on an ongoing struggle against the physicians of the University of Paris medical establishment.[78] Departure from the teachings of the Ancients was regarded with suspicion. In reaction we find Paré claiming that:

The arts are not yet so perfected that one cannot make any addition; they are perfected and polished in the course of time. It is sloth deserving blame to stop with the inventions of the first discoverers, only imitating them in the manner of lazy people without adding anything and without increasing the legacy left to us ... More things are to be sought after than have been found.[79]

In Paré's mind there was no question but that he had surpassed the achievement of Antiquity in his own field: 'For God is my witness, and all good men know, that I have now laboured fifty years with all care and pains in the illustration and amplification of Chirurgery and that I have so certainly touched the mark whereat I aimed, that Antiquity may seem to have nothing wherein it may exceed us.'[80]

The disparagement of the authority of the Ancients is especially evident in the Parisian lectures of the potter Bernard Palissy. Against the prestige of the

[76] Ibid., Cf. Keller, 'Mathematical Technologies', I, 18.

[77] *De philologia* (1532), quoted in Samuel Kinser, 'Temporal Change and Cultural Process in France', *Renaissance Studies in Honour of Hans Baron*, ed. Anthony Molho and John A. Tedeschi (De Kalb, Ill., 1971), p. 709.

[78] Ambroise Paré, *Des monstres et prodiges*, ed. Jean Céard (Geneva, 1971), pp. xiv–xviii.

[79] Paré, *Œuvres*, ed. J.F. Malgaigne (Paris, 1840), I, 8. See Edward Zilsel, 'The Genesis of the Concept of Scientific Progress', *Journal of the History of Ideas* 6 (1945), 342.

[80] Paré, *Des monstres et prodiges*, I, 2.

Ancients, Palissy invoked his own experience. Contrary to those who asserted that gold could be dissolved in boiling water, Palissy argued that an experiment which entailed the evaporation of water into which gold had been placed would prove the opposite. He continued:

Perhaps you will say that one must believe the learned and the ancients who have written of these things many years ago, that one ought not to accept my teaching insofar as I am not a Greek or Latin and that I have not read the works of the physicians. To which I answer that the ancients were men just like the moderns and that they made mistakes.[81]

The assertion, not only of equality with the Ancients, but even of superiority over them, is also to be found in the work of the Parisian architect Philibert De l'Orme. According to him, the Romans did not have the capacity to put up large vaulted structures. The expense of the long lengths of timber necessary to this kind of vaulting was prohibitive. In his *Des œuvres et nouvelles inventions pour bien bastir et a petit frais* (1561) De l'Orme claimed to have discovered a new method which resolved the problem.[82] Indeed, he maintained that if Julius Caesar had known of his invention it would have been far easier for him to construct the bridges described in his *Commentaries*. De l'Orme believed that, using his invention, it would be possible to bridge a river with a structure made of a single arch of 700 or even 1,400 feet without even sinking piles into a stream.[83]

Brunelleschi, Alberti and Bramante had done much to elevate the prestige of the architect in Italy. De l'Orme was consciously attempting to do the same thing in France. Likewise, Palissy and Paré were trying to raise the dignity of their crafts. Proclaiming the superiority of their achievements to those of Antiquity was one manner of doing so. To be sure these claims should be seen as reflecting an attempt at self-aggrandizement by those who made them. Paré, De l'Orme and Palissy were without a doubt trying to enhance their social position by challenging the wisdom of the Ancients. But one ought to note that their achievements, nevertheless, did represent not only an important advance towards the integration of practical knowledge with theory, but a true reflection of the real material progress being made in sixteenth-century France.

A sense of equality, even superiority, with respect to the Ancients manifested itself even with regard to the progress of agriculture. One of the most important works on agriculture published during the sixteenth century was Charles Estienne and Jean Liébault's *L'agriculture et maison rustique* (1564), a work notable for its understanding of the agriculture of the regions around Paris.[84] Steeped in the classics as he was, Estienne did not hesitate to assert the independence of French agriculture from that of Antiquity. According to Estienne, French agriculture is as

[81] *Les œuvres de Bernard Palissy*, ed. Anatole France (Paris, 1880; Geneva, 1969), p. 74.
[82] *Œuvres*, Books x and xi (Rouen, 1648; Ridgewood, N.J., 1964).
[83] Ibid., fo. 307r–v.
[84] The first edition of Estienne and Liébault's work was considerably emended in successive printings. I have used the Paris edition of 1572.

different from that of Antiquity as is the manner in which the houses and edifices of the French kingdom are built. The agriculture of France varies from that of the Ancients according to differences of region, soil and geography in the same way that language, clothing, tools and implements differ from region to region. It would be pointless, therefore, in this work to review the agricultural practices of the Ancient world in order to understand those of present-day France. This does not prevent Frenchmen from living as well as or better than those who lived in the past.[85]

The development of a certain idea of material and intellectual progress among Parisian scholars, architects, mathematicians, surgeons and highly skilled craftsmen must be seen as part of the larger struggle between the Ancients and the moderns which characterized sixteenth-century French intellectual life. Animated by a sense of nationalism, the moderns attempted to make the French vernacular a vehicle for philosophical, religious and scientific discussion which could rival and surpass both Antiquity and Italian humanism.[86]

In its fullest articulation the notion of progress advanced by the moderns linked the intellectual advance of France with its material and technological development. An excellent example of this combined point of view can be found in the French poet and mathematician Jean-Pierre de Mesmes' *Institutions astronomiques* (1557).[87] In this work Mesmes celebrates the development of vernacular poetry and history and the beginnings of a distinctively French philosophy and mathematics. The advancement of intellectual disciplines including astronomy in the vernacular would obviate the need for French students to waste their early years studying Latin and Greek.[88]

France is making every effort to liberate itself from the domination of foreign influence. To the advantages it possesses by virtue of its martial prowess, trade, agriculture, manufacture and technology it is adding a reputation for science. The savants of France are competing with others by means of emulation while they celebrate the progress achieved since Antiquity. In particular, Mesmes celebrates the contributions of George Puerbach, Copernicus, Erasmus Reinhold and Oronce Finé to making modern astronomy easier, simpler and more exact than that of the Ancients through their use of superior instruments.[89]

---

[85] Estienne and Liebault, *L'agriculture et maison rustique*, fo. 1r.
[86] Cf. Hubert Gillot, *La querelle des anciens et modernes* (Paris, 1914; Geneva, 1968), pp. 1–171. For the general historical context cf. Hans Baron, 'The *Querelle* of the Ancients and the Moderns as a Problem for Renaissance Scholarship' in *Renaissance Essays*, ed. Paul Oscar Kristeller and Philip P. Wiener (New York, 1968), pp. 95–114.
[87] *Les institutions astronomiques* (Paris, 1557). See Emile Picot, *Les Français italianisants aux XVIe siècle* (Paris, 1908; New York, 1968), I, 295–311.
[88] Mesmes, *Les institutions astronomiques*, fo. sig. c.
[89] Ibid., p. 285. See A.R. Hall, *The Scientific Revolution: 1500–1800* (London, New York, 1954), p. 53.

TECHNOLOGICAL INNOVATIONS

The economic dynamism of the first part of the sixteenth century also found expression in the willingness of entrepreneurs to invest in technological improvement. The first part of the century was admittedly not a period of particularly remarkable invention. Rather it was a period in which inventions made earlier were adopted on a large scale in the expectation of making further profits. It therefore corresponds to the Schumpeterian model of a period of relatively high profits where the inventions of a prior period of economic stagnation are finally absorbed.[90] As a result mining, milling and iron manufacturing as well as printing, cloth and silk manufacturing underwent a certain degree of technological improvement. Although powered by human labour it is nevertheless the case that the printing press itself was a kind of machine.[91] The productivity of this machine amazed contemporaries: 'it would appear to be incredible if experience did not prove it to be true that four or five workers can produce in one day as much excellent script as three or four thousand of the best scribes of the whole world by means of this most excellent art of printing.'[92] In the course of the century the press was improved by the introduction of tympans to hold paper in place, the use of friskets to ensure clean margins and the employment of a pressing stone that could be rolled.[93]

The alarming rise in the cost of using wood as a fuel stimulated the search for more efficient furnaces. In 1543 at Amiens, for example, Hector Palet offered to supply brewers and dyers with a new, more efficient kind of furnace. The city council agreed to pay Palet six *écus* if the furnaces proved to be useful.[94] The same year two other inhabitants of the city invented a machine for rolling satin.[95] The advantage of the machine lay in the substitution of manpower for horsepower, the employment of manpower at this point being apparently less expensive as a result of the rising cost of grain and the elasticity of wages.

Mechanical silk spinning, using water-power, was introduced into France in the late fifteenth century. It arrived at Avignon between 1464 and 1470 introduced by Italian manufacturers. It made its way subsequently into the Lyonnais on the Gier, at Saint-Chamond and at La Valla.[96] In 1539 such mills were installed at Lyons itself. In the meantime a mill for spinning and twisting silk was established at Tours as early as 1514. Orders for the construction of other such mills were

---

[90]   J.P. Gourlaouen, Y. Perraudeau, *Economie, croissance, et cycles économiques* (Paris, 1987), p. 216.
[91]   Hauser, *La modernité du XVIe siècle* (Paris, 1963), p. 77.
[92]   *Plaidorie pour la reformation de l'imprimerie* (Paris, 1572), fo. 3r–v.
[93]   Natalie Zemon Davis, 'A Trade Union in Sixteenth Century France', *Economic History Review* series 2, 19 (1966), 53.
[94]   *Recueil des monuments inédits de l'histoire du Tiers Etat*, ed. Augustin Thierry (Paris, 1853), II, 607–8.
[95]   Ibid., II, 620.
[96]   Richard Gascon, *Grand commerce et vie urbaine au XVIe siècle: Lyons et ses marchands* (Paris, 1971), I, 322–3.

given in 1530 and 1542.[97] While on the subject of milling, we should not neglect a major innovation in the more efficient processing of grain which was introduced first of all in the Ile-de-France. Thus, the so-called 'economic milling' of grain was being practised in the Beauce and around Senlis by 1550.[98] Technical progress is evident also in the increased use of water power in the working of metals and the growing use of coal, especially at Saint-Etienne and Saint-Chamond.[99] The use of the blast furnace in iron production made rapid progress in northern France in the first part of the sixteenth century. Indeed, it is entirely likely that this new process, which spread like wildfire in England from the 1540s, was introduced there from France.[100] In mining the hundred years between 1450 and 1550 saw impressive technical innovations, encouraged in part by the high nominal salaries of the period. Over this period the metallic toughness of chisels as well as the quality of other tools and techniques for the cutting of shafts reflects demonstrable improvement. The widespread adaptation of wooden tracking in and around the mines made possible dramatic gains in productivity.[101] Finally, we should note that Italian artisans and craftsmen introduced new techniques in the manufacture of ceramics and glassware into France in the course of the sixteenth century.[102]

The extent of rural industry or proto-industrial activity that developed in the sixteenth century must be reiterated. There was scarcely a region of the kingdom from which rural industrial activity was absent. The Ile-de-France had its paper, glass and wool cloth manufactures. Nearby Normandy was the site of manufactures of wool cloth, linen, canvas, iron, glass and paper. The Auvergne may have been the province which was least touched but even it had its important paper manufacturing industry. The Southwest, hardly a focal point of industrial activity, nevertheless, saw the development of mining in the Pyrenees, iron manufacture in the Limousin, Pyrénées, and Périgord, leather manufacture in the Périgord and the wool cloth industry in Poitou. The production of pastel, a speciality of the Lauragais as we have seen, was regarded by contemporaries as a quasi-industrial activity. Yet it was the Southeast, including lower Languedoc, Dauphiné, Lyonnais and Forez, with their mining, iron manufacture, wool, canvas and silk manufacture, which had perhaps the most diversified forms of manufacturing.

But the dynamism of the period cannot be fully understood if we confine our view to the mere multiplication of productive facilities or to the introduction of

---

[97] André Coudouin, 'Recherches sur les métiers de la soierie à Tours dans la première moitié du seizième siècle' (University of Tours, Ph.D. Thesis, 1976), pp. 39–40.

[98] Arpin, *Histoire de la meunerie*, I, 124.

[99] *Histoire économique et sociale de la France*, Part I, vol. I, 265.

[100] Gille, *Les origines de la grande métallurgie*, pp. 17–18.

[101] Paul Benoît, 'Les techniques minières en France et dans l'Europe aux XVe et XVIe siècles', *Journal des Savants* (1988), 82–3.

[102] Boissonade, *Le socialisme d'état* (Paris, 1927; Geneva, 1977), p. 92; Devèze, *La vie de la forêt française*, II, 49.

improvements in technology. Such changes were a superficial aspect of a much more profound process. The real key to the economic progress of the period was the reorganization of the processes of production.[103] This reorganization was sparked above all by the intrusion of merchant capital. Everywhere the tentacles, especially of Lyonnaise and Parisian merchant capital, reached out to gain control of economic activity. Here, merchants gained control of the food supply of a town or, indeed, of an entire region. There, merchants bought up the cloth production of hitherto independent producers, reducing these producers to a condition of economic dependence. In other places merchants actually introduced increasingly hard-pressed rural producers to the system of putting-out. In other cases still, entrepreneurs bought up land or opened mines in which those who worked found themselves under the direct control of their employers. Such processes were only beginning, were resisted by the working population, and had scarcely reached completion in any economic sector. Indeed, rendering producers totally dependent on wages was often beyond the means or goals of merchant capital. Nevertheless, this encroachment of merchant capital on economic life, or, to put it in other terms, the still quite partial subsumption of labour to capital, is the single most important economic and social development of the sixteenth century. In the first half of the sixteenth century it was the half-Italian merchants of Lyons who took the lead in this movement. But the merchant class of Paris was not very far behind. These merchants of the Seine, furthermore, successfully resisted attempts on the part of the Italians of Lyons to dominate them. Moreover, the Parisian merchant elite, in close touch with the monarchy and in intimate relation with the merchants of Rouen and Antwerp who were pioneering the Atlantic trade, had its finger on the pulse of the future.

[103] Jones, *Growth Recurring*, pp. 15, 54. For an overview of this phenomenon from the perspective of proto-industrialization see Maxine Berg, 'Markets, Trade and European Manufacture' in *Markets and Manufactures in Early Industrial Europe* (London, 1991), pp 3–26.

2

Labour in Paris in the sixteenth century

> I am a jack-of-all-trades
> Who only wants a job.
> If anyone has need of me
> Behold! I am ready to work.
> Christophe de Bordeaux, *Valet à louer à tout faire*

To what extent can we speak of the French economy of the sixteenth century as capitalist? If we confine ourselves to looking at the heights of the economy, namely, banking and international commerce, the answer is an unqualified affirmative. Quite clearly, the circulation of credit and commodities at the highest level was more and more under the control of bankers and merchants from Paris and Lyons. The issuing of *rentes* on the Hôtel de Ville of Paris and the creation of that vast financial syndicate known as the Grand Parti of Lyons bespeak an ability to organize credit operations on a grand scale. Paris and Lyons were centres of international commerce on the level of Antwerp, Florence and Venice in the first half of the sixteenth century. Moreover, French banking and commercial activities were increasingly linked with those of the rest of Europe. On the other hand, it is not enough to confine our perspective simply to that of the circulation of large amounts of money, credit and commodities when speaking of capitalism. However much a necessary condition, the development of the European market into a world market in the first part of the sixteenth century is not a sufficient condition for us to speak of France as a capitalist economy. Nor is the appearance of new kinds of industry, the development of new relations of industrial production under the control of merchants, the introduction of new technology, or even the investment of substantial amounts of capital in an industry like mining, to be taken as determinative. Industry, after all, represented only a relatively small percentage of total economic output in this period.

Agriculture was by far the most important economic activity. Consequently, the question of the degree to which the French economy was capitalist must be determined by examining changes in the nature of productive relations in agriculture. Two studies have directly addressed the question of rural capitalism in sixteenth-century France, Le Roy Ladurie's *Les paysans de Languedoc* and Guy

Bois' *Crisis of Feudalism.*[1] These authors concur on the emergence of a kind of rural capitalism in the first half of the sixteenth century. Bois speaks of a process of expropriation of the peasantry to the benefit of landlords and merchants beginning as early as 1510–20. The peasantry in eastern Normandy became increasingly differentiated, with proletarians emerging at one end of the hierarchy, and a kind of rural bourgeoisie at the other. Individual small commodity production – the cornerstone of feudalism – was weakened, while tendencies became evident towards the separation of labour from the means of production, the latter increasingly directed towards the accumulation of profit. The development of tenancy in place of *cens*, of a growing dependence on wages, and of bourgeois ownership of land seem unambiguous.[2]

But Bois warns against too hasty a conclusion:

Pauperization, on the one hand, concentration of wealth, on the other, these then are the new characteristics of the first third of the sixteenth century: without a doubt they bear the mark of an emerging capitalism. Let us, however, guard against forcing the connection. However vivid the force of money in the countryside, however clear the tendencies to the accumulation of land, they did not overthrow the old agrarian structure. Does not the major difficulty lie precisely in comprehending the contradictory nature of the process: the growth of capitalism and at the same time the victorious resistance in considerable degree of the old structures?[3]

Bois points to the continued interest of landlords in seigneurial dues, the persistence of communal rights and, even, the perpetuation of archaic mental attitudes as factors retarding the full development of capitalism in the Norman countryside. More importantly Bois underlines the failure to reorganize agriculture so as to make possible larger-scale and more efficient production as an even more fundamental hindrance to the progress of agrarian capitalism.[4] In a subsequent essay, Bois remarks that the persistence of middle-sized peasant holdings and the hypertrophy of the state were distinctive inhibitions on capitalist relations in early modern French society.[5]

Le Roy Ladurie's account of sixteenth-century Languedoc is not unlike that of Bois' treatment of Normandy. In Languedoc, as in Normandy, one has the same tendencies towards rural polarization. The most striking difference between Le Roy Ladurie and Bois is the former's portrayal of an emergent capitalism in Languedoc based on the profits of an emergent class of farmers and leaseholders who operated on large, consolidated holdings quite unlike those in Normandy.[6]

---

[1]   *Les paysans de Languedoc*, 2 vols. (Paris, 1966); *The Crisis of Feudalism: Economy and Society in Eastern Normandy* (Cambridge, Paris, 1984).

[2]   Bois, *The Crisis of Feudalism*, pp. 384–5.

[3]   Ibid., p. 155.

[4]   Ibid., pp. 393–7, 408.

[5]   'Against the Neo-Malthusian Orthodoxy' in *The Brenner Debate: Agrarian Class Structure and Economic Development in Pre-Industrial Europe*, ed. T.H. Aston and C.H.E. Philpin (Cambridge, 1985), pp. 111, 114.

[6]   Le Roy Ladurie, *Les paysans de Languedoc*, I, 251–2, 255–6.

The existence of these large-sized holdings in Languedoc would seem to reflect a capitalism which had gone beyond the stage of development reached in Normandy. Nevertheless, Le Roy Ladurie regards this sixteenth-century agrarian capitalism as being equally unable to break through the fundamentally traditional structures of the countryside. According to him, a progressive kind of agrarian capitalism would have raised the level of surplus value extraction by making improvements on the land or by introducing new technological means of exploiting it. Instead, the agrarian capitalism of Languedoc attempted to increase surplus value by continually depressing the standard of living of wage-earners.[7] The limits of this type of surplus value extraction were reached by about 1580, signalled by a decline in the level of profit in relation to rent.[8] In Le Roy Ladurie's view, the failure to introduce new productive forms of exploiting the land was rooted in the persistence of a certain traditional *mentalité* in the Midi. Both Le Roy Ladurie and Bois see the agrarian capitalism of the sixteenth century as immature and incomplete. Bois puts the stress on the survival of the middle peasantry and seigneurial class and the consolidation of a bureaucratic state, while Le Roy Ladurie emphasizes the importance of a kind of mental inertia, especially among the mass of increasingly impoverished small peasants.

Recognizing the immaturity of this new economic order, it is, nevertheless, important to reiterate the existence of a type of agrarian capitalism in sixteenth-century France. True, the nobility and clergy were still predominant as seigneurial landlords. Communities in both Languedoc and Normandy jealously hung on to their communal rights. Agricultural output increased, but not as fast as did population.[9] The urban bourgeoisie nevertheless steadily increased its hold on rural property in the course of the sixteenth century. At the same time, a class of rural bourgeoisie made up of wealthy peasants, notaries and rural merchants was able to consolidate itself in the countryside. Simultaneously, an increasing fraction of the rural population found itself reduced to the level of landless, or nearly landless, peasants increasingly dependent on wages in order to live. It is in this context that we must understand the development, over wide areas of the French countryside, of the proto-industrial wool cloth, linen and canvas industries as well as industries based on water- and wind-power.

PROLETARIANIZATION

Capitalism requires the extension of control by entrepreneurs over productive activity. But as a complement to this process, it also demands the existence of increasing quantities of wage labour. Indeed, it is the emergence of a growing pool of wage labour in the countryside of the Ile-de-France as well as in Paris itself

---

[7]   Ibid., I, 327.
[8]   Ibid., I, 465.
[9]   Jacquart, *Paris et l'Ile-de-France au temps des paysans*, p. 30.

which must be emphasized at this point. For it was the increasing availability of this kind of workforce which explains in significant measure the expansiveness of the Parisian economy in the first half of the sixteenth century which we have described. The process of rural dispossession was no doubt critical to the creation of this pool of labour. But also important was the continuing rapid expansion of the rural population in the first half of the sixteenth century. Young migrants streamed towards Paris from all over the northern part of the kingdom during this period, swelling the population of the city. Largely unskilled and desperate to escape the general poverty that prevailed among newcomers, they were prepared to work for whatever wages they could get. As we have suggested, the accessibility of this relatively cheap labour force goes far to explain the dynamism of the Parisian economy in the first half of the century. At the same time, the process of developing such a supply of labour was far from being a smooth one. The authorities attempted to assure the obedience of such a workforce through a variety of mechanisms. It was even prepared to experiment with training it at public expense where necessary. But certain of those who were being forced into the position of becoming wage workers resisted the process. Some peasants as well as artisans tried to provide themselves with alternative means of subsistence. Others tried to fight back by organizing themselves and on occasion even by withholding their labour altogether.

The emergence of rural capitalism in the Ile-de-France has been carefully documented by Jacquart.[10] Its characteristics seem to parallel more closely capitalist development in Languedoc rather than in Normandy. From the late fifteenth century, a distinct opposition developed between a comparatively small group of well-off *laboureurs* and the mass of small-scale producers, the so-called *censitaires*. The latter element barely held enough land to eke out a subsistence living for themselves and their families. Meanwhile, *laboureurs* were able to use their substantial allotments to produce surpluses of food for sale on the expanding markets of Paris. This fundamental division in the rural population was confirmed and accentuated throughout the sixteenth century. Population increase and equal division of inheritance among male heirs reinforced the tendency to parcelling out of land and immiseration among the mass of the peasants. At the same time, only *laboureurs* had the capital, equipment and expertise to take up the leases offered by the nobility and the religious houses on their lands in the Ile-de-France. Between 1540 and 1560 the practice developed among the aristocracy and the monastic clergy of renting their *réserve en bloc* to prosperous *laboureurs*. Buying out the properties of the poor, leasing out still others, marketing food, fodder and cattle, loaning equipment or money, the most wealthy of these *laboureurs* emerged as a new stratum of rural capitalists. In contrast, the mass of the rural population, including *manouvriers*, *vignerons*, shepherds and rural artisans, were forced to turn

[10] Jacquart, *La crise rurale en Ile-de-France*.

31

to wage labour and to purchasing an increasing proportion of their food in the course of the sixteenth century.[11]

The emergence of a wage-earning class in France did not occur overnight. On the contrary, in a country like France the development of a proletariat can only be understood as the result of a long-drawn-out process that took place over centuries. Moreover, it cannot be said that those who kept written records paid particular attention to this phenomenon. Like the history of women, the history of the emergence of wage workers is in good part a hidden one. As a result, one has to search here and there and everywhere in order to uncover their traces.

One especially alert sixteenth-century observer, who did take note of the process of proletarianization in his region, was a merchant from Le Puy, Etienne de Médicis.[12] His chronicle represents a remarkable attempt to capture and even to quantify, as far as possible, the social and economic life of his town and the Velay region surrounding it. It is Médicis who provides us with a rare, indeed perhaps unique, description of the process of proletarianization during the sixteenth century. In the first place, Médicis observed how relatively infertile and heavily populated a region was the Velay. As a result of the ensuing economic difficulties, he noted that many of the rural folk moved to Le Puy. Some of these newcomers became servants and domestics. Others tried to learn a craft or even how to read. Still others earned their livelihood as wage workers. But the ranks of such wage labourers, Médicis noted, were not made up only of migrants from the countryside. They were also composed of craftsmen who had been reduced to this condition by economic circumstances. Some of the artisans became poor because of their large families or the high cost of living. Others were forced into this condition as a result of heavy taxation or poor management of their affairs. Médicis himself was a moneylender. Nevertheless, he was honest enough to admit that it was possible that some of these unfortunates were ruined because of the accumulated burden of their debts. All of these sorts of people, of whom, Médicis noted, there were many in the town, were forced to earn their living by working for wages as porters, stevedores or labourers. Every day these workers assembled in one of the principal public squares of the city which served as a labour market.[13] As a token of their vocation, they each wore a cord which they hung from their belt as they waited to be hired for the day. Indeed, as they waited in the square to be taken on to load, unload or to carry freight, they assembled together, in what Médicis described as a *collège*, which was full of vain, if amusing, talk and story-telling. Indeed, in the pious and paternalistic city of Le Puy, the authorities

---

[11] Jacquart and M. François, 'Le beau XVIᵉ siècle' in *Histoire de l'Ile-de-France et de Paris*, ed. Mollat (Toulouse, 1971), pp. 208–10.

[12] *Livre de Podio ou chroniques d'Etienne Médicis, bourgeois du Puy: 1475–1565*, ed. A. Chaissang, 2 vols. (Le Puy, 1869).

[13] On urban labour markets see Bronislaw Geremek, *La salariat dans l'artisanat Parisien aux XIIᵉ–XVᵉ siècles* (Paris-La Haye, 1968), p. 126.

attempted to help them find their place by allowing them to create their own confraternity with their special patron saint.[14]

Elsewhere in his chronicle, Médicis takes notice of the so-called 'rayols', agricultural workers who came down from the mountains of Gevaudan and Haut-Vivarais to harvest the grain in the Velay.[15] Thomas Platter, likewise, spoke of the workers in the vineyards of Languedoc, who rose at two o'clock in the morning to stand in the public square of Montpellier in hope of finding work. The hours of these vine-dressers were so long and hard that it was necessary for their employers to feed them six times a day in order to keep them going.[16] In the salt-works of Peccais many seasonal labourers from the Cevennes found work during the hottest months of the summer. They were joined by hundreds more from Provence itself. The intense heat and difficult work was relieved by a quaint custom. These workers had the right to curse any passer-by, no matter how elevated his rank, who happened to travel past by the way.[17] At Marseilles the authorities annually brought in up to 2,000 migrants in February and March to take care of the vines in and around the city.[18] Indeed, the migration of wage labourers throughout the Midi assumed the form of a kind of human transhumance. Many workers, especially from the Comminges, crossed the Pyrenees to work in Catalonia, where wages were higher than they were in France.[19]

The significance of wage work in agriculture becomes evident if one examines the diaries of the Sire de Gouberville in Normandy.[20] Perusing this record, it seems clear that Gouberville was accustomed to hiring labour by the day, week, month and year. In the spring the work of ploughmen was necessary. They were taken on along with their ploughs and draught animals in order to prepare and plant the fields. But the great bulk of the labour employed by Gouberville appears to be related to the mowing of hay and the harvesting of the crops, which involved

[14] *Livre de Podio*, I, 366–7.

[15] Ibid., I, 462. See Abel Poitrineau, *Remues d'hommes: essai sur les migrations montagnards en France aux XVIIe et XVIIIe siècles* (Paris, 1982); Pior Paolo Viazzo, *Upland Communities: Environment, Population and Social Structure in the Alps since the Sixteenth Century* (Cambridge, 1989), p. 40; Eugène Sol, 'La propriété en Quercy avant le XVIIe siècle', *Revue d'histoire économique et sociale* 23 (1936–7), 80.

[16] *Felix et Thomas Platter à Montpellier, 1552–1559, 1595–1599: notes de voyage de deux étudiants bâlois* (Montpellier, 1892), p. 201.

[17] Ibid., pp. 365–6.

[18] *Histoire du commerce de Marseille*, ed. Gaston Rambert, vol. III: *De 1480 à 1599* by Raymond Collier and Joseph Billioud (Paris, 1951), p. 185.

[19] Jorge Nadal and Emile Giralt, *La population catalane de 1553 à 1717: l'immigration française* (Paris, 1960), pp. 62, 126, 157–9; Christine Langé, 'L'emigration française en Aragon, XVIe siècle et première moitié du XVIIe siècle' in *Les Français en Espagne à l'époque moderne (XVIe–XVIIe siècles). Colloque Toulouse, 7–8 octobre 1987* (Paris, 1990), pp. 26–44.

[20] *Journal manuscrit d'un sire de Gouberville et du Mesnil au Val gentilhomme campagnard du Cotentin de 1558 à 1562* 2nd edn (Rennes, 1879; La Haye, 1972); Madeleine Foisil, *Le sire de Gouberville: un gentilhomme normand au XVIe siècle* (Paris, 1985), pp. 153–7. See also *Le journal de Guillaume Paradin ou la vie en Beaujolais au temps de la renaissance (vers 1510–1589)*, ed. Mathieu Méras (Geneva, 1986), pp. 35–6, 77, 81, 83–4, 88–9, 92.

hiring scores of both males and females from neighbouring villages. Gouberville also engaged house servants who would remain in his service for periods of up to three years. It is clear that payment in kind, or partly in kind, did play its part. But it seems evident that payment in coin was increasingly the norm. The spread of wage labour is exemplified at Le Havre, where the construction of the port in the first part of the sixteenth century was initiated with the use of *corvée* labour. Soon, this system proved to be ineffective and was replaced by the hiring of wage labour, whose wages were paid by imposing tax levies on the surrounding communities.[21]

Le Roy Ladurie has carried out a systematic study of the economic circumstances of agricultural workers in Languedoc. Real wages, paid in money or kind, did not cease to deteriorate throughout the sixteenth century.[22] Particularly hard hit were the wages of women agrarian workers, who were overwhelmingly preponderant among those employed outside the vineyards. Traditionally, their wages had been half those of their male counterparts. But in the course of the sixteenth century, their wages fell to one-third of those of male workers.[23]

The mining industry in France never achieved a level of development comparable to Germany and Central Europe. Nevertheless, as we have noted, from the middle of the fifteenth century there was a rapid development of mining in Dauphiné, Lyonnais, Nivernais and the Pyrenees.[24] At Pampelieu in the mid-fifteenth century, the mine and forge there employed 376 workers.[25] At the beginning of the sixteenth century, the mine at Suchel à Ancy operated with a work force of 400 men.[26] Wage workers were required in substantial numbers to operate the iron smelters and forges which, as we have seen, grew so rapidly in the first part of the sixteenth century. Nicolas de Nicolay spoke of the forges of the Forez in the 1570s as 'much frequented by an infinity of certain poor foreign forgers who come and go like birds of passage'.[27] Quarries, likewise, required large numbers of workers. The quarries around Angers, for example, produced several hundred thousand slates a year which were used to cover the roofs of houses, chateaux and churches. Several hundred workers found steady employment at these work sites.[28]

The shipyards of the kingdom, which, generally speaking, were small in size and scattered along the coast of northern and western France, would nevertheless have required a substantial number of wage labourers to produce the 200–400

---

21 *Histoire du Havre et de l'estuaire de la Seine*, ed. André Corvisier (Toulouse, Privat, 1983), p. 48.
22 Le Roy Ladurie, *Les paysans de Languedoc*, I, 263–76.
23 Ibid., I, 276–7.
24 Hesse, *La mine et les mineurs en France*, p. 401.
25 Ibid., p. 581.
26 Ibid., p. 582. A recently published *règlement* (1560) for the mines of Pontgibaud (Puy-de-Dôme) provides extensive information on conditions of employment in the mining sector. See *Catalogue des Actes de François II*, ed. Marie-Thérèse de Martel (Paris, 1991), II, 763–81.
27 Nicolay, *Description générale de la ville de Lyon*, p. 162.
28 F. Soulez Larivière, *Les ardoisières d'Angers* (Angers, 1979), p. 28.

ships a year constructed in the first half of the sixteenth century.[29] Sailors were another form of wage labourers. The general rule was that a ship of 100 tons required a crew of 100 sailors.[30] In practice this rule was not adhered to. Merchants and captains sought to economize on the size of crews as much as possible. Likewise, they tried to pay those employed as little as they could. Brittany was a favourite recruiting-ground since experienced sailors could be found there most cheaply.[31]

The first part of the sixteenth century thus saw a significant expansion of wage labour. However, it is important to reiterate that the process of proletarianization was only at its beginning during this period. Only a small proportion of the population was totally dependent on wage labour for a livelihood. Many more combined occasional or seasonal wage labour with other means of subsistence. Many avoided wage labour, preferring other kinds of subsistence where possible. A preference for leisure as against working for subsistence wages likewise posed a problem to employers. In his study of the relationship between demography and proletarianization in European history, Charles Tilly has attempted to characterize this complex process by arguing that the rate of proletarianization can be understood as a product of the change in the rate of dependence on wage employment added to the change in the rate of expropriation.[32] Historically, expropriation and dependence on wages are quite distinct phenomena. The loss of the land through expropriation is not automatically followed by the offer or the acceptance of wage employment. Likewise, families can become partially dependent on wage labour without, necessarily, losing their land. Tilly, particularly, underlines the connection between proletarianization and higher rates of fertility. This relationship was even commented on in the sixteenth century. Thus, a councillor in the Paris Parlement in the 1540s disapprovingly noted the precocious fertility of young Parisian workers. He observed that the majority of the apprentices in the city had abandoned their apprenticeships and were working outside the system of apprenticeships. No longer being apprentices, such men had no hope of becoming masters. These young men without property married before they reached the age of twenty, attaching themselves to girls that were as poor as they were. Soon after, they had large families which they could not support, so that they and their children often became beggars.[33] Implicitly, this magistrate was comparing the reckless behaviour of these young workers with the more cautious procreative

---

29 Devèze, *La vie de la forêt française*, II, 54; Isambert, *Recueil générale*, XIII, 587. On naval construction see Jacques Bernard, *Navires et gens de mer à Bordeaux (vers 1400–vers 1550)* (Paris, 1968), I, 317–48.

30 Henri Lapellinière, *L'Amiral de France* (Paris, 1584), pp. 54–5, 60–2; Mollat, *Le commerce maritime normand à la fin du moyen âge: étude d'histoire économique et social* (Paris, 1952), p. 345.

31 Charles de la Roncière, *Histoire de la marine française* (Paris, 1900), II, 458; Bernard, *Navires et gens de mer*, II, 589–90.

32 'Demographic Origins of the European Proletariat' in *Proletarianization and Family History*, ed. David Levine (Orlando, Florida, 1984), p. 18.

33 Coll. Lamoignon, VII, fo. 324r.–v.

stance of his own class. Despite such interesting titbits of evidence, it is one of the curiosities of the French school of demography that it does not seem to pay much attention to differences of class in studying the reproductive activity of the population of the sixteenth and seventeenth centuries.[34]

SUBSISTENCE, PROTO-INDUSTRY AND THE POOR

Dependence on wage labour and the expropriation of small peasant producers both increased in the first half of the sixteenth century in the Ile-de-France.[35] But neither of these processes had yet advanced very far at this stage. Most rural workers or *manouvriers* normally had a garden, patch of land, and rights of grazing, gleaning and pasturage to supplement their wages. The forests, where they still stood, offered all sorts of subsistence possibilities to hard-pressed peasant families for foraging, pasturing and poaching. Many found a livelihood, or part of a livelihood, through cutting and hauling timber, making ash or charcoal, and manufacturing all kinds of wooden shoes, utensils, tools, barrels and furniture.[36]

The role of the forests in providing non-wage means of subsistence is vividly described by Jean Du Choul. Part of the population of the region of Mont Pilat, according to him, earned their livelihood in the underground coal-mines that had developed in the region. A part of the workforce of the region was thus at least partially proletarianized. But wage work, being still quite scarce and other means of subsistence being available, the population was far from being significantly proletarianized. The vast forests in which they lived offered them immense resources. Du Choul describes these mountain folk as at once poor and deeply religious. According to him, the poverty of these people was far from being a dishonourable state for it stimulated their eagerness to earn a living and increased their sense of economy. Rather than remaining idle, the population manufactured all sorts of articles out of wood. The children of these people carried this merchandise to the city for sale. Du Choul concludes that it was the very lack of grain and money which helped to make these mountain people so industrious.[37] From our point of view, the lack of sufficient available wage employment and the existence of alternative means of subsistence retarded the degree of proletarianization.

The development of proletarianization must thus be seen in the light of the growth of such rural industry or proto-industrialization which spread so widely in

---

[34] French population studies for this period are hampered by a lack of baptismal records. Those investigations that have been carried out lack a class dimension as compared to those of the eighteenth century. See Bernard Derouet, 'Une démographie differentielle: clés pour un système auto-régulateur des populations rurales d'*ancien régime*,' *Annales: ESC* 35 (1980), 3–37; Moriceau, *Les fermiers de l'Ile-de-France*, pp. 145–6.

[35] Jacquart, *La crise rurale en Ile-de-France*, pp. 140–1, 145.

[36] Devèze, *La vie de la forêt française*, II, 130–48.

[37] Du Choul, *Description du Mont Pilat*, p. 21.

the sixteenth century. So, likewise, in the Hurepoix region south of Paris, the spread of rural industry represented a partial solution to the problem of the increasing immiseration of the majority of the population.[38] Proto-industrialization represented in part an alternative to proletarianization and in part a half-way house on the way towards it. In the event, there clearly emerged in the sixteenth century the phenomenon known as a wage-earning peasantry or a peasantry dependent, to a greater or lesser degree, on wages which had become necessary to its continued existence.[39]

Despite the greater opportunities for wage employment, there were far more people looking for such work than could find it in the first part of the sixteenth century. Expropriation from the land, partial though it was, and, especially, population increase were responsible for this situation. Increasing supplies of relatively low-cost labour help to explain the economic dynamism of France during this period. On the other hand, problems of unemployment and under-employment were chronic, especially in the all too frequently recurring periods of economic crisis. The poor were thus an increasingly serious problem, especially noticeable in the towns from the 1520s onwards.[40] The poor made up a large and growing part of the population of the towns. Robert Favreau, for example, estimated those who could be classified as poor in Poitiers at mid-century at well over 50 per cent of the population, while in a recent work on poverty at Bordeaux, Martin Dinges concluded that fully 80 per cent of the population were susceptible to poverty.[41]

The poor as a problem were an ever-expanding, although largely urban, phenomenon. As a category the poor certainly included wage workers like journeymen, *manouvriers*, *valets* and servants. Jean-Pierre Camus, indeed, in the seventeenth century, would define the poor as those who have no other means of livelihood except their work or industry.[42] But the poor as defined even by Camus included far more than wage-earners. In reality, the 'poor' was a vast, hetero-genous and amorphous underclass which included not only wage-earners, but also encompassed small-scale artisans, pedlars, street vendors, widows, orphans, cripples, invalids, old people, beggars and vagabonds. Their efforts at survival

---

[38] Jacquart, *La crise rurale en Ile-de-France*, pp. 144–5; Bezard, *La vie rurale*, pp. 176–8.
[39] On the nature of a wage-earning peasantry see Douglas R. Holmes, *Cultural Disenchantments: Worker Peasantries in Northeast Italy* (Princeton, 1989), p. 57.
[40] Geremek, 'Criminalité, vagabondage, pauperisme: la marginalité à l'aube des temps modernes,' *Revue d'histoire moderne et contemporaine* 21 (1974), 337–75; Geremek, 'La populazione marginale tra il medioevo e l'era moderna', *Studi storici* 9 (1968), 23–40; Heller, *The Conquest of Poverty*, pp. 18–20, 146–7.
[41] *La ville de Poitiers à la fin du moyen âge* (Poitiers, 1978), II, 559; Martin Dinges, *Stadtarmut in Bordeaux 1525–1675: Alltag-Politik, Mentalitäten* (Bonn, 1988), p. 67. At Grenoble the figure in this category is 73 per cent. *Histoire de la France urbaine*, ed. Georges Duby, vol. II: *La ville classique*, ed. Roger Chartier *et al.* (Paris, 1981), p. 201.
[42] Jean-Pierre Gutton, *La société et les pauvres: l'exemple de la généralité de Lyon, 1534–1789* (Paris, 1971), pp. 10–11.

37

often aroused the antipathy of the powerful. In 1539, for example, the Chambre des Tournelles of the Paris Parlement ordered the clearing of street vendors, idlers, beggars and vagrants who were infesting the steps of the Palais de Justice. The peddling, begging, gambling and thieving of this motley gang had become a direct nuisance to the elite.[43]

The poor were categorized by the authorities as *valides* or *puissans*, those who were capable of work but were unable for some reason to find any, and the *invalides* or *impuissans*, who because of injury, illness or age were unable to work. There were also among the poor the so-called *honteux*, the feared and despised vagrant and beggar population who made idleness a way of life. Economic crisis periodically swelled the ranks of the poor with craftsmen and workers unable to find work. But it seems clear that the number of people overall in the category of the poor increased as the sixteenth century wore on. Urban governments regarded the expanding mix of poor people as their single greatest challenge. At times the sheer number and desperation of the poor induced a sense of panic among the elite.

The vast number of such people is illustrated by an analysis recently made of the population of Paris subject to the so-called free gift of 1571.[44] According to Robert Descimon, the 16,000 names which appear on the list could not amount to more than 40 per cent of the city's households. He calculates that this number did not represent more than 140,000 of the total of an estimated 300,000 inhabitants. But of those on the list nearly 19 per cent could not afford to pay any tax. Excluded altogether were the other 60 per cent of the population, many of whom lived in rented rooms. By no means all of this latter group can be regarded as poor, but undoubtedly most were. Of this number, a large fraction were people who worked for a wage or who were seeking such work.

It is impossible to estimate the total number of wage workers in the city. Such an estimate involves too many variables and unknowns. On the other hand, there does exist a contemporary estimate of the number of unskilled workers. In 1536, a year which saw yet another outbreak of the Habsburg–Valois conflict, the king ordered the strengthening of the defences of the capital. The bishop of Paris and the king's *lieutenant*, Jean Du Bellay, commanded the bourgeoisie to furnish *manouvriers* and *gens de peine* to work on the city's fortifications. A councillor in the Parlement noted that this should have totalled 16,000 men, which amounts to 20 or 25 per cent of the total male workforce.[45]

The control of the poor was among the highest priorities of the government. Of the 247 police decrees of the Paris Parlement in the Collection Dupré for the period 1536–1559, 17 per cent deal with the poor. That figure is exceeded only by

---

[43] AN U 448.
[44] 'Paris on the Eve of Saint Bartholomew: Taxation, Privilege and Social Geography' in *Cities and Social Change*, ed. Benedict, pp. 69–104.
[45] *Reg. BVP* II, 253, n. 1.

the number of decrees devoted to public security. Indeed, the issue of the poor and that of public security were matters which were closely connected in the minds of the magistrates. All other questions of administration trailed far behind.[46]

Many of those who actually enrolled among the ranks of the poor were newcomers to the city. Thus, for example, in 1556, of the 5,000 on the rolls of the Bureau des Pauvres most were from Normandy. Only a minority came from Paris.[47] Likewise, it was reported in 1580 that only one in ten on the rolls of the poor relief were Parisians.[48]

Throughout the century the standard way of dealing with the swelling numbers of the poor in periods of economic crisis was through public works. The authorities made sure that the poor were employed at building or repairing the fortifications of the towns. In 1542 the Parlement suggested that the poor of Paris be set to work through the establishment of a cloth manufacture to be funded by the city drapers.[49] Such a manufacture would have replaced much of the cloth imported from the towns of northern France, while providing productive employment to the poor. Two years later, the municipal government established a Bureau des Pauvres, modelling the reform of poor relief on that carried out at Lyons a decade earlier.[50]

The Parlement showed itself to be particularly solicitous of the fate of the children of the poor. Its consistent aim was to find the means of turning such children into productive workers. In 1535 the Parlement set aside the existing guild regulations on employment in an effort to do so. The guild statutes normally restricted training to those enrolled as apprentices. In addition to their accustomed apprentices, the court now allowed masters to take both male and female children of the poor into their employ and to instruct them in their craft.[51] Six years later, the Parlement decreed that the poor were to send their children to school to learn the elements of the Catholic religion and to read and write.[52]

In 1545 the Parlement took the lead in the creation of the Hôpital de la Trinité.[53] The creation of the Hôpital was the most important initiative of the Parisian authorities to try to create a trained and docile supply of workers for the skilled trades. The purpose of this foundation at first was to implement the

[46] BN MS Fr. 8066. The problem of the Parisian poor is briefly considered in Barbara B. Diefendorf, *Beneath the Cross: Catholics and Huguenots in Sixteenth Century Paris* (New York, 1991), pp. 20–1.

[47] BN MS Fr. 8075, fo. 339r.–v.

[48] BHVP MS CP 5168.

[49] BN MS Fr. 8075, fos. 11v.–12r.

[50] Coyecque, 'L'assistance publique à Paris au milieu du XVIᵉ siècle', *Bull. soc. hist. Paris* 15 (1888), 105–18; Marcel Fosseyeux, 'L'asssistance parisienne au milieu du XVIᵉ siècle', *MSHP* 43 (1916), 83–128; Dom Michel Félibien, *Histoire de la ville de Paris* (Paris, 1725), II, 1018–19.

[51] Coll. Lamoignon, VI, fo. 332r., BN MS Fr. 8075, fo. 429r.

[52] Coll. Lamoignon, VI, fo. 674v.

[53] Félibien, *Histoire de la ville de Paris*, II, 1018–19; Fosseyeux, 'Les maisons d'apprentissage à Paris sous l'*ancien régime*', *Bull. soc. hist. Paris* 40 (1913), 36–56.

parlementary decree of 1535 which aimed to place poor children in the shops of the craftsmen. Some 300–400 were so placed in following years. But the majority of these children soon left these workplaces, either because of the hostility they encountered from the apprentices, or because of interference by their parents.[54] The new policy of the Hôpital became to separate the children as much as possible from their parents. In 1549 the Parlement forbade parents from trying to remove their children from the Hôpital.[55] The originality of this cruel policy has been underlined in a work recently published by Maurice Capul.[56] In order to break the bonds of poverty, the authorities had come to the conclusion that the new generation had to be separated from their parents, who had sunk into a life of indolence and dissolution.

The new policy required the enclosure of the children of the poor of both sexes until their late twenties. Indeed, the regime imposed on the children was one of almost monastic rigour.[57] The Hôpital was run by a board made up of three bourgeois, a councillor of the Parlement, a cleric and a representative of the governor of the city.

Boys and girls were kept strictly segregated by an iron grille placed between their dormitories. The youngest were sent to school, the older ones set to work learning a craft from a master. Those inmates of the Hôpital who had reached their twenties helped the masters to teach the younger children a trade. Late marriage was one of the objectives of the institution. Precocious marriage, before a young man or woman had learned a craft and acquired a material stake, was believed invariably to lead to poverty.[58]

The older boys and girls rose at five o'clock in summer and six o'clock in winter. Younger children were allowed an hour's respite. After hearing Mass in the chapel, inmates were provided with a ration of bread and then proceeded to school or to work. Prayers and a simple meal marked the mid-day and the early evening, with work or instruction continuing until nine o'clock at night. Daily rations were one pound of bread, six ounces of meat and a bowl of soup. The Hôpital provided a simple uniform, including shoes and socks, although the children were to go barefoot during the summer months.[59]

The purpose of this austere regime, which was marked by constant religious training and exercises, was to instil a sense of obedience and discipline which would properly prepare the children for the requirements of the workplace. No secret was made of the expectation that a steady supply of such young workers to the Paris labour market would make it possible for masters to hold down wages. Policies of wage restraint were made more attractive to consumers by the promise

---

[54] Coll. Lamoignon, VII, fo. 321r.–v.
[55] Fosseyeux, 'Les maisons d'apprentissage', p. 40.
[56] *Abandon et marginalité: les enfants placé sous l'ancien régime* (Toulouse, 1989), p. 128.
[57] *Institution des enfants de l'hospital de la Trinité* (Paris, 1553).
[58] Coll. Lamoignon, VII, fos. 383v.–384r.
[59] *Institution des enfants*, pp. 253–5.

of lower prices. It was asserted that high prices were the result of the debauched behaviour of apprentices who absented themselves on work-days. These young workers spent their time in taverns, forcing the masters to pay higher wages. On the contrary, the hope was that the Hôpital would provide the city with an enlarged pool of skilled workers from which the masters could choose their employees. Moreover, it was believed that the graduates of the Hôpital, who had been raised in sobriety and discipline, would have a deeper sense of responsibility than many of those apprentices and journeymen currently employed.[60]

Given that such ideas lay behind the establishment of the Hôpital, the violent reaction of the Parisian apprentices towards it is not surprising. Somewhat more unexpected is the hostility of the masters as well. The Hôpital employed craftsmen, some of whom maintained their own shops, to teach the children a large variety of the trades practised in the city. Indeed, the products manufactured by the children were put on sale in competition with those produced by the masters of the craft guilds. The result was that the Hôpital became the target of the hostility of the masters as well as the apprentices. Both groups together staged demonstrations in front of the Hôpital in the rue Saint Denis. Stones were thrown at the Hôpital and at the workshops of the teachers. Teachers and children from the Hôpital were roughed up in the streets. Indeed, the tapestry masters and apprentices threatened the lives of the instructors.[61] Opposition continued into the 1570s, particularly as the monarchy took the further step of exempting the graduates of the Hôpital from the usual requirements for receiving masterships in the guilds.[62]

DOWN AND OUT IN PARIS

The migration of would-be workers to Paris from the Ile-de-France and beyond is a striking reality of the first half of the sixteenth century. An outstanding, if somewhat unexpected, source of information about this workforce is the verse of the minor poet Christophe of Bordeaux.[63] Towards the middle of the century, Christophe published *Varlet à louer à tout faire*, a farcical treatment of the experiences of a young emigrant worker to Paris. The success of this piece no doubt encouraged him to follow it up with a complementary poem on a young female worker, the *Chambrière à louer à tout faire*.[64] Both poems purport to describe newly arrived workers to the city prepared to do just about anything to earn a living. Both pieces were written for the amusement of the middle class and

[60] Coll. Lamoignon, VIII, fos. 323v.–324r.
[61] Fosseyeux, 'Les maisons d'apprentissage', pp. 41–3.
[62] Coll. Lamoignon, VII, fos. 389r.–390v., IX, fos. 214r.–215r., 217r.
[63] On Christophe de Bordeaux see *DBF* VI, 1074; *Dictionnaire des lettres françaises*, ed. Monseigneur Georges Grente; *Le seizième siècle*, ed. A. Pauphilet *et al.* (Paris, 1951), pp. 119–20.
[64] *Recueil de poésies françoises des XVe et XVIe siècles*, ed. Anatole de Montaiglon (Paris, 1855), I, 73–108.

cannot be taken as a direct representation of working-class experience. Nevertheless, accuracy of detail is intrinsic to the very method of the poems. Both are based on the principle of *accumulation*, or the enumeration, in as amusing a fashion as possible, of as many examples of a phenomenon as conceivable. Thus, in offering himself for employment, the *valet*, or wage worker, claims, among innumerable other things that he can do, to do the impossible such as make two devils out of one,[65] take the moon between his teeth, cause the sun to eclipse, make the old run and goats dance,[66] give haircuts to goats and put spurs on rats.[67] In the course of listing these *congeries* or variations, however, Christophe, as a keen observer of Parisian life, provides us with some significant information about working-class existence. His need to introduce as many variations as possible in his poem helps to ensure that the list of occupations where wage labour was employed is probably fairly comprehensive. He enumerates at least 108 different categories of employment in which male wage labourers were employed. Of these some 62 were in manufacturing, another 32 in services and 14 in food provision.

The wage employment open to women was apparently far more restricted. It is true that a Swiss visitor to Paris in the 1570s noted that the women of Paris were more involved in commerce than women elsewhere. According to him, this reflected the remarkable freedom enjoyed by Parisian women.[68] Yet this freedom does not seem to have translated into a variety of occupational choices comparable to those of men. Christophe mentions about forty occupations carried on by women. It is not clear exactly how many of these could be pursued outside domestic service. We know that there were at least three guilds reserved exclusively for women: wigmakers and hairdressers, cheese and butter vendors, and linen and canvas makers. Three more guilds were of mixed sex: lingerie makers; embroiderers and chasuble makers; hatters and sheet makers.[69] Christophe mentions these as well as other female employments like dressmaker, ribbon maker, belt maker, street vendor, singer, musician and midwife which we know were carried on outside domestic service. Young girls were frequently apprenticed as lingerie makers, dressmakers, belt makers, embroiderers and butter and cheese vendors. Taken together, these tabulations of male and female occupations drawn

---

[65] Ibid., I, 76.
[66] Ibid., I, 86.
[67] Ibid., I, 86.
[68] 'La liberté des femmes est grande à Paris; elles sont fort entendues aux affaires commerciales': this is a quotation from the description of Paris by Théodore Zwinger, whose account has been translated and published by J. Cousin, 'Etat de Paris au XVIe siècle', *MSHP* 1 (1875), 111. See Cynthia Truant, 'The Guildswomen of Paris: Gender, Power and Sociability in the Old Regime', *Proceedings of the Annual Meeting of the Western Society for French History* 15 (1988), 130–8. On the limitations on women in the trades see Davis, 'Les femmes dans les arts mechaniques au XVIe siècle' in *Mélanges en hommage de Richard Gascon* (Lyons, 1980), I, 139–67; Evelyne Berriot-Salvadore, *Les femmes dans la société française de la renaissance* (Geneva, 1990), pp. 207–24.
[69] René Pillorget, *Nouvelle histoire de Paris: les premiers Bourbons* (Paris, 1988), p. 120. See BN MS Fr. 8607, fo. 219r.; Diefendorf, *Beneath the Cross*, pp. 19–20.

from Christophe make clear how far wage employment had developed in a city like Paris.

Christophe clearly understood that all of these employments had the common characteristic of the sale of labour for money. Part of the force of his poetry lies in demonstrating the great variety of things the *valet* or maid was prepared to do in exchange for this single and universal commodity. The *valet*'s first lines at the beginning of the poem make this clear:

> I am a jack-of-all-trades
> Who only wants a job.
> If anyone has need of me
> Behold! I am ready to work.[70]

The necessity of selling their labour for money leads the *valet* and maid to offer themselves in endless ways to whoever will pay them. The *valet* literally turns himself inside out offering an endless number of services that he is prepared to perform for the would-be employer. Indeed, a good part of the humour of both pieces from the perspective of the bourgeois reader lies in the recognition of the infinite variety of ways in which the *valet* tries to ingratiate himself. While his object is to amuse the reader through this enumeration, Christophe, in so doing, conveys the precariousness and insecurity of wage labour:

> It is true and I do not lie
> There is nothing that I will not do.[71]

The *valet* and maid are presented as young, living by their wits, and needing to hustle in order to gain a livelihood. They are certainly represented as not being above criminality. The *valet* is portrayed as a thief, counterfeiter, philanderer, gambler, drunk and abortionist. The maid is depicted as a thief and prostitute. As such, it is clear that these characters are thought of as part of the underworld of criminality.[72] At the same time there is an engaging quality to their mischief:

> I enrage but I also do marvels.[73]

With little to lose, the maid and *valet* are pictured as being prepared to do what respectable people cannot or will not do. In other words, the suppressed impulses of those with property are projected onto the behaviour of those without any means.[74]

---

[70] *Recueil des poésies françoises*, ed. Montaiglon, I, 73.
[71] Ibid., I, 82.
[72] The identification of the labouring classes with the dangerous classes in bourgeois opinion dates back at least to the sixteenth century. See Louis Chevalier, *Labouring Classes and Dangerous Classes in Paris During the First Half of the Nineteenth Century*, tr. Frank Jellinek (New York, 1973), pp. 359–72.
[73] *Recueil des poésies françoises*, ed. Montaiglon, I, 83.
[74] Gutton, *Domestiques et serviteurs dans la France de l'ancien régime* (Paris, 1981), p. 154.

The fact that Christophe made the *valet* and maid the subject of poetry testifies to the growing importance and visibility of wage workers. Contemporaries made a fundamental distinction in this respect between skilled and unskilled workers. It is, therefore, remarkable that Christophe makes no such distinction with respect to the *valet* and maid. In his poem a wage labourer who works as a shepherd, gardener or waiter appears to enjoy the same prestige as one who works for a weaver, shoemaker or mason. Working for a wage makes him assign them to the same stratum. *Valets*, in particular, existed in a realm below the level of the guild system of apprentices and journeymen. As such, they could never accede to masterships. While those who were part of the system still had the real or imagined expectation of such advancement, Christophe's *valet* had no possibility of it if he remained in that station. The *valet*'s fondest wish, with which Christophe concludes the poem, is therefore to be taken into domestic service. Entry into such service would represent a major step up in standard of living and security of employment.[75] Furthermore, domestic service held out the prospect for the still young *valet* of one day being taken on as an apprentice in a skilled trade.[76] In other words, the *valet*, who is the subject of Christophe's poetry, is part of an expanding pool of labour which was excluded from the apprenticeship system and so more or less permanently consigned to proletarian status.

SKILLED WORKERS

Skilled workers, who were part of the system of apprenticeship were thus a privileged minority of the actual labour force. An important source of information on the skilled working class in Paris in the sixteenth century is the collection of notarial contracts published by Ernest Coyecque at the beginning of this century.[77] Of the 6,610 contracts in this collection, 864 are apprenticeship agreements. Such apprenticeships were normally for two or three years in the late middle ages according to Bronislaw Geremek.[78] However, based on an analysis of the contracts in the Coyecque collection, the average length of apprenticeship increased to 3.75 years in the first half of the sixteenth century. The span of such contracts averaged 3.5 years for men, while it was slightly more than four years for women. Overwhelmingly, these young workers training for skilled occupations were recruited from Paris and the Ile-de-France, with almost 70 per cent coming from Paris alone. The north of France supplied most of the rest, with only a handful coming from the region south of the Loire valley.[79]

[75] *Recueil des poésies françoises*, ed. Montaiglon, I, 87–8.
[76] Pillorget, *Nouvelle histoire de Paris*, pp. 110–12.
[77] *Recueil d'actes notariés*.
[78] Geremek, *La salariat*, p. 31.
[79] It is noteworthy that two centuries later it was still from north of the Loire that the Parisian working class was recruited. See Daniel Roche, *The People of Paris: An Essay in Popular Culture in the 18th Century*, tr. Marie Evans and Gwynne Lewis (Berkeley, 1987), p. 26.

Of the 864 contracts of apprenticeship in Coyecque seventy-one, or 8 per cent, involved women. A few of these female apprenticeships were cases of hardship. Thus, for instance, we have the example of Jeanne Hebert of the faubourg Saint-Marcel.[80] Jeanne was the wife of a mercer, Jean Louvere, who had been absent from the city for more than a year. After months of waiting for her husband's return, Jeanne found herself destitute. Accordingly, another mercer, Andre Willerme, and his wife, Phillipes Musnyer, a belt maker by vocation, consented to take Jeanne into apprenticeship out of pity for her situation. They agreed to apprentice her for three years, providing bed and board, promising to show her how to make belts and other articles and consenting to pay her 17 *livres tournois*. It is noteworthy that, although she was to learn Phillipes' vocation, Jeanne nevertheless had to be apprenticed to both Phillipes and her husband.

Most females who were apprenticed were much younger than Jeanne. Normally, they were pre-adolescent girls. Having a vocation would eventually represent a substantial asset when they entered the marriage market. The apprenticeship of Marion Chaperon at the age of five is typical in this respect.[81] Her father, the fuller Pierre Chaperon, apprenticed her until the age of fourteen to the mason, Jacques Regnault, of the faubourg Saint-Marcel. The agreement stipulated that she be taught hat-making by Regnault's daughter or by someone equivalently qualified. The apprenticeship would end in nine years, at which time Marion would be given cloth and linens in payment. It was further provided that her apprenticeship could be prolonged until the age of twenty, at which time she need not be paid provided Regnault could arrange a marriage for her comparable to that to be provided for his daughter.

Coyecque's collection of notarial documents also records numerous agreements involving *compagnons*. These include contracts for employment by the piece,[82] by the week[83] or by the year.[84] A not untypical annual contract is one in which Augustin Bassier of the faubourg Saint-Marcel promised to serve as a fuller in the faubourg Saint-Marcel as well as at a fulling mill at Essones. Bassier was to live at the mill, full hats there and transport them to Paris.[85] At times the language of such employment agreements has an ambiguous quality. Thus, Philibert Goyer is described in one such contract as both a *compagnon* and apprentice mason.[86] Obviously, Goyer had a certain qualification and age. Nevertheless, he agreed to apprentice himself for six years to master mason Nicolas Menager, who would teach him the craft and pay him 3 sols per day when he required him on a job.

[80] Coyecque, *Recueil des actes notariés*, no. 460.
[81] Ibid., no. 4678.
[82] Ibid., no. 205.
[83] Ibid., no. 206.
[84] Ibid., no. 1336.
[85] Ibid., nos. 1445, 4048, Fuller bonnetiers were explicitly subordinated to the master bonnetiers by the statutes of 1550. See Lespinasse, *Les métiers et corporations*, III, 252.
[86] Coyecque, *Recueil des actes notariés*, no. 2857.

Otherwise, it was agreed that he could work elsewhere, subject to being called to work with Menager at two days' notice. Such an arrangement implied a tight labour market in which the *compagnon* had to compete with other more or less qualified employees, hoping, eventually, to be recognized as a master mason. That masterships in the construction industry were especially difficult to obtain is confirmed by royal letters of 1568 which noted that an 'infinitude' of *compagnon* pavers had been unable to achieve masterships.[87]

It is true that the social and economic circumstances of the majority of Parisian *compagnons* tended to decline alongside that of the rest of the working population. Nevertheless, it is a mistake to see this upper stratum of the workforce as all suffering the same fate. The economic and social prospects of a *compagnon* draper like François Jacquet, who married Jeanne Grouyn in 1552, were evidently far superior to those of most *compagnons*. Jacquet was already a junior partner in his father's cloth business. The bride's father was a merchant bourgeois of the city who provided a dowry of 200 *livres tournois* along with making available a house as well as part of an interest in a rural property to the newly-weds.[88] Jacquart's experience as a *compagnon* was only a stage in a life cycle in which he could expect eventually to become part of the Parisian merchant elite.

If not every *compagnon* had such rosy prospects there were, nevertheless, doors which still stood wide open. The possibilities of Abel Regnier, a *compagnon* cooper, if not so auspicious as those of François Jacquet, were by no means inconsiderable. Regnier emigrated to Paris from the Brie. In 1554, he agreed to marry Perine Pasquier, who hailed from Picardy where her father was a *laboureur*. Her uncle Jean Pasquier was a master cooper in the rue Serpente. According to the marriage contract, it was Jean Pasquier, the uncle, who provided his niece's trousseau. Furthermore, he agreed to provide Pasquier with employment as well as lodgings for the next six years.[89] Many *compagnons* were the owners or heirs to bits of property, usually located in the regions from which they had migrated.[90] In 1551, for example, Jean Du Pont, a *compagnon* tapestry maker, handed over to his nephew, Pierre Picart, his rights to the major portion of a house and land near La Flèche in Anjou. Pierre was the son of Simon Picart *gaigne denier* and was a student at the University of Paris.[91] Indeed, some *manouvriers* were not without property. Thus, in 1551, we find Remy Le Marche *manouvrier* transferring title to a piece of land held by him and his wife to their son, a student at the University.[92]

Madeleine Jürgens has prepared a list of the inventories after death in the

87 BN MS Fr. 8081, fo. 329r.
88 *Inventaire des registres des insinuations du Châtelet de Paris, règnes de François I⁰ʳ, et de Henri II*, ed. Emile Carpardon and Alexandre Tuetey (Paris, 1906), no. 4313.
89 Ibid., no. 5345.
90 Ibid., nos. 1441, 1474, 1523, 1597, 1707.
91 Ibid., no. 3911.
92 Ibid., no. 3274.

Minutier Central for the late fifteenth and early sixteenth centuries.[93] Of the 1,532 Parisians on this list, only fifty-eight were *compagnons* or the wives of *compagnons*. The small percentage of such inventories must be taken as reflecting more than the relatively young age of this social category. Most *compagnons*, apparently, had too few worldly goods worth the expense of preparing an inventory. Thus, the meagre number of inventories in this category listed by Jürgens can hardly be taken as representative of the possessions of the group as a whole.[94] A sample of these inventories nevertheless indicates ownership of a considerable number of household items and a certain level of material comfort. Among these better-off *compagnons* oak beds, canopies, chairs, benches, tables, chests, tableware, linens, shirts and robes were common household items.[95]

MASTERS AND WORKERS: DEPENDENCY AND RESISTANCE

Masters and workers, especially in the skilled trades, continued to be linked by ties of significant mutual interest. They were attached to one another, in the first place, by shared vocational concerns and the hope of many apprentices and *compagnons* of one day becoming masters themselves. Many apprentices and *compagnons* continued to live under the same roof as their masters, sharing their tables. Even where this was no longer the case, the relationship between a master and his workers continued to have something of the aspect of the patriarchal family to it. At the least, the worker continued to be looked upon as a kind of domestic servant.[96]

The term 'servant' was, in fact, commonly used to refer, not only to domestics, but to wage workers in general. Indeed, employers sometimes made use of the confusion for their own purposes. An illuminating example is to be found in the Parisian dyeing industry in which a dispute in 1514 between the masters and apprentices led the masters to lock out the apprentices and to replace them with non-Parisian workers. The dyeing of cloth in large quantities was fast becoming Paris' leading industry. This dispute was in fact an important stage in the transformation of this traditional craft into a major capitalist industry in the first half of the sixteenth century. The dismissed employees, many of whom had been at the point of completing their apprenticeships, refused to accept the lock-out by their employers. For years thereafter, they sought to induce the new workers to walk out and join those already thrown out of their work. The master dyers, especially, complained about the repeated attempts of the discharged apprentices

[93] Madeleine Jürgens, *Documents du Minutier Centrale des notaires de Paris. Inventaires après décès*, vol. I: *1483–1547* (Paris, 1985).

[94] On this point see Dinges, 'Materielle Kultur und Alltag. Die Unterschichten in Bordeaux im 16/17 Jahrhunderts', *Francia* 15 (1987), 262.

[95] Inventories consulted in AN Min. Cent.: in étude III, 117, étude IX, 129, 130, étude XIX, 60, 267, étude XX, 34, étude XXXVI, 9, étude LXXXVI, 91.

[96] Geremek, *La salariat*, pp. 38, 101; Gutton, *Domestiques et serviteurs*, p. 14.

to seduce the new employees by getting them to go off to the taverns. The taverns in the sixteenth century, it should be noted, often served as safe havens where wage workers could assemble and discuss their grievances against their employers. More colourfully, the taverns were considered by the authorities to be places of *debauch*, redoubts of plebeian excess to which workers would defiantly flee from unsatisfactory work.[97]

The locked-out apprentices in this dispute carried on a legal battle which went on for years. Defending their dismissal of the apprentices in the courts during the 1530s, the masters described their former employees as corrupt and ill-humoured servants whom no respectable bourgeois would keep in his home in the midst of his wife and children.[98] The employers thus defended themselves by stressing the threat to the family posed by such domestic servants. In fact, the dyers' guild was in the process of freeing itself from most of the restrictions which had limited the medieval corporation.[99] Dyers like the Gobelin and Canaye were operating large-scale establishments based on wage labour rather than domestic enterprises.

Despite this confusion between domestics and wage workers, more thoughtful contemporaries clearly understood that a distinction between the two was necessary. Bodin, for example, notes the difference in the course of his discussion of slavery in the *Six Books of the Commonwealth*.[100] Servants, he observes, are not slaves since they have the right to do most of the things that free men can do. On the other hand, they are not like *mercenaires* or *gaigne deniers* who work by the day. The employers of such people have no power or right of command or punishment over them. Masters, on the other hand, have such powers over their domestics.[101]

The distinction made by Bodin seems to depend, in part, on whether or not the wage worker was a member of the household. Such a line was easy to draw when it came to so-called *gaigne deniers, mercenaires, journaliers, crocheteurs, aides, gens de peine, gens de labeur, gens de bras* and *manouvriers*. These were names commonly given to wage workers who clearly worked outside the household. The master had no disciplinary rights over these workers other than the discipline of the market. It was much more difficult to make the distinction with respect to *compagnons, valets, valets servans, servans de boutique,* and *servans de metier*. Some of these workers continued to live with their masters, although many others, evidently, did

---

[97] On the tavern as a site of working men's sociability see Davis, 'A Trade Union in Sixteenth Century France', *Economic History Review* 19 (1966), 52; Keith Wrightson, 'Alehouses, Order and Reformation in Rural England, 1590–1660' in *Popular Culture and Class Conflict 1590–1914: Explorations in the History of Labour and Leisure*, ed. Eileen and Stephen Yeo (Sussex, 1981), p. 17; Peter Clark, *The English Ale House: A Social History: 1200–1830* (London, 1983), pp. 145–8.

[98] Coll. Lamoignon, VI, fo. 378r.–v.

[99] Lespinasse, *Les métiers et corporations*, III, 114.

[100] *The Six Books of a Commonweale*, ed. Kenneth Douglas McRae (Cambridge, Mass., 1962).

[101] Ibid., p. 33. On a similar distinction in English law see Robert J. Steinfeld, *The Invention of Free Labor: The Employment Relation in English and American Law and Culture, 1340–1870* (Chapel Hill, 1991), pp. 19–20.

not. In so far as they were part of the household or continued to be regarded as part of it, they were subject to its discipline. On the other hand, among the latter category of workers, the terms *compagnons* or even *servans de metier* also imply access to a level of training not available to other kinds of workers.

In many towns like Paris, Orléans, Beauvais, Tours and Chartres the guilds continued to play a predominant role in economic life. In towns like these which were commercially important, they were used as a means of assuring the dominance of merchant capital over the working population. In Paris the so-called six guilds – drapers, grocers, mercers, tanners, hatters and jewellers – dominated all of the others. On the other hand, Lyons, the economic capital of the kingdom in the first half of the sixteenth century, was almost entirely free from guilds, as were a majority of other towns in the kingdom.[102] Indeed, even in Paris where the guilds were relatively strong, apprentices and *compagnons* struggled to free themselves from the controls imposed upon them in the name of the masters.

The masters in the guilds were especially wary of the attempts of *compagnons* to set up workshops outside the control of the guild. There were many cases of *compagnons* who, having accumulated some capital, tried to operate a clandestine enterprise or, as it was said, strove to work *en chambre*. In secret workshops the *compagnon*, assisted by his wife and children together with other less well-off workers, would begin to turn out manufactures in competition with the shops of the masters. Even masters were not beyond operating workshops which violated the statutes of the corporation of which they were members. In 1510, for instance, the *balanciers* complained that one of the new masters of the guild was violating the statutes of the corporation, which allowed only one apprentice. In secret, he had set up a workshop in which he employed a large number of shoemakers who, in fact, were married men over the age of thirty. Indeed, this renegade was conspiring with another master to establish a string of such illegal operations.[103] The statutes of the embroiderers of 1551 likewise complained about production being carried out illegally in clandestine shops. Not only were the workers in such enterprises quitting their legitimate masters but their example was leading those *compagnons* who remained with the masters to refuse to work at the established wage rates. Orders from aristocratic clients were being left unfilled, finally forcing the masters to pay higher wages to get the work done.[104] In the next few years some of the masters appear to have reached an accommodation with the illegal operators. The statutes of the embroiderers in 1566 claimed that it had become the established practice for masters to put out orders to *compagnons* who worked independently of the masters. The new statutes tried to prohibit this practice. Indeed, the statutes forbade *compagnon brodeurs* from working *en chambre*, asserting that, in doing so, they were stealing the services of other *compagnons*

[102] Hauser, *Ouvriers du temps passé: XVe–XVIe siècles* (Paris, 1899; Geneva, 1982), pp. 111–12.
[103] Coll. Lamoignon, v, fos. 537r., 543r.
[104] Ibid., VII, fo. 351r.

from the masters.[105] In 1574 the master shoemakers of Paris complained about so-called *compagnon cordonniers chambrelans* who were producing shoes clandestinely and selling them to master shoemakers.[106]

At a later stage in the history of capitalism, the guilds would be viewed as restricting the free movement of labour.[107] But in this early period, the problem seems to have been the tendency of workers to flee from wage labour altogether. Craftsmen in the faubourgs were entirely escaping from the control of the guilds. It was this problem which caused Henri II, in November 1548, to issue an edict completely prohibiting the further extension of the faubourgs of Paris.[108] The text of this edict begins by noting the large number of new houses which had been built in the faubourgs of the city in the last twenty-five years. As a result, according to the edict, a great multitude of people had migrated from other towns and villages in the kingdom to Paris. Such places had suffered as a result of this exodus towards the capital. But since these newcomers inhabited the faubourgs and, as a result, did not pay the *taille*, the inhabitants of Paris derived no benefit from them.

Many of the migrants had opened workshops which escaped visitation by the guilds. The craftsmen who worked in the suburbs were not required to provide proof of apprenticeship. As a result, the masters of the Parisian guilds were having difficulty in retaining their apprentices and *valets*, who were also opening workshops in the city's faubourgs. The workmanship of such craftsmen was poor. Meanwhile, the price of manufactures and other commodities in the city had risen because of the need to raise wages in order to retain workers. In the meantime, many of the houses put up in the faubourgs were in fact taverns, bordellos and gambling dens in which young men were becoming dissipated and ruining themselves.[109]

Flight to the greater freedom of the suburbs was one way in which the young sought to resist being reduced permanently to wage labour. But the economically vulnerable in the countryside, it should be noted, proved to be equally resistant to this process. Gleaning had long been a way of providing for the poor. In the mid-sixteenth century, especially in the wake of the famine of 1545–6, the practice became a serious problem to landlords and *laboureurs*. Throngs of the needy from both the town and the countryside were seizing part of the harvest under the pretext of gleaning.[110] Such actions were clearly a reaction to the scarcity of grain,

---

[105] BN MS Fr. 8607, fo. 211r.

[106] Hauser, *Ouvriers du temps passé*, p. 118.

[107] William H. Sewell, *Work and Revolution in France: The Language of Labour from the Old Regime to 1848* (Cambridge, 1980), pp. 62–3. Sewell's treatment of the guilds under the *ancien régime* ibid., pp. 16–39, is an excellent summary.

[108] *Edict du roy touchant les defenses de ne plus bâtir es faux-bourgs de la ville de Paris* (Paris, 1549).

[109] The edict of 1548 was a dead letter by the mid-1550s. See Nicolas de La Mare, *Traité de la police* (Paris, 1705–38), I, 96.

[110] Edict of 1554; see ibid., V, 68.

but were also a way in which the rural poor could resist accepting low wages. Working together, a poor family could gather enough grain to keep it going for three or four months of the year.[111]

The ability of the rural population to live in part off gleaning or other subsistence activities made it possible for them to limit their dependence on, or altogether to refuse to take, wages or excessively low wages. Hence, it became necessary for the monarchy to intervene on the side of rural entrepreneurs. By an edict of 1554, only the very young, the aged and the crippled were allowed to continue to glean at harvest. Healthy men and women were ordered to present themselves for employment in the harvest during the month of August and to ask for reasonable salaries in doing so.[112]

In 1567 and again in 1577 the monarchy drew up edicts in order to shore up the control of the guilds over labour. But Henri III's edict in 1581 admitted that the majority of artisans in the kingdom were working outside the control of the guilds.[113] The failure of this legislation testifies to an economy whose dynamism made it difficult to control the workforce by administrative means. It also reflected the determination of many *compagnons* to escape the control of organizations which were increasingly regarded as antagonistic to their interests. By increasing the lengths of apprenticeships, raising the costs of masterships or complicating the production of masterpieces, the masters of many guilds were making it increasingly difficult for *compagnons* to accede to the status of masters.[114] Many masters made it their practice to employ unrestricted numbers of *aides* and *valets* in their workshops. In the Parisian construction industry the employment of large numbers of unskilled workers had been the norm since the late middle ages. This practice was confirmed by a royal ordonnance of 13 September 1574 which asserted that masons, plasterers and bricklayers could employ as many workers as they wished provided that they did not teach them their craft.[115] The master pavers of Paris refused to hire *compagnons*, preferring instead to use *manœuvriers* and apprentices, one master having as many as sixteen apprentices.[116] In the printing industries of Paris and Lyons, the master printers made it their strategy to try to offset the power of the *compagnons* in the workshops by taking on more and more apprentices.[117]

The increasing polarization of labour and capital within the guilds led to the

---

[111] Micheline Baulant and Corinne Beutler, 'Les droits de la communauté villageoise sur les cultures: glanage et chaume en France, XVIIᵉ siècle' in *Agricultura e trasformazione dell'ambiente secoli XIII–XVIII*, ed. Annalisa Garducci, *Atti della Undicesimo Settimana di studio (25–30 aprille 1979) Istituto Internazionale di Storia Economica – 'Francesco Datini'* (Florence, 1984), p. 71.

[112] La Mare, *Traité de la police*, v, 68. See Liana Vardi, 'Construing the Harvest: Gleaners, Farmers and Officials in Early Modern France', *American Historical Review* 98 (1993), 1432–4.

[113] Coornaert, *Les corporations en France avant 1789* (Paris, 1968), pp. 112, 122.

[114] Hauser, *Ouvriers de temps passé*, pp. 119, 121–6.

[115] BN MS Collection Joly de Fleury 1422, fo. 10v.

[116] Hauser, *Ouvriers du temps passé*, p. 36.

[117] Ibid., p. 184.

emergence as early as the end of the fifteenth century of confraternities of journeymen organized to protect the interests of workers against the masters.[118] The hostility of the authorities to such organizations at first expressed itself by a generalized hostility to all confraternities. Such popular organizations had emerged in the late middle ages as religious, confraternal and vocational associations among the urban plebian population. In 1498 an *arrêt* of the Paris Parlement ordered that all banquets and assemblies under the auspices of confraternities be prohibited.[119] Two years later the creation of any new confraternities was forbidden.[120] In 1506 a decree of the Châtelet attempted to prohibit the *compagnon couturiers* of the city from electing a king and organizing themselves into a confraternity. The forms and ceremonies of this new organization appear to have been borrowed from those of the urban religious, neighbourhood and confraternal associations. The *compagnons* held regular meetings in the form of suppers and banquets presided over by an elected king. A showdown apparently occurred between the masters and the king of the *compagnon couturiers*, Philibert Rue, as a result of which the latter was accused of verbal and physical assaults on the masters.[121]

As the century continued, the authorities became increasingly punitive. Workers could be prosecuted for blasphemy, carrying weapons, wearing capes and hats, gambling, and socializing in taverns and cabarets. Lists of room rentals were compiled in each quarter of the city and the casual rental of rooms more strictly regulated.[122] In 1524 the Council of Sens condemned confraternities whose saints' days, far from being religious occasions, 'only appear ... to have been established in order to foster combinations ... and the excesses of debauchery'.[123] The confraternity of shearers was suppressed in 1534.[124] The next year the Parlement outlawed confraternities and in 1539 this ban was confirmed by the edict of Villers-Cotteret issued in the throes of the strikes in the printing industries of Paris and Lyons.[125]

But only two years later the powerful merchant drapers of Paris appealed to the king to allow the restoration of their confraternity. They pointed to its antiquity and to the fact that they had their own chapel and priests, who were supported

---

[118] Geremek, *La salariat*, pp. 116, 118; Etienne Martin Saint-Léon, *Le compagnonnage* (Paris, 1901), p. 33.

[119] La Mare, *Traité de la police*, I, 405; Coll. Lamoignon, v, fo. 435r.

[120] La Mare, *Traité de la police*, I, 405.

[121] Coll. Lamoignon, v, 496r.–503v.; Geremek, *La salariat*, p. 116. On social polarization among couturiers see Georges Dumas, 'Les tailleurs d'habits et les bonnetiers de Paris du XIIIe au XVIe siècle', *Ecole des Chartes, position des thèses* (1951), pp. 5–6.

[122] *Reg. BVP* IV, 200; VI, 292; VII, 37; Coll. Lamoignon VI, fos. 203r., 387r.–388v., 606r.–607v.; BN MS Fr. 8080, fo. 241r.; *Recueil des privileges, concessions et reglemens de commissaires, enquesteurs et examinateurs des Chastellet de Paris* (Paris, 1509), pp. 12–13.

[123] La Mare, *Traité de la police*, I, 406.

[124] BN MS Fr. 8075, fo. 417r.

[125] Ibid.; Coll. Lamoignon, VI, fos. 304r.–307r.; BN MS Fr. 8075, fo. 503r.–v.

from the revenues of the organization. The king allowed the re-establishment of this confraternity. Other merchant confraternities were then able to restore themselves in the wake of the master drapers.[126] However, alongside the middle-class confraternities, more popular and tumultuous organizations attempted to reappear. In 1551 the Parlement had to order the *compagnon* shoemakers to dissolve their newly re-established confraternity.[127] Ten years later, in letters-patent of 5 February 1561, Charles IX took note of the re-emergence of confraternities in many towns. At Lyons and elsewhere, according to this document, the *gens de métier* of these confraternities were organizing so-called 'kingdoms' for the purpose of staging parades on Sundays and feast-days. During these popular processions, holy wafers decorated with tiny painted flags would be carried through the streets by men in masks or dressed in some outlandish fashion. These individuals would proceed on their path to the sound of fifes and drums, while accompanied by a host of craftsmen, who were often armed. Following a religious service in a church, the procession would repair to a tavern or to the home of the so-called *courier* of the confraternity for a banquet.[128] The festive, carnivalesque and religious character of this workers' culture is striking. By reason of these disorderly public manifestations, the king once again banned confraternities. However, it proved necessary to repeat the ban in 1566 and again in 1567 and 1577. In the latter instances confraternities of *compagnons* were expressly singled out as proscribed.[129]

In the first part of the sixteenth century, then, the resistance of workers to their masters expressed itself through the creation and maintenance of their own culture of opposition in the face of official and clerical hostility. Confraternities, in addition to providing material help to workers and their families, enabled *compagnons* to escape to a degree from the paternalistic control of the masters. One cannot overestimate, for example, the importance to the *compagnon* shoemakers of Paris of the legal victory they won that allowed them to continue to celebrate their patron saint's day with a church service separate from that of the masters.[130]

The ultimate recourse of workers faced with a decline in their standard of living or working conditions was to withdraw their labour. The strikes of 1539–41 of the Paris and Lyons *compagnon* printers are too well known for us to recall at length.[131] The workers in this industry were clearly empowered by their high

---

[126] La Mare, *Traité de la police*, I, 406; Coll. Lamoignon, VI, fos. 36or., 649r.–651v.; BN MS Fr. 8080, fos. 479r.–480v., 525r.–532v.
[127] Coll. Lamoignon, VII, fos. 450r.–451v.
[128] La Mare, *Traité de la police*, I, 406.
[129] Ibid., I, 407.
[130] Hauser, *Ouvriers du temps passé*, pp. 173–4.
[131] Ibid., pp. 177–234; Paul Chauvet, *Les ouvriers du livre en France des origines à la Revolution française de 1789* (Paris, 1942), pp. 7–58; Davis, 'A Trade Union in Sixteenth Century France', pp. 48–69; Davis, 'Strikes and Salvation in Lyons' in *Society and Culture in Early Modern France* (Stanford, 1975), pp. 1–16; M. Audin, 'Les grèves de l'imprimerie à Lyon au seizième siècle' in *Gutenberg Jahrbuch* 1938, pp. 172–89.

level of skill and literacy as well as the considerable amount of material resources at their disposal. But the strikes of the journeymen printers were far from being isolated instances. We know, for example, of a strike by the *compagnon* bakers of Paris just prior to the walk-out of the printers.[132] Indeed, the late 1530s seem to have been exceptional years for walk-outs. The excellent grape harvest of 1539 endowed the Parisian working population with strong bargaining power. The master coopers complained that their *compagnons* were leaving to work in the *vendange*. Other masters reported that their workers were doing likewise. Parlement ordered that workers were not to leave their masters until the conclusion of the grape harvest.[133] At Dijon in 1552 the Parlement there acted to quell labour unrest. It ordered the *compagnons*, many of whom were foreigners, either to work at their vocations or to leave the city. The warning had to be repeated eight years later.[134]

But what is surprising is that less well-organized and well-positioned workers were also capable of taking strike action. In 1511 a gang of *manœuvriers* in the Bordelais struck for higher wages. At the canonry of Saint-André in the autumn of that year, the *manœuvriers* at the site were engaged in digging a trench to take the pile of a flying buttress. The heavy rains of that season made the work hard and dangerous, particularly as the trench kept filling with water. On 10 November the workers refused to continue to work at the going wage. Two days later, the canons agreed to raise the wage of the *manœuvriers* from 10 to 15 *liards* for those prepared to work night-shifts as well as day-shifts. Although this offer appears to have been accepted by the workers, tension between them and the canons continued just below the surface. On 23 November the workers were able to work only part of the night-shift owing to the inclement weather. The treasurer of the canonry thereupon docked the workers part of their pay. The following night some of the workers sabotaged the pump set up to drain the trench. The canons then agreed to pay for night-work separately and to buy boots for those who had to work in the wet trench at night.[135] In 1535 sailors on board ships of the royal navy went out on strike, claiming that their monthly pay of 60 sols was inadequate. They had to be given 25–40 sols a month additional pay.[136] In 1536 the city of Paris employed thousands of workers to build fortifications protecting the town. Many of these workers were in fact drawn from the construction industry. Failing to obtain an increase in wages, the workers on this project staged a work stoppage. Indeed, to back up their demands they organized marches and demonstrations at which they paraded in organized units under flags of their own devising. The city council was able to control this outbreak without too much difficulty. But nearly

---

[132] Luc Benoist, *Le compagnonnage et les métiers* (Paris, 1980), p. 32.
[133] Coll. Lamoignon, VI, fos. 507v.–508r.; BN MS Fr. 8080, fo. 427r.
[134] Coornaert, *Les corporations en France*, p. 115.
[135] A. Brutails, 'Deux chantiers bordelais (1486–1521)' *Le moyen âge* 13 (1900), 188.
[136] La Roncière, *Histoire de la marine française*, II, 458–9.

two decades later, in 1553, it seems clear that the intensity of protest had sharpened. It was reported that every day saw tumults and outcries on the part of day-labourers who complained that their wages were being sequestered. The demonstrations and strikes troubling the city on this occasion were aimed at contractors who made it a practice to pocket part of the workers' wages for themselves. The city council ordered the contractors to hire labour on the basis of a wage agreed to before work began and to pay the agreed wage in full to the workers.[137]

The ports of La Grève and the Ecole Saint-Germain where much of the grain, wood and straw indispensable to the life of Paris was unloaded, were particular hot spots. At times, especially in the first part of the century, the day-labourers stampeded onto the boats and fought with one another for work.[138] Stevedores had to be prohibited from double-charging merchants and consumers for unloading and transporting merchandise.[139] A tendency towards a more organized expression of common interests seems apparent among the dock workers as the century progresses. In 1558 Parlement prohibited such dock workers from attempting to unload boats without permission or from demanding wages which were higher than those already fixed.[140] In 1563 the court prohibited certain *gaigne deniers* from trying to monopolize the unloading of wood.[141] Eight years later, the court intervened to prevent the dockers from combining to raise their wages.[142] The increasing sense of organization among the workers on the docks reflects the growing permanence in the condition of wage workers even in this largely unskilled activity.

In the first part of the sixteenth century, then, a partial proletarianization of the workforce took place in the kingdom of France. This process was based on both the incomplete expropriation of the peasantry and a steady increase in the population. In the Ile-de-France the growing dependence of an increasing fraction of the rural population on wage labour seems evident.[143] Some limited steps were taken in the introduction of technological innovation in industries like mining, printing, the milling of grain and the spinning of silk. The development of industry was facilitated by the overall increase in the availability of wage labourers. The reorganization of production in a more capitalist sense was manifest in agriculture as well as in the rapidly growing putting-out system of industry. It is, nevertheless, necessary to emphasize the limited extent of this process at this stage. The amount of capital invested in new means of production was quite restricted in both agriculture and industry. Much of the rural labour force was

[137] *Reg. BVP* II, 245, 271, 283; IV, 176–7.
[138] AN Z^{14} 567.
[139] *Reg. BVP* IV, 232.
[140] BN MS Fr. 8066, fo. 502; AN F^{14} 9776.
[141] BN MS Fr. 8067, fos. 123v.–124r.
[142] Ibid., fo. 387r.–v.
[143] Jacquart, *La crise rurale en Ile-de-France*, pp. 140–1, 145.

only partially or seasonally dependent on wages. Some resisted being reduced to dependence on wage labour. In the towns many of those seeking wage employment were unable to find it and were consigned to that large urban underclass known as the poor. A sharp distinction was drawn between those who were considered to be part of the system of apprenticeship and the much larger group of workers, skilled and unskilled, who were not. But in the final analysis, one is struck by the increasing modernity of outlook apparent in those who were caught up in these changes. A certain objectification of labour as a factor of production is evident. Opening an arithmetic published at the end of the 1540s, we note that the author Jacques Peletier devoted the fourth book to the practical computational problems faced by businessmen. The very first problem he considers is 'If eight workers earn twelve *écus* in fifteen days, how many *écus* will eighteen workers earn in twenty-four days?'[144] Wage labour as never before had become an important fact of economic life.

[144] *L'arithemetique*, Book I, ch. I. On the diffusion of business manuals in France see Jochen Hoock and Pierre Jeannin, 'La contribution de l'imprimerie à la diffusion du savoir commercial en Europe au 16ᵉ siècle' in *La ville et l'innovation en Europe: 14ᵉ–19ᵉ siècles*, ed. B. Lepetit and J. Hoock (Paris, 1987), pp. 48–9, 56. See also Paul Benoît, 'Calcul, algèbre et marchandise' in *Elements d'histoire des sciences*, ed. Michel Serres (Paris, 1989), pp. 197–222.

3

Civil war and economic experiments

> ... how many great inventions were there not only to the profit of His Majesty, but, indeed, for the benefit of his whole people ...
>
> Philibert De l'Orme, *Instructions* (1563)

As we have seen confidence in the notion of progress was widespread among the middle class of France during the first part of the sixteenth century. No one expressed this idea more fully than the humanist Louis Le Roy. It is in his work that the sixteenth-century idea of progress was most completely developed. In his *Consideration sur l'histoire ... universelle* of 1568, Le Roy expressed himself as follows with respect to the achievements of his own age:

However, balancing the bad with the good, there has not been in the past an age where knowledge and the arts have reached a higher perfection than the present. Not at the time of Cyrus during which Pythagoras and Thales lived ... not at the time of Alexander the Great when Greece produced what it had of the highest excellence in letters, arms and all the arts, when Plato, Euripides, Demosthenes and Aristotle lived. Not at the time of Augustus ... Caesar, Pompey, Horace and Ovid ... Not at the time of the Saracens among whom there flourished Averroes, Avicenna and Abenzonar ...

For in the past one hundred years, not only have things which were previously hidden by shadows been brought to light, but also many other things have become known which were entirely unknown to the ancients: new seas, new lands, new kinds of men, morals, laws, customs, new plants ... trees ... minerals ... newly discovered inventions, like printing, cannons, and the use of the compass ... the restoration of ancient languages ... These things being taken into consideration, one ought to be able to bear more easily the calamities which have occurred and which are occurring in this age ... Certain individuals think that men have been continuously in decline and human affairs changing for the worse. If this was so during the long period during which the world has lasted, we should have been by now totally annihilated and nothing of value would have remained among us.[1]

In this passage Le Roy provides us with a fully articulated version of the Renaissance conception of progress, which stressed advances in learning, invention and discovery. At the same time, it is noteworthy that this notion of progress

---

[1] Cited in Geoffrey Atkinson, *Les nouveaux horizons de la renaissance française* (Geneva, 1935, 1969), pp. 404–5. On Le Roy's theory of progress see Abraham Henri Becker, *Un humaniste au XVI* *siècle: Louis Le Roy* (Paris, 1896), pp. 256–68; Werner L. Gundersheimer, *The Life and Work of Louis Le Roy* (Geneva, 1966), pp. 111–21.

was defended by Le Roy at a time of growing troubles induced by the civil wars and his own sense of the instability of the historical process. By the time Le Roy came to write *De la vicissitude ou varieté des choses en l'univers* (1575), he gave way to an overwhelming sense of pessimism about the prospect of further progress:

If the memory and knowledge of the past is the instruction of the present, and the foreshadowing of the future, it is to be feared that having arrived at such excellence, the power, wisdom, disciplines, books, industry, work and knowledge of the world may plunge headlong, and perhaps perish as they have done in the past; and that confusion will succeed the order and perfection of today, rudeness will replace civility, ignorance knowledge, and barbarity elegance.[2]

DARKENING HORIZONS

Le Roy thus had a strong sense of the greatness of his own time, especially when it was compared with classical Antiquity. But his sense of the mutability of human affairs, evidently reinforced by the accumulating tragedies and disasters of the civil wars, led him back towards a theory of cycles and decline. Indeed, Le Roy gives way to a deep sense of pessimism with respect to the future:

I foresee wars everywhere, springing up at home and abroad, factions and heresies arising to profane every human and divine thing they find, famines and plagues menacing mortal men. I foresee the order of nature, the rule of the celestial movements, the harmony of the elements breaking asunder, while, on the one hand, floods occur, and on the other, excessive heat and very violent earthquakes. And I foresee the universe approaching its end by one form of unruliness or another, bringing with it the confusion of all things, and leading them back to their former chaos.[3]

A whole series of thinkers, as we have seen, had sketched out a theory of human progress based on the advances of the first part of the century. This positive outlook reached its highest expression in Le Roy's work and then surrendered to a mood of increasing pessimism and anxiety. This change of tone, evident among French authors from the 1550s, was closely related to the growth of religious strife and darkening economic perspective.

Bernard Palissy, who began to publish in the opening years of the religious wars, shared nothing of Le Roy's initial optimism. A persistent critic of the Ancients, Palissy, as a modern, was convinced of the superiority of his own views to those of the past. However, unlike many of his contemporaries, he was far from drawing optimistic conclusions about the present or the future based on this sense of intellectual superiority. Despite its promise of wealth, Palissy's *Recepte veritable par laquelle tous les hommes pourront apprendre à multiplier et augmenter leurs tresors*

---

[2]   Cited in Gundersheimer, *The Life and Work of Louis Le Roy*, p. 116. On Le Roy's sense of the vicissitude of things see Jean Céard, *La nature et les prodiges: l'insolite au XVIᵉ siècle en France* (Geneva, 1977), p. 375.

[3]   Cited in Gundersheimer, *The Life and Work of Louis Le Roy*, p. 116.

(1563) was marked by a profound pessimism about the human prospect.[4] Experience of persecution and violence at the beginning of the religious wars only deepened Palissy's sense of humanity's wickedness:

I pray to God that it please Him to give us peace, but if you had seen the horrible crimes committed by men during the troubles there is not a hair on your head which would not have quivered for fear of falling prey to the malice of men. And he who was not a witness to these things cannot conceive what a great and terrible thing war is.[5]

It is for this reason that Palissy thought of escaping into an imaginary garden and citadel of his own devising.[6] This garden was partly conceived of as a utopian project and partly as a redemptive economic enterprise.[7] As such it is redolent with a specifically Protestant sense of approaching Apocalypse.[8]

Palissy's sense of pessimism with respect to humanity is embodied in his dream of the quarrel of the instruments which forms part of the *Recepte veritable*.[9] In a way which is most unusual for the times, Palissy singles out in this dream man's capacity as toolmaker as his most distinctive and noble attribute. Asked what tools he required to construct his garden, he responds that he would need the tools of geometry as well as those of agriculture. He then remembers that only a few nights earlier he had dreamed of the quarrel of these tools. About midnight one evening of the previous week, as he recalled, his tools of themselves rose up against one another and began to argue with each other over which had precedence over the others. Involved in this dispute for superiority were the compass, rule, plumb-line, level, bevel square and astrolabe. Each instrument in turn vaunted its own superiority over the rest. Thus, for example, the compass claimed primacy because it guided and measured all things. The compass pointed out that it was so influential in human affairs that when, for example, a man lived beyond his means, he was commonly admonished by other men to live within his own compass. The rule answered the compass by noting that the latter could only deal with things circuitously while the rule dealt with things directly. Furthermore, the rule pointed out that if a man lived in a dissolute way it was said that he lived without a sense of rule. The plumb-line, on the other hand, argued for its own superiority because it was necessary to the construction of all buildings erected by men and that without it not a single wall could be properly erected at the proper right angle. For good measure the plumb-line airily noted that it could often be used to take the place of the rule altogether. The last word went to the astrolabe, which raised itself to its full

---

4 Palissy, *Recepte veritable*, ed. Keith Cameron (Geneva, 1988).
5 Ibid., p. 186.
6 Ibid., p. 54.
7 Frank Lestringant, 'Le prince et le potier: introduction à la "Recepte veritable" de Bernard Palissy (1563)', *Nouvelle revue du XVIe siècle* 3 (1985), 5–24; Heller, *The Conquest of Poverty*, pp. 247–52.
8 Lestringant, 'Le prince et le potier', p. 18. See Jean Delumeau, *Le péché et la peur. La culpabilisation en Occident: XIIIe–XVIIIe siècles* (Paris, 1983), pp. 129–63, 586–623.
9 Palissy, *Recepte veritable*, pp. 174–7.

dignity and claimed its right to first place by virtue of its ability to measure the heavens and to understand the weather and the seasons. The quarrel of the instruments is clearly Palissy's metaphor for humanity divided against itself.

The noise of these disputes, Palissy claimed, finally woke him up. He found himself appointed by the instruments to settle the dispute. However, when he went on to assert that pre-eminence ought to go to none of the instruments, but to man who had created them, the tools retorted in chorus that they could not be expected to honour or obey a creature who himself was so wicked and imbued with folly. The tools, no longer quarrelling with one another, then collectively proposed to turn against the humans who had originally created them by measuring the skulls of various specimens of humankind in a kind of phrenological study designed to reveal mankind's foolishness.

It was Palissy's master, Calvin, who had not only praised labour as one of humanity's distinctive pursuits but who had actually sanctified it as a divinely ordained activity. While convinced of humanity's essential depravity, Calvin nevertheless believed in the godly consecration of human labour.[10] Palissy takes Calvin's view a stage further. Harking back to the Renaissance idea of the dignity of man, he emphasizes the notion that man's dignity is rooted in the fact that he has invented tools able to measure all things including the heavens themselves. But Palissy also notes, in accord with Calvin, that man's dignity is tragically flawed by his corruption.

Reflecting the influence of Erasmus' *Praise of Folly*, he attempts to measure the various kinds and degrees of human folly, using man-made implements. He discovers, however, that human foolishness is so various and inconstant that it is not subject to common measure. Not being able to measure human folly, he is forced instead to resort to the foolishness of alchemy in order to putrefy, calcine, examine, sublimate and distil the human spirit.[11]

Palissy then surveys a cross-section of French society providing us with a catalogue of human wilfulness and misdeeds. He meets a merchant who buys pepper cheaply and sells it dear, while adulterating the product to gain still more profit. He encounters a young man who, to keep up with the fashionable mode, slits his clothes and boots and claims that they will accordingly wear better that way. He remonstrates with the wife of a magistrate who wears dresses designed deliberately to expose her charms. In return for what he considers his well-intentioned reproaches, she denounces him for being a Huguenot. He then interviews her husband, the magistrate, who explains his official larceny by the need to maintain his estates and please his wife. When Palissy questions an ecclesiastic as to the reasons why he attacks those who teach the Gospel, the cleric answers that it is not because he is against such teaching in principle, but simply to preserve his benefice. Again, he encounters a judge who sits in a *présidial* court and who persecutes those who follow the Gospel in order to preserve his share of

---

10 André Biéler, *La pensée économique et sociale de Calvin* (Geneva, 1959), pp. 390–403.
11 Palissy, *Recepte veritable*, pp. 177–8.

ecclesiastical revenue. In like manner, he meets a *conseiller* in the parlement who admits to opposing the evangelicals in order to protect his property. This man of laws attempts to justify his attitude by pointing out that the nobility do likewise, in order to hold onto their estates, honours and possessions. In the end, Palissy cries out in despair at the prospect of the great of the world ranged against the followers of the Gospel in this manner. He urges the evangelicals to return to their simple ways, since those who take up the quarrel of God must expect persecution. This dark view of the future is qualified somewhat by the prospect of apocalyptic intervention. For, he notes in a concluding passage, God will determine the time and place to take vengeance for the injuries done to the evangelicals.[12] Palissy's sense of despair at the future is rooted in the thoughtless immorality and intolerance of the elites in French society.

Palissy's dismal view of the present in part reflected the perspective of Calvin, who wrote: 'the world always deteriorates and becomes gradually more vicious and corrupt: the world grows worse as it becomes older'.[13] According to Calvin, it is the coming of the Lord, not the works of men, which will effect the deliverance of humanity: 'the confusion of things revealed in the world today will not last forever, for the Lord, by his coming, will summon the world again to order'.[14] But Palissy's pessimism was not simply rooted in the theology of his master. It was based on his reaction to the violence and persecution which threatened the Huguenot movement. His catalogue of humanity's foolishness is therefore followed immediately by a paragraph entitled 'Histoire', in which he explains that it was after he understood the folly and malice of men and had taken into consideration the horrible riots and attacks that had broken out recently against the evangelicals that he determined to plan a fortress of refuge.[15] At the beginning of the 1560s, Palissy was overcome by a sense of impending disaster which was given expression as a religiously based sense of despair and expectation of eventual deliverance.

Jean Céard has noted the sense of anxious foreboding that seems to affect so many of the writers of the period marked by the onset of the wars of religion. According to one of these, Jean de Marconville, the onset of the religious wars had been preceded by an infinitude of premonitions like crop blight, hail, thunder, lightning storms and interminable rains. These were all premonitions of divine wrath or foretastes of God's anger. During this same period, Ronsard likewise occupied himself with ever more complete lists of gloomy omens of the approaching wars.[16] Fears of impending disaster were not confined to the intellectual and artistic elite. The chronicler Claude Haton reported in the 1550s that there was a widespread expectation of impending calamity in the towns and villages among

---

[12] Ibid., pp. 178–85.
[13] *Commentaries on Daniel 2:31–35*, cited in William J. Bouwsma, *John Calvin: A Sixteenth Century Portrait* (New York, 1988), p. 82.
[14] *Commentaries on James 5:7*, cited in ibid., p. 73.
[15] Palissy, *Recepte veritable*, p. 185.
[16] Céard, *La nature et les prodiges*, pp. 336–7.

the older people. Indeed, he notes that his father, Pierre Haton, a *laboureur* aged sixty-five or sixty-six, from Melz-sur-Seine, predicted the coming of the wars.[17]

Palissy's expectation of the Apocalypse was shared by another Huguenot master craftsman, the Burgundian engraver Jean Duvet. An even more overwhelming sense of impending doom than that found in Palissy emerges from the masterful engravings in Duvet's *L'Apocalypse figurée*, published at Lyons in 1561. Duvet, who was trained as a jeweller, had fled to Geneva from Dijon because of the persecution of heretics in France. In 1541 he was accepted into the bourgeoisie of Geneva and five years later he became a member of the Council of Two Hundred. But fear of persecution and involvement in the affairs of Geneva did not prevent him from returning to France for long visits. In 1544, 1552 and 1556 he was resident at Langres, where he conducted himself, ostensibly, as a Catholic. At the beginning of the 1560s, he lived for some months in Lyons in order to oversee the printing of his masterpiece.

The quality of the engravings in *L'Apocalypse figurée* are comparable to those of Dürer by whom Duvet was obviously deeply affected. The excellence of these engravings reflects the skills of a master craftsman who had become adept at an impressive array of specialities: architecture, engineering, design and painting on glass, tapestry and mural, set design, enamelling, jewellery-making and minting. These engravings embody much of the craft technique of the French Renaissance at its highest level. At the same time, they reflect the profound influence of the two great pillars of French Renaissance culture, biblical religion and humanism.[18]

Duvet's engravings, of which *The Four Horsemen of the Apocalypse* (Plate 1) is a good example, reflects a world profoundly troubled by the conflict between the forces of light and the forces of darkness. In successive engravings we are witness to scenes of surging conflict between these forces, which clearly announce the imminent arrival of the Last Days. These engravings can thus be read both as a remarkable artistic and religious vision of the Apocalypse and an amazingly prophetic anticipation of the French religious wars.

Behind the expectations of Apocalypse which loomed so large at the beginning of the 1560s lay the reality of increasing economic malaise and social conflict. For this decade was to see not only the start of the religious wars, but also the onset of economic troubles of major proportions and prolonged duration. The symptoms of this malaise are well known: war, financial anarchy, rampant inflation and a constriction of the internal market. The causes which lay behind these phenomena are likewise evident, being rooted in stagnant productivity, falling real wages and declining profit margins.[19]

17 Claude Haton, *Mémoires*, ed. F. Bourquelet (Paris, 1857), I, 17.
18 Colin T. Eisler, *The Master of the Unicorn: The Life and Work of Jean Duvet* (New York, 1979), pp. 1–34.
19 The genesis of this crisis is sketched in Heller, *The Conquest of Poverty*, pp. 12, 18, 21, 23–6, 62–3 and *passim*.

Plate 1   Jean Duvet, *The Four Horsemen of the Apocalypse*, *L'Apocalypse figureé* (Lyons, 1561).

Famine and plague were already serious problems in the first half of the sixteenth century. Paris and the Ile-de-France, along with the rest of northern France, were experiencing serious food shortages and outbreaks of disease already in the early 1520s.[20] Far from disappearing, these scourges recurred in the following decades, reaching their peak in the crisis of 1545–6, which was arguably the most terrible year in the history of sixteenth-century Paris until the siege of 1590.[21] Indeed, it is notable that four decades later the memory of that terrible year had not disappeared. In 1586 Christophe de Bordeaux, by then an old man, published an account of that year entitled *Discours lamentable et pitoyable.*[22] Writing in the wake of all the accumulated suffering of the wars of religion, Christophe nevertheless recalled the crisis of the 1540s as an unprecedentedly frightful catastrophe for his city: 'those who are still alive today and who remember it know well that it was so venomous and cruel in Paris and its environs that nearly half the population died of it'.[23] No doubt there is some hyperbole in this claim. But there is little question that the mortality from this plague as well as from the accompanying famine must have been extremely serious.

The years of famine and plague were no doubt only the most acute phases in the suffering of the poor and working classes in a period marked by a dramatic fall in living standards. By the 1540s the gravity of the situation began to be reflected even in the medical literature. Jacques Dubois, one of the most celebrated Paris physicians of the first half of the century, turned his attention to the plight of the poor. Dubois, himself of humble circumstances, undertook to offer advice to the poor on how to preserve their health and avoid disease despite their economic problems. But, as Gerhard Baader has noted, Dubois' works teach us more about the plight of the poor than about how they could possibly have maintained their well-being by following his suggestions.[24]

The diet of the poor, as described by Dubois, consisted of various kinds of gruel of bread and water, bread and broth, or bread and beer. Sheep's blood or pig's blood stewed with onions and fat provided a soup. Gristle, small bones, tendons and sinews, minced together and cooked, was a common meal. Trying to look on the bright side of this situation, Dubois argued that by eating such food the poor avoided the rich and unhealthy diet of the wealthy. He also observed that, in contrast to the unhealthy leisure of the wealthy, the often arduous work of the poor served as a form of exercise.

---

[20] Ibid., p. 54.

[21] See 'Disette de 1545–1546' in Baulant and Meuvret, *Prix des céréales extraicts de la Mercuriale de Paris,* I, 133–50.

[22] *Discours lamentable et pitoyable sur la calamité, cherté et necessité du temps présent ...* (Bordeaux, 1586).

[23] Ibid.

[24] Gerhard Baader, 'Jacques Dubois as a Practitioner' in *The Medical Renaissance of the Sixteenth Century,* ed. A. Wear, R.K. French and I.M. Lonie (Cambridge, 1986), p. 152; Jean Dupèbe, 'L'alimentation des pauvres selon Sylvius' in *Pratique et discours alimentaires à la renaissance: actes du colloque de Tours 1979,* ed. J.C. Margolin and Robert Sauzet (Paris, 1982), pp. 41–56.

In the preface to his treatise on famine (1546), a work published significantly in the vernacular, and directly inspired by the dearth of that year, Dubois noted how everything was growing worse as a result of diseases, shortages of money and resources, lost wars and scarcity of food, especially, grain. According to Dubois, the poor might mitigate their hunger and thirst through an understanding of humoral physiology, which suggested that they should try to subsist on gaseous rather than humid and solid food.[25]

The looming prospect of religious conflict and the experience of growing economic difficulties caused the notion of progress to fade from consciousness. It was replaced by a pervading sense of pessimism. But despite the general sense of gloom, there were individuals who began to cast about for remedies, which included proposals for improvements in agriculture and manufacturing. These initiatives were given shape under Charles IX, who entertained proposals for an overall reform of the French economy. Many of those who interested themselves in economic improvement were sympathetic to the Reformation. Moreover, it appears that the monarchy's interest in such measures was partly prompted by a desire to conciliate the Huguenot party.

AGRICULTURAL REFORMS

Towards the middle of the sixteenth century the provision of an adequate food supply became urgent. Beyond assuring the subsistence of the population, it was also critical to maintaining the momentum of the burgeoning manufacturing sector of the economy. Sustaining profit margins in industry depended on controlling wages. Relatively low wages were only possible if the cost of grain – which had been rapidly rising – could be contained. As a result, one notes a growing preoccupation with agriculture among humanist authors. To be sure, initially the influence of Antiquity overshadowed this concern. Thus, for example, in order to prove the worth of an interest in agriculture, André Tiraqueau found it necessary to point out that it had attracted the attention of no less than 150 ancient writers.[26] Indeed, the works of classical authors remained the central preoccupation of publishers until the middle of the century. Prior to the middle of the sixteenth century, eight Latin editions of the works of Cato, Varro, Columella and Palladius were published in Lyons and Paris. Vernacular translations of Columella (1551, 1558), Palladius (1551), and Vegetius (1563) marked the middle decades of the century.[27] This preoccupation with the classical world was taken to its limit by Lucas Frenelle, a teacher of law at Bordeaux, who was preparing to

25   *Conseil tres-utile contre la famine* (Paris, 1546).
26   *De nobilitate* (Paris, 1549), pp. 210–11.
27   For these Latin and French editions see *Scriptores rei rusticae veteres Latini Cato, Varro, Columella, Palladius*, ed. Johann Matthias Gesner (Leipzig, 1735), I, xliii–xlviii.

publish a comprehensive manuscript on ancient agriculture at the time of his death at the beginning of the religious wars.[28]

In the meantime, contemporary authors began to exhibit a growing interest in assuring the provision of adequate amounts of food. Such matters are at the heart of Robert Breton's *Agriculturae encomium* (1539).[29] Breton, the humanist schoolteacher, his ideas still heavily coloured by classical influences, nevertheless emphasizes the need to combine practical and theoretical learning in agriculture. Furthermore, this knowledge should be used to improve the fertility of the soil so as to increase agricultural output.[30] The food produced in the countryside, he pointed out, was absolutely essential to the existence of the towns and the state itself.[31]

Le Roy Ladurie has pointed out how vital the ongoing spread of the chestnut in Languedoc was to the continuing progress of the economy of that region in the sixteenth century.[32] Indeed, the potential of the chestnut in meeting the food requirements of the population is the theme of Jean Du Choul's work on the chestnut which appeared in 1555.[33] More significant still was Claude Bigottier's *Rapina, seu raporum encomium* (1540).[34] Bigottier was born in a village near Bourg-en-Bresse. Having taught at a school in Dauphiné, Bigottier found employment as a regent in the *collège* of Lyons at the time his encomium on the turnip was published. The poem is characterized by a conventional Catholic piety. Yet this orthodox appearance is belied by our knowledge of Bigottier's unavowed earlier involvement with the Protestant cause. As early as 1531 he had converted to the reform movement and had been admitted as an inhabitant of Geneva serving as a rector of the schools.[35] He then resurfaced as a schoolmaster in Lyons, where a Nicodemist attitude towards religion was a common posture among humanists.

Bigottier felt it necessary to apologize for taking as the subject of his verse so lowly a thing as the turnip, the staple food of his beloved native Bresse. Indeed, as he explained, the inhabitants of Bresse used the turnip for just about any purpose, including drink, nourishment, medicine, skin care, and even sexual arousal, to the point that their neighbours ridiculed them with the nickname 'turnips'.[36] Bigottier was determined to defend his compatriots, whose land had been incorporated into the French kingdom only a few years earlier:

---

[28] Cf. François Roaldès, *Discours de la vigne*, ed. Philippe Tamizey de Larroque (Bordeaux, 1886), p. 34.

[29] Published in Paris, 1539. On Breton see M. Prevost, 'Robert Breton', *DBF* VII, 247–8.

[30] Breton, *Agriculturae encomium*, fos. Sig. Dii r., Ei v.

[31] Ibid., fos. Iii v.

[32] Le Roy Ladurie, *Les paysans de Languedoc*, I, 211–13.

[33] 'Hoc in ore omni populo est ... sat quercus' (Du Choul, *De Varia quercus historia accesit Pylati Montis Descriptio* (Lyons, 1555), fo. 4).

[34] Ed. Joseph Brossard (Bourg-en-Bresse, 1891).

[35] A.-L. Herminjard, *Correspondence des réformateurs dans les pays de langue française* (Geneva, 1866–97), II, 425; Henri Delarue, 'Olivetan et Pierre de Vingle à Genève, 1532–1533', *BHR* 8 (1946), 105–6; Giovanni Gonnet, 'Le premier synode de Chanforan de 1532', *BSHPF* 99 (1953), 211.

[36] Bigottier, *Rapina*, p. 21.

Let some sing of war, Bacchus or the Furies,
Let them crown their times with laurel,
Let others, veritable fools, usurp the titles and attributes
Of royalty,
Make themselves into gods hurling harmless thunderbolts.
As for me I will chant the virtues of my compatriots,
The glories of my country and of my beloved turnips.
If this threefold subject appears ridiculous to the reader,
Let him recall that often times great things are hidden behind
The apparently insignificant.
It is in the smallest details that nature reveals itself
As most admirable.[37]

Bigottier's intention with respect to the turnip was to inform others of its qualities in the hope that they would benefit from what the people of Bresse already knew. Not only was the turnip an excellent food, its juice even being a worthy alternative to wine, but its cultivation greatly increased the fertility of the soil. According to Bigottier, improving the fecundity of the land was critical to the avoidance of famine. Indeed, to underline this point he includes in his poem a harrowing description of the ravages of famine and of the plague which, he explains, frequently accompanies it.[38] In contrast, cultivation of the turnip assures an abundance of nourishment. Indeed, Bigottier goes on carefully to describe how to cultivate turnips, including the method for choosing appropriate seeds and the way to plant them, and their different varieties and uses.[39]

As I suggested in *The Conquest of Poverty*, it was Bernard Palissy who perhaps understood the economic and social causes and consequences of insufficient agricultural output better than any of his contemporaries.[40] In the dedication of the *Recepte veritable* to François de Montmorency, governor of Paris, who had the ultimate responsibility for feeding the more than 250,000 inhabitants of the city, Palissy noted that he had included the secrets of agriculture in his work in order to incite those who worked the land to exploit it more effectively. Indeed, he guaranteed that the French kingdom could produce 4 million bushels more of grain a year if his advice was followed.

Palissy's practical proposals included the intelligent use of manuring and, in a later work, the application of marl as a means of improving the fertility of the soil. More generally, he demanded the application of what he called philosophy to farming, or the development of agriculture on a more rational basis. In order to introduce a more rational approach to agriculture, it was necessary to end the practice of leaving the cultivation of the land to the most miserable and ignorant peasants. On the contrary, what was required was for the rich peasants and the urban

---

[37]   Ibid., p. 18.
[38]   Ibid., pp. 85–6.
[39]   Ibid., p. 24.
[40]   See Heller, *The Conquest of Poverty*, pp. 247–51.

elites to devote themselves to farming. Now we know that in fact there was some movement in this direction, which continued throughout the sixteenth century. However, Palissy quite rightly decried the fact that too many of the rural and urban bourgeoisie were trying to transform themselves or their offspring into office-holding notables, members of the nobility, or ecclesiastics living off their rents. The diversion of capital which resulted was having disastrous effects on agriculture.

Palissy's appeal for reform in this respect included not only the richer peasants and merchants but the nobility itself. He bemoaned the fact that too many of the nobles squandered their fortunes in wasteful expenditure, display and extravagance after the manner of the court. Their time would be better spent instructing and working closely with their tenants. He decried the effects of the concept of derogation on French society. It led to the view that manual labour was incompatible with nobility. Rather, he called upon the nobles to work with their hands and to regard their agricultural implements as more valuable than their weapons. In effect, Palissy called upon the nobles to transform themselves from being feudal into capitalist landlords. Indeed, he recommended that the king create special offices, honours and rewards for those who invented new tools and machines which would be useful to agriculture. He lamented the fact that armourers were constantly inventing new kinds of halberds, swords and other weapons of war, while agricultural invention was neglected. He recounted that recently he had travelled through the regions of Béarn and Bigorre, where the sight of the clumsy ploughs being used by the peasants had infuriated him.

The importance of agriculture to the rest of the economy is suggested by Palissy's final remarks. He wondered why young men of good family could not invent new tools or devices which would be useful to agriculture, instead of spending their time finding new and fanciful ways of cutting cloth, as they were doing. Here Palissy was referring to the textile industry, in which fashion was already an important economic consideration. He was trying to suggest that profitability in this industry ultimately depended on reasonable food prices. Like a good Calvinist, he attacked the preoccupation among cloth manufacturers with fashion, or what we today would call product innovation. The innovators in that industry, he suggests, ought to occupy themselves instead with inventing new agricultural implements which would make agriculture more productive. They would thereby be ensuring the viability of cloth manufacturing itself.

The recommendations in Palissy's *Recepte veritable* are a testimony to the urgency of the agricultural problem at the time of the beginning of the wars of religion. Another contemporary, Jean de Marconville, went so far as to argue that the blight which had affected the harvests in the ten years preceding the wars were really a premonition of the wars themselves.[41] At the end of the

---

[41] See Céard, *La nature et les prodiges*, p. 336.

religious wars Olivier de Serres pointed out in retrospect that a shortage of grain could be the very cause of civil wars.[42] In any case it seems evident that increasing agricultural output was a preoccupation of a number of writers in this period.

Palissy's work was undoubtedly outstanding in comprehending so clearly the importance of increasing agricultural productivity to the whole of French economic and social life. But from the point of view of agronomy, the actual content of his writings was relatively slight. A much more substantial contribution was Charles Estienne and Jean Liébault's *L'agriculture et maison rustique* (1564). This work, according to one recent student of French agronomy in the age of Enlightenment, has been unfairly slighted:[43] for instance, it introduced a classification of different types of land (stony, sandy, clay, chalk, light, heavy, and newly cleared) which remained in use until the first half of the eighteenth century. Furthermore, the work abounds in judicious advice on how to treat, cultivate, manure and fertilize these different kinds of terrain. Its observations, especially on agriculture in the Ile-de-France, are a remarkable demonstration of the complex and painstaking techniques required for working the land properly. Advice is offered on the cultivation of many different kinds of plants, some of which were newly discovered. Indeed, certain of the new plants recommended by Estienne and Liébault would be forgotten, to be rediscovered only in the eighteenth century after a long period of neglect.

Estienne and Liébault's work marked the growing independence of French agronomy from classical influence. As we have seen, the agricultural practices of Antiquity were regarded by these two as largely useless in dealing with the conditions of sixteenth-century France. But this treatise had its rivals, notably, Agostino Gallo's *Le vinti giornale dell'agricultura* ..., translated into French by François Belleforest.[44] In recommending his translation to his readers, Belleforest even went so far as to suggest that Etienne and Liébault had based their work on Gallo.[45] A native of Brescia, Gallo came from a region of Italy in which the most advanced techniques of cultivation were practised. In particular, his work helped to introduce the cultivation of rice and lucerne into France.[46]

That agricultural reform was a preoccupation of this period may be seen from a treatise already published by the reign of Henri II, Raoul Spifame's *Dicaearchiae Henrici, regis christianissimi, progymnasmata* (1556).[47] Spifame, a member of a

---

[42] Serres, *Le théâtre d'agriculture* (Paris, 1600), p. 57.
[43] André J. Bourde, *Agronomie et agronomes en France au XVIII⁴ siècle* (Paris, 1967), I, 40–1, 42–3.
[44] *Secrets de la vraye agriculture* (Paris, 1572).
[45] Ibid., fo. sig. a iii r.
[46] See *Nouv. biog. univ.* ed. Michaud, v. 20, pp. 323–4.
[47] *Dicaearchie Henrici, regis christianissimi, progymnasmata* (n.p., 1556). Despite its Latin title, the treatise is in French. The prose being difficult and confused, I have used an eighteenth-century paraphrase faithful to the original published under the title *Vues d'un politique du XVI⁴ siècle sur la législation de son temps*, ed. Jean Auffrey (Amsterdam, 1775).

distinguished family of notables and magistrates, had the effrontery to lay out and publish a series of 306 so-called royal edicts for the reform of the kingdom. His temerity led to the seizure of his work and his arrest on a charge of *lèse-majesté*. He was only able to escape the royal anger by spending the last seven years of his life confined under house arrest and treated as a madman.[48] Committed to a policy of high taxation, religious persecution and war abroad, Valois absolutism under Henri II was not prepared to entertain any proposals for political and social reform, especially those stemming from members of the parlementary elite.[49] The publication of Spifame's proposals in the form of a series of royal edicts might well have been seen by the king as the rash act of an insane person. Still, one cannot help but observe the curious modernity of this manner of dealing with political opposition.

Spifame, despite being accused of challenging royal authority, nevertheless wrote as part of that stream of absolutizing writers which marked the reigns of Francis I and Henri II. Unfortunately for him, he chose to substitute his will for that of the king, even styling himself dictator at various points in the text. It is unclear whether he might have been inspired thus boldly to present himself by the model of the wise fool in Erasmus' *Praise of Folly* or by Sébastien Brant's *Ship of Fools* or whether there is, indeed, a lunacy at work which is more than a literary device.

Despite elements of mania in Spifame's way of presenting himself, his proposals for reform are of considerable interest. A thoroughgoing Gallican, he proposed that the king carry out a sweeping reform of the Church. Simony, pluralism, ecclesiastical courts, fees for clerical services, collections in churches and clerical begging were to be abolished.[50] Ecclesiastical property was to be secularized and the clergy to receive reasonable annual salaries as state servants. Clerics without benefices, or otherwise idle, were to be made into what he called public serfs, to be paid by the day or at the rate of other wage workers.[51] The regular clergy was to help with the harvest.[52]

Despite his call for these reforms and for the abolition of most saints' days, there is no evidence of explicitly Protestant assumptions behind Spifame's proposed reforms. There is, instead, some trace of the influence of Machiavelli's *Discourses*, the first book of which had appeared in a French translation in the previous decade.[53] Spifame, furthermore, insists on the abolition of the office of

---

[48]   Yves Jeanclos, *Les projets de réforme judiciare de Raoul Spifame au XVIᵉ siècle* (Geneva, 1977), pp. 9–12. Cf. J. Mathorez, 'Un radical-socialiste sous Henri II. Raoul Spifame', *Revue politique et parliamentaire* (1914), 538–59.

[49]   On the tension between the parlement and the crown in the first half of the sixteenth century see the somewhat overdrawn but nonetheless deeply interesting and challenging essay by J.-L. Bourgeon, 'La Fronde parlementaire à la veille de la Saint-Barthélemy', *Bibliothèque de l'école des Chartes* 148 (1990), 17–89.

[50]   Spifame, *Vues d'un politique du XVIᵉ siècle*, pp. 33, 66–7, 73, 78–80, 85, 136, 139, 142, 202–3.

[51]   Ibid., p. 71.

[52]   Ibid., pp. 200–1.

[53]   Machiavelli, *Le premier livre des Discours de l'estat de paix et de guerre de messire Nicolas Macchiavegli* (Paris, 1544).

the dead as well as the existing funeral ceremonies, to be replaced by celebrations of joy and thanksgiving at the entry of the dead into the realm of eternal felicity.[54] Echoing Machiavelli's admiration of Roman civic religion, Spifame advocates the establishment of a cult of heroes in order to inspire the nobility to fight for the state.[55] The roll call of these heroes should be read out at church services, as was currently the martyrology of the saints.[56] A royal historian and poet should be appointed to support this cult.[57] Inspired no doubt by the great tide of public-school foundations which was then sweeping urban France, Spifame called for the establishment of a national system of public schools.[58] Such schools were to be maintained by the parish, through collections and by additional taxation at the local level. Tuition was to be free so as not to exclude the poor. Schooling was to begin at the age of six and to run through nine classes or grades. The core of the curriculum was to be the three ancient languages, to be taught by regents who had acquired a master of arts degree. Girls would be taught a curriculum suitable to them through the convent schools.[59] Spifame insists on the rights parents should have over children. The law ought to compel the obedience of children to the will of parents. Marriages were to be arranged for unmarried males over the age of twenty-five and for unmarried females aged fourteen and over.[60]

While calling for a uniform nation-wide system of weights and measures, Spifame also demanded a unified system of laws for the kingdom.[61] *Monts-de-piété* were to be established to provide small loans at reasonable interest rates, there was to be a thirty-year jubilee on debts, and the principal on presently outstanding loans was to be redeemed without further interest.[62] The idle of all social classes were to be forced to work. Those who were unable to find work were to be employed in municipal workshops established to produce all kinds of manufactures.[63]

Spifame's proposals on agriculture must be seen as part of his overall scheme of reform, which emphasizes political rather than economic solutions to problems. His agrarian reform measures address themselves to the problem of improving productivity, while rejecting a solution based on the further development of capitalism. In this respect, his views were entirely opposed to those of Palissy who was calling precisely for a solution to the problem of food scarcity by the further development of a capitalist agriculture. Indeed, for Spifame the capitalist relations

---

[54] Spifame, *Vues d'un politique du XVIᵉ siècle*, pp. 12–13.
[55] Ibid., pp. 14–15.
[56] Ibid., p. 16.
[57] Ibid.
[58] On the development of municipal schools and colleges cf. George Huppert, *Public Schools in Renaissance France* (Urbana, Chicago, University of Illinois, 1984); Paul F. Grendler, 'Schools in Western Europe', *Renaissance Quarterly* 43 (1990), 775–87.
[59] Spifame, *Vues d'un politique*, pp. 117–25.
[60] Ibid., p. 110.
[61] Ibid., pp. 174, 177.
[62] Ibid., pp. 5–6, 189.
[63] Ibid., p. 45.

of production which had developed in the countryside were part of the problem. According to him, the landlords who were making use of tenants and wage labour to exploit their land were not well served. The infertility of the soil, as he put it, was the result of their neglect.[64] The lack of productivity of the land accounted for the high price of food, from which the poor in particular suffered. The rural poor ought to be given land to cultivate. Even the proprietors of the soil would benefit, as the poor do all they can to cultivate well the little land that they have.[65] Spifame thus praises the industriousness of the poor and calls for a redistribution of land in their favour as a way of producing more food. Contrast this attitude with that of Palissy, who ridicules the ignorance and lack of capacity of the poor who remain on the land.

In order to foster agricultural improvement, Spifame urged that agrarian chambers be established in every *élection*. These chambers were to be composed of mixed bodies of wealthy and experienced peasants, merchants and lawyers. The members of these chambers would be charged with carrying out regular visitations and inspections to see to the implementation of agricultural improvements. In addition, there would be local courts to redistribute the land and adjudicate disputes.[66] It is assumed that the resultant increase in the productivity of the land would allow for the support of this whole new layer of bureaucracy in the countryside.[67]

According to Spifame, each tract of land has its own characteristics. Improvements in output can only be founded on first-hand knowledge of its qualities. Proper fertilization of the land requires large amounts of manure. A great expansion of livestock would be necessary to produce sufficient amounts of fertilizer. In order to help to support such expanded herds of cattle and sheep, vineyards between fields were to be replaced by hedgerows. These would provide not only feed for livestock but also kindling. Fruit-bearing trees, hedges and vineyards were to be planted along all paths, roads and highways, to be maintained by the local inhabitants.[68]

Another work of this period of more than passing interest is *De laudibus Provinciae* (1551) by Quiqueran de Beaujeu, bishop of Senez.[69] It contains an excellent description of the livestock of the Camargue, emphasizing the strength of its bulls and oxen, the fine bloodstock of its cows and horses, and the high-quality wool produced by the sheep of the region. The quality of the vineyards of Crau and of Arles is stressed, as is the excellence of the olive oil produced in the province generally. The great variety of fruits and vegetables produced throughout the area is also enumerated.

[64] Ibid., pp. 154–5.
[65] Ibid., p. 156.
[66] Ibid., pp. 161–3, 165.
[67] Ibid., p. 152.
[68] Ibid., pp. 159–60.
[69] I have relied on the account to be found in Bourde, *Agronomie et agronomes en France*, I, 40–6.

The subject of productivity comes up in Quiqueran de Beaujeu's discussion of rice culture. Grain yields normally did not exceed 5 or 6:1 anywhere in France. Because rice culture can produce yields of up to 40:1, the cultivation of rice was increasing rapidly in Provence according to Quiqueran de Beaujeu. At the same time, he notes that the large quantities of moisture required for this kind of cultivation and the malarial disease accompanying it were hampering this expansion. Finally, he urges the development of sugar-cane as a lucrative crop. Indeed, this treatise was published in the very year that the first attempts were being made to establish sugar plantations at Hyères.[70] Similarly, experiments in the production of cotton were going on in the province at the same time.[71]

Jacquart has noted that increases in agricultural productivity were to emerge from the market gardening practised in and around Paris and the other large towns. In the Ile-de-France, as elsewhere in northern France, market gardeners, anxious to augment their revenues, experimented with the cultivation of peas, beans and other nitrogen-rich plants which helped make possible the eventual elimination of the fallow. Such developments were to come, however, only at the beginning of the next century.[72] But the possibility of a more intensive agriculture was already visible in the mid-sixteenth century in the exploitation of commercial crops such as grapes, pastel and saffron. The growing of such cash crops not only directly increased know-how but indirectly stimulated the commercialization, specialization and intensification of agriculture. In Jacques Gohory's *Devis sur la vigne, vin et vendanges* (1550), for example, a Rabelaisian celebration of the joys of wine is combined with a businesslike approach to the cultivation of grapes.[73] In addition to all kinds of advice on the practice of viticulture in the Ile-de-France, the commercial advantages of an investment in vineyards over *rente* are mathematically demonstrated.

In the eyes of the merchants of Paris, the production of pastel was not simply a matter of cultivation but one of processing and manufacture. According to their remonstrance of 1565 against a proposed monopoly on the export of pastel, the quality of pastel did not simply depend on the fertility of the soil, as was the case with wheat or wine, but was the result of skill and technique no less than was the manufacture of linen and canvas.[74] Indeed, the Lauragais, where most of the pastel was produced, supported a large population on small plots of land cultivating pastel with an almost Asiatic intensity which involved careful preparation, manuring and harvesting of the crop, followed by washing, drying, milling,

[70]   *Histoire du commerce de Marseille*, ed. G. Rambert, III, 437.
[71]   Boissonade, *Le socialisme d'état*, pp. 89–90.
[72]   Jacquart, *Paris et l'Ile-de-France au temps des paysans*, p. 27.
[73]   *Devis sur la vigne, vin et vendanges d'Orl, de Suave, auquel la façon ancienne du plant, labour et garder este descouverte et reduicte au present usage* (Paris, 1550).
[74]   *Reg. BVP* v, 511.

fermenting, assaying and weighing of the product.[75] What is interesting about the cultivation and processing of pastel from our perspective is the relationship between the commercialization of the product and the development of an intensive form of agriculture which could support a larger population than was normally sustained by the cultivation of grain. The Parisian merchants, attempting to defend the commerce in pastel, made the point that its production could profitably be extended to other parts of the kingdom.[76]

It was with the same idea of advantageously extending the production of saffron to other parts of France that Elie Vinet published *Le safran de Roche-Foucaut. Discours du cultivement de safran, des vertus, proprietes et profit d'icelui* (1568).[77] The work was, in fact, written in 1560 at the château of Jean Benoit, seigneur of Lagebasten, *premier président* of the Parlement of Bordeaux, at Montignac in the Charente.[78] Prior to 1520, according to Vinet, little saffron was grown in the Angoumois. Spanish Aragon and the French Toulousain were the principal areas from which the merchants of Lyons and south Germany obtained supplies of this dye. But, in the succeeding years, the inhabitants of Rochefoucauld began to cultivate saffron and were soon imitated by their neighbours in the rest of the Angoumois. Merchants from Lyons and Germany were buying 100,000 *livres tournois* of saffron annually from the merchants of Rochefoucauld who controlled the trade. Profits were so great that a producer could pay back the price of the land used to raise the crop in a single year.[79]

Vinet's text is mainly devoted to explaining how saffron was cultivated. As such it is one of the most detailed pieces of agronomic literature produced in the sixteenth century. Saffron, Vinet explains, is grown on small plots which are intensively worked. By preference the soil should be light without too much clay or sand. It is a crop which is best grown in the Midi in areas where it is both warm and humid. Saffron does best in soil which is left fallow for a year. The land should be ploughed three or four times, six or seven months prior to planting. The soil can be turned with a plough, but it is better to work it carefully with hand implements. The best crops are produced where the land is manured at least six times.[80] Money is to be made not only by selling the flowers to the merchants but also from marketing the bulbs to the growers.

The degree to which a kind of capitalist logic had penetrated the rural economy is perhaps most succinctly illustrated through the title of Prudent Le Choyslet's *Discours economiques, non moins utile que recreatif, monstrant comme, par le mesnagement de pouilles, de cinq cens livres, pour une fois employees, l'on peut tirer par an*

[75] Gilles Caster, *Le commerce de pastel et l'épicerie à Toulouse de 1450 environ à 1561* (Toulouse, 1961), pp. 39–42, 67–76.
[76] *Reg. BVP* v, 509.
[77] (Poitiers, 1568).
[78] Vinet, *Le safran de Roche-Foucaut*, p. 40.
[79] Ibid., pp. 3–4.
[80] Ibid., p. 2.

quartre mil cinq cens livres de proffit honneste.[81] Published for the first time in 1572, the treatise was to see four more French editions up to 1612. An English translation appeared in London in 1580.[82] The text of less than twenty pages is a straightforward and unadorned account of how to run a successful poultry-farming operation located close to an urban market.

But of the works published in the middle of the century, second only to that of Palissy's in importance was Pierre Belon's *Les remonstrances sur le default du labour et culture des plantes* (1558).[83] This treatise was clearly the fruit of Belon's extensive travels throughout Europe and the Near East. His patrons being predominantly aristocrats, it is to them that Belon addresses himself in the first instance. Thus he makes a point of arguing that nobles are capable of thinking in the long term and of practising economy, contrary to the common view that they are impulsive, money-hungry and spendthrift. He takes this wishful thinking a stage further, being at pains to prove the somewhat dubious proposition that war is no necessary impediment to agricultural improvement.[84] This, at a time when France was being bled white by the bellicose ambitions of its king supported by his nobility. Despite these notions meant to flatter the elites, Belon nevertheless makes it clear that he is writing 'not for the moment, nor for any particular person, but for the duration of time and for the whole world'.[85] Moreover, the *Remonstrances*, as we have them, deal with silviculture as part of a larger project which includes agriculture. At several places in the text, Belon notes that he is postponing the discussion of a subject. He promises instead to deal with it in a work on agriculture which he announces as forthcoming.[86] This treatise, if it ever existed, appears to have been lost.

Belon's treatise directs itself to resolving the related problems of a growing shortage of food and an increasing scarcity of wood. For him the land is the source of all wealth. The land provides the necessities of life, the materials with which craftsmen work, and the revenues off which the nobility lives.[87] Belon argues that the introduction and cultivation of large numbers of new plants and trees will augment the incomes of both peasants and nobles while increasing knowledge among men of letters.[88] It would be no small thing, Belon argues, to provide at little expense the means to raise many different kinds of trees which could vastly increase income.[89] The parks and enclosures of the nobility would make perfect sites for nurseries, where new species of plants and trees could be

[81]   (Paris, 1572).
[82]   *A Discourse of Husbandry*, tr. Richard Eden (London, 1580; Reading, 1951).
[83]   (Paris, 1558).
[84]   Belon, *Les remonstrances*, fo. 31v.
[85]   Ibid., fo. 33v.
[86]   Ibid., fos. 38r., 49r., 61v.
[87]   Ibid., fos. 13v.–14r.
[88]   Ibid., fo. 5r.–v.
[89]   Ibid., fo. 6r.

planted and improvements to the soil could be tried out.[90] In this connection, he observes that the cultivation of trees is preferable to that of plants because they require much less labour. Through these means new species of trees can be domesticated in France, not on a scale of thousands but on a scale of millions.[91] Clearly, Belon had in mind a vast programme of reforestation designed to resolve not only the problem of the shortage of wood, but also to provide more and different kinds of food. According to Belon, land which is at present lying fallow because it is unsuitable for the growing of grain could become the most valuable land of all if it were planted in vines and woodland.[92]

Belon then proceeds to enumerate a whole series of different kinds of trees from Italy, Savoy, Switzerland, Asia Minor and Syria which might be brought to France and raised in nurseries in whatever quantities were desired.[93] Many of these trees would be fruit-bearing and could be used to increase the supply of food. Among these, he notes plantains from Italy,[94] wild pine, the seeds of which the peasants of Grisons use to nourish themselves,[95] conifers from Embrun,[96] the seeds of balsam which are eaten with bread in Syria,[97] and lemon, lime and pistachio trees.[98] Many of these are already cultivated on French soil. It is only a question, according to Belon, of developing their culture more systematically.

Belon notes with dismay the growing resort to coal as a fuel in place of increasingly scarce wood. His observation tends to confirm the view that the mining of coal had already assumed considerable proportions by the middle of the sixteenth century. Belon regarded coal as a noxious substance and regretted its increasing use. For him the answer to the growing fuel shortage lay in increasing the supply of wood. The extensive planting of trees on waste land was part of the answer, as was the more effective transport of wood by river from the forests to the towns.[99] Finally, he remarks on the possibility of using oil from beechwood, noting its utility as a fuel.[100] No doubt it was concern with finding new supplies of energy to supplement firewood which stimulated his interest in petroleum, which he pursued particularly during his Italian travels.[101]

Henri II had already ordered the planting of elms along the roadside

[90] Ibid., fo. 15r.–v.
[91] Ibid., fo. 30v.
[92] Ibid., fo. 48v.
[93] Ibid., fos. 39v.–48r.
[94] Ibid., fo. 44v.
[95] Ibid., fo. 33v.
[96] Ibid.
[97] Ibid., fo. 46v.
[98] Ibid., fo. 47v.
[99] Ibid., fo. 48v.
[100] Ibid., fos. 48v.–49r.
[101] See R.J. Forbes, *Pierre Belon and Petroleum* (Leiden, 1958).

throughout the kingdom as one way of alleviating the growing shortage of wood.[102] Belon was sceptical of this administrative approach to the problem. He argues, instead, that teaching the peasants the elements of silviculture would be more effective.[103] Like Palissy, Belon believed that developing a sense of industry among the peasantry was crucial to economic improvement. In this regard, he tells a story which seemed to him to be exemplary. A bishop, who had accompanied Francis I on his punitive expedition to La Rochelle (1542), was the source of the tale. The bishop was probably René Du Bellay, whom we know to have been interested in agriculture, and who was one of Belon's most important patrons. Returning to Paris from La Rochelle, the bishop heard of a peasant who his neighbours believed possessed a mandrake by means of which he had become wealthy. Le Roy Ladurie has attempted to demonstrate the significance of the mandrake in the rural society of southwestern France in his study of Francouneto, Jasmin's witch.[104] The mandrake was thought to give its possessors supernatural or witch-like powers that enabled them to enrich themselves at the expense of their neighbours. Having heard the tale of the wealthy peasant reputed to have conjured with a mandrake, the bishop travelled out of his way on his return from La Rochelle in order to interview him and asked him to let him see the mandrake. The peasant replied that the only mandrake he had had in the twenty years that he had lived in the region was to make sure that he rose earlier than any of the male or female workers he employed to cultivate the land. It was as a result of his own diligence, he maintained, that he and his farm had prospered.[105]

Le Roy Ladurie makes use of the notion of the mandrake to illustrate his view that the *mentalité* of the peasants of the *ancien régime* was based on what anthropologists call the notion of limited good. In other words, the world-view of the mass of the population of the *ancien régime* was a static one. According to Le Roy Ladurie, a society of limited good clung to the notion that the wealth available in the community was fixed and limited. If an individual acquired something, it was always at the expense of someone else.[106] But, as James Dow has pointed out, the concept of limited good itself is the product of a peasant society which is not static but is under pressure from the development of capitalist relations of production, hence hardly in a state of inertia.[107] It is the defensive reaction of a community that is not necessarily against growth or inherently conservative but,

---

[102] Antoine Fontanon, *Les edicts et ordonnances depuis S. Loys jusques à present* (Paris, 1585), p. 786.
[103] Belon, *Les remonstrances*, fo. 52r.
[104] *Jasmin's Witch*, tr. Brian Pearce (London, 1987), pp. 32–7, 58, 60.
[105] Belon, *Les remonstrances*, fo. 31r.–v. On the association of rural entrepreneurship with magic cf. Davis, *The Return of Martin Guerre* (Cambridge, Mass., 1983), p. 60.
[106] Le Roy Ladurie, *Jasmin's Witch*, p. 25; Le Roy Ladurie, *Love, Death and Money in the Pays d'Oc*, tr. Alan Sheridan (New York, 1982), pp. 511, 568, n. 6.
[107] 'The Image of Limited Production: Envy and the Domestic Mode of Production in Peasant Society', *Human Organization* 40 (1982), 361–3.

on the contrary, feels itself threatened by change, which it regards as exploitative and therefore illegitimate and unnatural. Peasant societies are not automatically opposed to the accumulation of wealth based on hard work. Indeed, the appeal made to the work ethic by the rich peasant in Belon's story is cast in terms of the values of the peasants themselves.

The point of the story, as Belon tells it, is that there were in the French countryside those who rejected the idea that their prosperity meant that they were taking advantage of others and who claimed that they were creating new wealth out of their own labour or by properly organizing the labour of others. At the very least the existence of such ideas in the stratum of rich peasants in the countryside must put us on guard against the idea that everyone in the *ancien régime* implicitly accepted the idea of a society of limited good in Le Roy Ladurie's static sense of the term. Rather, the conflict lay between those who were reacting against capitalist relations of production and those who attempted to justify these capitalist activities by insisting on their non-exploitative and positive aspects. In any case, it is evidently wrong to believe that we are dealing with a static society.

Palissy's plan to increase grain output by 4 million bushels annually and Belon's scheme to plant millions of new trees to provide more food, fuel and materials for housing and furnishings hardly reflect a society which is inert. Indeed, to the jaundiced eye of the late twentieth century watching the disappearance of the rainforests and the depletion of the ozone layer, the plans of Palissy and Belon, which were designed to increase the food supply while renewing the forests, appear to be a beautiful and noble prospect.

French writers of the mid-sixteenth century, we may conclude, clearly had some sense of the notion of economic growth. This conception found expression in ideas of technological and intellectual progress with respect not only to the middle ages, but even to Antiquity. How did such ideas emerge? They arose, in the first place, through the experience of the positive results of roughly a century of economic advance. But a consciousness of material progress seems to have been especially a product of a sense of growing economic difficulty in the aftermath of a long period of prosperity. It is at the point when economic growth seemed to be jeopardized that Palissy and Belon began to develop a clearer sense of the notion of economic growth and what might be done to maintain or restore it.

Belon closes his work with two grand proposals. The first is to establish a botanical garden attached to the medical faculty of the University of Paris.[108] Although he puts the stress on the scholarly aspect of this endeavour, Belon also alludes to the practical agricultural benefits which might follow from such a project.[109] His second proposal was a call to Frenchmen to seek out plants and seeds from all over the world to be acculturated on French soil. Taking this a step

---

[108] Belon, *Les remonstrances*, fo. 70v.
[109] Ibid., fo. 75r.

further, he urged that this become a truly international exchange with France trading its plants for those of other kingdoms and nations to the benefit of all.[110]

It is noteworthy that even Guillaume Rondelet, considered the founder of the school of natural history at Montpellier, turned to consider the problems of agriculture towards the end of his life: Laurent Joubert, who inherited Rondelet's books and manuscripts and wrote his biography, noted an unfinished treatise on agriculture among his writings.[111] It would seem, therefore, to be a mistake to see the emergence of a scientific interest in natural history in France in the second half of the sixteenth century as entirely divorced from practical considerations. While on the subject of the school of French Renaissance naturalists, we should not overlook the importance to agriculture of artists and illustrators who often worked in collaboration with scholars. Jacques Le Moyne de Morgues is one of these illustrators whose work has recently become better known. Le Moyne's *Œuvres* have been collected and critically studied in a magnificent catalogue published in 1977 by the British Museum.[112] Le Moyne was born *c.* 1533 at Dieppe and by the early 1560s had become a Calvinist. In 1564 he sailed with the Huguenot expedition to Florida as a cartographer and illustrator.[113] Although the French monarchy was not directly involved in organizing the expedition, the political and economic significance of this attempt to found a Huguenot colony in Florida was undoubtedly considerable.[114] A survivor of the Spanish assault on the colony, Le Moyne migrated to England to escape further religious persecution. The Sydney family became his principal patrons. In 1581 he received letters of naturalization while living in Blackfriars in London with his French wife. As is pointed out by William T. Stearn in his study of Le Moyne as plant illustrator and herbalist, it is scarcely possible to separate the aesthetic, scientific and economic motives in his work.[115] Le Moyne's botanical drawings were never embodied in a comprehensive set of illustrations accompanying a learned text. Most are scattered in unpublished collections.

The earliest of these studies were undoubtedly executed prior to his departure for Florida.[116] They are unquestionably part of that tradition of plant illustration which began with Dürer and continued through the work of Leonard Fuchs, Rondelet, Charles L'Escluse and Matthieu L'Obel. Artists who worked in this stream sought realistic and accurate representations of the vegetable kingdom.

---

[110] Ibid., fos. 75v.–76v.

[111] Laurent Joubert, *Operum latinorum tomus primus ... Cui subjectus est tomus secundus, nunc primum in lucem proditus*(Lyons, 1582), II, 192–3. I owe this reference to the kindness of Professor Gillian Lewis, St Anne's College, Oxford.

[112] *The Work of Jacques Le Moyne de Morgues: A Huguenot Artist in France, Florida and England*, ed. Paul Hutton, 2 vols. (London, 1977).

[113] See Lestringant, *Le Huguenot et le sauvage* (Paris, 1990), pp. 150–4, 183–202.

[114] See D.B. Quinn, 'The Attempted Colonization of Florida by the French, 1562–65' in *The Work of Jacques Le Moyne de Morgues*, ed. Hutton, I, 17–18, 21.

[115] Stearn, 'Le Moyne as Plant Portraitist and Herbalist', in *Jacques Le Moine*, ed. Hutton, I, 55–7.

[116] Ibid., I, 13.

But, in addition to scientific and aesthetic concerns, an interest in the value of plants as food or medicine is clearly in evidence.[117]

Jean Bodin addressed the question of food scarcity as part of his discussion of the causes for the general rise in prices which had reached alarming proportions in the 1560s. *La responce de Jean Bodin à monsieur de Malestroit* (1568) attributes the price inflation to the increase in the money supply arising from the influx of bullion from the New World.[118] Bodin opposed any outright ban on the export of grain in the name of international free trade. But in spite of his commitment to the principle of free trade, his solution to the problem of grain shortages was to regulate supply by increasing export duties and by establishing urban granaries which would help regulate supply and prices.[119] Not only did he advocate managing supply, he was prepared to argue that the high price of beef and poultry could be dealt with by restricting demand. The common people should reduce their new taste for meat in favour of a return to fish consumption. But Bodin turns this seemingly traditional approach into a proposal advocating a huge expansion in the supply of fish. Inspired by the work of Guillaume Rondelet, he calls for the development of pisciculture as a means of dramatically increasing food resources. France, he argues, is filled with streams, ponds, lakes and rivers, as well as being surrounded by seas which could be used for this purpose. A shift towards the consumption of fish, whose variety, Bodin notes, is far greater than that of animal species, would increase the supply of food, lower prices and stimulate the development of the fishing industry.[120]

How important was this literature we have been considering in improving the supply of food? Jean Meuvret, the great expert on the agriculture of the *ancien régime*, was rather pessimistic, stressing the limited number of original works on agriculture published by Frenchmen during the sixteenth century.[121] One may wonder, however, whether Meuvret was aware even of all the works we have mentioned to this point.[122] Indeed, Corinne Beutler, who has studied the agronomic literature of the sixteenth century in its European context, criticizes Meuvret for not taking translations into account.[123] When one does take translations into consideration, France emerges as second only to Italy in the amount of

---

[117] Ibid, I, 56.

[118] Bodin, *La response*, ed. Hauser (Paris, A. Colin, 1932).

[119] Ibid., pp. 35–7.

[120] Ibid., pp. 37–40.

[121] 'Agronomie et jardinage au XVIᵉ et au XVIIᵉ siècle,' *Etudes d'histoire économique* (Paris, 1971), pp. 153–61.

[122] Important to the study of French agronomic literature is the catalogue produced by Marc Bloch and Charles Bost and others for an exposition on the history of French agriculture which was held at the Bibliothèque Nationale on the eve of the Second World War. *Les travaux et les jours dans l'ancienne France, exposition organisée sous les auspices des chambres d'agriculture avec le concours du Musée nationale des arts et traditions populaires par le comité national constitué pour commemorer le IVᵉ centenaire d'Olivier de Serres* (Paris, June–September, 1939).

[123] 'Un chapitre de la sensibilité collective: la littérature agricole en Europe continentale au XVIᵉ siècle,' *Annales: ESC* 28 (1973), 1281.

such published literature. Of 600 works on agriculture published in the course of the sixteenth century, Paris and Lyons published no less than 245. This compares to only 41 for the Low Countries and a mere 20 for England. Moreover, as Beutler stresses, this literature was not meant to distract and entertain, but rather was designed to transform nature in the sense of increasing and diversifying agricultural production.[124] Furthermore, as will be demonstrated, this is precisely what did occur, at least in those parts of France like the Ile-de-France, Normandy and Dauphiné which have been investigated carefully.[125]

Efforts at improving the food supply were not confined to theoretical proposals advanced through the printing press. Under Charles IX a series of measures was taken to try to maintain or increase the grain supply. In 1566 an edict was issued ordering the alienation of royal lands to those prepared to cultivate them.[126] Obviously, this sell-off of land by the crown was designed to raise revenue. However, the wording of the edict makes it plain that the possibility of an increase in the grain supply was an important consideration. The year following, the king sought to increase grain production by restricting the cultivation of grapes. Two-thirds of the arable land in the kingdom was to be reserved for the cultivation of grain.[127] Again in 1567, the king fixed the interest rate at 6 2/3 per cent, claiming that high interest rates were encouraging cultivators to abandon their fields as well as merchants to abandon their trade in favour of loaning money at high interest rates.[128] In 1571 Charles IX issued a three-year moratorium on the payment of agricultural debts.[129] The next year the king prohibited the seizure of land or possessions for debts accumulated as a result of the wars. The ordonnance took note of the fact that much land was not being cultivated or was being poorly cultivated because of a lack of capital available to would-be producers. Accordingly, the ordonnance prohibited property seizure or foreclosures on those cultivators who remained on the land.[130] Stocks of grain and other raw materials were to be inventoried every six months and export prohibited if they were found in short supply.[131]

The crown interested itself in diversifying and increasing agricultural output. In January 1565, Charles IX accorded two entrepreneurs from the Low Countries the right to cultivate a new plant that they claimed to have discovered for the

[124] Ibid., p. 1289.
[125] See below, p. 123.
[126] Robert Estienne, *Les edicts et les ordonnances du roy très chrétien Charles IX de ce nom* (Paris, 1568), pp. 536–7; AN X^{ia} 8629, fo. 184r.; AN X^{ia} 8630, fo. 91r.–v.
[127] La Mare, *Traité de la police*, III, 524. Bodin, *La response*, p. 36 opposed this measure. It had to be reintroduced in 1577.
[128] *Edict et ordonnance du roy touchant les usures* (Rennes, 1567), fo. sig. Aii r.
[129] Guillaume Blanchard, *Compilation chronologique contenant un recueil en abregé des ordonnances, édits, declarations et lettres patentes des rois de France* (Paris, 1715), I, 997.
[130] Pierre Rebuffi, *Les édicts et ordonnances des roys de France depuis l'an 1226 jusques à present* (Lyons, 1573), p. 1489.
[131] Isambert, *Recueil général*, XIV, 241.

production of oil. It was noted that such oil was useful in soap manufacture and in the manufacture of textiles and the tanning of leather. They were to be given a monopoly on the sale of this oil throughout the kingdom.[132] Two years later the king opened the royal gardens at Hyères to the cultivation of sugar-cane in order to bolster the faltering efforts of entrepreneurs who were trying to develop sugar-cane as a commercial crop in the Midi.[133] In 1566 the king issued a patent for a new plough to Henri Rambault of Marseilles. As the text of the patent explains, Rambault 'had invented a form of agricultural machine or tool by which land can be much more quickly, cheaply and easily cultivated and worked than by the plough or other device presently in use in the Kingdom'.[134]

Initiatives towards agricultural improvements were taken quite independently of the monarchy. Interest seems to have been particularly marked in the Midi. Especially notable in Provence was the development of irrigation as a result of the efforts of the engineer Adam de Crapponne. In 1554 he received permission to divert part of the waters of the Durance into a canal designed to irrigate the arid plain of the Crau. An entirely private enterprise based on a pooling of capital by a group of partners, the first stage, which brought the canal as far as Salon, was inaugurated in 1557.[135] As a result of this irrigation project, some 13,000 hectares of land were made available for cultivation. Extensions of the canal were undertaken in 1559, 1564, 1567 and 1569. Provision for the development of water-mills for industrial purposes along the course of the canal was also made. In addition to this ongoing project, Crapponne involved himself in the construction of the port of Nice (1564), the canal of Bouc (1567), and the drainage of the swamps of Tarascon and Fréjus.[136] Between 1568 and 1570 Crapponne undertook the drainage of a part of the Camargue.[137] The execution of these projects, we may suggest, was no doubt facilitated by an expanding population, which was increasingly dependent on wage labour. The water made available through these endeavours undoubtedly helped to increase the agricultural output of Provence.

Nowhere does the impetus to agricultural improvement in the kingdom seem to have been greater than in Languedoc. The sixteenth century there saw the introduction of a bewildering variety of new plants and food crops: 'siesse' wheat, maize, potatoes, alfalfa, lucerne, green beans, cauliflower, artichokes, pimentos, green peppers, tomatoes, melons, pumpkins, cucumbers and new kinds of cabbage, lettuce, pears, figs and plums.[138] Towards the middle of the sixteenth century, we

---

[132] Alexandre Tuetey, *Inventaire analytique des livres de couleurs et bannières du Châtelet de Paris* (Paris, 1899), no. 3054; BN MS Fr. 8081, fos. 205v.–206r.

[133] *Histoire du commerce de Marseille*, ed. Rambaud, III, 437.

[134] Léon Menard, *Histoire civile, ecclésiastique et littéraire de la ville de Nîmes* (Paris, 1744–58), V, appendix pp. 21–2.

[135] Felix Martin, *Adam de Crapponne et son œuvre* (Paris, 1874), pp. 15, 18–22, 28.

[136] Adam de Crapponne, art. *DBF* IX, 1171, Edouard de Dienne, *Histoire du dessèchement des lacs et marais en France avant 1789* (Paris, 1891), p. 367.

[137] Martin, *Adam de Crapponne et son œuvre*, p. 50.

[138] Le Roy Ladurie, *Les paysans de Languedoc*, I, 55, 60–76.

hear of the construction of irrigation ditches and drainage schemes around Narbonne, experiments with the use of the scythe instead of the traditional sickle, and the gradual adoption of the *charrue mousse* with mould-board in place of the age-old *araire* of the Midi.[139] The drive towards opening up new land to the plough is illustrated by the case of Rochefort (Gard). In 1552 a project to drain the pond of Rochefort was instigated. In 1561 the consuls of the town petitioned the king to allow the drainage of the pond to proceed 'in order that they would be able to till and seed the land of the pond which at present earns no revenue'.[140]

At Nîmes in 1566, after the city had passed into Huguenot hands, an attempt was made to put the new plough invented by Henri Rambault into actual use. The introduction of the new plough was part of a standing policy of local political intervention (begun in the 1550s) to support a faltering economy. Nîmes, like other towns in the kingdom, was already feeling the economic pinch at that time. The town tried to counter the growing sense of economic malaise with a programme of municipal initiatives and financial incentives. In 1552 the city fathers established a weekly livestock market.[141] Two years later they subsidized the establishment in the city of a pin manufacture from Le Puy.[142] In 1557 two Italian merchant manufacturers from Avignon were induced to set up a velvet manufacture. The city provided a house, loans and tax exemptions to induce the foreigners to set up an enterprise in the town.[143] The following year Pierre Dupont was able to establish a silk manufacture, again with the help of the municipal government.[144] Raw silk, which had to be imported into Nîmes from Italy, represented a large fraction of the costs of production. In 1564 François Traucat appealed to the city fathers to support the planting of mulberry trees and the raising of silkworms in the diocese to create local sources for the supply of raw silk.[145]

Thus, when in 1567 the town council agreed to try to promote the use of Henri Rambault's plough in the region, the initiative represented a continuation of past policy. The town agreed to pay the inventor 60 *livres tournois* for the right to employ his agricultural device in the countryside around the city.[146] The authorities apparently had an understanding of the connection between increasing the food supply and the prosperity of manufacturing.

At Pradel north of Nîmes, meanwhile, it is noteworthy that the Calvinist agronomist Olivier de Serres was beginning his first experiments in agricultural improvement in the 1560s. It is more than likely that his early attempts to irrigate

---

[139] Ibid., I, 80, 83, 86–7.
[140] Robert Bailly, 'L'assèchement des étangs de Rochefort-Pujaut: XVI–XVIIe siècles', *Rhodanie* 6 (1989), 37.
[141] Menard, *Histoire de ... Nîmes*, IV, 223.
[142] Ibid., IV, 240.
[143] Line Teisseyre, 'L'industrie lainière à Nîmes au XVIIe siècle: crise conjuncturelle ou crise structurelle?' *Annales du Midi* 88 (1976), 396.
[144] Menard, *Histoire de ... Nîmes*, IV, 242.
[145] Teisseyre, 'L'industrie lainière à Nîmes', p. 397.
[146] Menard, *Histoire ... de Nîmes*, V, 8.

his land were assisted by the presence in the Vivarais of the Calvinist engineer Jacques Besson. In the late 1550s Besson had helped the town of Lucerne install a new system of water-pumps.[147] By then he had become a militant follower of Calvin and underwent training as a minister of the new faith. Besson, indeed, was swept up in the movement of Geneva-trained ministers who invaded France at the beginning of the religious wars. Summoned to Villeneuve-le-Berg at the instance of Olivier de Serres, Besson ministered to the Calvinist community while he and his family lived on Serres' estate.[148]

Serres may well have become involved in experiments with a new kind of plough which Besson pictures in his *Théâtre des instrumens mathematiques et mechaniques* (1578) (Plate 11).[149] He characterizes this plough as 'a by no means common artifice for ploughing the land in a marvellously short time using three ploughshares by the use of two lengths of cord attached to the plough and rewound either at the plough or at the end of the field'.[150] The accompanying engraving shows a heavy wheeled plough equipped with three ploughshares moved forward by oxen. In addition to the ploughman, there are two workers who guide the plough while turning a side winch. The winch is located behind the oxen and is attached to guide wires fed by pulleys fixed at either end of the field. If we are to believe the description given in the text, the pulleys at either end of the apparatus were designed to reinforce the pull of the oxen on the plough.

Many years later Serres was to express himself as certainly not opposed in principle to the use of machinery in agriculture. In his *Théâtre d'agriculture* (1600), he allows, without any qualification, that it is entirely possible and, indeed, desirable to improve on the agricultural practices of the past by new inventions whose worth has been tested. However, he notes that one should be cautious in doing so in order not to abandon oneself to what he describes as 'all manner of new inventions'.[151] It is difficult to avoid the conclusion that he had Besson's contraption in mind when he wrote these lines. Indeed, disagreements over such matters as well as over the way Besson was carrying out his ministerial duties may have been responsible for the rupture of relations between Besson and Serres which caused the former to leave Villeneuve-le-Berg.

INDUSTRIAL PROJECTS

Initiatives to counter the growing economic malaise were not confined to agriculture. As we have seen in the case of Nîmes or the irrigation projects of Crapponne, attempts at improving agricultural output coincided with efforts to

[147] Eugénie Droz, *Chemins de l'hérésie. Textes et documents* (Geneva, 1976), IV, 271.
[148] Ibid., IV, 284–89.
[149] [Lyons, 1578].
[150] Besson, *Théâtre des instrumens mathematiques*, proposition xxxiii.
[151] Serres, *Théâtre d'agriculture*, pp. 81–2.

Plate II   Jacques Besson's Mechanical plough, *Théâtre des intrumens mathématiques et mechaniques* (Lyons, B. Vincent, 1578).

stimulate industry as well. One of the most illuminating initiatives in this latter respect is to be found in the proposals of the architect Philibert De l'Orme.[152] De l'Orme's efforts to counter the increasingly adverse economic climate are embodied in his *Nouvelles inventions pour bien bastir et a petits fraiz*, which he published for the first time at Paris in 1561. The title of the treatise, which succinctly describes its contents, can be translated as *New Inventions for Building Well at Low Cost*. Later, the work was reprinted as Books x and xi of De L'Orme's monumental *L'architecture*.[153] Building was the second most important industry in the kingdom after agriculture and without a doubt the most important industrial activity carried on in the towns. Evidence of a slow down in this sector is apparent as early as 1545.[154] The factors behind the difficulties in this area of the economy were similar to those affecting all of French industry: reduced demand, higher costs and a squeeze on profits. But the problems of this sector were undoubtedly made more serious by the increasing scarcity of wood

[152] On De l'Orme see Anthony Blunt, *Philibert de l'Orme* (London, 1958); Naomi Miller, 'Philibert de l'Orme' in *Macmillan Encyclopedia of Architects*, ed. Adolf K. Placek (New York, London, 1982), I, 542–56.

[153] I have used the text in Books X and XI of *L'architecture* (Rouen, 1648), which is virtually identical to that of the edition of 1561. (Ridgewood, 1964). See Blunt, *Philibert de l'Orme*, p. 100.

[154] See Marcel Couturier, 'Investissement culturelle à Chartres: 1480–1600', *Bull. de la société archéologique de l'Eure-et-Loir* 72 (1978), 22.

resulting from deforestation.[155] The steadily rising price of wood on the Paris market in the sixteenth century directly reflected this problem. Over the course of the century the cost of wood for construction increased by 700 per cent. In the late 1540s a Parisian entrepreneur had succeeded in partially alleviating the shortage of wood by creating a new source of supply. Opening the rivers of the Nivernais to water traffic, he began to float huge rafts of timber from the forests of this region to Paris.[156] Nevertheless, by 1566 the price of lumber at Paris was already 300 per cent of what it had been at the beginning of the century, with at least one-third of the increase occurring in the 1550s and early 1560s.[157]

Palissy was as aware of the shortage of wood as he was of the shortage of grain. In the *Recepte veritable* he decried the way the forests were being cut down indiscriminately without any concern for replenishing the supply of trees. He was particularly scathing at the extent of the destruction of forest resources on the lands of the upper clergy and appealed to the aristocracy to reafforest their estates, which would be a means of enhancing the value of their land. He observed, correctly, that virtually all manufacturing was dependent on wood as a raw material and no industry more so than in the construction industry. Deforestation threatened to destroy the basis of French industrial activity.[158]

De l'Orme's *Nouvelles inventions*, like Palissy's *Recepte veritable*, is the product of not only the economic but also the religious and political crisis of the early 1560s. It was a moment in which a significant proportion of the population was swept by religious expectations and infused with evangelical enthusiasm without being necessarily committed to the Calvinist Church.[159] De l'Orme was evidently one of those who was momentarily caught up in this excitement. Evangelical influence is manifest in this treatise in a way in which it is not in his other writings. Thus, at the beginning and end of this work, he attributes his own achievement to the grace of God.[160] Citing Saint Paul (1 Cor. 12), he asserts that the gift of understanding the principles of geometry is itself a product of God's grace.[161]

---

[155] On the crisis of deforestation in the first half of the sixteenth century see Devèze, *La vie de la forêt française*, II, pp. 9–55; Boissière, 'La consummation parisienne de bois' in *Forges et forêts*, ed. Woronoff, pp. 29–56; Belhoste, 'Une silviculture pour les forges: XVIᵉ–XIXᵉ siècles,' in *Forges et forêts*, pp. 222–31. The negative impact of the shortage of wood on the metallurgical industry is noted in Belhoste, ibid., pp. 70–1.

[156] Babelon, *Nouvelle histoire de Paris*, p. 313; Johann Beckmann, *History of Inventions, Discoveries and Origins*, tr. William Johnston (London, 1797), II, 320.

[157] Beckmann, *History of Inventions*, II, 381.

[158] Palissy, *Recepte veritable*, ed. Cameron, pp. 170–2. See *Les œuvres de Bernard Palissy*, ed. Anatole France (Paris, 1880; Geneva, 1969), pp. 225–6.

[159] Denis Richet, 'Aspects socio-culturels des conflits religieux à Paris dans la seconde moitié du XVIᵉ siècle', *Annales: ESC* 32 (1977), 767–80.

[160] De l'Orme, *Nouvelles inventions*, fos. 279, 327.

[161] Ibid., fo. 301. Perhaps it is not too far-fetched to suggest that de l'Orme's openness towards evangelical influences at this point may not be unrelated to his quarrel with the Guise and the loss of some of his ecclesiastical benefices. See Blunt, *Philibert de l'Orme*, pp. 88–9.

De l'Orme announces in this treatise that he has discovered a method of joining together relatively small lengths of wood with connectors. Such a system made it possible to build much larger vaulted structures than was possible using large single lengths of timber, which in any case were becoming increasingly rare. Not only was this technique more effective from the point of view of the construction of vaulting, but, because it was based on shorter lengths of wood, it was also considerably cheaper. The importance that De l'Orme attributed to this new method of construction is reflected in his *Instruction* drawn up in 1563 to defend himself against his enemies. In this text, he noted that 'beside all the beautiful works that I carried out, how many great inventions were there, not only to the profit of His Majesty, but, indeed, for the benefit of his whole people, like the invention of timber-work for roofs that one can build from all sorts of wood, even from the smallest pieces'.[162] According to De l'Orme, his new invention made possible savings not only in the use of wood but of other materials as well, including iron, tile and masonry.[163]

While De l'Orme was concerned to discover more economical and improved techniques of construction, he was also interested in achieving lower costs and higher quality work by acquiring better control of the labour force. From the time he was an adolescent, he informs his readers, he was accustomed to super-intending work sites where there were as many as 300 construction workers.[164] In the conclusion to *L'architecture*, he sets out what he thinks the relationship ought to be between the patron of the building project, the architect, the masters of the works, and the other workers involved in the construction of an edifice. In particular, he undertakes to lay out the rules of obedience which ought to exist between the architect and the patron, on the one hand, and all the workers, controllers and assistants to the architect on the other.

The primary objective in ordering the labour process, according to De L'Orme, is to ensure that the orders of the architect are executed. In order to guarantee that the master mason and other workers follow his orders, it is necessary to employ a controller on the site. The controller ought to know something about construction in order to be able to judge the character of the materials being used and the quality of the work which has been carried out. The activities of the controller are thus vital to holding down the costs of construction as well as ensuring the quality of the work on the site. It is particularly important that the controller consult regularly with the architect in order to ensure that the work has been properly performed.[165]

---

[162] Cited in Blunt, *Philibert de l'Orme*, p. 150.
[163] De l'Orme, *Nouvelles inventions*, fos. 325r.–326v.
[164] Ibid., fo. 307v.
[165] Ibid., fos. 327v.–328r. On control of workers at construction sites see the interesting account of the role of master masons in the construction of the Hôtel de Ville of Paris in the 1530s in Louis Auvray, *Dictionnaire générale des artistes de l'école française* (Paris, 1895; New York, 1976), v, 17–18.

De l'Orme makes a particular point of the necessity to master geometry if the architect is to control the master masons and workers as well as to build properly. If he does not have a proper grasp of the rules of geometry, what the architect undertakes or orders to be done will be ridiculed or distorted and he will become in effect the slave of the master mason or workers.[166] It is the architect's mastery of theory which separates him from the workforce and allows him to command it. Indeed, De l'Orme explicitly ties his mastery over the classical and Renaissance architectural repertoire to his power of command over the labour force.[167]

The development of architectural theory from the time of Brunelleschi to De l'Orme obviously played a great role in the enhancement of the prestige of the architect.[168] Indeed, the first use of the term 'architect' as against 'master mason' in France dates from 1511 and reflects the increasing influence of Italian ideas. In fact, the profession of architect in France was entirely a creation of the growing popularity of the Renaissance style in sixteenth-century France. But humanist learning in architecture not only raised the status of the architect, it also helped to foster a new division of labour in construction or, at least, in the construction of large edifices.[169]

The development of architectural theory was thus hardly innocent, however much it may have also improved the appearance or enhanced the structural qualities of buildings. De l'Orme, indeed, played a particularly important part in the development of a more theoretical approach to architecture. His writings not only expressed the importance of geometry, but attempted to demonstrate the complex architectural forms which could be realized by employing its theoretical principles.[170] He reproved architects and even masons for ignorance of mathematics, for which there could be no excuse, especially after the publication of Euclid's *Elements* in a French translation by Pierre Forcadel in 1564. De l'Orme proposed an ambitious programme to incorporate Euclid's teachings into architecture. This included a deductive theory on how to fit stones of complex shape together (stereotomy) as well as the resolution of other analogous architectural

---

[166] De l'Orme, *Nouvelles inventions*, fo. 309r.

[167] Ibid., fo. 307v.

> Ce que ie cognois en moy, qui de iour en iour experimenté, trouvé et excogité nouvelles inventions, m'estant employé et addonné dès ma première jeunesse à tousjours chercher les plus doctes en Geometrie,[et] autres sciences requises à l'Architecture qui fussent en Europe: [et] visitant les excellentz antiquitez [et] d'icelles prenant extraicts, mesures [et] proportions, pour l'illustration de l'architechture. En quoy par la grace de Dieu i'ay ordonné [et] ay faict construire Temples, Chasteaux, Palais, [et] Maisons par vray art d'Architechture en divers lieux tant pour Roys, Princes, Cardinaux qu'autres, voire dès l'aage de quinze ans, auquel ie commencay avoir charge et commander tous les jours à plus de trois cents hommes.

[168] Paolo Rossi, *Philosophy, Technology and the Arts in the Early Modern Era* (New York, 1970), p. 30.

[169] On the evolution of relationships in the construction industry see Maurice Bouvier-Ajam, *Histoire du travail* (Paris, 1967), I, 339.

[170] Sergio Luis Sanabria, 'From Gothic to Renaissance Stereotomy: The Design Methods of Philibert de l'Orme and Alonso de Vandelvira', *Technology and Culture* 30 (1989), 266–99.

problems. In addition, he attempted to integrate Vitruvius' *Ten Books on Architecture* and Euclid's *Elements*. These two works were juxtaposed by De l'Orme to form a coherent and comprehensive theory of architecture.[171] Based on this revamped architectural theory, De l'Orme suggested the creation of a geometrical morphology or a classification of architectural forms using geometrical invariance as a criterion.[172] Likewise, he advocated a kind of functionalism, to be achieved by the application of geometrical forms to functionally defined initial conditions.[173]

De l'Orme, we may conclude, thus made it evident that the way to build with greater economy and style was, among other things, to employ new technology and theoretical concepts the better to command the workforce by achieving more rational control and supervision over it. Indeed, as we have attempted to make clear in discussing the development of French industry in the sixteenth century, the reorganization of the workforce was at least as important as, if not more important than, the introduction of technological improvements in enabling manufacturers to produce more efficiently or more cheaply. The construction industry in this respect proves the rule.

Private initiatives to overcome the negative conjuncture in manufacturing were not lacking. One of the most successful was the development of stocking manufacture in the Hurepoix and Beauce south of Paris. Typically, it took the form of a further extension of the putting-out system. The production of wool cloth and the manufacture of knitted caps were well established at Dourdan and in the surrounding countryside prior to the wars of religion.[174] At the beginning of the wars, according to an account published fifty years later, an officer of the château of Dourdan noted the expertise with which a young boy knitted a woollen cap and induced him to try his skill in making a wool stocking. The youth taught the other cap makers to do the same and soon the whole town and the rural population for six leagues in all directions was busy making stockings. Some years later, the stocking makers in Dourdan itself began to produce high-quality silk stockings in the Milanese fashion, leaving the manufacture of woollen stockings to the rural population.[175] This manufacture was still going strong at the beginning of the seventeenth century.

CROWN ECONOMIC INITIATIVES

But it was the monarchy itself which took the most concerted action to try to resist the increasingly negative economic conjuncture in trade and industry. We

[171] Ibid., p. 281.
[172] Ibid., p. 298.
[173] Ibid.
[174] Bezard, *La vie rurale*, pp. 172–82; Joseph Guyot, *Chronique d'une ancienne ville royale Dourdan, capitale de Hurepoix* (Paris, 1864), p. 335.
[175] Jacques Lescornay, *Mémoires de la ville de Dourdan* (Paris, 1624), pp. 10–12.

have already discussed some of the initiatives taken by Charles IX to try to stimulate a flagging agriculture. Under his rule the monarchy sought to hold down interest rates, place a moratorium on the foreclosure of farms, make available land for grain farming while encouraging the production of commercial crops, and encourage the invention and use of new agricultural implements. These measures, we would maintain, were part of a concerted policy on the part of the crown to try to strengthen the economy. Under Charles IX the state undertook to aid private enterprise in whatever ways its limited financial resources permitted. It was a policy which was part and parcel of a general royal policy of trying to end the civil wars by a reconciliation of Catholics and Huguenots, a policy which endured until the Massacre of Saint Bartholomew.

Interventionist economic policies on the part of government were by no means confined to France in the latter half of the sixteenth century. Across the Channel, in response to adverse economic trends, the English government under Elizabeth adopted a policy of protectionism and royal patents and monopolies which spurred the development of English industry.[176] In Switzerland hard times arrived in 1560 at about the same time as the first great downturn in the French economy. But the existence of the bank of Basle and the public debt of the other cities made it possible for urban governments to intervene actively to sustain the Swiss economy.[177] The credit made available through these bodies helped to stimulate the textile and the construction industry through the second part of the sixteenth century.[178] If government in Switzerland and England was used to sustain private enterprise, in Spain the weakness of the private economy under Philip II led the state itself to try to fill the vacuum. One notes the interest of the Spanish crown in promoting the study of navigation, naval construction, reafforestation and mining.[179] On the other hand, these royal economic initiatives were hampered by a shortage of capital, the high cost of labour and the scarcity of technical skills and knowledge. Furthermore, the political preoccupations of the state led to an overemphasis on military technology and warfare.[180]

Previous kings had shown a concern with the geography of France; Francis I and Henri II had manifested a certain amount of interest in learning more about the population, topography and economy of the kingdom. But it was Charles IX who ordered the publication of Louis Le Boulenger's census, *Le projet et calcul faict par commandement du roy, de la grandeur, longeur et largeur de son royaume, pays, terres, et seigneuries* (1566).[181] It was also Charles IX who appointed Nicolas de Nicolay royal geographer, commissioning him to carry out a detailed survey of

---

[176] Thirsk, *Economic Policy and Projects.*
[177] Martin H. Korner, *Solidarités financières suisses au XVIᵉ siècle* (Paris, Lucerne, 1980), pp. 431–2.
[178] Ibid., pp. 437–8.
[179] David C. Goodman, *Power and Penury: Government, Science and Technology in Philip II's Spain* (Cambridge, 1988), p. 101.
[180] Ibid., pp. 100, 114, 120, 159.
[181] *Archives curieuses de l'histoire de France*, VI, 345–9.

all the provinces and regions of the kingdom. Nicolay's project called for the preparation of a series of volumes for the king which would include a description of the land, rivers, forests, justices, fairs and *greniers à sel* of each of the kingdom's provinces.[182] The royal tour of the kingdom by Charles and the Queen-Mother in 1564–6 was no doubt undertaken with a view to trying to pacify a troubled kingdom. But it also had the effect of providing Charles with an uncommon grasp of the French economy. Arnaud Sorbin, who wrote a history of the reign, noted that the king acquired an understanding of the industries in each province of the kingdom.[183] In his eulogy of the dead king, Ronsard praised Charles' knowledge of the mechanical arts.[184]

Private enterprise was far stronger in France than in Spain. Nevertheless, starting as early as the reign of Francis I, the state interested itself in public projects aimed at strengthening the economy. Following his return from his victory at Marignano in Italy, the young Francis I initiated the construction of the port of Le Havre designed to provide a safe harbour in the English Channel and to support a fleet of warships to protect French commerce.[185] During his stay in Lombardy, Francis I had been much impressed by the irrigation canals he had seen there. As a result, he commissioned Leonardo da Vinci to plan an irrigation canal to bring water to the Sologne. The king and Leonardo spent some days travelling the countryside of Touraine planning the diversion of the Loire system towards the Sologne.[186] In his notes dating from this period, Leonardo also refers to a proposal for a canal of the Centre which would link Tours, Amboise and Lyons.[187] Ten years later, the Parlement of Paris launched a project to make the Ourcq, a small tributary of the Marne, navigable. This involved dredging, straightening the channel, and easing bends by cutting the banks along a 27-mile stretch of the river. It was in the reign of Charles IX that this project was finally completed.[188]

In 1539 a royal commission had approved a plan to link the Atlantic and the Mediterranean by means of a canal through upper Languedoc.[189] Nothing came of this scheme under Henri II, but it was revived in the reign of Charles IX.[190] Henri II's reign, likewise, saw the elaboration of plans for a canal of the Centre. Adam de Crapponne was commissioned to develop a scheme for a canal to join the

---

[182] Jean Bautier, Alain Dewerpe, Daniel Nordman, *Un tour de France royale: le voyage de Charles IX, 1564–1566* (Paris, 1984), pp. 48–54.

[183] *Histoire véritable des choses memorables advenues tant durant la règne que le jour de trepas du très haut et très puissant roy très chretien Charles IX*, Archives curieuses de l'histoire de France, VIII, 304.

[184] *Le tombeau de feu Roy très-chrestien Charles IX* (Paris, 1574), verse 110.

[185] *Histoire du Havre*, ed. Corvisier, pp. 46–8.

[186] Edouard Fournier, *Le vieux-neuf, histoire des inventions et decouverts modernes* (Paris, 1859), II, 164–5.

[187] William Barclay Parsons, *Engineers and Engineering in the Renaissance* (Cambridge, Mass., 1968), p. 18.

[188] Ibid., pp. 424–5.

[189] See Germain de Lafaille, *Annales de la ville de Toulouse* (Paris, 1687–1701), II, 133.

[190] Parsons, *Engineers and Engineering*, p. 439.

Loire and the Rhône. The financial priorities of the crown, especially its overriding commitment to war, frustrated this design.[191]

What strikes one about the reign of Henri II is a quickening of interest in economic improvement and technological innovation based on the final advance of a still expanding commercial economy. Amidst growing signs of exhaustion at the local level, the most far-reaching plans for economic rationalization were proposed. Invariably, these proposals were frustrated by a lack of political will and financial means.

In 1549 the king proposed the establishment of a bank in the city of Paris. An assembly-general seriously debated the proposal, which had been brought forward by an Italian banker Vincent de Saint Donyno. A number of objections were raised against the proposition. In the first place, it was argued that the establishment of such a bank went against God's prohibition against usury. Secondly, it was suggested that the ease of borrowing which a bank would allow would ruin the nobility. More seriously, it was asserted that merchants would abandon their commerce if the returns on bank deposits were too attractive. Fear was expressed that, as a result of the establishment of a bank, its officers, rather than parents, would come to control the inheritances of minors. This would be all the more reprehensible as the bank would be controlled by foreigners. Indeed, it is an anti-Italian bias which largely explains the opposition to the bank by the Parisian merchants. It was to be feared, some said, that those who controlled the bank would through intermediaries, ultimately control the commerce of the city, raising prices and ruining trade as a result. The proposal for a bank at Paris was accordingly turned down.[192] The Parisians thus resisted being entirely absorbed into the Italian-Lyonnaise orbit which dominated the major part of French economic activity until the wars of religion.

This initiative on the part of Henri II to provide freer access to capital was followed by an attempt at establishing free trade in commodities. In 1551 Henri published an ordonnance which proclaimed complete freedom of commerce within the borders of the kingdom in all products with the exception of grain. In this text is conveyed the sense of France as an economically unified entity in which 'each should (freely) seek his gain from his land, his labour, his industry, or his commerce, and that in doing this he should serve himself, his country, and others, by the benefits flowing from trade'.[193] This measure was followed by another which attempted to provide France with a unified system of weights and measures. Local systems of measurement were to be replaced by the system in use at Paris.[194]

Under Henri II attempts were made to eliminate the circulation of debased coin

---

[191] Martin, *Adam de Crapponne et son œuvre*, pp. 43–4.

[192] Félibien, *Histoire de la ville de Paris*, II, 1022–3; *Reg. BVP* II, 107–8; Paul Harsin, *Crédit public et banque d'état en France du XVIᵉ au XVIIIᵉ siècle* (Paris, 1933), pp. 7–8.

[193] Quoted in Abbot Payson Usher, *The History of the Grain Trade in France 1400–1710* (Cambridge, Mass., 1913; New York, 1973), p. 340.

[194] Fontanon, *Les edicts et ordonnances*, p. 786.

and to create a stable national currency.[195] It was in this context that the monarchy interested itself for the first time in the possibility of minting coins by machine rather than by hand. In the reign of Francis I an Italian, Matteo del Nassero, had constructed a mill in Paris on wooden pilings over the Seine, for polishing precious stones. In 1552 this mill was purchased by the royal mint on orders of the king to house new water-powered minting machines designed and built at Augsburg. According to the royal edict, the machines were expected to produce more and better coins than could be made by hand.[196] Their introduction was opposed by the guild of coiners, which, following the death of Henri II, was able to limit the use of the machines to the production of medals.[197]

The most notable inventor in this reign was Abel Foulon, who in 1551 was appointed *valet de chambre du roi*.[198] He had apparently attracted the notice of the king as a result of having discovered a new and efficient method of minting *testons* with a minimal silver content. In 1551 he received a royal privilege to print *Usaige et description de l'holomètre pour scavoir mesurer toutes choses qui sont soubs l'estandue de l'œil*.[199] The *holomètre* was a device equipped with field glasses and two rulers which made it possible to solve problems in elementary trigonometry. In the preface dedicated to the king, Foulon also claimed to have invented a new method of casting bronze, devices for raising water and a self-propelled vehicle.[200] The latter was apparently based on the unwinding of a clock-like spring.

Between 1545 and 1554, as we have seen, the royal Hôpital de la Trinité in Paris created a training school for poor apprentices. Some fifty children in the school were involved in the production of fustian. The raw material came from cotton grown in Provence, the production of which was being introduced by the monarchy on its estates there.[201] In 1558 the monarchy and the municipality of Paris attempted to establish a municipal lighting system. The scheme failed, 'owing to the difficulties of the times and the poverty of the citizens'.[202] It was under the same king that a method of cleaning the streets of Paris using water under pressure was proposed.[203]

---

[195] Frank Spooner, *The International Economy and Monetary Movements in France, 1493–1725* (Cambridge, Mass., 1972), pp. 138–43.

[196] Fernand Mazerolle, *Les médailleurs français du XVᵉ siècle au milieu du XVIIIᵉ* (Paris, 1902), I, 20.

[197] This incident is used by Lynn Whyte to argue that the obstruction of the guild of coiners succeeded because they were dealing with a 'brutally enforced royal monopoly'. See 'Technology, Western' in *Dictionary of the Middle Ages*, ed. Joseph R. Strayer (New York, 1988), XI, p. 654. But a state monopoly over the coinage rather than competing currencies would seem to be a *sine qua non* of a modern market economy. It was the absence of a strong government following the death of Henri II rather than its presence which was the real obstacle. At a more profound level it would seem that it is the economic policies pursued by a strong government which are the important factor in stimulating or retarding technological innovation in the early modern period.

[198] St Le Tourneur, 'Abel Foullon', in *DBF* XIV, 670; Haag, *La France protestante*, V, 157.

[199] (Paris, 1555).

[200] Foullon, *Usaige st description de l'holomètre*, fo. sig. A.ii v. See Tuetey, *Inventaire analytique*, no. 2750; AN Coll. Lenain MS 63, fos. 49, 99.

[201] Boissonade, *Le socialisme d'etat*, pp. 89–90.

[202] Franklin, *Dictionnaire historique*, pp. 422–3.

[203] Parsons, *Engineers and Engineering*, p. 273.

In February 1557 Charles Prudhomme was issued a patent for a device which economized on the use of wood as a fuel. No doubt Prudhomme had invented a new kind of furnace which burned wood more efficiently. Evidently, Henri thought Prudhomme's invention of sufficient importance to permit him to call together the heads of the guilds of Paris in order to give them a demonstration of its utility.[204]

Belon had campaigned for a vast programme of reafforestation. Palissy likewise called for conservation and reafforestation, while bitterly complaining about the indiscriminate cutting down of trees on the lands of rich ecclesiastics. As early as 1537 the monarchy had prohibited ecclesiastics from cutting down the forests on their lands without royal permission.[205] But so many exceptions were made that this prohibition remained ineffective.[206] Under Charles IX the preservation of the forests became a priority. By his ordonnance of Saint-Germain-en-Laye (October 1561) one-third of immature timber on ecclesiastical and royal lands was set aside and allowed to become fully grown forest.[207] By the ordonnance of Meulan (September 1563), immature timber could only be cut every ten years.[208] Taking things a step further, Charles IX ordered a survey of all the forests of the kingdom and the enactment of a comprehensive forest code.[209]

Mining was in serious difficulties by the 1560s. Especially hard hit was the mining of precious metals, which had to compete with the increasing flow of New World bullion. But even the mining of base metals had difficulty in maintaining itself in the face of lower costs and the production of higher quality ore from Central Europe. Here, too, we find the government of Charles IX doing all it could to sustain the industry in France.[210] In 1568 Antoine Vidal, seigneur de Bellesaigues, a tax collector, was named grand master of the mines. In his commission the king recalled that in the previous twenty years some thirty new mines had been opened. He demanded an increased pace of exploration and development, calling upon Vidal to see to it that no less than forty new mines were opened during the six-year term of his office.[211]

In order to facilitate trade, an edict of November 1563 created the Tribunal des juges consuls, a court which was to hear all commercial cases in Paris in the first instance. Its purpose was to speed up the settlement of commercial disputes. The *prévôt des marchands* designated one hundred electors from among the merchants of Paris, who in turn named a judge and four consuls to serve a one-year term. Overwhelmingly, the majority of electors were chosen from the ranks of the six dominant guilds of Paris, especially the powerful guild of the mercers. The

---

[204] AN Coll. Lenain MS 63, fo. 38.
[205] Devèze, *La vie de la forêt française*, II, 202.
[206] AN Coll. Lenain MS 63, fos. 147–200.
[207] Devèze, *La vie de la forêt française*, II, 201–2.
[208] Ibid., II, 202.
[209] Ibid., II, 203–6.
[210] AN Coll. Lenain MS 63, fos. 12, 672–84; BN MS Fr. 21789, fo. 19.
[211] AN F¹⁴ 9774.

establishment of this court thus confirmed the predominance of the six guilds over the economic life of the capital.[212]

The establishment of this commercial court at Paris was only a part of a much larger plan to establish such courts in all the principal towns so as to facilitate commerce and manufacturing. In total, thirty-four such tribunals were established in French cities during the reign of Charles IX:[213]

Abbeville	Laon
Amiens	Laval
Angers	Montferrand
Auxerre	Niort
Bar-sur-Aube	Orléans
Beauvais	Paris
Billom	Poitiers
Bourges	Reims
Calais	Riom
Châlons-sur-Marne	La Rochelle
Chartres	Saumur
Châtellerault	Senlis
Chaumont	Sens
Clermont	Soissons
Compiègne	Thiers
Felletin	Villefranche-en-Beaujolais
Fontenay-le-Comte	Vitry-le-François

Meanwhile, to the north in Rouen, a commercial bank was founded in 1566 with the support of the monarchy.[214] In the face of the growing protectionism of the English, the king negotiated the Anglo-French commercial treaty of 1564, designed to safeguard French exports, particularly manufactures. Renewed in 1572, this treaty was matched by protective measures against the export, first of raw wool, and, then, of all textile fibres.[215] Montchrétien would later comment acidly on the disastrous consequences for France of this treaty.[216]

Charles IX in principle supported the organization of as much as possible of industry through the guilds. Nevertheless, for the sake of useful inventions, he was on occasion prepared to limit their powers. During the 1560s, for example, three Parisian coppersmiths began to produce morions or casques which were of higher quality and lighter to wear than those already in use. However, it was the

---

[212] Babelon, *Nouvelle histoire de Paris*, pp. 320–1.
[213] Bernard Barbiche, *Ordonnances enregistrées au parlement de Paris sous le règne de Charles IX*; AN MS 1967, 'Consul des Marchands'.
[214] Harsin, *Crédit public*, p. 7.
[215] AN X^{ia} 8629, fo. 305v.; AN X^{ia} 8625, fo.181r.–v.
[216] Antoine de Montchrétien, *Traicté de l'œconomie politique*, ed. Th. Funck-Brentano (Paris, 1889; Geneva, 1970), p. 71.

armourers who held the monopoly on the production of defensive weapons. As a result, the coppersmiths were unable to profit from their invention, nor to allow the public to benefit from it. In 1568, accordingly, Charles IX issued letters-patent overriding the ordonnances of the guild of armourers 'wishing', as he said, 'to increase the desire of all and everyone of our subjects to exercise themselves on things which would be good and profitable to the people of our Kingdom ... and to give them the means to make use of the favours and abilities that they have acquired through their work and industry'.[217] At the same time Charles attacked the flagrant abuses that had developed in the guilds in the construction industry. Noting that there were infinite numbers of *compagnon* pavers in the city of Paris who were not being allowed to accede to masterships, he ordered that their mastership examinations be expedited and that they be received as masters by the guilds without delay if they were qualified.[218]

Charles IX also endeavoured to facilitate the development of traffic on the rivers of the kingdom. In 1564 the work of making the river Ourcq navigable (which had been initiated under François I) was brought to completion.[219] In every possible way, the king tried to clear obstacles impeding the use of the Loire for navigation.[220] A royal privilege was granted to Robert Hérault to operate galleasses and galleys of his own invention on the Seine and other waterways.[221] A campaign was then launched to rid the Seine, too, of obstructions to water-borne commerce.[222] According to Joseph Scaliger writing at the beginning of the reign of Henri IV, the king's Privy Council appointed a commission of experts to inspect every river in the kingdom to determine which ones could be opened to shipping. The council ordered the removal of all obstacles to navigation on the rivers. This reflects the national scope of the campaign to improve the conditions for economic activity. However, Scaliger pointed out that this programme was stopped in its tracks by the Massacre of Saint Bartholomew, 'which broke the neck of all these enterprises and so the rivers have remained useless as in the past down to the present day'.[223] Saint Bartholomew really appears to have been something of a watershed, marking the end of serious royal initiatives not only to clear the rivers, but more generally to counter the onset of the first major and prolonged economic crisis of the sixteenth century. Likewise, it seems to mark an end to the monarchy's effort to conciliate the Huguenot interest, not only religiously but economically as well.

---

[217] AN X^{ia} 1568, fo. 292v.; Coll. Lamoignon, VIII, fos. 400r.–401v.
[218] BN MS Fr. 8081, fo. 329r.; Coll. Lamoignon. VIII, fo. 502r.–503r., AN F^{14} 9774.
[219] *Reg. BVP* V, 435.
[220] See list of letters-patent in *Catalogue des livres imprimés de la Bibliothèque du Roy. Jurisprudence* (Paris, 1753), II, 310–12. Cf. AN F^{14} 9774.
[221] Tuetey, *Inventaire analytique*, no. 3032.
[222] BN MS Fr. 8067, fos. 381r.–v., 383r.–v.
[223] Joseph Juste Scaliger, *Opuscula varia antehac non edita* (Paris, 1610), p. 559.

4

Inventions and science in the reign of Charles IX

> It is not enough to know how to express the rules of navigation, construction and farming ... one must put one's hand to the task ...
>
> Ramus, *Remonstrance au Conseil Privé* (1567)

The economic and political crisis into which the French kingdom was plunged in the 1560s spurred technological innovation and economic rationalization. Schemes and proposals to produce more food or to conserve or develop sources of energy were put forward. All kinds of machines and inventions were designed with the intention of producing manufactures which were cheaper and therefore potentially more profitable. A fascination with machinery became pervasive. An inventor came forward to offer the city of Rouen an underground diving bell of his own devising to repair a recently collapsed bridge.[1] The Hermeticist bishop François Foix de Candale spent his leisure contriving all sorts of mechanical devices including wheels, levers and pulleys, clocks and measuring instruments.[2] A mock castle with ninety-nine mechanical artifices toured the kingdom, its mechanically operated cannon, jousting knights, water fountains and windmill astounding the population. The mathematician Henri de Monantheuil, viewing this spectacle, took it as a portent of more important things to come.[3] The monarchy, although hamstrung by its own insolvency and distracted by the civil wars, tried as best it could to encourage such initiatives. At the same time, the shock of the wars and economic crisis encouraged a growing number of attacks on traditional learning. An increasing number of writers began to attack scholastic philosophy and Galenic medicine as too theoretical. During the reign of Charles IX and in the opening years of the following reign, a trend towards a more empirical, practical and even experimental learning began to become evident. It is the theme of this chapter to trace the outlines of this new tendency which arose out of the economic, political and religious crisis of the second half of the sixteenth century.

---

[1] Benedict, *Cities and Social Change*, p. 46.
[2] Jeanne Ellen Harrie, 'François Foix de Candale and the Hermetic Tradition in Sixteenth Century France', (University of California, Riverside, Ph.D. Dissertation, 1975,) pp. 35, 37.
[3] Keller, 'Mathematical Technologies', I, 18.

PALISSY'S EMPIRICISM

The most outspoken advocate of a more empirical approach to learning in this period was Bernard Palissy. In the preface to his *Discours admirables de la nature des eaux et fontaines*, Palissy denounced those teaching the priority of theory over practice. The proponents of this view, according to him, believe that it is necessary to imagine or conceive the task at hand before setting one's hand to it. Palissy attempts to refute this point of view by force of counter-example. If this view were correct, he asserts, alchemists would rapidly be able to create beautiful things based on the conceptions in their minds without spending fifty years at the task as many have done.[4] If military leaders, he notes, could execute what they conceived in their minds they would never lose a battle.[5] Lastly, he observes that those who have spent a lifetime studying the theory of navigation would never themselves actually venture to sail a ship to different parts of the globe the way that an experienced and practical sailor does.[6]

The point of these examples was to insist that at the end of all argument it must be conceded that practice in fact gives birth to theory. Moreover, it seems evident that this argument of Palissy's is not merely a philosophical one. Rather, he adopts the position to counter the social prejudice against empirical and practical knowledge. Indeed, he adds that he has raised the argument in favour of practice in order to silence those who assert that no one has the right to speak of nature without knowledge of the Latin learning of the philosophers.[7] He concludes by claiming that by practice he can, in fact, demonstrate the falsity of the ideas of the most famous and ancient of philosophers.[8]

Defending himself against the reigning social prejudice, Palissy placed practical knowledge ahead of theory. Indeed, the *Discours admirables de la nature des eaux et fontaines* is presented as a dialogue in which *Practice* always comes out on top against *Theory*. Indeed, the latter is made the object of continual ridicule. With its heavily didactic tone, Palissy's dialogue bears the mark of the sixteenth-century school-book. It is conceivable, too, that he may have adopted this dialogue form from the model provided by Huguenot vernacular treatises, humanist texts translated into French, or even from the example of alchemical writings.[9] But the principal point that Palissy insists upon in this dialogue is that, contrary to the supercilious assumptions of *Theory*, *Practice* itself has a philosophical component built into it. Unlike the kind of abstract philosophy that emerges from *Theory* divorced from experience, *Practice*, in fact, creates its own theory. He tries to

4   Palissy, *Œuvres*, pp. 165–6.
5   Ibid., p. 166.
6   Ibid.
7   Ibid.
8   Ibid., p. 168.
9   On Palissy's use of dialogue see Mustapha Kemal Bénouls, *Le dialogue philosophique dans la littérature française du seizième siècle* (Paris, La Haye, 1976), pp. 73–91.

demonstrate this with respect to his own craft of pottery. At a certain point in the dialogue, *Theory* denounces the potter's craft as mechanical or manual, with the implication that it is marked by a lack of theory as well as social baseness. In response, *Practice* admits that certain aspects of this craft are mechanical, i.e., they involve manual labour. However, according to *Practice*, the firing of pottery requires an 'exact philosophy' and a 'distinctive geometry' that is far from being mechanical. Arts which require the use of compass, ruler, numbers, and weights and measures ought not to be considered mechanical.[10] Palissy attempts to elevate the social prestige of his craft by stressing the mathematical or intellectual element in it.

A like desire to raise the prestige of the crafts by stressing their need to employ mathematics, we may note, is found in the writings of the architect Jean Bullant, which date from the 1560s. He particularly emphasized the notion of tying together theory and practice by using geometry. Bullant, whose father was an architect, was sent to Italy to complete his studies.[11] Upon his return to France in 1537, he entered the service of Constable Montmorency, for whom he constructed the magnificent château of Ecouen. During the 1560s, while in residence at Ecouen, he published the *Recueil d'horlogiographie* (1561),[12] the *Petite traicte de geometrie et d'horlogiographie pratique* (1562)[13] and the *Reigle generalle d'architechture des cinq manieres de colonnes* (1564).[14] In the *Recueil d'horlogiographie*, which deals with the construction and use of quadrants and solar clocks, Bullant includes a discussion of some of the elements of geometry for craftsmen who would not otherwise be aware of them.[15] He goes on to make the rather astonishing claim that the liberal arts, which include geometry and arithmetic, ought to be of service to all, i.e., the rustic as well as the learned.[16] Geometry and arithmetic, to be sure, are of special use to those who aspire to the so-called higher arts. But Bullant by no means excludes ordinary craftsmen from an understanding of these loftier studies. For, he asserts, all craftsmen and men of experiment (*gens mercurieux*) who aspire to discover new secrets of nature must, above all, know how to measure things. For God has created all things, including organic and inorganic matter, by means of harmonic number, weight and measure.[17] Bullant simply takes it for granted that craftsmen are capable of grasping the higher arts and discovering the secrets of nature.

[10] Palissy, *Œuvres*, p. 362. See also Céard, 'Relire Bernard Palissy', *Revue de l'art* 78 (1987), 78.
[11] On Bullant see Miller, 'Jean Bullant', *Macmillan Encyclopedia of Architects*, I, 329–30; Blunt, *Art and Architecture in France, 1500–1700* 2nd edn. (London, 1970), pp. 78–80.
[12] *Recueil d'horlogiographie, contenant la description, fabrication et usage des horloges solaires* (Paris, 1561).
[13] (Paris, 1562).
[14] (Paris, 1560).
[15] *Recueil d'horlogiographie*, fo. 3.
[16] Ibid., fo. 4.
[17] Ibid.

On a more mundane level, an understanding of the rudiments of arithmetic and geometry by craftsmen was seen as indispensable to their work. Thus, when Elie Vinet travelled through Guyenne in the 1550s, he was appalled by the ignorance of the surveyors in the region. *L'arpenterie d'Elie Vinet, livre de geometrie enseignant à mezurer les champs et plusieurs autres chozes* (1577) was his answer to the situation he found.[18] Indeed, Palissy's appreciation of the importance and utility of mathematics appears to derive from his own experience as a surveyor in this region of France.[19] But theory, as Palissy understood it, was not confined to mathematics: theory or philosophy could mean as little as having a sense of overall circumstances. Thus, for instance, when speaking of preserving the forests from deforestation, he remarks that the notion that no manufacture would be possible without wood is a 'philosophy' that even a chambermaid could understand.[20] He praises a certain Italian aristocrat who by 'philosophy' had discovered that a forest is a good long-term investment.[21] Indeed, the knowledge that a farmer has of the seasons, fields and crops constitutes for Palissy a form of conceptual knowledge which he considers philosophy. The lack of this kind of philosophy, according to him, leads to the violation of the land and the dilution of its fertility.[22]

But it seems apparent that Palissy's understanding of the meaning of philosophy extended beyond practical knowledge and an understanding of technique. Thus *Practice* accuses *Theory* in the dialogue of mocking him when the latter suggests that he hates philosophy. On the contrary, *Practice* retorts, he is constantly searching for philosophy, for the kind of knowledge which he seeks is not opposed to philosophy which is real and worthy of the name. Thus he denounces alchemists who, he claims, seek to transform metals without understanding any of their properties. These alchemists deserve to be called anti-philosophers rather than philosophers. On the other hand, he praises those who distilled essences and substances because they presumably understood the properties of the materials they were manipulating.[23] Palissy was certainly predisposed to the practical and empirical, given the prejudices and errors of the scholars who blindly invoked the traditional learning based on untested theory. On the other hand, it seems clear that he did not reject theory, but aspired to a *rapprochement* of theory and practice for the sake of both knowledge and utility.

---

[18] (Bordeaux, 1577), fos. sig. A¹–A¹¹¹.

[19] Bernard Dufay, Yves de Kisch *et al.*, 'L'atelier parisien de Bernard Palissy', *Revue de l'art* 78 (1987), 58.

[20] Palissy, *Œuvres*, p. 115.

[21] Ibid., pp. 115–16.

[22] Ibid., pp. 24–6.

[23] Ibid., pp. 258–9. Despite his denunciation of the alchemists, Palissy may in fact have been under their influence for a considerable period. See W. Kirsop, 'The Legend of Bernard Palissy', *Ambix* 12 (1961), 136–54.

THE UNITY OF THEORY AND PRACTICE

Palissy's preoccupation with the relationship between theory and practice was shared by the humanist and mathematician Jacques Peletier du Mans. We have already seen how he endeavoured to make his *L'arithemetique* (1549) of use to merchants. Peletier takes up the question of the proper relationship between theory and practice in his *De l'usage de geometrie* (1573).[24] He begins his discussion by noting that whether theory or practice is preferable is perennially in dispute between men of learning and experience. Peletier took the view that it is impossible to understand a craft without both theory and practice. A craftsman, no matter how accustomed he is to handling things, would nevertheless find it impossible to carry out his designs without speculation. On the other hand, the more that a man of theory gives himself up to pure speculation, the less able he is to resolve matters taking into account considerations of use, i.e., utility and profit. If speculation has always found more favour among philosophers, one should not conclude that nature itself favours contemplative men over men of practice (*hommes ouvriers*), since nature itself is a continual and indefatigable actor. There are those who prefer contemplation over action. But what does virtuous contemplation amount to, after all, if it is not applied? Are there not, in fact, more contemplators of virtue than executors of it?

It seems that nature has wished to excite our reverence and admiration through its works, rather than making available to us its ultimate causes. It keeps most of these to itself. It seems that only those things which are most simple are accessible to our understanding. We should therefore proceed to know things prudentially in a step-by-step fashion.[25] Peletier, indeed, believed that man's principal role in the universe was that of a discoverer who gradually uncovered the secrets of nature. Nature is always several steps ahead of humanity and so humankind must proceed by a series of approximations towards the truth.[26]

Francisco Sanches, although best known as a sceptic, nevertheless helped to foster a more empirical approach to learning. Sanches, the scion of a Marrano family, spent decades teaching in the medical faculty of the ultra-Catholic University of Toulouse. However, his contacts with the medical humanists of Italy and perhaps of Montpellier imbued him with an empirical approach to the study of nature.

Sanches is remembered as a great sceptic whose philosophical work helped put into doubt the a priori systems of Plato and Aristotle. Sanches categorically denied the possibility of acquiring absolute knowledge. On the other hand, basing himself on the study of medicine, he strongly defended a type of knowledge which was

[24] (Paris, 1573). See Cifoletti, 'Mathematics and Rhetoric', pp. 74–5.
[25] Peletier, *De l'usage de géométrie*, fo. 2.
[26] D.B. Wilson, 'The Discovery of Nature in the Work of Jacques Peletier du Mans', *BHR* 16 (1954), 298.

probabilistic, approximative and cumulative.[27] It goes without saying that such knowledge had to be based on empirical observation.

According to Reijer Hooykaas, the birth of experimental science was the consequence of the union of ancient rational philosophy and the empirical and practical learning of craftsmen, alchemists and engineers dating from the middle ages and the Renaissance.[28] The unification of these two streams, the penetration of rational philosophy by experimentation, and the entry of rational method into workshops of craftsmen and artisans, began to occur in the sixteenth century.

In the case of Palissy, we have an example of craftsmanship being elevated towards science through a recognition of the need for a kind of theory which was more closely based on practice. Pierre de la Ramée (Ramus) affords an instance of a rational philosopher moving towards a method based on experience. Like Palissy, Ramus was of humble origin, and like him, too, he was attracted to the evangelical religion of the Calvinists. But, unlike Palissy, Ramus had immersed himself in the world of Latin scholarship and Aristotelian philosophy which continued to dominate his alma mater, the University of Paris. Ramus began his onslaught on scholastic Aristotelianism in the 1530s. But, it is significant that it is only in the 1560s, with the onset of religious and economic crisis, that Ramus began to urge the application of the liberal arts to the problems of daily life.

Ramus had been appointed to a commission to study the reform of the University of Paris in 1557. Growing impatient with the slow pace of reform, he published his reform proposals anonymously, in both Latin and French in 1562. The publication of Ramus' proposals has thus to be seen as part of that general upsurge of interest in the reform of economic, political and religious life that marked the onset of the religious wars. Ramus called for a reform of the University of Paris which would make its curriculum more relevant to practical life.[29] Notable among his proposals was his appeal to reduce the cost of university education to make it more accessible to poor students.[30] But his call to make university studies more relevant to practical life is also noteworthy. He was especially insistent on the need to reform medical studies by means of botanical field trips, the teaching of anatomy through dissection and the introduction of practical internships.[31]

All the great thinkers of Antiquity, according to Ramus, were guided by the

---

27 Francisco Sanches, *That Nothing is Known*, ed. Elaine Limbrick and Douglas F.S. Thomson (Cambridge, 1988), pp. 53–4, 67, 69.

28 Reijer Hooykaas, *Humanisme, science et réforme, Pierre de la Ramée: 1515–1572* (Leiden, 1958), p. 91.

29 Peter Sharratt, 'Peter Ramus and the Reform of the University: The Divorce of Philosophy and Eloquence', *French Renaissance Studies: 1540–70, Humanism and the Encyclopedia*, ed. Sharrat (Edinburgh, 1976), pp. 4–20.

30 Ramus' ideal polity, which he called a timocracy, was one in which careers would be open to talent. Cf. James Veazie Skalnik, 'Ramus and Reform: The End of the Renaissance and the Origins of the Old Regime in France' (University of Virginia, Ph.D. Dissertation, 1990), pp. 298–315.

31 Ibid., p. 14.

principle of reason, whether applied to mathematics and philosophy or to the practical judgements and conduct of men. Thus the reason Ramus has in mind is one which is not confined to abstract theory but one which is practical or employed in resolving the actual problems of daily life.[32]

In his *Remonstrance au Conseil Privé* (1567) Ramus cited Socrates as an exponent of practical philosophy:

Among the great and admirable elements of the wisdom of Socrates one was that he maintained that all of the liberal arts ought to relate to human life in order to make man better able to deliberate and act well and that in the schools there is too much teaching and too many books, too much of subtleties and disputes without utility, without use: that to be a sailor, mason, farmer, it is not enough to know how to express the rules of navigation, construction and farming but one must put one's hand to the task and navigate well, construct well, farm well: that mathematics (which at that time was the most practised and celebrated of the arts) ought to be demonstrated, arithmetic in order to count well, geometry in order to measure well, astrology in order to navigate, heal and farm well.[33]

Ramus here tries to turn the humanist preference for action over contemplation into a kind of pragmatism. Indeed, he goes so far as practically to abolish the distinction between the liberal and the mechanical arts, the one being reserved for the learned and the other for craftsmen. In his *Geometria* (1569), he reiterates that the purpose of geometry is to measure well, and that this end is served more in usage and in geometric works than by precepts and rules. Astronomers, geographers, surveyors, navigators, mechanics, architects and painters make use of geometry in the description and measurement of the heavens, countries, the land, machines, seas, buildings and paintings, just as grammar, rhetoric and logic are to be observed more fully and abundantly in their use by poets, orators and philosophers than in the rules of grammarians, rhetoricians and logicians.[34]

The purpose of geometry, Ramus argued, is to enable men to measure well; consequently, its realm is the whole of land surveying and mechanical or manual activity. There are many little machines, for example pincers and scissors, which are in fact great inventions, making life easier, but which, because they are commonly used, are taken for granted. Instruments of mechanical geometry, like the vice and the lever, are used to lift weights, to saw wood, cut marble and to press oil. They are employed by navigators, architects, stonecutters, jewellers, miners, surgeons and shepherds, with the result that artisans, 'mechanics', those who work with their hands, are practitioners of geometry, even though they are not aware of it.[35]

[32] Hooykaas, pp. 20–1. On Ramus' method and its relation to Bacon's see Craig Walton, 'Ramus and Bacon on Method', *Journal of the History of Philosophy* 9 (1971), 289–302; W.S. Howell, *Logic and Rhetoric in England* (Princeton, 1956), pp. 146–72, 342–97; L. Girard, 'La production logique au XVIᵉ siècle', *Etudes philosophiques* 59 (1985), 303–24.

[33] Quoted in Hooykaas, *Humanisme, science et réforme*, p. 21.

[34] Ibid., p. 25.

[35] Ibid., p. 83.

Ramus believed that mechanical inventions were in great part due to mathematics. He also held that mathematics had developed out of the mechanical arts. His aspiration was to make known the secrets of the liberal arts to craftsmen. In like fashion, the practice of the mechanical arts could furnish precious clues which could make possible the restoration of the liberal arts.[36]

Ramus was struck by the honour and esteem with which mathematics was regarded in Germany. No country had so many well-paid chairs of mathematics in its schools as had Germany. Ramus' explanation of this phenomenon was a strictly economistic one. According to him, the greater part of the income of the German princes and cities was derived from the gold, silver and other mines of the country. These mines have been developed and maintained by the operation of innumerable machines whose operations are based on geometric principles. 'It is, thus, by means of geometrical hands that the Teutonic Pluto draws to itself the riches of the soil of Germany.'[37] Furthermore, the art of war is totally founded on geometry. The great military inventions are German. Every day Germany invents and manufactures new weapons and sells them to its neighbours. Germany is 'thus the true school of Mars and the office of Vulcan'.[38] Economic circumstances thus impel the governments of Germany to promote mathematics and mathematical learning. Conversely, Ramus held to the proposition that where the schools of mathematics are good, the engineers and military strategists as well as the mathematicians will likewise be good. If the schools of France would imitate Germany in founding chairs of mathematics, according to Ramus, the mines of France would bear fruit once again.[39]

Hooykaas judiciously concludes that Ramus' explanation of the superiority of German mathematics seems plausible, containing a part, if not all, of the truth. But what needs to be emphasized are the reasons which caused Ramus to offer such an argument, which smacks of economic determinism. If we review the state of French mining at the time when Ramus was writing, the reasons emerge plainly enough. The mining industry expanded rapidly in France after 1450. Never as robust as the industry in Central Europe, the industry nevertheless saw substantial growth based on the investment of capital and the application of new techniques over the next century. Many kinds of ore were mined, among the most valued being gold, silver and copper. The decline of the industry dates from 1550, when the enormous flood of bullion from the New World abruptly made French mining uneconomic.[40] Ramus therefore offered this argument in order to hold out the prospect that the encouragement of mathematical learning might lead to the revival of the mining industry.

---

[36] Ibid., pp. 92–3.
[37] Quoted in ibid., p. 96.
[38] Quoted in ibid.
[39] Ibid., p. 88.
[40] Hesse, *La mine et les mineurs*, p. 421.

In the event, it seems to us that it was the intensifying pressure of economic difficulties in the 1560s that encouraged Ramus to seek a *rapprochement* between theory and practice. In his case this took the form of trying to open the liberal arts to the revitalizing influence of the practical arts.

However, despite their laudable intent, it does not seem that Palissy or Ramus had a firm idea of how theory and practice should relate to each other. Both appeared to favour a kind of inductivism that of itself would produce knowledge. Indeed, in the case of Ramus, this inductivism led him to take a rather negative view of Copernicus' theory. While allowing that Copernicus was the greatest astronomer of his time, Ramus the empiricist nevertheless criticized Copernicus for making the mistake of basing his ideas on hypotheses.[41]

A much more positive assessment of Copernicus was made by Jacques Besson. Besson praised the very thing in Copernicus which Ramus decried, namely, the making of hypotheses. Like Ramus and Palissy, Besson was a Calvinist who was also interested in providing useful knowledge. Thus his *L'art et science de trouver les eaux et fontaines* (1569) aimed at developing a method for finding subterranean sources of water.[42] His object was to provide a basis for doing so which would be more certain than the empirical methods that had been utilized until then by architects and agriculturists. These empirical methods, more often than not, had led to vain and useless expenditures by more than one property owner.[43] Besson therefore fully understood the limits of a strictly empirical method.

Given the limitations of empiricism, Besson puts forward his own method for searching for water. His procedure is to bring empirical facts together with first causes, the two together being, according to him, more conclusive than each separately. He stresses the novelty and utility of this approach, comparing it to what he considers to be the hypothetical-deductive method of Copernicus, which led the latter to the heliocentric view of the universe.[44]

Once again, in Besson as in Palissy, Peletier and Ramus, we find the desire to combine theoretical and practical knowledge in a way which could provide useful knowledge. It would seem, however, that Besson had an understanding of how they ought to be combined which was superior to any of his French contemporaries. Indeed, Besson's hypothetical-deductive method seems to approach that of the Italian Aristotelians whose classrooms he may have haunted during his sojourn in Italy.[45]

[41] Hooykaas, *Humanisme, science et réforme*, pp. 64–5.
[42] *L'art et science de trouver les eaux et fontaines cachées soubs terre, autrement que par les moyens vulgaires des agriculteurs et architectes* (Orléans, 1569), fos. sig. B v.–Bi r.
[43] Ibid, fo. sig. Bi r.
[44] Ibid. On literary and philosophical Copernicanism at Paris see Edward A. Gosselin, 'Bruno's French Connection: A Historiographical Debate' in *Hermeticism and the Renaissance: Intellectual History and the Occult in Early Modern Europe*, ed. Ingrid Merkel and Debus (Washington, 1988), pp. 166–81.
[45] *Cambridge History of Renaissance Philosophy*, ed. Charles Schmitt *et al.* (Cambridge, 1988), pp. 708–9.

BESSON'S MACHINES

The details of Besson's life were for a long time shrouded in darkness. They have been lately brought to light through the magnificent research efforts of Denis Hilliard, Eugénie Droz and Alexander Keller.[46] Keller has scored a breakthrough by discovering a manuscript copy of Besson's *Théâtre des instrumens mathématiques et mechaniques* in the British Library. Droz has uncovered a considerable body of new information on the details of Besson's career as a result of her patient archival research. Hilliard has not only found additional biographical information, he has introduced a welcome rigour and precision into our knowledge of Besson.

Besson came from Colombière, a village in the valley of Oulx in Dauphiné. At some point, he moved to northern Italy, where he studied engineering and physics. He may have been briefly enrolled in the Universities of Bologna, Ferrara or Padua.[47] In 1557 he was living in Lausanne, where he undertook to install pumps to supply the town with water.[48] In the autumn of that year, he visited Conrad Gesner at Zurich.[49] The next year, 1558, he married Nicolarde Dongon in Geneva, the ceremony being presided over by Calvin himself.[50] By 1559 he was a *habitant* of Geneva. During his residence at Geneva, Besson made the acquaintance of the French humanist François Berauld. Berauld was teaching Greek, while Besson was giving lessons in science and mathematics.[51]

As we have seen, between 1562 and 1564 Besson served as a minister to the Calvinist congregation of Villeneuve-le-Berg in the Vivarais. Having quarrelled with Olivier de Serres and the other elders of the church there, he moved first to Lyons and then, at the invitation of his friend Berauld, to Orléans, at that point a Protestant bastion. There he worked on perfecting his cosmolabe, a device for taking measurements on land, on sea and in the heavens.[52]

In 1569 he presented a manuscript version of his work on machines to Charles

---

[46] Hilliard, 'Jacques Besson et son "Théâtre des instruments mathématiques"', *Revue française d'histoire du livre* NS 48 (1979), 5–38; Hilliard, 'Jacques Besson et son "Théâtre des instruments mathématiques", recherches complémentaires', *Revue française d'histoire du livre* NS 50 (1981), 47–77; Droz, *Chemins de l'hérésie*, IV, 271–372; Keller, 'A Manuscript Version of Jacques Besson's Book of Machines' in *On Pre-Modern Technology and Science: A Volume of Studies in Honor of Lynn White Jr*, ed. Bert S. Hall and Delno C. West (Malibu, Calif., 1976), pp. 75–103; Keller, 'The Missing Years of Jacques Besson, Inventor of Machines, Teacher of Mathematics, Distiller of Oils and Huguenot Pastor', *Technology and Culture* 14 (1973), 28–39.

[47] Droz, *Chemins de l'hérésie*, IV, 281.

[48] Ibid., IV, 271.

[49] Ibid., IV, 272.

[50] Ibid., IV, 274.

[51] Ibid., IV, 280.

[52] *Le cosmolabe, ou instrument universel concernant toutes observations qui se peuvent faire par les sciences mathématiques, tant au ciel, en la terre, comme en la mer* (Paris, 1567). See Droz, *Chemins de l'hérésie*, IV, 299.

IX.[53] In his dedication to the king, Besson made clear the utilitarian purpose of his work, which presents 'new machines and inventions for geometers, mariners, merchants, artisans and gentlemen, in brief for rich and poor, who wish to understand all that for the conservation, utility and maintenance of the common-weal'.[54] Besson's work must be appreciated as something more than a do-it-yourself guide for the construction of machines. It was based on the sometimes admittedly fancifully expressed idea that machines could help to improve society. The engravings for Besson's volume were almost certainly the work of Jacques Androuet Du Cerceau, who shared Besson's Protestant sympathies as well as his desire to make a contribution to the improvement of the common good.[55] Indeed, Du Cerceau's engraved illustrations play as important a part, or a more important one, in Besson's work than does the accompanying text. They suggest the closest kind of collaboration between the two men based on a common purpose.

Besson was attempting to find technological solutions to meet underlying economic needs. However, it should be pointed out, as our discussion of his mechanical plough has already suggested, that there is an impractical and fantastical element in many of the machines that he devised. Thus the original impetus to create these mechanisms may have been economic, but it seems that in many of them a sense of fantasy and whimsy has taken over. Indeed, George Basalla has recently emphasized how important it is that we do not fall into a narrow utilitarianism with respect to the spirit of Renaissance invention. Economic need played its part, but did not inhibit or repress a sense of playfulness and imagination.[56]

The *Théâtre des instrumens mathématiques et mechaniques* as published omits all reference to the theoretical premises on which Besson's machines were based. But the manuscript version discovered by Keller contains a preface which lays down their theoretical foundation.[57] Besson knew the pseudo-Aristotelian *Mechanics* as well as the pseudo-Euclidean *On the Light and Heavy Bodies* translated and commented on by Pierre Forcadel. He was also familiar with Archimedes' *Livre . . . des pois qui aussi est dict des choses tombantes en l'humide*. Two other translations by Forcadel which may have influenced Besson are *Le premier livre d'Archimede* (1565) and *Deux livres de Proclus du mouvement*.[58] Besson's physics is not

---

53 Keller, 'A Manuscript Version of Jacques Besson's Theatre of Machines', p. 76; Hilliard, 'Jacques Besson et son "Théâtre des instruments mathématiques"', recherches complémentaires', pp. 47, 50.

54 Quoted in Hilliard, 'Jacques Besson et son "Théâtre des instruments mathématiques"', recherches complémentaires', pp. 62–3.

55 See the dedication in Du Cerceau's *Livre d'architecture* (Paris, 1559), fos. sig. A ii r., A iii r. See also Naomi Miller, 'Du Cerceau', *Macmillan Encyclopedia of Architects*, I, 603–8; *Harvard College Library. Catalogue of Books and Manuscripts: French Sixteenth Century Books*, compiled by Ruth Mortimer (Cambridge, 1964), I, 76–7.

56 George Basalla, *The Evolution of Technology* (Cambridge, 1988), pp. 14, 66–8.

57 Keller, 'A Manuscript Version of Jacques Besson's Book of Machines', pp. 78–80.

58 Hilliard, 'Jacques Besson et son "Théâtre des instruments mathématiques"', recherches complémentaires', pp. 52–3.

innovative. His fundamental premise is the traditional Aristotelian one that inertness is normal and that violent motion is to be accounted for by the intrusion of some external force. His attempts to account for the motion of his machines by means of the mathematical understanding of efficient causes thus clearly failed.[59] What is memorable, however, is his sense of the need to integrate theory and practice.

The first edition of Besson's work appeared in 1571 or at the beginning of 1572.[60] By that time he had moved to Paris. There we know him to have participated in the philosophical and scientific discussions of the circle of Jacques Gohory.[61] No doubt he was attracted to Gohory's little academy by his interest in iatrochemistry. This interest was reflected in his *L'art et moyen parfait de tirer huyles et eaux de tous medicaments simples et oleogineaux*, which appeared in a French version in 1573.[62] This was of good enough quality to be reprinted at the end of Andreas Libavius' *Praxis alchymiae* at the beginning of the seventeenth century.[63] Besson died in Paris, probably in 1573, leaving his wife and children virtually penniless.[64]

It was left to his friend and colleague François Berauld to arrange for a second edition of his work on machines. It was Berauld who entitled it the *Théâtre des instrumens mathématiques et mechaniques* which he arranged to have printed at Lyons in 1578.[65] The term 'theatre', in the sense of a panorama of objects displayed in an amphitheatre, was becoming increasingly fashionable in the second half of the sixteenth century.[66] Besson's work became a best-seller for its time, running through nine editions in five languages before the start of the new century. Its popularity is attested by the fact that more than 150 copies survive in public libraries on both sides of the Atlantic.[67] Its impact may also be measured by the fact that it found many imitators in France, including Jean Errard's *Le premier livre des instruments mathématiques mechaniques* (1584),[68] Agostino Ramelli's *Le diverse et artificiose machine* (1588),[69] Ambroise Bachot's *Le gouvernail* (1598)[70] and Joseph

---

[59] Vernard Foley, Darlene Sedlock, Carole Vidule and David Ellis, 'Besson, Da Vinci and the Evolution of the Pendulum: Some Findings and Observations', *History and Technology* 6 (1988), 1–43.

[60] Hilliard, 'Jacques Besson et son "Théâtre des instruments mathématiques"' p. 14.

[61] E.T. Hamy, 'Un précurseur de Guy de la Brosse, Jacques Gohory et le Lycium Philosophal de Saint-Marceau-les-Paris, 1571–1576', *Nouvelles archives du museum*, 4th series, 1 (1899), 20.

[62] Besson had published a Latin edition at Zurich in 1559. A shortened Latin edition was printed in 1571, followed by a French translation two years later.

[63] (Frankfurt, 1604).

[64] Hilliard, 'Jacques Besson et son "Théâtre des instruments mathématiques"', recherches complémentaires', p. 59; Droz, *Chemins de l'hérésie*, IV, 343.

[65] (Lyons, 1578).

[66] Droz, *Chemins de l'hérésie*, IV, 349.

[67] Hilliard, 'Jacques Besson et son "Théâtre des instruments mathématiques"', p. 3.

[68] (Nancy, 1584).

[69] *Le diverse et artificiose machine* (Paris, Ramelli, 1588); See also *The various and ingenious machines of Agostino Ramelli*, tr. Martha Teach Gnudi (Baltimore, 1976).

[70] (Melun, Bachot, 1598).

Boillot's *Modeles, artifices de feu et divers instruments de guerre avec les moyens d'en prevaloir* (1598).[71]

The list of machines included in Besson's work is remarkable for its variety: new measuring instruments, fire-extinguishers, coffer-dams, saw-mills, perpetual motion clocks, windmills, water-mills, hand mills, perpetual screws, wheelbarrows, cranes, pumps and presses.[72] Besson's machines are a mixture of serious technical inventions and fantastical contraptions. Many of his devices are not viable and were certainly not put into use. Others are workable, but were not realizable with the available materials and technology. Some of his devices are imitations of or improvements on Roman and Greek technology. On the other hand, his work played an important part in the transmission of certain technological ideas. For example, it was Leonardo who had the first conception in modern times of the mechanical screw. Leonardo's idea of this device was transmitted in the work of Cardano, but it was only made known generally through Besson's treatise.[73]

Towards the end of the sixteenth century, Thomas Platter saw a dredge at work in the harbour of Lates which was apparently based on Besson's design. In January 1596 he went to Lates to see the ships in the harbour. During his visit, he observed a dredge at work clearing weeds and other debris from the harbour. It struck him that the device was based on a design he had seen in a book published recently in Geneva. Rut Keiser, editor of a German edition of Platter's diary, correctly links the reference to the Geneva edition of Besson's work which appeared in 1594.[74]

The engraving in Besson (Plate III) shows a dredge operated by a system of winches which draws the dredge back and forth across a harbour by means of ropes.

Besson's panorama of machines and inventions was designed to appeal to technically proficient craftsmen or engineers. It was also meant, as I have pointed out, to stimulate the imagination of merchants, notables and aristocrats, conveying the idea that machinery could improve society. More to the point, the descriptions which accompany the illustrations of Besson's inventions repeatedly suggest that such devices could either carry out existing tasks more efficiently or perform tasks hitherto considered difficult or impossible. In the latter category are a design for a mine-shaft elevator,[75] various kinds of pumps,[76] a fire-extinguisher,[77] a ship

---

[71] *Modeles, artifices de feu et divers instruments de guerre avec les moyens de s'en prevaloir pour assieger, suprendre et deffendre toutes places* (Chaumont, Q. Mareschal, 1598).

[72] The full list of sixty is given by Droz, *Chemins de l'hérésie* I, 338–44.

[73] Hilliard, 'Jacques Besson et son "Théâtre des instruments mathématiques", recherches complémentaires' pp. 16–17.

[74] (Geneva, 1594). See Thomas Platter, *Beschreibung der Reisen durch Frankreich, Spanien, England und die Niederlande 1595–1600*, ed. Rut Keiser (Basle, Stuttgart, 1968), I, 93.

[75] Droz, *Chemins de l'hérésie*, IV, 342, n. 45.

[76] Ibid., IV, 343, nn. 47–50.

[77] Ibid., IV, 343, n. 52.

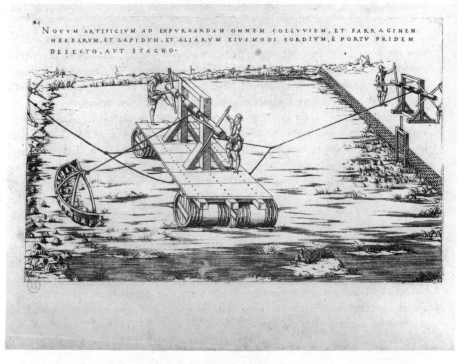

NOVVM ARTIFICIVM AD EXPVRGANDAM OMNEM COLLVVIEM, ET FARRAGINEM
HERBARVM, ET LAPIDVM, ET ALIARVM EIVSMODI SORDIVM, È PORTV PRIDEM
DESERTO, AVT STAGNO-

Plate III   Jacques Besson, Mechanical dredge, *Théâtre des intrumens mathématiques et mechaniques* (Lyons, B. Vincent, 1578).

salvage device,[78] a press based on an endless screw[79] and a mechanically driven boat.[80] These devices are marked by their supposed capacity to do great amounts of work which would be otherwise difficult or impossible to carry out.

But most of the machines designed by Besson were meant to save a relatively small amount of labour. I have already discussed his plough, which was intended to save labour by reducing time in ploughing.[81] More typical is a machine designed to brick and mortar a wall as quickly as a large number of masons.[82] Typical, also, is a device for moving weights as heavy as columns or obelisks with the help of a small number of workers,[83] and a mechanical saw in which two workers turning wheels would be able to saw as much wood as eight workers could ordinarily do.[84] Similarly,

[78] Ibid., IV, 343–4, nn. 53, 58.
[79] Ibid., IV, 4, n. 59.
[80] Ibid., IV, 344, n. 60.
[81] Ibid., IV, 341, n. 33.
[82] Ibid., IV, 341, n. 35.
[83] Ibid., IV, 341, n. 30.
[84] Ibid., IV, 339, n. 13.

he proposed a hand-mill employing a limited number of workers which could grind as much grain as a windmill or water-mill.[85] The appeal of these machines was that they were economical in their use of labour. They could potentially do more work than could be done previously while at the same time reducing the amount of labour necessary. Quite clearly, the greater productivity and efficiency of these machines was related to costs. According to Besson, their effectiveness could be estimated from the promptness and duration of their action and their low cost 'in order that the outlay should not surpass either the revenue or returns'.[86] At a time when the nominal cost of labour was rising owing to increasing food costs, while profits, for that reason as well as others, were under pressure, the devices proposed by Besson and others must have been attractive to manufacturers, provided, of course, they could have afforded them. From a historical point of view, it does seem that Besson's inventions were among the first in a long line of proposals designed, through the introduction of new technology, to enhance productivity and profitability in the face of declining profit margins. But the truth is that new technology is likely to be introduced not in periods of lowered profitability but, on the contrary, in periods of enhanced profitability when entrepreneurs can actually afford such innovations in expectation of still higher returns.

The growing influence of engineers, architects, physicians and skilled craftsmen we may conclude led to attacks on contemplative forms of knowledge and a growing demand for empirical and practical knowledge. This demand for a knowledge rooted in practice was catalysed by the intensifying pressure of economic adversity. Under the pressure of material hardship, a new collective scientific convention, to use the terminology of Barry Barnes, was thus in the process of substituting itself for the old.[87]

THE NATURALISTS OF MONTPELLIER

Paris was clearly the centre of innovation in French scientific thought during the latter half of the sixteenth century, attracting to itself men like Palissy, Ramus and Besson. But we should not ignore the flowering of botanical scholarship at the same time in the Midi, particularly at the medical school of the University of Montpellier.[88] Clearly beginning in the 1560s, a movement towards a more empirical approach to nature was developing there. At the centre of the study of natural history there was the great naturalist Guillaume Rondelet.[89] Rondelet inspired a whole generation of brilliant botanists and naturalists including Pierre Pena, Mathias de l'Obel, Jean Bauhin, Charles de l'Ecluse and Jacques

---

[85] Ibid., IV, 340, n. 26.
[86] Quoted in Keller, 'A Manuscript Version of Jacques Besson's Book of Machines', p. 77.
[87] 'Sociological Theories of Scientific Knowledge' in *Companion to the History of Science*, ed. R.C. Olby *et al.* (London, 1990), pp. 60–77.
[88] See Karen M. Reeds, *Botany in Medieval and Renaissance Universities* (New York, 1991).
[89] See A.G. Keller, 'Guillaume Rondelet', *DSB* XI, 527–8.

Daléchamps. In 1562, in the midst of the crisis which signalled the onset of the religious wars, Bauhin had begun the study of the flora of Languedoc through the systematic study of the plants of the region of Montpellier.[90] But it was Pena and l'Obel who extended this work to the whole of Languedoc and Provence.[91] In 1570 they published the *Stirpium adversia nova*.[92] Significantly, owing to the disturbed circumstances in their own country, these two Huguenot naturalists had to publish their work in England. It consists of notes and data on 1,200–1,300 plants that they had gathered and examined in Languedoc as well as in England and the Low Countries. Notable in their work is the presence of Neoplatonic assumptions which inspired their interest in every variety of plant species no matter how insignificant. In the preface to the *Stirpium adversia nova*, they urged students of botany who were seeking new medicines to study even the most insignificant plants. As God has created the natural world, there can be nothing in nature, however obscure, which is not of interest to rational beings. The most trivial plant still might have healing powers.[93] It is to be remarked that Pena, like Besson, became part of Gohory's Parisian circle in the 1570s.[94] Another notable French scholar was Jacques Daléchamps, who received his doctorate in medicine at Montpellier in 1547.[95] Daléchamps' *Historia generalis plantorum* (1586–7), which he published after decades of collecting and research, was the most complete botanical compilation of the sixteenth century.

PARACELSIANISM IN PARIS

The movement towards empiricism, such as it was, was made less sharp by the growing influence of the ideas of Paracelsus. The revival of Neoplatonism and Hermetic philosophy in the fifteenth century itself prompted interest in discovering God through study of the Book of Nature. The growing influence of Paracelsus' natural philosophy, itself rooted in neoplatonic assumptions, strongly reinforced a religiously inspired curiosity in exploring the details of the natural world.[96] Paracelsus' theories coexisted easily with a body of craft knowledge and technique and, indeed, encouraged empirical enquiry. On the other hand, it was a

---

[90] Charles Webster, 'Jean Bauhin', *DSB* I, 525–6; Roman D'Amat, 'Jean Bauhin', *DBF* V, 927–8; Conrad Gesner, *Vingt lettres à Jean Bauhin fils (1563–65)*, ed. Claude Longeon (Saint-Etienne, 1976).

[91] Ludovic Legré, *La botanique en Provence au XVIe siècle. Pierre Pena et Mathieu de Lobel* (Marseilles, 1899); Armand Louis, *Mathieu de l'Obel (1538–1616): épisode de l'histoire de la botanique* (Ghent-Louvain, 1980), pp. 29–68, 88, 94–121.

[92] (London, 1570).

[93] Quoted in Legré, *La botanique en Provence*, pp. 27–8.

[94] Pena had returned to Paris from England and the Netherlands in time to hear the celebrated public lectures of Palissy in 1575. See Désirée Leroux, *La vie de Bernard Palissy* (Paris, 1927), pp. 81–2.

[95] Charles B. Schmitt, 'Jacques Daléchamps', *DSB* III, 533–4.

[96] Debus, *Man and Nature in the Renaissance* (Cambridge, 1978), pp. 11–15.

theory which was compatible with more or less orthodox Christian ideas. At the same time, however, it conceived of nature in terms of magical affinities and sympathies.[97]

At the focal point of scientific activities in Paris in the 1570s was Jacques Gohory.[98] Born *c.* 1520 into a family of Tourangeaux notables of Italian descent, Gohory, like his two brothers, pursued a career as an *avocat* in the Parlement of Paris. In the 1540s he took part in diplomatic missions sent to the Low Countries, England and to Rome. Disenchanted with legal and courtly life, he decided to devote himself to the study and pursuit of literature, music, occult philosophy, natural history and medicine.

Gohory was a close friend of the Pléiade and of the circle of Jean Antoine de Baïf. From 1572 he established a private academy, the so-called Lycium Philosophal, at his home in the faubourg Saint-Marcel. Like the academy of his friend Baïf, Gohory's Lycium was devoted to the encyclopaedic cultivation of the arts. In the gardens of his home provision was made for games and ceremonies as well as for study and discussion. A sense of naive play and ritual was thus combined with the quest for learning. But in contrast to Baïf's stress on poetry and music, Gohory emphasized alchemy, botany and the magical arts. The Lycium had a botanical garden in which both exoticism and utility seem to have determined the choice of plants cultivated. He also maintained a chemical laboratory for the preparation of medicines and for alchemical experiments.

Gohory's importance lies especially in the dissemination of the ideas of Paracelsus in France. It is Paracelsus' ideas which are seen by today's historians of science as central to undermining the hold of Aristotle and Galen on natural philosophy and medicine, while stimulating the development of experimental philosophy.[99] In his *Compendium* (1568) of the philosophy and medicine of Paracelsus, Gohory reviewed the biography of Paracelsus, summarized his principal teachings, and commented on his *De vita longa*. Gohory noted with approval the microcosm–macrocosm analogy, insisted on following Paracelsus in claiming that all diseases are curable, advocated the use of minerals like gold and antimony in the treatment of disease, and rejected the humoral theory of physiology. He considered magic to be of great importance, including the notion of the Spirit of Life, cabalistic words and numbers, and the use of talismen, seals, characters and amulets.[100] He helped to disseminate Paracelsian notions which he

---

[97] On Renaissance Paracelsianism see Debus, *The Chemical Philosophy: Paracelsian Science and Medicine in the Sixteenth and Seventeenth Centuries*, 2 vols. (New York, 1977); Charles Webster, *From Paracelsus to Newton: Magic and the Making of Modern Science* (Cambridge, 1982). On the various currents leading to the Scientific Revolution see John A. Shuster, 'The Scientific Revolution' in *Companion to the History of Modern Science*, ed. Olby *et al.*, pp. 217–22.

[98] On Gohory cf. Hamy, 'Un précurseur de Guy de la Brosse'; Owen Hannoway, 'Jacques Gohory' DSB v, 447–8; A. Tetry, 'Jacques Gohory', *DBF* xvi, 502–3; Enea Balmas, 'Jacques Gohory, traduttore del Machiavelli' in *Saggi e studi sul rinascimento francese* (Padua, 1982), pp. 23–73.

[99] Debus, *The Chemical Philosophy*, i, 102; Webster, *From Paracelsus to Newton*, pp. 1–12.

[100] Debus, *The Chemical Philosophy*, i, 147.

discussed with such Parisian medical luminaries as Jean Fernel, Ambroise Paré, Jean Chapelain, Honoré Chastellan and Leonardo Botal.

Palissy, too, must be understood to have been inspired not only by religious belief but also by certain elements in the thought of Paracelsus. Like Besson and Pena, Palissy appears to have been part of the periphery of Gohory's circle. Indeed, he learned of Paracelsus through the works of Jacques Gohory as well as through *Le Demosterion de Roch le Baillif Edelphe ... medecin spageric ...* (Rennes, 1578) and from Alexandre de la Tourrete's *Bref discours des admirables vertus de l'or potable* (1578).[101] Palissy, as is well known, recommended the use of manure and marl to improve the fertility of the soil. However, what is notable is his attempt to explain the fertilizing effects of these substances in Paracelsian terms.[102] Following Paracelsus, he attributes the nutritive influence of manure and marl to the salt which they contain. The presence of salt is indispensable to vegetative matter, according to him.

Palissy's views on the origins of streams and rivers are of interest. He refuted the older theories that held that streams came from sea water or from the air that had condensed into water.[103] He had no real sense of the enormity of geological time. Nevertheless, he believed that the mineral world was ceaselessly in flux. The petrifaction of plants and animals into fossils, some of which he recognized as extinct species, was a fundamental aspect of his thought.[104] He was the first to develop a real collection of such fossil remains. Indeed, Jean Claude Plaziat has discovered that Palissy included representations of such fossils from the Tertiary period among the rustic figurines on his pottery.[105] As a result of experimentation, Palissy concluded that all minerals with geometric crystal forms must have crystallized in water. His classification of salts turned out to be nearly correct. Finally, he was the first to suggest the concept of superposition to explain the development of sedimentary rocks.[106]

AMBROISE PARÉ: SURGERY AND PHILOSOPHY

At first sight, Ambroise Paré's work, like that of Palissy's, seems to exemplify the triumph of a purely empirical approach to medicine and nature. Paré was born *c.*

---

[101] Kirsop, 'The Legend of Bernard Palissy', p. 148.

[102] 'Palissy, Plat and English Agricultural Chemistry in the Sixteenth and Seventeenth Centuries' in Debus, *Chemistry, Alchemy and the New Philosophy, 1550–1700* (London, 1987), p. 73; Céard, 'Bernard Palissy et l'alchimie' in *Actes du colloque Bernard Palissy (1510–1590): l'écrivain, le réformé, le céramiste. Journées d'études 29 et 30 juin 1990. Saintes–Abbaye-aux-Dames*, ed. Lestringant (Saintes, 1992), pp. 157–61.

[103] See Aurèle Le Roque, 'Bernard Palissy' in *Toward a History of Geology*, ed. Cecil J. Schneer (Cambridge, Mass., 1969), pp. 226–41. Margaret R. Biswas and Asit K. Biswas, 'Bernard Palissy', *DSB* x, 280–1; François Ellenberger, *Histoire de la géologie* (Paris, 1988), pp. 133–4.

[104] Ellenberger, *Histoire de géologie*, p. 137.

[105] Ibid., p. 142.

[106] Biswas and Biswas, 'Bernard Palissy', pp. 280–1.

1510 at Laval, the son of a craftsman.[107] He became an apprentice barber-surgeon at Angers or Vitré. Moving to Paris, he spent three years working in the Hôtel-Dieu, where he acquired unrivalled experience as a surgeon as well as knowledge in other aspects of medicine. His long years of following the French armies in the field enabled him to perfect his knowledge of surgery. His most celebrated achievement was to revolutionize the treatment of gunshot wounds, which, until then, were usually cauterized with boiling oil. Instead, he substituted a dressing made of egg yolk, oil of roses and turpentine. He reported his discovery in *La methode de traicter les playes faites par les arquebuses et autres bastons a feu* (1545). Its publication brought him instant celebrity.

Paré's empiricism is manifest in his *Anatomie universelle du corps humain*, which he published at Paris in 1561. As he himself admitted, many of the engravings were based on Vesalius' *De fabrica*. On the other hand, the text relied on his own anatomical investigations. But in order to ensure the accuracy of these observations, he attempted to verify them by consultation with his colleague J. Rostaing de Binosque, also highly experienced in the art of dissection. Indeed, checking his own observations against those of Rostaing de Binosque constituted an essential part of his procedure:

> For given the diversity of bodies that he had seen, on the one hand, and those that I had elsewhere seen, on the other hand, he at times disagreed with my viewpoint. In order to be more certain, we have sometimes several times a day resorted to examining corpses in order to settle disagreements over a detail of anatomy, which having been reviewed in this manner, we have thanks to God emerged with a unanimous conclusion of the points of view which have been adopted in this work of mine.[108]

Paré attempted as much as possible to join together the practical and theoretical aspects of medicine. The practical side of his craft is exemplified in the wide array of instruments he used in working on the human body. He refers to this inventory of surgical tools in a poem at the beginning of his *Dix livres de la chirurgie avec le magasin des instrumens necessaires a icelle* (1564). In it he claimed that his 'shop' of surgical tools contained more than 300 instruments, some of his own invention and others devised by his predecessors.[109] Indeed, he devoted the last thirty-two pages of this work to engravings that would demonstrate what some of these instruments looked like and how they ought to be employed. With Paré we are far from the use of such tools as the laser and computer as practised in modern surgery. Nevertheless, it is important to recognize that surgery in the sixteenth

---

[107] On the life of Paré see *Œuvres complètes*, ed. J.F. Malgaigne (Paris, 1840–1), vol. I, introduction; W.B. Hamby, *Ambroise Paré: Surgeon of the Renaissance* (Saint Louis, Mo., 1967); Joseph François Malgaigne, *Surgery and Amboise Paré*, tr. Wallace B. Hamby (Norman, Okla., 1965).

[108] *Œuvres complètes*, ed. Malgaigne, I, ccxii; Malgaigne, *Surgery and Amboise Paré*, p. 325.

[109] *Œuvres complètes* ed. Malgaine, I ccxiv; Malgaigne, *Surgery and Amboise Paré*, p. 329. See also Alain Ségal, 'L'instrumentation chirurgicale à l'époque d'Ambroise Paré', *Histoire des sciences medicales* 25 (1991), 109–26.

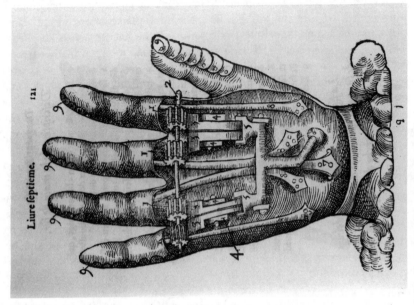

Liure septieme. 121

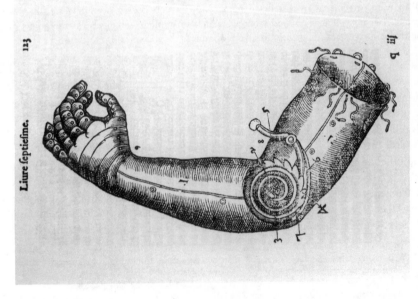

Liure septiesme. 123

Plate IV Artificial arm and hand, Ambroise Paré. *Dix livres de la chirurgie* (Paris, 1564).

century was very much an artisanal vocation, the tools of which were fundamentally important. Certainly, the medical profession thought of it in that way and was outraged by the attempt by Paré and others to dignify it with theoretical pretensions.

The 'mechanical' aspect of Paré's work is nowhere better exemplified than in his *Des moyens et artifices d'adjouster ce qui defaut naturellement ou par accident*. Accompanied by engravings, this treatise forms chapter 17 of the edition of his *Œuvres* published in 1579. It is a work devoted to prosthetic devices, including artificial eyes, noses, ears, palates, legs and penises. But especially notable are his artificial arm and hand (Plate IV), which are really complex pieces of machinery comparable to the devices of Jacques Besson.[110] However fanciful these devices were, with their gears and springs, they nevertheless serve to demonstrate how interested contemporaries were in the relationship between human and mechanical forms of power. They were fascinated by the possibility of using mechanical means to extend or improve what could be achieved by human labour or effort.

Paré's increasing success was based on his fresh approach to medicine from the standpoint of practical experience. But his growing fame excited the animosity and jealousy of the medical faculty of the University of Paris. In May 1575, shortly before the publication of the first edition of his collected works, the faculty of medicine demanded that they not be put on sale prior to their being examined by a committee of its members. At the trial before the Parlement of Paris which took place in mid-July, Paré was accused of plagiarism and indecency. Behind these accusations lay the hostility of the faculty towards an upstart surgeon who had the audacity to deal with questions of medical theory in the French vernacular.[111]

Our discussion of Paré to this point has stressed the empirical and practical aspect of his activity. However, it would be a great oversight to view him simply in this light. Paré, we know, was part of the circle of Jacques Gohory. As a consequence, he was fully conversant with the ideas of Paracelsus. Indeed, as early as 1568 he had recommended the use of antimony in the treatment of plague. The reaction of the medical faculty was so hostile that he was forced partially to retract his approval: 'some heartily approve and recommend the use of antimony alleging many cases of its positive effects that they have witnessed. But because the usage of it is reproved by several members of the faculty of medicine, I will desist from writing anything about it at this point.'[112]

Beyond the traces of Paracelsian influence in Paré's work, it is important to stress the religious assumptions that underlay his conception of nature. A number of scholars including Malgaigne, the great nineteenth-century editor of his works,

---

[110] On Paré's contribution to an understanding of the body as a mechanism see Bruce Mazlish, *The Co-evolution of Humans and Machines* (New Haven, 1993), pp. 17–18.

[111] See Paré, *Des monstres et prodiges*, ed. Céard (Geneva, 1971), pp. xiv–xv.

[112] *Œuvres complètes*, ed. Malgaigne, I, cclxxii–cclxxiii;, Malgaigne, *Surgery and Ambroise Paré*, p. 282.

have attempted to deny Paré's Calvinism. It does seem to be the case that Paré held aloof from formally joining the Reformed Church. However, the later references to Paré by Sully, his close relationship to Admiral Coligny, and the fact that his publisher was a Huguenot who specialized in Calvinist publications, make it highly probable that Paré was indeed a Calvinist.[113] Moreover, any serious reading of his work must confirm the powerful influence of Calvin on his thought. In particular, one is struck by the similarity between Calvin's and Paré's sense of the natural world as a manifestation of divine grace, power and order.

Céard has studied Paré's conception of nature, particularly as it appears in his best-selling *Des monstres et prodiges*.[114] In this work Paré presents a pantheon of human and animal monsters, anomalies and prodigies, not in order to demonstrate the capriciousness of nature, but rather to display its grandeur, especially in so far as nature should be seen as the 'caretaker' of God's activity. According to Paré, these creatures, horrible as some of them may appear, nevertheless, testify to the incomprehensible grandeur of the works of God.[115] His aim was to try to naturalize the monstrous, stripping it of all sense of imperfection. The monstrous he considered as the extreme form of that variety so pleasing to the natural order which, in the last analysis, is the construction of God.[116] Paré's study of monsters is thus meant to reinforce a sense of divinely ordained design in nature. Moreover, his empiricism must be understood as informed by a strongly religious sensibility.

In conclusion it is important to appreciate the efforts made in science and technology in the reign of Charles IX as a response, in part, to the overall climate of economic and political crisis. They must be set within the overall context of urgent efforts to improve the economy and reform society and the Church. It is noteworthy that, for example, Ramus addressed his call for the reform of the university curriculum to the same Privy Council that was interesting itself in the patenting of all sorts of new inventions. Finally, it seems evident that this drive towards technological improvement and a more empirical approach to the study of nature was strongly informed by Calvinist religious assumptions. Palissy, Ramus, Besson, Foulon, du Cerceau, Rondelet, Pena, L'Obel, Bauhin, Paré and even Peletier and Bullant appear to have been inspired by evangelical ideas. Sanches had Marrano roots. Certainly Belon, who had made his career prior to the 1560s, held aloof from Calvinism. Nevertheless, it does seem that, as elsewhere in Europe, sympathy for the teachings of Calvin and a desire to reform or create knowledge and improve society went hand in hand.

[113] Janet Doe, *A Bibliography of the Works of Ambroise Paré, 1545–1940* (Amsterdam, 1976), pp. 12–15.
[114] Paré, ed. Céard.
[115] Ibid., p. 308.
[116] Ibid., p. 309.

5

Expropriation, technology and wage labour

... In this place my best income is derived from manual labour. The work of a hundred men produces a profit which lasts a long time.

Montaigne, Essais

In the 1560s, as we have seen, many initiatives were taken to try to reverse the onset of economic crisis. Indeed, the initial crisis of the early 1560s was followed by a partial recovery. It is only from 1575 to 1580 that one sees the full onslaught of economic depression.[1] By then there is no question that the combination of the ravages of war, the burden of heavy taxation, the decline in population, and the lowering of profit margins was responsible for a serious economic regression. Le Roy Ladurie characterizes the period of the religious wars as a crisis of the second degree. By crisis of the second degree, he means one that was more serious than an ordinary cyclical downturn, but less severe than the total collapse of the fourteenth and fifteenth centuries.[2] No doubt the difficulties of these concluding years of the sixteenth century were somewhat less serious than the catastrophic decline of the late middle ages, a crisis of the first magnitude. Still, there is little question that we are dealing with a severe economic setback.

WAR AND ECONOMIC DECLINE

One of the most serious aspects of this economic regression was the migration of skilled craftsmen, merchants and small-scale manufacturers out of the kingdom. The value of fixed capital in early modern industry was generally negligible. What counted most was keeping the skills and techniques of merchants and craftsmen. Innovations in the means of production or in the product were more often the product of the ingenuity of craftsmen than the result of the designs of engineers. In the highly competitive textile industry, there was an acute sense of competition and a continuous need to innovate.[3]

Attempts to manufacture a more competitive product as well as to reduce the

---

[1] *Histoire économique et sociale de la France*, ed. Chaunu and Gascon, Part I, vol. I, 326–7.
[2] Ibid., ed. Le Roy Ladurie and Michel Morineau, Part I, vol. II, 693–4.
[3] Pierre Deyon, 'La concurrence internationale des manufactures lainières', *Annales: ESC* 27 (1972), 20, 22.

cost of labour were frequent. Paradoxically, one of the most common excuses for making masterships more difficult to obtain was the need for the masters of a guild to learn more and more varied techniques than had been necessary in the past in order to meet the competition. Nevertheless, when necessity required it, the guild system itself was modified in order to keep an industry competitive. At Amiens in 1570, for example, the cloth industry introduced a new product in order to meet the competition at home and abroad. Manufacturers at Beauvais, Orléans, as well as in England and the Low Countries, had successfully combined two kinds of thread to create a cloth which had the properties of both say and wool. At Amiens the producers of says and wool cloth were organized in separate guilds. After negotiations with the town council, some manufacturers in the two crafts were allowed to create a new guild to produce the new mixed kind of cloth.[4] The guild system, on the basis of which manufacture was organized at Amiens, proved to be no real barrier to change when the need to meet the challenge of competition seriously presented itself.

Keeping control of the secrets of a craft was a matter of rivalry between states. Thus, in 1570, Louis Drera brought the technique of Venetian scarlet secretly to Marseilles. On this basis, the highly successful Compagnie drapiere de l'Escarlate was created.[5] Likewise, in 1592 Drera was able to fabricate a cloth to rival English kersey, threatening thereby to steal the market in the Levant from the English. Writing to his nephew at Aleppo on the dispatch for the first time of this new fabric to the East, Drera exulted: 'you will see a most beautiful and good thing ... which in finesse, width and colour is superior to that of the English or the Venetians'.[6]

But against these positive French initiatives must be set the massive exodus of Huguenot merchants and craftsmen to Switzerland and England. At least 12,000 refugees, most of whom were craftsmen, migrated to Geneva, subsequently playing an important role in the transformation of the city's economy. The development of printing, silk manufacture, watch- and instrument-making in Geneva was in good part the result of the skills supplied by these refugees from France.[7]

Driven by economic hardship and religious persecution, some 5,000 Huguenots emigrated from France to England during the religious wars.[8] The government of England provided these migrants with a refuge as a matter of religious principle. But it also welcomed them as a way of building up its own industry.[9] French,

---

[4]   *Recueil des monuments ... du tiers état*, ed. Thierry, II, 782–9.
[5]   *Histoire du commerce de Marseille*, ed. Rambert, III, 461–2.
[6]   Ibid., III, 462.
[7]   See William Monter, 'Historical Geography and Religious History in Sixteenth Century Geneva', *Journal of Interdisciplinary History* 9 (1979), 399–437; Heller, *The Conquest of Poverty*, pp. 252–4.
[8]   Robin D. Gwynn, *Huguenot Heritage: The History and Contribution of the Huguenots in England* (London, 1985), p. 51.
[9]   Thirsk, *Economic Policy and Projects*, pp. 43–4.

Flemish and Walloon migrants played a critical role in the development of the so-called 'new draperies' at Norwich, Canterbury, Colchester, Halstead, Maidstone and Southampton. As early as 1577 one English observer noted:

By reason of the troubles grown in other countries, the making of 'baies, friesadowes, tuftmoccadowe' and many other things made of wool, is mightily increased in England ... For this cause we ought to favour the strangers from whom we learned so great benefits because we are not so great devisers as followers of others.[10]

In 1590 the French Calvinist church at Southampton reported that its entire congregation was made up of serge weavers.[11]

The emigration from France saw the loss not only of merchants and skilled workers but also of those who possessed the secrets of design. By the early 1580s, as we have seen, the illustrator Jacques Le Moyne had established himself in England in flight from religious persecution. In 1586 he published in London *La clef de serfs*, containing ninety-six woodcuts of plants, birds and animals 'which might serve all those who would like and desire to learn good and honest matters among whom is the youth noble as well as artisan, the one to instruct in the art of painting or engraving, the others to become jewellers, sculptors, embroiderers or carpet makers, and indeed all manner of needle work for all of which portraiture is the point of departure'.[12]

The new draperies, as well as stocking and ribbon manufacture, were introduced to England by the French, among others. They provided much needed employment and increased family incomes. At a time of increasingly intense commercial rivalry abroad and stagnating internal markets, one nation's gain really was, more and more, another nation's loss.

Even south Germany provides an example of a success story at the expense of France. In 1570 Antoine Fournier arrived in Nuremburg from France. He brought with him the secret of drawing fine wire in gold and silver. This technique was well known in France at the time but apparently unknown in Germany until then. Accordingly, he was able to improve on the existing machinery for this purpose and established a factory for manufacturing silver and gold wire at Freistadtlein about 6 kilometres from Nuremburg. In the process he was able to accumulate considerable wealth.[13]

Economic decline, the disruption of war and the migration of those with skill and talent thus, must undoubtedly, leave us with a dismal impression of the French economy during the religious wars. Yet I will argue that the economic crisis of this period imposed a restructuring process that would ultimately have important positive consequences on the French economy. In response to the

[10] Quoted in Gwynn, *Huguenot Heritage*, p. 61.
[11] Ibid., p. 62.
[12] *The Work of Jacques Lemoyne*, II, plate 65.
[13] Beckmann, *History of Inventions*, II, 230.

economic malaise, established industries were restructured, while new industries were created, particularly in the countryside, in the midst of the civil wars. There is also growing evidence of improvements in agricultural productivity and diversification. More importantly, the violence and fiscal oppression of the religious wars actually strengthened the middle class. It allowed them to buy up land, while making available growing pools of labour from the dispossessed population with which to exploit it.

NEW ECONOMIC INITIATIVES: LIGHT IN THE DARK

The notion of unrelieved economic decline must be qualified in the first place by drawing a distinction between the situation in the Midi and that in the north of the kingdom. While the wars ravaged the south of France in the 1560s and 1570s, the north escaped serious devastation. During these decades, the economic consequences of the wars were felt mainly in the Midi. Only in the 1580s and 1590s did the armies move north of the Loire and wreak havoc there. Overall, the major negative economic effects of the war on the kingdom as a whole were experienced between 1585 and 1595.[14]

One must be cautious abut the notion of economic decline even on this basis. Lyons was clearly badly hit from the 1570s and Paris suffered severely under the control of the League. But can one say the same of ports like Nantes, La Rochelle, Marseilles and Rouen?[15] La Rochelle under Huguenot control behaved much like an independent city-state republic and enjoyed an unprecedented economic growth.[16] During the religious wars Marseilles assumed leadership in the Levant trade. Its commercial pre-eminence was reinforced by the development of cloth, soap and sugar manufacturing.[17] Despite ups and downs, Rouen enjoyed periods of great prosperity during the religious wars. The affluence of Rouen's merchants in this period was based on the Atlantic trade, including an emerging tie with the Dutch. Rouen's problems only became chronic when the Catholic and Huguenot armies moved their campaigns to the north of France.[18] Indeed, during this period Normandy as a whole witnessed a surprisingly high level of economic activity. Spurred by Rouen's export trade, the manufacture of canvas and ironware in the Norman countryside attained levels not seen again until the

---

[14]   See Mark Greengrass, 'The Later Wars of Religion in the French Midi' in *The European Crisis of the 1590's: Essays in Comparative History*, ed. Peter Clark (London, 1985), p. 106; Philip Benedict, 'Civil Wars and Natural Disasters in Northern France' in ibid., p. 84.

[15]   *Histoire économique et sociale de la France*, Part I, vol. I, 325–6.

[16]   Etienne Trocmé and Marcel Delafosse, *Le commerce rochelais de la fin du XVᵉ siècle au début du XVIIᵉ* (Paris, 1952), pp. 143–71.

[17]   *Histoire de Marseille*, ed. Edouard Baratier (Toulouse, 1989), p. 145.

[18]   Benedict, 'Rouen's Trade During the Era of the Religious Wars (1560–1600)', *Journal of European Economic History* 13 (1984), 29–73; Gayle K. Brunelle, *The New World Merchants of Rouen: 1559–1630* (Kirksville, Mo., 1991), pp. 25–6.

eighteenth century.[19] Likewise during this period there are unmistakable signs in Norman agriculture of innovation, diversification and increases in output.[20] In Dauphiné Daniel Hickey has discovered a like diversification out of grain into pasture, vineyards, orchards and animal husbandry.[21] The Ile-de-France records increases in agricultural productivity in the late sixteenth and the early seventeenth century, interrupted temporarily by the intensification of the religious wars after 1570.[22]

The vast putting-out industry engaged in manufacturing linen and canvas appears to have maintained itself throughout the religious wars, not only in Normandy but in Brittany, Maine, Anjou and Poitou as well.[23] Nicolas de Nicolay, writing in the 1570s, described an immense rural industry of linen and canvas manufacture in Lyonnais, Beaujolais, Forez, Charlieu, Charrolais and parts of Dauphiné producing for export to the Levant.[24] A royal edict of 1586 describes the canvas and linen manufacture as the largest single trade in the kingdom.[25] Around Saint-Chamond a rural silk industry with a trade of up to 100,000 *écus* a year flourished. In the town itself there were more than a hundred mills which spun the raw silk into thread.[26] Between 1580 and 1590 the silk industry began to expand in lower Languedoc. From Nîmes it spread into the Lodévois and the Uzège, based on a partnership of merchants, landlords and peasants which operated on a system of *metayage*.[27] Laffemas spoke of this system as having extended itself to the foot of the Cevennes by the beginning of the seventeenth century.[28]

By the 1570s the prosperity of the silk and wool hosiery manufacture

[19] Jacques Bottin, 'Structures et mutations d'un espace proto-industriel à la fin du XVIᵉ siècle', *Annales: ESC* 43 (1988), 975–95; Bottin, 'Les jeux de l'échange et de la production en Normandie à la fin du XVIᵉ siècle', *Histoire, économie et société* 9 (1990), 373–7; Bottin, 'Grand commerce et produit textile à Rouen, 1550–1620', *Bulletin du centre d'histoire des espaces atlantiques* NS 5 (1990), 265–79; Jean Vidalenc, *La petite métallurgie rurale en Haute-Normandie sous l'Ancien Regime* (Paris, 1946), p. 35.

[20] Bernard Garnier, 'Pays herberger et pays "ouvert" en Normandie, XVIᵉ – début du XIXᵉ siècle,' *Revue d'histoire économique et sociale* 53 (1975), 493–525; J.M. Pavard, 'Production et rendement céréalières à Cheux au début du dix-septième siècle', *Annales de Normandie* 26 (1976), 41–65.

[21] 'Innovations and Obstacles to Growth in the Agriculture of Early Modern France: The Example of Dauphiné', *French Historical Studies* 15 (1987), 208–40.

[22] Philip T. Hoffman, 'Land Rents and Agricultural Productivity: The Paris Basin 1450–1789', *Journal of Economic History* 51 (1991), 791–3.

[23] Gustave Charles Fagniez, *L'économie sociale de la France sous Henri IV: 1589–1610* (Paris, 1897; Geneva, 1975), p. 84. See also James B. Collins, *Classes, Estates and Order in Early Modern Brittany* (Cambridge, 1994), pp. 34, 49.

[24] Nicolay, *Description générale de la ville de Lyon*, p. 210.

[25] *Edict et reglement du roy sur les abus qui se commettent es manufactures de lin ...* (Paris, 1586), BN F.46881 (6).

[26] Nicolay, *Description générale de la ville de Lyon*, p. 210.

[27] Le Roy Ladurie, *Les paysans de Languedoc*, I, 438.

[28] Barthélemy de Laffemas, *Lettres et exemples de feu la reine mère, comme elle faisoit travailler aux manufactures et fournissoit aux ouvriers de ses propres deniers* (Paris, 1602), p. 3. See Le Roy Ladurie, *Les paysans de Languedoc*, I, 438.

centred around Dourdan was well established.[29] Ribbon-making appeared in the Forez during the religious wars. From 1585 it began to penetrate the Velay, where it was established by the turn of the century.[30] At the same time, the first signs of a rural lace-making industry in the Velay were manifest.[31] In 1589 the monarchy was able to attract Flemish lace makers to Senlis.[32] It is from this period that we have the first evidence of a rural wool cloth industry in the Beauvaisis.[33] At Montpellier and Lyons the manufacture of fustian became a lucrative affair. In the latter city towards 1580, 4,000 workers were said to be employed in this industry, whose sales were in the millions of *livres*. Indeed, the latter half of the sixteenth century saw the foundation of French cotton manufacturing, which was subsequently to become one of the most dynamic sectors of French industry. [34]

In 1583 the crown helped a manufacturer of luxury glassware to establish himself at Mâcon.[35] The manufacture of fine crystal was introduced to Lyons by an Italian, Giacomo Sarrodo. A decade later he transferred his workshops to Nevers.[36] Under its duke Louis de Gonzague, Nevers appears to have come into its own as a manufacturing centre during the religious wars. Its coal-mines and forges seem to have operated at full blast, while under the patronage of the duke its economy expanded to produce glass, pottery and faience.[37] Indeed, the real development of faience at Nevers, and also at Lyons, Nîmes, Montpellier and Rouen, dates from the period of the civil wars.[38] The prosperity of the foundries and forges of Normandy during the religious wars has already been noted. Nicolas de Nicolay likewise remarked on the vitality of the ironware industry in the Lyonnais.[39] Indeed, given the demand for weapons during the religious wars, Nef's and Gille's assumption of a decline in the manufacture of iron during this

---

[29] Lescornay, *Mémoires*, pp. 10–12.

[30] Germain Martin, *Le tissage du ruban à domicile dans les campagnes du Velay* (Paris, 1913).

[31] Louis Lavastre, *Dentellières et dentelles du Puy* (Le Puy, 1911).

[32] Boissonade, *Le socialisme d'état*, p. 90.

[33] Pierre Goubert, *Beauvais et la Beauvaisis de 1600 à 1730: contribution à l'histoire sociale de la France du XVIIᵉ siècle* (Paris, 1966), pp. 130–1; *Documents pour servir à l'histoire de Beauvais et du Beauvaisis* , ed. Victor Leblond (Paris, 1909), p. 4.

[34] Boissonade, *Le socialisme d'état*, p. 90; Franklin, *Dictionnaire historique*, pp. 328, 351. See also Maureen Fennell Mazzaoui, *The Italian Cotton Industry in the Later Middle Ages: 1100–1600* (Cambridge, 1981), pp. 159–61.

[35] Boissonade, *Le socialisme d'état*, p. 77; Paul M. Bondois, 'Le développement de l'industrie verrière dans la régionne parisienne de 1515 à 1665', *Revue d'histoire économique et sociale* 23 (1936–7), 51.

[36] Francesco Savorgnandi Brazza, *Tecnici e artigiani italiani in Francia* (Rome, 1942), p. 66.

[37] François Boutiller, *La verrerie et les gentilshommes verriers de Nevers* (Nevers, 1885); Louis Gueneau, *L'organisation du travail à Nevers aux XVIIᵉ et XVIIIᵉ siècles* (Paris, 1919), pp. 295, 319–20; Coquille, *Histoire du pays ... de Nivernais*, p. 353; Destray, 'Les houillières de la Machine', pp. 361–92.

[38] Henry-Pierre Fourest, *L'œuvre des faïenciers français du XVIᵉ à la fin du XVIIIᵉ siècles* (Paris, 1966), pp. 1–39; Jeanne Giacomotti, *French Faience* (New York, 1963), pp. 13–14, 17.

[39] Nicolay, *Description de la ville de Lyon*, p. 210.

period is open to question.[40] Under Henri III the monarchy showed a continuing interest in the introduction of new technology. In 1575 it licensed a new process for the manufacture of soap.[41] It supported the attempt of the ex-mariner Etienne de L'Escot and others to perfect new furnaces which would economize on the consumption of wood as a fuel.[42] Moreover, it backed the attempts of L'Escot's associate, François des Troyes, to develop L'Escot's other devices, engines and inventions to process mineral ore, mill grain and build bridges.[43] In October 1581 it granted Nicolas Cheville of Besançon the right to construct furnaces he had designed at various sites in the kingdom on payment of 10 *écus* per furnace.[44]

It was Catherine de Medici, according to Laffemas, who played an outstanding role in encouraging the development of industry in the troubled reign of Henri III.[45] It was the Queen-Mother who promoted the production of lace at Moulins and the manufacture of satin in the style of Genoa at Paris. In a letter to the city fathers of Orléans, she urged them to attract foreign entrepreneurs and technicians, to subsidize those who came and to exempt the enterprises which they established from taxation. Not only were such enterprises useful in themselves, they were particularly helpful in providing work for the large numbers of the otherwise unemployed poor.[46]

At the Assembly of Saint-Germain-en-Laye (1583), the king himself envisaged various means of stimulating the economy, above all through the encouragement of the textile industry. It was indispensable in this respect to prohibit the export of raw silk, linen, canvas and wool. It was likewise necessary to prohibit the import of finished cloth. Because of commercial agreements, it was impossible to prohibit the import of English cloth. On the other hand, it would be possible to fix its price so low that merchants would be discouraged from importing it. The king agreed to consider the cancellation of the newly introduced sol/*livre* tax on cloth which had caused the closure of many enterprises and the migration of workers abroad. The importation of raw materials, notably raw silk, wool, linen, canvas and indigo, was to be promoted. Likewise, the immigration of foreign craftsmen, especially Italians, who would help to bring French industry up to date, was to be encouraged.[47]

In the wake of the Assembly of Saint-Germain, Henri III issued letters-patent in favour of those inventors or entrepreneurs who were prepared to apply water

---

[40] Gille, *Les origines de la grande métallurgie*, pp. 11, 17; John U. Nef, 'A Comparison of Industrial Growth in France and England from 1540 to 1640', *Journal of Political Economy* 44 (1936), 518–19.

[41] AN Coll. Lenain MS. 63, fo. 807.

[42] Ernest-Jules-Frédéric Lamé Fleury, *De la législation minérale sous l'ancienne monarchie* (Paris, 1857), p. 64; AN Coll. Lenain, MS 63, fo. 107.

[43] BN MS Fr. 16444, fos.108r.–109v; BN MS Fr. 21225, fo. 286 r.–v.

[44] BN MS Fr. 21225, fo. 177v.

[45] Laffemas, *Lettres de feu la reine mère*, p. 3.

[46] Ibid., pp. 15–36.

[47] *Articles et propositions lesquelles le roy a voulu estre deliberées par les princes et officiers de son conseil, qui se sont trouvez en l'assemblée pour ce faicte à Saint-Germain-en-Laye au mois de novembre, mil cinq cens quatre vingts et trois* (1583), BN Ll³⁴220; Aline Karcher, 'L'assemblé des notables de Saint-Germain-en-Laye, 1583', *Bibliothèque de l'école des chartes* 114 (1956), 151.

power to the development of industry.[48] The king's privilege called for the use of water power to create grain mills, fulling mills, tanneries, gunpowder mills, paper mills, saw-mills and to operate the bellows and hammers of forges for the reduction of all kinds of ores. The royal letters speak of experiments with devices to carry or lift weights more effectively, of fuel-efficient furnaces used in breweries and by fullers, and of machines based on perpetual motion which could be used for an infinitude of good purposes.

An attempt was launched to supply Paris with water. Exclusive rights were granted to Nicolas Wasser Hun, Jehan Desponde and Paul La Treille to use engines for the raising of water and the working of various mills. The patentees proposed taking the water from a canal which tapped the Seine, probably located above the city.[49]

RAMELLI'S INVENTIONS

The privilege mentioned above celebrates the fact that foreign engineers had been attracted into the kingdom. Of these, the most outstanding was Agostino Ramelli, whose *Le diverse e artificiose machine*, dedicated to Henri III, was published in French and Italian in Paris in 1588. It proved to be the only serious sixteenth-century rival of Jacques Besson's *Théâtre des instrumens mathématiques et mechaniques*. The relative lack of interest in military technology in Ramelli is striking given his background as a military engineer. Unlike other works on technology published during the religious wars, such as Errard's *Le premier livre des instruments mathématiques mechaniques* or Boillot's *Modeles, artifices de feu et divers instrumens de guerre*, its concern with military inventions and technology is secondary. Of its 195 illustrations only thirty-four are devoted to military devices. Such a lack of interest lends support to the notion that Ramelli's work, like Besson's, aspired to promote the use of technology to bolster the French economy. Given Henri III's patronage of Ramelli, it is highly likely that this was the aspiration of the king himself.

Ramelli was born at Maranza in the Duchy of Milan about 1521. At school he excelled at natural philosophy and mathematics. He then entered the military under the warlord, the marquis de Marignano Giacomo de' Medici, attaining the rank of captain in the course of the campaigns of Charles V. Following the death of his patron, he entered the service of the duke of Anjou. He was wounded and taken prisoner by the Huguenots at the siege of La Rochelle. His son was looked after and his ransom paid by Anjou. When Anjou went to Poland as king, he kept in touch with his engineer, writing him frequent personal letters. When Anjou ascended the French throne as Henri III, he conferred a generous life pension on him. Ramelli died in Paris in 1590.[50]

The 195 devices in Ramelli's work are distributed as follows:[51]

---

[48] *Lettres de privilege du roy pour l'elevation des eaues et autres belles et utiles inventions* (Paris, 1585), BN F.46879 (3).
[49] Parsons, *Engineers and Engineering*, p. 47.
[50] Ibid., pp. 108–9.
[51] Ramelli, *The Various and Ingenious Machines*, p. 27.

Classification of devices

	Total number	Description	Prime movers	Plates
Water-raising devices	110	62 piston pumps 10 rotary pumps 17 ordinary well buckets 21 other devices	54 by manpower 55 by water-power 1 by wind-power	1–110
Grain mills	21	20 with conventional millstones 1 portable iron mill	9 by manpower 3 by horsepower 7 by water-power 2 by wind-power	113–33
Other mills	4	2 stone saw-mills 1 timber saw-mill 1 forge hearth	1 by horsepower 3 by water-power	134–7
Cranes	10		10 by manpower	168–77
Machines for dragging heavy objects	7	6 for columns and monoliths 1 for artillery	6 by manpower 1 by horsepower	178–83, 189
Machines for raising excavated earth	2		1 by manpower 1 by horsepower	138–9
Coffer-dams	2			111–12
Fountains and bird calls	4	3 automatic fountains 1 with hidden operator		184–7
Book wheel	1			188
Military bridges	15		12 by manpower 3 by horsepower	140–53, 195
Military screwjacks and breaking devices	14		14 by manpower	154–67
Military hurling engines	4		4 by manpower	190–3
Gunner's quadrant	1			194
Totals	195		110 by manpower (58%) 9 by horsepower (5%) 65 by water-power (35%) 3 by wind-power (2%)	

Plate V   Revolving bookcase, Agostino Ramelli, *Le diverse e artificiosie machine*
(Paris, 1588).

Plate VI Treadmill, Agostino Ramelli, *Le diverse e artificiosie machine* (Paris, 1588).

Among the devices of Ramelli's own inventions were the horizontal vertical treadwell, the bellows pump, the sliding vane rotary pump, the gated lobe rotary pumps, the epicyclic gear train and, perhaps, the oscillating wing pump.[52] The importance of water as a source of power is notable. Some 35 per cent of Ramelli's devices were powered by water, while only 2 per cent were based on wind-power. The attention devoted to pumps and water-mills simply reflects the importance of water for urban life, manufacturing and agriculture. But what is especially striking is that 58 per cent of Ramelli's devices are founded on the more efficient exploitation of human labour.

Ramelli's revolving bookcase (Plate v) represents a notable application of epicyclical gearing to a practical if somewhat fanciful device. Ramelli probably learned the principle of this type of gearing from clock making.[53] This invention, alongside the scores of other mills and pumps in his work, reflects the aspiration of a new kind of Renaissance intellectual to technical mastery over the world. In striking contrast stands Ramelli's engraving of a worker on a treadmill (Plate vi): his perpetual brute effort supplies the power to the machine, while he remains for ever a prisoner of its demands. A more vivid contrast between those who aspired to control the new world which was developing and those who were being reduced to being its slaves is difficult to imagine.

Under the League, Paris experienced its most difficult period of the century. But even then the city was not without its innovations. New large paving-stones were installed as an experiment in the rue Planche-Mibray, rue de la Juiverie and rue de la Lanterne. The contractor who undertook this installation proposed to pave the whole city with this new kind of pavement which he promised would save the city enormously in maintenance. A century later Parisians still referred to it as 'the pavement of the League'.[54]

Pierre Dupont, who was to be enormously successful under Henri IV manufacturing Turkish and Persian carpets, traced his success to the time of the League. During that period of suffering and misfortune, he was later to recall, he sought to busy himself by experimenting with the manufacture of all kinds of tapestry and carpeting. It was during this period that he discovered his highly successful method for manufacturing Turkish and Persian carpets.[55]

We have seen that the mining industry began to run into difficulty in the 1550s. Charles IX did what he could to try to resuscitate it. That this effort had a certain success is reflected in the fact that there were at least ten mines being actively worked in the Lyonnais in the 1570s, including at least six

---

[52] Ibid., pp. 573–5.
[53] Bert S. Hill, 'A Revolving Bookcase by Agostino Ramelli', *Technology and Culture* 11 (1970), 389–400.
[54] Henri Sauval, *Histoire et recherches des antiquites de la ville de Paris* (Paris, 1724; Farnborough, 1969), I, 185.
[55] *La stromatourgie*, ed. Alfred Darcel and Jules Guiffrey (Paris, 1882), p. 36.

silver-mines and a gold-mine.[56] Later in the decade, the new King Henri III actively supported the efforts of L'Escot to revive the mining and processing industry. These efforts included the introduction of new machinery for mining and processing ores as well as the undertaking of a survey of mines throughout the kingdom.[57]

In 1579 the community of Chitry in the Nivernais received a royal privilege to exploit the silver ore discovered in its vicinity.[58] At that time, François Garrault, *trésorier de l'épargne* and controller general in the Cours des monnaies, published an interesting memoir on Chitry and the French mining industry.[59] Notable in Garrault's account is his generally positive view of France's economic position, especially with respect to the Iberian peninsula. He admits that real mineral wealth is to be found more outside than within France's borders. However, he points out that through its commerce France is able to attract bullion from the Iberian peninsula owing to Spain's need for French exports with which it cannot dispense.[60] Thus, France is able to feed and clothe itself from what it produces, while at the same time it is able to obtain bullion to carry on its commercial activities.[61] The ability of France to supply itself with all its needs, according to Garrault, is called by some France's 'inexhaustible mines'. They renew themselves every year, while those of silver and gold such as Spain's exhaust themselves.[62]

ECONOMIC RESTRUCTURING

Indeed, the natural wealth of France is what impressed contemporaries. The unqualified abundance with which nature had endowed France helps to explain the apparent signs of prosperity in the countryside in the midst of the civil wars. Certainly, this was the essential feature of the account of the Venetian ambassador Friuli in 1582. According to him, the natural wealth of France was never more evident than during the wars. The kingdom of France was so inherently rich that war simply did not have the same impact on it as it did on other countries. Notwithstanding the ravages of the armies passing to and fro across the landscape, not a corner of the kingdom had been left uncultivated in a single year. Despite their destructiveness, argues Friuli, armies have had difficulties ruining the regions they have traversed. Soldiers who have moved into regions in the wake of other armies have found fresh resources to exploit. Not only does the kingdom

---

[56] Nicolay, *Description générale de la ville de Lyon*, pp. 210–11.
[57] Fleury, *De la législation minérale*, pp. 63–5.
[58] Boissonade, *Le socialisme d'etat*, p. 69.
[59] Garrault, *Des mines d'argent trouvée en France, ouvrage et police d'icelles* (Paris, 1579); see also P. Faure, 'François Garrault', *DBF* xv, 554–5.
[60] Garrault, *Des mines*, fo. sig. C iv v.
[61] Ibid., fo. sig. D r.
[62] Ibid.

provide the king with 10 million *livres* a year, its resources are enough to supply the needs of local governors and the extortions of the soldiers as well.[63]

There is evidently considerable truth in this view which stressed the natural bounty of the kingdom in explaining its economic resilience. More to the point in explaining the strength of certain sectors like the manufacture of canvas or the production of ironware, is to stress the importance of exports and foreign trade. While the internal market withered, the centres of export like Marseilles, La Rochelle, Saint-Malo and Rouen retained a certain economic vitality. Exports of French wine, salt, canvas, linen, books, paper, cloth and ironware to Spain, the Levant and to the Baltic were critical to maintaining whatever dynamism the French economy retained during the religious wars.

If the period as a whole was marked by economic regression, it is a mistake to see it as marked solely by decline. Economic depressions in capitalist economies do have their creative aspects which cannot be ignored. In certain sectors, difficult restructuring processes entailing considerable human cost went on, which nevertheless helped to make those enterprises which were able to endure these changes more viable in the long run. The enterprises which survived these upheavals found themselves in a stronger economic position at the end of them. The printing industry in Paris is a good example. The industry had grown spectacularly in the first part of the sixteenth century, based on competition between a large number of firms. But the industry was in serious trouble by the 1560s and early 1570s. However, the crisis of these two decades led to a certain weeding-out process which left eight or ten firms to dominate the entire industry. On this altered basis, the printing industry experienced a renewed period of prosperity between 1575 and 1585.[64]

What is notable about this period is that the prosperity in the industry was quite unevenly distributed. The book dealers at the head of these few powerful firms, whose organization and operations were international in scope and involved trading in books as well as other merchandise, prospered.[65] The printers, to whom the book dealers put out the production of books, did less well. The book dealers demanded that the books produced be relatively cheap, free of typographical errors and rapidly produced. But the printers found that their profit margins were squeezed by higher material costs, wages and taxes.[66] At the end of the religious wars, a great many of the printers, small book dealers, binders and journeymen in the industry found themselves in precarious circumstances.[67]

The situation in the printing industry thus highlights an important feature of

---

[63] Fagniez, *L'économie sociale*, p. 8.
[64] Denis Pallier, *Recherches sur l'imprimerie à Paris pendant la Ligue, 1585–1594* (Geneva, 1975), p. 9. A comparable rationalization occurred in iron manufacturing. See Belhoste, 'Une silviculture pour les forges: xvie–xixe siècles' in *Forges et forêts*, ed. Woronoff, p. 231.
[65] Pallier, *Recherches sur l'imprimerie*, pp. 22–3.
[66] Ibid., p. 29.
[67] Ibid.

the French economy during the wars of religion. The prosperity of some of the merchants of Paris, La Rochelle or Marseilles coexisted with the continuing erosion of the living standards of craftsmen, skilled and unskilled workers. Whatever economic growth there was tended to come at the expense of the small producers and wage-earners. Moreover, when money could not be made through commerce, merchants turned to loaning money, to purchasing land or to buying offices.[68]

MONTAIGNE AND TECHNOLOGY

But the buoyancy of certain sectors of the economy can be understood in another way as well. The period of the religious wars accelerated certain profound changes that were taking place in French society at that time. We can begin to appreciate what those changes were by returning to our discussion of the widespread interest in technology which characterized the later half of the sixteenth century. Montaigne, curiously, can serve as our point of departure in this discussion. Montaigne's *Essais* are of course for the most part 'philosophical' discussions, i.e., concerned with the perennial questions of the life of humankind in relation to the eternal truths of the natural order. They have little or nothing to say about matters technical or 'mechanical'. Such questions, however, are at the forefront of Montaigne's *Journals*. Only the state of his own health, the nature of his therapy and matters of religion occupy more space in this private record of his journey through France, Switzerland and Italy.[69]

Montaigne, like Besson and Ramelli, was especially interested in hydraulic technology – mills, pumps, fountains and canals.[70] In Constance, he described a huge water-mill equipped with twelve or fifteen wheels, which raised a massive quantity of water some 50 feet high. The mill dumped the water into a man-made canal which fed a large number of industrial mills in the city. What particularly seemed to impress Montaigne was that this gigantic mechanism which did so much work was run by a single millwright who had an annual salary of 5,700 florins and his wine in addition.[71]

In Sciaffusa, he remarked on a device made of iron, by means of which heavy stones could be moved without the use of human labour.[72] In Basle, he noted the superior quality of the work of the ironmasters. He observed that the roasting spits in most of the houses in the town operated by means of springs or weights,

[68] BN MS Fr. 18780, fos. 4r.–5v.
[69] G.G. Ellerbroek, 'Montaigne et les applications de la technique', *Neophilologus* 28 (1943), 1–6; Line Pertile, 'Montaigne in Italia: arte, technica e scienza dal *journal* agli *Essais*', *Saggi e ricerche di letteratura* 13 (1973), 49–92.
[70] Ellerbroek, 'Montaigne et les applications de la technique', pp. 2–4; Pertile, 'Montaigne in Italia,' p. 60.
[71] Pertile, 'Montaigne in Italia', pp. 60–1.
[72] Ibid., p. 69.

like clockworks. Some spits also worked by means of a windmill-like device on their chimneys which was turned by the draught of the fire in the chimney, causing the spit itself to revolve.[73] In Florence, he visited the workshops of the silk manufacturers and noted how a spinning-machine operated by a single woman could make fifty spindles turn at the same time.[74] Once again, it was the enormous economy of labour effected by the machine which amazed Montaigne.

Throughout his journey to Switzerland and Italy, Montaigne commented on the number and character of the clocks that he saw, especially compared to those in France. In this respect, he noted the superiority of the towns in Switzerland. The town clock seems to have symbolized to Montaigne the overall level of mechanical capacity and level of material well-being of a country.[75] Throughout the regions he visited, he did not fail to notice the quality of craftsmanship, especially in iron, glass, lead and clay.[76] Magistrate that he was, he showed a great interest in examining public works of all kinds, including bridges, roadways, gardens, canals, public squares, and fountains. Overall, he esteemed the accomplishments of the Swiss most highly.[77]

With respect to the city of Rome, he noted the general absence of cultivated land in and about the city. He attributed it to the overall absence of rural and unskilled workers in the region. On his way to Rome from Ostia, he encountered several troops of migrant workers who he learned migrated annually all the way from Savoy and the Grisons to work in the vineyards and gardens around the city. They earned enough, so these migrant workers explained to him, to be able to pay the rent on their land back at home. The shortage of manpower in Rome was certainly not due to an insufficient population, but to an unwillingness of even the lower classes to do any kind of heavy manual labour. The source of this attitude, according to Montaigne, was the domination of the city by the nobility and the papal court. Above all, he concluded, the population of the whole city was affected by the reluctance of the clergy to work. According to him, there existed in the city no real market street like the rue de la Harpe or rue St Denis in Paris. The activity of the city was no different, no matter what day of the week it was. Thus, during the whole of Lent, people spent their days carrying out the stations of the Cross. The streets were as crowded with worshippers on work-days as on holy days. One saw coaches, ecclesiastics and ladies in the streets rather than merchants, craftsmen and workers.[78]

Montaigne's positive attitude towards work, his hostility towards clerical idleness and his interest in technology have been attributed to the bourgeois roots of his family, to his Marrano connections and to his Calvinist relatives, whose

---

[73] Ibid.
[74] Ibid., p. 70.
[75] Ibid., pp. 71–2.
[76] Ibid., p. 74.
[77] Ibid., p. 73.
[78] Ibid., pp. 75–6.

attitudes presumably influenced him.[79] None of these explanations should be lightly dismissed. But with respect to his interest in work and technology, the management of his own estates ought also to be considered. In Book Three, chapter XII of the *Essais*, Montaigne recalls a devastating plague in Guyenne which carried off, it was said, at least 14,000 people.[80] As a result of the terrible mortality, he says, grapes lay idle on the vine. In his neighbourhood, most of the population was carried away by the plague. This was all the more serious as 'in this place my best income is derived from manual labour. The work of a hundred men produces a profit which lasts a long while.'[81] The employment of wage labour on a considerable scale was the norm in a wine-growing region like the Bordelais. Montaigne's interest in technology was no doubt fed by a growing consciousness of the availability of this kind of labour. The use of wage labour was in itself profitable. The employment of such labour, which could be made more productive, or more profitable, by the use of machinery, as in the case of the millwright of Constance, or the Florentine silk spinner, was even more attractive.

The religious wars, to be sure, were a period of religious conflict and of aristocratic reaction. But despite their apparently archaic character, these wars were also, as we shall see, a period of major advance for both the rural and the urban bourgeoisie. The form of this advance was that of the acquisition of large amounts of land transferred to them from the nobility, the Church and, above all, from the less well-off peasantry. The acquisition of this land and its inclusion in the circuits of market exchange, as well as the growing availability of wage labour in the form of the work of expropriated peasants, redounded to the benefit of this bourgeoisie.

BODIN AND WAGE LABOUR

The growth of wage labour during the religious wars is apparent in the writings of Bodin as well as Montaigne. Bodin's attempt to come to grips with this phenomenon is manifest as a sub-theme in his celebrated discussion of slavery. In the first book of his *Six Books on the Commonwealth*, Bodin devoted a large section to the history of slavery in the Ancient world, to the rights and wrongs of servitude, to its gradual disappearance in the middle ages, and to its recent revival by the Portuguese and Spaniards, especially in the New World.[82] Bodin, however, is at pains to demonstrate that slavery disappeared from France in the late thirteenth century.

Despite vestiges of servitude in the French kingdom, Bodin observed that it

[79] Ibid., p. 77.
[80] Montaigne is referring to the plague of 1586. See Géralde Nakam, *Les Essais de Montaigne, miroir et procès de leurs temps: témoignage historique et création littéraire* (Paris, 1984), pp. 84–5. See also Jean-Noel Biraben, *Les hommes et la peste en France et dans les pays européens et méditerranéens* (Paris, La Haye, 1975), I, 385.
[81] Montaigne, *Œuvres complètes*, ed. Maurice Rat (Paris, 1962), p. 1025.
[82] *The Six Books of a Commonweale*, ed. McRae, pp. 32–41.

was generally abhorred by the French population. He noted, furthermore, that, whereas the French courts were prepared to recognize payments in labour which were the vestiges of personal servitude, magistrates were not willing to admit the legality of personal servitude itself. Thus he recalled that the Parlement of Toulouse had refused the right of a seigneur to force tenants to return to his estates which they had moved off, while admitting that the seigneur had the right to all kinds of labour services from those of his tenants who remained on the land.[83]

But far from assuming that slavery was continuing to lose ground in his own lifetime, Bodin believed that it was in fact on the march once again. Not only was slavery gaining ground in the New World but it was advancing even in Europe. Nevertheless, he regarded its progress with distaste, and showed himself to be quite hostile to its being accepted once again in France. Slavery, according to Bodin, was in the final analysis an attack on natural human dignity, an affront to reason and a threat to political and social order. As to the argument that slavery, or the threat of enslavement, would forestall or drive away debtors, thieves and the poor in general, who were the source of many contemporary problems, Bodin answered in a curiously modern fashion. According to him, the best solution to such evils was not the imposition of perpetual servitude, but the institution of proper vocational training for poor children, as was done in Paris, Lyons and Venice.[84]

Bodin thus appears to take a stand in favour of free labour in the first book of his work. Moreover, his discussion of the subject remained substantially unchanged through the successive French editions of the work. But in the Latin edition of 1586, Bodin breaks new ground by adding an eighth chapter to Book I.[85] There he takes up the subject of slavery once again in an apparent effort to take recent developments into account.

What he is concerned to argue in this new chapter is that, contrary to the views of the Greeks and the Romans of Antiquity, slaves ought to be considered citizens of the commonwealth. He hastens to add that he is not in fact advocating the restoration of slavery in France, from which it had disappeared. But, in an apparent reference to the religious wars going on around him, he notes that 'as the force and boldness of men is so far broken out, as that we see servitude and slavery by little and little to creep in, and to return again'.[86] In other words, as a result of the wars, men are once again being forced into servitude. Bodin believed that such men should continue to be regarded as citizens.

But what kind of servitude or slavery did Bodin have in mind? He was preoccupied by the question of the political rights of those citizens of the

83 Ibid., p. 42.
84 Ibid., pp. 45–6.
85 Ibid., p. A 129.
86 Ibid., p. 388.

commonwealth who fell into a condition of servitude or slavery. No doubt during the civil wars the nobility was trying to revive all sorts of feudal customs and seigneurial exactions as tokens of personal servitude. Bodin thus appears to be referring in part to preserving the political rights of those threatened by the revival of traditional forms of servitude. But, in this context, it is clear that Bodin also had in mind a new kind of servitude, namely, that arising from wage labour.

Bodin attempted to demonstrate that wage labour, especially apparent in agriculture, was in fact a new kind of servitude. In his view it was axiomatic that all those in base or mechanical occupations involving manual labour ought to be excluded from participating in government, while still being considered citizens.[87] He admitted that in ancient times, especially during the Roman Republic, agriculturalists had participated in the government of the state. He allowed, following the early Roman writers, that husbandry and pasturage indeed became a free-born man. Agriculture would therefore be ennobling, were it not for the fact that 'these most notable arts, in servile manner [are] continuously let out onto base men for wages hired. Now we have said those arts to be accounted base whose wages is the earnest penie of their slaverie.'[88] Accordingly, such men involved in wage labour ought not to be included in government. On the other hand, Bodin was anxious to preserve the rights of such individuals to citizenship in the commonwealth.

Bodin seems to extend the notion of slavery here to those who work for wages as well as those in other kinds of personal servitude. In doing so he is simply reflecting the growing prevalence of wage labour in the rural economy which was developing in the midst of the religious wars. Indeed, his remark about the gradual return of slavery during the wars, probably refers not only to the attempted revival of older forms of servitude but to the growing importance of wage labour as well. Bodin wishes to exclude such men from government. On the other hand, he is anxious to continue to regard men who fall into the category of wage labourers as citizens of the commonwealth, since they live in the midst of it and are clearly part of it.

EXPROPRIATION AND PRIMITIVE ACCUMULATION

During the religious wars the process of peasant expropriation which had begun in the first part of the sixteenth century accelerated. The partial or complete loss of land experienced by producers, which continued into the first part of the seventeenth century, entailed a growing dependence on wage labour. Daniel

---

[87] Ibid., p. 397.
[88] Ibid., p. 401. Charron follows Bodin's discussion of slavery closely. Referring to the development of wage labour, he notes that the growth of poverty has led to the appearance of what he describes as voluntary slavery in which the poor freely place themselves in servitude in exchange for food and security. See *Œuvres* (Paris, 1635; Geneva, 1970), I, 171.

Hickey's study of the duchy of Valentinois-Diois clearly reflects this process of expropriation.[89] The holdings of wealthy merchants, officials and nobles of commoner lands were already considerable in this region prior to 1560. The wars of religion led to a dramatic acceleration of the concentration of property into the hands of this elite at the expense of the major part of the peasantry. Pillaging, taxation and debt forced a sell-off of land by the least well-off of the peasantry to those with capital.[90]

In Poitou, the nobles and bourgeoisie – the latter including merchants and notables from the towns, but also rich peasants – bought up more and more land at the expense of the small and middle peasants. During the civil wars *metayage* and the rate of turnover in *métairies* increased notably.[91] The number of day labourers and wage workers grew as well.[92]

Increasing concentration of land ownership was accompanied by growing proletarianization. Jonathan Dewald has studied these trends as complementary phenomena in his work on the seigneurie of Pont-Saint-Pierre in Normandy.[93] For the history of landholding he focuses on the large agricultural village of la Neuville-Chant-d'Oisel, where most of the arable land in the seigneurie was to be found. Dewald found that the tendency towards an increasing concentration of ownership was virtually continuous from the late fourteenth century until the Revolution. But the critical point in the process came in the late sixteenth and early seventeenth centuries. The previous two hundred years had seen a gradual and steady erosion of the small landowner's situation. Between 1587 and 1635 the process accelerated dramatically. In this half century, from the Catholic League to the French entry into the Thirty Years War, the leading 5 per cent of the village landowners increased their share of the land by nearly 70 per cent. The share of the middle group of the village landowners fell by about 50 per cent, from nearly a quarter of the arable land to only 12 per cent. The pattern of land holding established during this period remained unchanged until the end of the Old Regime.[94] Such a process inevitably led to an increased dependence on wage labour. Thus, as late as 1587 the lowest 25 per cent of landowners owned 38 per cent of the arable land. By 1600 they controlled only 1.3 per cent. By 1635 16.4 per cent of the property owners of la Neuville owned only a house and garden.[95] Such people would have had to resort to wage labour in order to eke out a living.

One of the most striking expressions of this process of bourgeois appropriation

89 Hickey, 'The Socio-Economic Context of the French Wars of Religion. A Case Study: Valentinois-Diois' (McGill University, Ph.D. Dissertation, 1973).
90 Ibid., pp. 144, 147.
91 Léon Merle, *La métairie et l'évolution agraire de la Gâtine poitevine de la fin du moyen âge à la Révolution* (Paris, 1958), pp. 70–1, 91.
92 Boissonade, *Histoire de Poitou* (Paris, 1925), p. 183.
93 *Pont-St.-Pierre, 1398–1798: Lordship, Community and Capitalism in Early Modern France* (Berkeley, 1987).
94 Ibid., p. 56.
95 Ibid., pp. 54–6.

of the land was the sudden spurt of interest during the religious wars in the art of measurement and in devices for measuring and surveying. Foulon's discussion of the *holomètre*, Besson's on the cosmolabe and Oronce Finé's on the geometric square were among the first such treatises in the vernacular.[96] In 1572 Toussaints de Bessard published a description of his *canomètre*.[97] Jean de Merliers followed with his text on the geometric square.[98] Elie Vinet published his work on land surveying and quadrants in the late 1570s and 1580s.[99] This was followed by Jacques Chauvet's book on measurement, which contained a description of his *cosmomètre*.[100] Nor should we forget the optical compass of Miles Denorry,[101] the first volume of Errard's *Geometrie* (Paris, 1594),[102] and Philippe Danfrie's *Declaration de l'usage du graphomètre*.[103] Last but not least we should take note of Henry de Suberville's *L'Henrymètre instrument royale et universel*, named in honour of the new king.[104] Suberville lists most of these measuring instruments, as well as those invented by the Ancients, declaring that the *Henrymètre*, his own invention, surpassed them all.[105] Obviously such devices were used for navigational, military and engineering purposes. But the proliferation of these new instruments coincidentally with extensive land acquisition by the bourgeoisie suggests their widespread use as well in the surveying of freshly appropriated land.

In the Ile-de-France, according to Jacquart, the years of war saw an intensification of the trends already manifest in the first part of the sixteenth century. Rural notaries and lawyers, together with rich peasants, appear to have benefited from the crisis by loaning money, marketing grain and livestock, and serving as rent collectors of both tithe and rent.[106] But these gains by the rural bourgeoisie were put in the shade by the windfalls enjoyed by the Parisian elites. Through speculation and money-lending, the merchants and notables of the city made extraordinary gains, especially between 1575 and 1585.[107] At the same time, the transfer of land from the peasantry, but also from the nobility and Church, into

---

[96] Finé, *La composition et usage du quarré géometrique* (Paris, 1556).

[97] *L'aigle-compas* (Paris, 1572).

[98] Jean de Merliers, *L'usage du quarré géométrique amplement descrit et demonstré* (Paris, 1573).

[99] Following the edition of 1577 Vinet published *L'arpenterie et la maniere de fere les solaires que communement on apele quadrans* (Bordeaux, 1583).

[100] Jacques Chauvet, *Instruction et usage du cosmomètre, ou instrument universel pour les dimensions, tant géometriques que optiques, astronomiques et géographiques* (Paris, 1585); Chauvet, *La pratique universelle de l'arpenterie ... contenant l'explication de parfaictement mesurer, arpenter, toiser, aulner et prendre le plant de la superficie de tous corps et figures de telles formes qu'ils soient* (Paris, 1585).

[101] Miles Denorry, *L'usage de compas optique* (Paris, 1588).

[102] Jean Errard, *La géometrie et la pratique générale d'icelle* (Paris, 1594).

[103] Philippe Danfrie, *Declaration de l'usage du graphomètre, par la pratique duquel l'on peut mesurer toutes distances ... et pour arpenter terres, bois, prez, et faire plans de villes et fortresses, cartes géographiques* (Paris, 1597).

[104] *L'Henrymètre* (Paris, 1598).

[105] Ibid., fo. sig. a iir.

[106] Jacquart, *La crise rurale en Ile-de-France*, pp. 234–40.

[107] Ibid., pp. 241–2.

the hands of the urban bourgeoisie continued at an accelerated pace.[108] Jacquart's findings are amplified by a number of local studies of the Hurepoix and the Brie.[109] The religious wars saw a massive expropriation of peasant property in favour of the bourgeoisie. It is notable that the exodus of the poor towards Paris was slowed where rural industry had implanted itself.[110]

Jacquart, in fact, finds the transfer of land towards the bourgeoisie during the wars of religion in the Ile-de-France to be comparable to that which occurred during the French Revolution.[111] Summing up this transfer of land from the peasantry to the bourgeoisie on a national level, Jacquart notes 'that the great wave of appropriation of the soil by the bourgeoisie took place between 1530 and 1600. Afterwards there ensued a continuation and consolidation of a hold which has never since been brought into question despite political, economic and social revolutions.'[112] As to the effects of this appropriation on the peasantry, Jacquart notes that at the end of the process it was left on average with 50 per cent of the soil and in some places with as little as one-third.[113] Moreover, this decline in the amount of land available to the rural producer was intensified by the continuing subdivision of the land into smaller and smaller units. To quote Jacquart once again: 'one can affirm that from the seventeenth century onwards three-quarters of the French peasantry were not able to exploit enough land to reach let alone to approach what we today call the vital minimum'.[114]

France, in contrast to England, continues to be viewed by historians as the land of the small producer. The peasant in France supposedly escaped the ravages of the enclosure movement to which the English peasant was subject. But Jack Goldstone, comparing the agrarian history of the two countries, argues that this idyllic view of the history of the French rural population is largely a myth. As he

---

[108] Ibid., pp. 240–2.

[109] Omer Tulippe, *L'habitat rurale dans l'ouest du département de Oise: essai de géographie du peuplement* (Liège, 1934), pp. 61–128, 149–51, 179–80; Frédéric-Auguste Denis, *Lectures sur l'histoire de l'agriculture dans le département de Seine-et-Marne* (Meaux, 1881); Emile Mireaux, *Une province française au temps du grand roi. La Brie* (Paris, 1958); Gombert-Alexandre Rethoré, *Recherches historiques sur Jouarre et ses environs. La Commanderie de Bibartaut et ses environs* (Meaux, 1877); Rethoré, *Recherches historiques sur Jouarre et ses environs. Territoire de Jouarre* (Meaux, 1895); Rethoré, *Histoire de Saint-Cyr-sur-Morin et des hameaux environnants compris dans la censive de l'abbaye de Jouarre* (Paris, 1896).

[110] Tulippe, *L'habitat rurale*, p. 149.

[111] Jacquart, *La crise rurale en Ile-de-France*, p. 247. On the social aspirations of the rural bourgeoisie of the Ile-de-France see Jean-Marie Moriceau, 'Le laboureur et ses enfants. Formation professionnelle et mobilité sociale en Ile-de-France (second moitié du XVIe siècle)', *Revue d'histoire moderne et contemporaine* 40 (1993), 353–86.

[112] *Histoire de la France rurale*, ed. Georges Duby and Armand Wallon, II *L'Age classique: 1340–1789*, ed. Hugues Neveux, Jacquart and Le Roy Ladurie (Paris, 1975), p. 274. See Jacquart, 'Les problèmes de la paysannerie française au temps de Henri III' in *Henri III et son temps*, ed. Robert Sauzet (Paris, 1992), pp. 282–3.

[113] *Histoire de la France rurale*, II, ed. Neveux, Jacquart, Le Roy Ladurie, p. 275.

[114] Jacquart, *Paris et l'Ile-de-France au temps des paysans*, p. 34.

points out, the amount of peasant dispossession by 1650 in France and England was more or less comparable.[115]

The period of the civil wars, paradoxically, was thus a period of overall economic decline and increasing social and political power for the bourgeoisie. It was the bourgeoisie who most benefited from the expropriation of part of the peasants' land, the appropriation of their property and its inclusion in the circuits of commercial exchange. The increased dependence of this expropriated peasantry on wages ensured the availability of abundant supplies of cheap labour for agricultural work.

The emergent bourgeoisie that we are speaking about was hardly a homogeneous and unified class. The office-holders, *rentiers* and wealthy merchants who collected capitalist rent were in a state of inherent economic opposition to rich peasants who rented the land from them in order to exploit it for profit. Moreover, the urban elite which got hold of most of the freshly expropriated land lived in a starkly different world from that of well-to-do peasants, rural merchants and notaries. The economic resources, social aspirations and cultural pretensions of the urban rich put them on a social plain far above the more restricted horizons of prosperous peasants and rural merchants and notaries. The latter element lived close to and were often involved in the processes of rural economic production. Indeed, urban economic domination and cultural snobbery, inequitable assessment of taxes and high-handed execution of justice on the countryside by city office-holders and lawyers sharpened the antagonism between the two groups. Those who increasingly lived off capitalist rent behaved in a way which was quite different from that of those who made most of their living from profits realized in the marketplace. On the other hand, the two groups were united inasmuch as the development of this new kind of rent, like the growth of profit, depended on the same process of progressive expropriation of the land, denial of access to it and consequent appropriation of the fruits of the work of the rural poor through the expansion of the system of wage labour.

This process, from which those who owned or rented land benefited, can best be described as one of primitive accumulation. By primitive accumulation I refer to the process sketched by Marx at the end of the first volume of *Capital*.[116] It is through this process of primitive or original accumulation that Marx endeavoured to explain the constitution of the bourgeoisie as a class and the initiation of the process of capitalist accumulation. In order to do so, he outlined by way of example the course of the seizure of the means of production and the expropriation of the peasantry by the English middle class in the sixteenth and seventeenth

---

[115] Jack A. Goldstone, 'Regional Ecology and Agrarian Development in England and France', *Politics and Society* 16 (1988), 312.

[116] *Capital*, ed. and tr. Ben Fowkes (New York, 1977), I, 876–95. See Michael Perelman, *Classical Political Economy: Primitive Accumulation and the Social Division of Labour* (London, 1983), pp. 6–59; Ross Thomson, 'Primitive Capitalist Accumulation' in *The New Palgrave: A Dictionary of Economics*, ed. John Eatwell, Murray Milgate and Peter Newman (London, 1987), III, 963–6.

century. The separation of producers from the means of production was crucial to this process. The land seized became a form of capital which could then be valorized by the growing use of wage labour extracted from an expropriated and subordinated rural population. Without the separation of the peasantry from the land, its exploitation as capital is unthinkable. The result of this process is the expansion of the role of profit in the economy and the emergence of a substantial class of rural capitalists. It is through this essentially coercive process that a capitalist class in England consolidated itself. But in fact, primitive accumulation was a phenomenon not confined to England, but one which affected much of Western Europe during this period and has proved a continuing and world-wide historical process. In the case of France it would seem the religious wars played an important part in the process of primitive accumulation. The apparently senseless violence of the period thus contained a surprising core of economic logic within it.

The French economy then, declined dramatically during the wars of religion. But despite its material losses, the middle class was greatly strengthened by restructuring processes that attended these wars. These processes and their strengthening effect on the middle class help to explain the political pugnacious-ness of the bourgeoisie throughout the period of the civil wars, as expressed in the upheavals of the 1570s, the period of the League and the Revolts of the 1590s.[117] Indeed, the strength and organization of rural leagues, notably in Dauphiné, Normandy, Brittany and Guyenne, appear to have been based on the growing weight of a rural bourgeoisie made up of richer peasants and small-town bourgeoisie. At the same time, these protest movements appear to have developed in regions where rural proto-industrialization had taken root.

By the beginning of the seventeenth century, a few rich peasants dominated each village. Most of the peasants owned, or were able to rent, only a small amount of land, often not enough to sustain a family.[118] Inevitably, an increasing fraction of the population was dependent on wages for a livelihood. However, it is important not to exaggerate the degree of dependence on wages. Some peasants still owned land and many more could still manage to lease or sharecrop enough to maintain themselves and their families in partial independence of wages. The spread of the putting-out system, together with seasonal agricultural work, helped to keep most of the population in the countryside in a condition of semi-proletarianization. Moreover, the wars and economic decline which accompanied them, however much they increased and intensified misery, reduced opportunities for wage employment or movement towards full proletarianization. At the same time, such conditions tended to create a growing army of the poor, who were prone to invade the cities as beggars, posing a problem for municipal govern-ments. Complaints against this influx of the poor into Paris grew increasingly loud

---

[117] See Heller, *Iron and Blood: Civil Wars in Sixteenth Century France* (Montreal, 1991).
[118] James B. Collins, *Fiscal Limits of Absolutism: Direct Taxation in Early Seventeenth Century France* (Berkeley, 1987), pp.184–6,189–90.

in the latter half of the sixteenth century. Under fire, the *lieutenant* of the *prévôté* of Paris, Anthoine Seguier, noted that 'the wealth of a good part of France flows into Paris. The poor who cannot get alms where they live flock there to seek out those who have carried off the substance of the countryside.'[119]

RURAL RESISTANCE: STRIKES AND RELIGION

The period of the religious wars saw an intensified resistance to the imposition of wage work on the part of the rural population.[120] In 1566, to the south and east of Paris, the belief spread in the countryside that to honour the Virgin work must stop in the fields at noon on Saturdays. This repose, it was said, had been formally ordered by the Virgin in a series of apparitions. At the centre of the religious excitement was a young woman from Charly-sur-Marne deep in Joan of Arc country.[121] It was she who claimed to have been the recipient of these revelations from the Virgin and who had been able to convince many rustics through various miraculous signs. She was arrested and interrogated by order of the Cardinal of Lorraine, who put an end to the movement by having her burned as a witch and Vaudois.[122] It is noteworthy that the charges against her – heresy and sorcery – were identical to the charges brought against Joan of Arc herself.[123] But more intriguing is the link made by the authorities between the heresy of the Vaudois and the witches' sabbath, a connection which Carlo Ginzburg dates back to the western Alps in the fourteenth century.[124]

This movement to shorten the work-day on Saturday embraced a wide area to the east of Paris, including the *bailliages* of Sens, Melun, Montereau, Bray, Nogent, Pont, Troyes, Sézanne, Châlons, Reims, Epernay, Château-Thierry, Meaux and Provins. The history of this movement is found in the chronicle of Claude Haton, who at the time was vicar of Ormes, a hamlet in the Brie. It is noteworthy that the nineteenth-century editor of Haton's chronicle, Felix Bourquelet, abbreviated Haton's account of these events to a single paragraph on the basis of what he regarded to be its historical insignificance. When we look at the manuscript itself, we find a detailed narrative of five densely packed pages

[119] 'Harangue faitte au roy en l'an 1580 par Maistre Antoine Seguier lorsque l'on vouloit distraire la police de la Prevosté de Paris, luy estant lieutenant civile', BHVP MS CP5168, fo. 3v.

[120] For the comparable case of resistance to the development of wage labour in England see Christopher Hill, 'Pottage for Freeborn Englishmen: Attitudes to Wage Labour in Sixteenth and Seventeenth Century England' in *Socialism, Capitalism and Economic Growth: Essays Presented to Maurice Dobb*, ed. C. Feinstein (London, 1967), pp. 338–50.

[121] For the Joan of Arc legend in the high culture of the sixteenth century see Marina Warner, *Joan of Arc: The Image of Female Heroism* (London, 1981), pp. 198–236.

[122] Haton, *Mémoires*, I, 418.

[123] *Early Modern Witchcraft: Centres and Peripheries*, ed. Bengt Ankarloo and Gustav Henningsen (Oxford, 1990), p. 2.

[124] 'Deciphering the Sabbath' in ibid., p. 132.

written in a compact hand.[125] Haton, in fact, was deeply involved in these events. He represents himself as having been the leading ideological opponent of this dangerous popular rural movement which embraced most of Champagne, Brie and part of the Ile-de-France.

The unrest began shortly before the feast of Saint John among, as Haton describes them, the simple people. Reviving a practice which Haton noted had weakened in recent years, those working for wages refused to plough, harvest, pick grapes or do any other kind of work after midday on Saturday. Resistance spread from village to village and soon embraced the whole region to the east and south of Paris. Those who worked in the fields where there were no clocks estimated the time to leave work by to the position of the sun in the sky. The cessation of work at Saturday noon, cutting short the working week by half a day, was apparently universally followed in the regions affected. This unilateral work stoppage was carried out in the name of the Virgin.

This revival of a Saturday half-day holiday began, according to accounts which reached Haton, following several apparitions of the Virgin. In the course of these miraculous appearances, the Virgin announced that only by stopping work on Saturday afternoons could an end be put to the ravages of the civil wars and the series of bad harvests from which the kingdom was suffering. Haton complained that those who had joined this movement had accepted these commands as articles of faith, from which no one could dissuade them. Indeed, to give what Haton termed this 'error' an air of sanctity, the simple folk were insisting on going to Saturday Vespers in their parish churches, as the Virgin had instructed them. He unhesitatingly stigmatizes the participants in this movement as being members of a sect which he calls the *sabatistes*, with the connotation of sorcery, heresy and Judaizing.[126]

Haton reports that serious investigations were begun by men of substance to determine the identities of those who were reported to have had these revelations from the Virgin. Rustics who were interrogated gave contradictory and conflicting testimony, but were unanimous in their refusal to do Saturday afternoon work. At last a young woman of humble origin from Charly-sur-Marne near Château-Thierry, whom Haton does not bother to identify by name, was found to be the source of these revelations.

As evidence that the Virgin had appeared to her, the young woman pointed out certain extraordinary signs marked on six or seven sheaves of wheat in her possession.[127] Haton claimed that she had set herself up as an authority on matters of faith, commenting in a scandalous way on the dignity of the Mass celebrated by

---

125 BN MS Fr. 11595, fos. 291v.–293v.
126 The links between accusations of sorcery, heresy and Judaizing are explored by Ginzburg, *Ecstasies: Deciphering the Witches' Sabbath* (London, 1991), pp. 63–88.
127 On the relationship of magic ritual to the fertility of crops see Ginzburg, *The Night Battles: Witchcraft and Agrarian Cults in the Sixteenth and Seventeenth Centuries*, tr. John and Ann Tedeschi (Baltimore, 1983), pp. 22–4.

her parish priest. It was reported that she had been able to turn the baptismal water in the village church red. Over the preceding months, she had performed various other miraculous acts as signs of her power. Her magical faculties included the ability to forecast future events. Her extraordinary deeds had become celebrated for a hundred miles in every direction. Crowds began to come to Charly to see and hear her. Haton compares her celebrity to that of the demoniac of Laon, who had caused a sensation all over northern France the same year.[128] On a single day, in mid-August 1566, as many as 2,000 people came to Charly in order to catch a glimpse of her. In September, on the Day of the Nativity of the Virgin, more than 4,000 pilgrims assembled at Charly, where it was reported that she caused the bells in the church to sound by themselves as she had promised that they would. By that time, she had become truly renowned, her prophecies having spread throughout northern France. Huguenots came to interrogate her and came away as confounded as did Catholics.

The arrest and execution of this woman as a witch must give us pause. Haton denounced her followers as *sabatistes*. It seems evident that the taint of sabbath worship is a reference not only to Judaizing but also to the witches' sabbath. Invented in the western Alps in the fourteenth century, the witches' sabbath quickly became associated with both the Vaudois and the Jews.[129] By the beginning of the fifteenth century, certain Jews and Christians in northern Italy, and also in Dauphiné and Comtat-Venaissin, were being accused of establishing and clandestinely spreading new sects and forbidden rituals contrary to the Christian religion.[130] In condemning the young woman of Charly who was accused of trying to sanctify the Sabbath as a Vaudois and witch, it seems plain that the ecclesiastical authorities were associating her with this plot against society.

The history of the origins of this myth of the demonic sabbath has been reconstructed in a remarkable scholarly book by Ginzburg. The really provocative aspect of Ginzburg's work is to argue that there may well have been something to the notion of a witches' sabbath. He notes, for example, the adherence of certain women to the ecstatic cult of the Madonna Oriente in upper Lombardy in the late fourteenth century, or to a similar group which followed the Bona Domina at Bressanone in the mid-fifteenth century. Ginzburg points, furthermore, to the veneration, especially by women, of a powerful female deity known as the Matron, the Teacher, the Greek Mistress, the Wise Sibilla and the Queen of the Fairies in the sixteenth century. He argues that this is evidence of the survival of a real cult, the central element of which was a mysterious and powerful female figure,

---

[128] Henri Weber, 'L'exorcisme à la fin du XVIe siècle, instrument de la contre-Réforme et spectacle baroque', *Nouvelle revue du XVIe siècle* 1 (1983), 79–101; D.P. Walker, *Unclean Spirits: Possession and Exorcism in France and England in the Late Sixteenth and Early Seventeenth Centuries* (Philadelphia, 1981), pp. 19–27.
[129] Ginzburg, *Ecstasies*, p. 79.
[130] Ibid., p. 68.

followed above all by women. Indeed, Ginzburg traces this cult back through the middle ages to the cult of the Mothers of Antiquity.[131]

It is possible that the anonymous young woman of Charly adhered to a Christianized version of this cult. Her invocation of the Virgin, her willingness to criticize the performance of the Mass, her ability to perform acts of magic and to foretell events, the comparison made between her and the ecstatic of Laon, are all suggestive if not conclusive. It is at least conceivable that the upheaval of the civil wars, the division of the elites into Catholic and Huguenot factions, and the traumatic economic changes going on in the countryside may have allowed such a cult to come to the surface and to challenge certain aspects of the established religion.

The execution of this young woman did not put an end to the boycott of Saturday afternoon work on the part of peasant workers. They argued that they were merely returning to ancient practice in refusing such work. In disgust, Haton observed that many parish priests, whether through ignorance or complacency, went along with them. At this point, he claimed, more rustics were going to Saturday Vespers than were attending Sunday Mass. It is significant that he and the vicar of Dommemarie, who denounced the work boycott from the pulpit, were labelled Huguenots by the simple people and even by some priests. This accusation incidentally tells us much about the economic attitudes of the Huguenots in the countryside. The boycott only came to an end when the Franciscan and Dominican Orders were mobilized to preach in the villages in the areas affected.

Haton felt vindicated by the collapse of the movement which, for a time, he had stood against virtually alone. The language with which he fought it reflects a willingness to label and exclude those who threatened the existing structure of society. In his sermons against those who followed the popular movement, he had especially insisted that to refuse Saturday work was to Judaize. He claimed that to work only half a day on Saturday was to attempt to be both Jew and Christian at the same time, which was impossible. Christians, who must abhor the Jews and their superstitions, could not observe the latter's Sabbath. Those who did so ran the risk of being taken for Jews. If one could afford the time, one could certainly go to Saturday Vespers, but those who are required to work ought not to do so. Having been denounced as a Huguenot, Haton retorted by vilifying his opponents as Jews or Judaizing sectarians.

Far from being inspired by Judaism, this movement of resistance to wage labour appears to have been rooted in rural folk culture which was half-pagan and half-Christian. It seems to have been part of a largely subterranean peasant opposition to the profound changes and upheavals that were taking place in the countryside of northern France in the second half of the sixteenth century.

---

[131] Ibid., p. 129.

Deprived of support from the better-off peasants, it fell short of becoming the kind of religiously inspired *jacquerie* which had shaken Hungary, Valencia, Castile and Germany earlier in the sixteenth century. Nevertheless, the fear among the elites that such a movement could develop was quite real.[132] It is this anxiety which largely explains the assimilation of this popular antagonism to sorcery and heresy in the latter half of the sixteenth century. Accusations of witchcraft became a characteristic form of pre-emptive attack by the ruling stratum in the villages, abetted by the ecclesiastical and secular authorities in the course of the civil wars.[133] Indeed, the great wave of witchcraft persecutions in the jurisdiction of the Parlement of Paris was initiated almost immediately after the crushing of the work stoppages of 1566.[134] The *processions blanches* of the 1580s should likewise be interpreted as attempts on the part of the authorities to pre-empt religiously inspired rural unrest and to confine it to channels under firm ecclesiastical control.[135]

The growing tension between rural wage-earners and employers is reflected in the writings of René Choppin, a lawyer in the Paris Parlement.[136] In 1574, Choppin published *De privilegiis rusticorum libri tres*, a work which he composed on his estate at Cachan just southwest of Paris. Amid the luxuriant fields and herds of plump livestock which surrounded his manor-house, Choppin began to reflect on how little men of law had done to recompense those by whose labour they lived. Accordingly, he decided to help the *fermiers* and *laboureurs* on whom the legal class depended by writing the first treatise on the law of the peasants. His interest in composing such a treatise, it should be noted, testifies, among other things, to the growing economic importance of the stratum of rich peasants in the countryside.

Choppin treats the problem of rural labour in his chapter 'On Harvesters and the Wages of Rural Workers'. The basic problem faced by such people was that, in so far as they were forced to seek wage labour, their wages failed to keep up with prices. Choppin admitted that the labour of agricultural workers was difficult and urged that they should be paid daily, rather than on a longer term basis, in order for them to be able to sustain themselves. He here appears to acknowledge the limited means of subsistence available to the rural workforce. On the other hand, he recalls that in 1350 the monarchy had fixed the wages and hours of such

---

[132] See Louis Ier Condé, *Mémoires* (London, 1740), IV, 390–1.

[133] Robert Muchembled, *La sorcière au village* (Paris, 1991), pp. 170–4, 257; Luciano Parinetto, *Streghe e politica: dal Rinascimento Italiano a Montaigne, da Bodin a Naude* (Milan, 1983), pp. 209–15.

[134] Alfred Soman, 'The Parlement of Paris and the Great Witch Hunt' in *Sorcellerie et justice criminelle: le Parlement de Paris (16e-18e siècles)* (London, 1992), pp. 31–44; Soman, 'Le procès de sorcellerie au Parlement de Paris (1565–1640)' ibid., pp. 790–814.

[135] Denis Crouzet, *Les guerriers de Dieu: la violence au temps des troubles de religion, vers 1525–vers 1610)* (Seyssel, 1990), II, 308–9.

[136] For the analysis of Choppin's work I am indebted to Davis, 'René Choppin on More's Utopia', *Moreana* 19–20 (1968), 91–5.

people. But nowadays stewards, husbandmen and rural workers were extracting enormous amounts of money from urban property owners. The solution, according to Choppin, was for the citizens of the towns regularly to commit some time to the supervision of agricultural work. He even had the temerity to cite Thomas More's *Utopia* as a precedent. The latter, of course, had proposed agricultural work for the citizens of the republic as a remedy for wage labour, not in order to make it more profitable. In any event, Choppin's treatise reflects growing unrest among agricultural workers.

In 1577, at Orly, Ablon, Villain, le Blois, Grignon, Chailly, Longjumeau and other villages in the area to the south of Paris the rural workforce finally went out on strike. According to the complaints of the 'poor labourers' to the Parlement, the servants, teamsters, harvesters and other employees whom they were accustomed to employ refused to work. Instead, they and their families were resorting to gleaning, especially at night, and, in doing so, were seizing grain which did not belong to them. Fearing a repetition of the strike the following year, the labourers appealed to the High Court to intervene. It responded by prohibiting those who were able-bodied from gleaning and by restricting the practice to the daylight hours. The able-bodied who refused to work were to be forced to do so on pain of imprisonment and seizure of their possessions.[137]

TERROR IN THE MINES

Resistance to proletarianization is also evident in François Garrault's treatise on mining which has already been mentioned, (p. 131) for the principal problem he deals with is the recruitment and maintenance of a labour force in the mines. The close connection between technology and proletarianization is especially evident in Garrault's work. The Romans, he recalls, used slaves to work the mines. But this, he claims, was not a good practice since slaves would do all they could to sabotage the mine.[138] Slavery did not mix well with investments of fixed capital and the use of machines.

The employment of paid workers has its risks. To illustrate this he tells the story of a merchant, who not long before had made 14,000 *livres* in a single year in the silver-mines of the Auvergne. But the next year he spent 7,000 *livres* looking for a vein of silver in a mine without finding it. The lesson Garrault draws from this incident is that the merchant should have employed less ignorant, or more skilful, workers in the undertaking.[139]

Garrault admits that there could be another explanation for the failure of this enterprise. The miners, in this instance, may have decided to work for themselves rather than for the merchant or, as he puts it, 'they were so wicked that they

---

[137] BN MS Fr. 8068, fos. 155r.–156r.; Coll. Lamoignon, IX, fos. 231r.–232r.
[138] Garrault, *Des mines d'argent trouvée en France*, fo. sig. C iv r.
[139] Ibid., fo. sig. D ii v.

wanted to take all the profit he [the merchant] had taken from their labour for themselves'.[140] Accordingly, they may have kept the location of the vein of silver a secret, claiming that it was lost. Garrault notes that several workers who worked in the mining industry had informed him in confidence that their fathers had told them of the location of mines with rich veins, which they were keeping secret in the hope of profiting from them in the future. They were prepared to reveal the secret of these mines if all the profit, or at least the traditional eight-tenths, was reserved for them.[141]

Many mines, he conceded, had been closed by the disruptions of the civil wars. But the more difficult problem seemed to be the high cost of food. The merchants who advanced the capital for the operation of the mine would by contract be obliged to supply the miners with food. At times the price of wheat would reach 45 sols per bushel and the merchants, as a result, would abandon the enterprise, being unable to meet the costs.[142] Food costs made wage labour too expensive.

Garrault was nevertheless optimistic about silver-mining in the Auvergne. The mines in the Auvergne, he argued, were as rich as those of Germany. The German mine of Leberthal, considered the most valuable in Europe, produced 1,500 *écus* of silver per annum. But Saint-Guillaume, or Chitry, in the Auvergne produced 1,100 *marcs* of fine silver and 100,000 *marcs* of lead.[143] The peasants of the Chitry region would open other mines, if the king would limit himself to the traditional tenth.

Garrault describes the mine at Chitry as a successful venture. The peasants themselves had apparently paid part of the capital costs out of their own pockets, especially those necessary for the refining of the ore. It is unclear who paid for the windmills which ran the ore elevators or pumped air into the shafts. According to Garrault, 80 per cent of the returns went to the workers in the form of wages or other expenditures.[144]

But it is precisely in the other expenditures where lies the rub. Chitry was hardly a miners' co-operative. Garrault notes that when the workers do not have the means to pay the costs, they have to be aided, as he puts it, by men of means and wealth, who provide them with all the necessities for the year. These men, who are often in partnership with others and enjoy all the privileges of the workers themselves, reimburse themselves from the workers' part of the mines revenue.[145] He appears to be describing a kind of corporation that had been in existence since the late fifteenth century in which workers were associated as minority share-holders.[146] But one wonders, after all, how much of their wages and return on their

---

[140] Ibid.
[141] Ibid., fo. sig. D iiii r.
[142] Ibid., fo. sig. D iii v.
[143] Ibid., fo. sig. D iiii r.
[144] Ibid., fo. sig. D iii v.
[145] Ibid., fo. sig. E r.–v.
[146] Gille, *Les origines de la grande métallurgie*, pp. 28–9.

investment the peasants of Chitry actually saw. One may well ask whether these peasants were driven more by necessity than opportunity into the mine.

According to Garrault, the most frequent reason for the abandonment of mines was not cave-ins or other accidents, but the sense of terror inspired by the presence of demons. Some of these so-called demons take on the form of a pale horse which, through its terrifying neighing and snorting, kills unfortunate miners. There are other spirits which assume the disguise of workers dressed in black. They carry off the miners to the top of the mine shafts and then let them fall to their deaths. On the other hand, there are the dwarfs, who are not dangerous. They dress themselves like miners, being no more than 2 feet 3 inches in height. They come and go in the mine, climb up and down as they please, and give the impression of working, although they are idle. They do no harm to those who work in the mine, if they are not molested. On the contrary, they take care of the workers and their families and livestock and speak with them in an easy and friendly way. There are at least six kinds of spirits in the mines, of which the most wicked are those dressed in black. Their evil intent can be overcome by prayers and fasts.[147]

Garrault's account is reinforced by that of Jean Malus, who explored the mines of the southwest of France at the end of the century.[148] Malus reports that the people of the Midi believed that evil spirits sought to prevent men from entering the mines. In the region of Couzerans, the local inhabitants told him of the terrible and awful noises and of the lightning and thunder that befell anyone who tried to open mines in the mountains of Poueg and Gouas.[149] These reports by Garrault and Malus parallel those to be found in the earlier works of George Agricola and Olaus Magnus about the mining regions of Central Europe and Scandinavia. They are in accord with accounts from Greece collected by Pierre Belon.[150]

Belief in demons in the mines is not a phenomenon confined to early modern Europe. Michael Taussig has studied this belief among the Bolivian tin-miners in his *The Devil and Commodity Fetishism in South America*.[151] According to Taussig, such beliefs are common to populations which are in transition from an economy based on use to one based on exchange. The demons which inhabit the mines are to be understood as projections of the sense of disruption and malaise felt by these workers who, accustomed to producing for subsistence, find themselves thrust into the bowels of nature in order to produce commodities for exchange.[152] The mines are not places where human beings can feel comfortable. Stooped over

---

[147] Garrault, *Des mines d'argent trouvée en France*, fos. sig. C iii r. – C iiii r. See the account in Paré, *Des monstres et prodiges*, ed. Céard, pp. 84–5.

[148] Jean du Puy, *La recherche et descouverte des mines des montagnes Pyrénées, faicte en l'an mil six cens* (Bordeaux, 1601). I have used the edition published by Nicolas Gobet in his *Les anciens minéralogistes du royaume de France* (Paris, 1779), I, 78–147.

[149] Du Puy, *La recherche et descouverte des mines*, p. 130.

[150] Paul Sébillot, *Les travaux publics et les mines dans les traditions et les superstitions de tous les pays* (Paris, 1894), pp. 443–51.

[151] Michael T. Taussig, *The Devil and Commodity Fetishism in South America* (Chapel Hill, 1980).

[152] Ibid., pp. xi–xiii, 10–11, 14–17, 20–1.

hacking at the earth in the narrow shafts and crevices of the mine, the unhappiness of the miners is in sharp contrast to the merry and idle dwarfs who are physically suited to a carefree life there. Indeed, human beings are forever at risk of being overwhelmed by monsters in such an environment.

PACIFYING LABOUR

The increasing availability of cheap labour and the expansion of foreign trade provided whatever dynamism the French economy had during the civil wars. But there seems little doubt that overall the period was marked by economic regression which became very pronounced between 1585 and 1595. Under such circumstances of economic decline, made worse by continuing inflation, wage-earners found it increasingly difficult to find work. Moreover, what work there was was only to be had under increasingly adverse circumstances.

Corporations in which no obligation of *compagnonnage* had existed now tended to make it obligatory. In Paris, between 1549 and 1582, the plumbers, purse makers, hat makers and jewellers imposed it. The royal edict of 1581 made it general throughout the kingdom. This edict, it is true, tried to limit the length of apprenticeship to three years, since masters were imposing terms of apprenticeship which averaged four to seven years. This attempt to restrict the length of apprenticeships had little, if any, effect.[153]

A royal edict of February 1565 had sought to limit the mobility of domestic servants by specifying that all such employees seeking new employment must provide prospective employers with a notarized record of past service. Domestic servants who left an employer without such a record would be treated as vagabonds.[154] The ordonnance of 1577 extended similar provisions to other workers. It prohibited workers from leaving their masters without reasonable and legitimate cause. It obliged workers to remain in the same employ for at least a year and to quit their employer only with the written permission of their master.[155]

Employee demands for higher wages were met with wage control legislation. The edict of 1567 specified that the wages of skilled and unskilled workers in the construction industry were to be fixed on an annual basis.[156] A *règlement* of 1572 fixed the wages of all skilled and unskilled workers in Paris and its environs.[157] Finally, the ordonnance of 1577 fixed the wages of both domestics and *valets*, while also attempting to limit prices.[158]

Charles IX's edict limiting the mobility of domestic servants was apparently inspired by the arguments of Philibert Bugnyon. Bugnyon, a lawyer from Lyons,

[153] Boissonade, *Le socialisme d'etat*, p. 131; Lespinasse, *Les métiers et corporations*, I, 84–5.
[154] BN MS Fr. 21800, fo. 2v.
[155] Boissonade, *Le socialisme d'etat*, p. 134; Pierre Deyon, *Les temps des prisons* (Paris, 1975), p. 58.
[156] Coll. Lamoignon, IX, fos. 139v., 143v.
[157] *Reg. BVP* VI, 451, n. 15.
[158] Boissonade, *Le socialisme d'etat*, p. 143.

drew up certain propositions for the regulation of coachmen, lackeys and servants prior to the legislation of February 1565.[159] Bugnyon begins his memorandum by noting that one of the problems that most interferes with the sweetness of life and which troubles society is the behaviour of servants, especially their licentiousness and thievery. These problems arise from the hatred that those in servitude feel towards their masters as well as the facility with which such servants are able to change their employment. As a result, servants do not do their work, they engage in licentious behaviour and rob their employers.[160] The trouble stems especially from the connection between servants and shoemakers, second-hand dealers, and fruit and vegetable vendors, who are incessantly encouraging them to change their masters. Some servants take as many as three or four positions in a month without giving their masters time to find new servants.[161]

Bugnyon's suggestions with respect to restricting the mobility of servants were substantially incorporated into the edict of 1565. As to the possibility that his recommendations gave too much authority to employers, he argued that no one could doubt that there was infinitely more justice, charity and reason exercised by masters than by servants.[162]

Bugnyon urged that servants be forced to give at least a month's notice before leaving their masters, noting that in the provinces a full year's notice is required and masters in Paris demand an apprenticeship of three to four years. It is not appropriate that those who hold power, i.e., the bourgeoisie of the metropolis of Paris, should be dependent on their servants, while the inhabitants of small towns are able to keep their servants dependent on them.[163]

In 1572 Bugnyon published a commentary on the edict of 1565.[164] In this work, he remarked that the edict had been made necessary as a result of the troubles. The civil wars had rendered servants less pliable, courteous, affectionate and obedient towards their lords and masters.[165] In every well-governed state, Bugnyon claimed, there must be those who command and others who obey. It is the same in every household. Not everyone can be a soldier or gladiator. There must be diverse kinds of men and different occupations, including those which demand labour. It is only right, therefore, that the powerful dominate and that the weak, or otherwise unfit, submit to the yoke of servitude. Apparently contradicting himself, Bugnyon claimed that in France servants in the past were, in fact, those who had the status of 'familiars', men of outstanding merit whom the lord

[159] BN MS Fr. 21800, fos.1r.–2v. On Bugnyon see Roman d'Amat, 'Philibert Bugnyon', *DBF* VII, 637–8.
[160] BN MS 21800, fo. 1r.
[161] Ibid.
[162] Ibid., fo. 2r.
[163] Ibid.
[164] *Commentaire sur l'édit du roi Charles Neufieme, roi de France, donné à Tholose, pour contenir les serviteurs et servantes en leurs devoirs et charges* (Lyons, 1572).
[165] Ibid., p. 2; see also BN MS Fr. 21800, fo. 26r.

took into his household as retainers or as members of his family. Between lord and domestic there was no sense of hatred or contempt. Bugnyon here is recalling for his own purposes the medieval sense of the relationship between lord and domestic. But in the final analysis, he admits that there are, in fact, two kinds of servants. There are those who are simple, open, truthful, faithful and frugal, and the others, who are stubborn, crafty, deceitful, morally defective and inert.[166]

To these attempts at controlling them, the workers responded with defiance, signalled by sedition in Paris in 1567, 1571, 1576, 1579.[167] In 1571–2 the *compagnon* printers of Paris and Lyons went out on strike once again.[168] The *compagnon* shoemakers were in a constant state of agitation, accused of holding illegal assemblies, engaging in collective action against their employers, and giving themselves over to licentious behaviour, while refusing to work.[169] The workers in the Parisian baking industry tried to intimidate their masters with threats. In 1579 they were prohibited from combining, holding meetings or wearing capes, hats and boots to work in order to try to cow their employers.[170]

Sumptuary defiance on the part of employees seems to have been particularly upsetting to employers. The bakery workers were enjoined to wear shirts, shoes and appropriate headgear to their work.[171] The third estate at Blois asked the king to enjoin workers (*gens de labeur*), vine-dressers and other village dwellers to wear only undyed cloth, to prohibit artisans from wearing black, scarlet or purple cloth and to prevent such artisans as well as domestic servants from wearing silk.[172]

Violent clashes between *compagnons* and masters took place between 1574 and 1583 at Bourges and at Troyes in 1580–94. At Bourges the *compagnon* shoemakers were accused of forcing newcomers to pay an entrance fee to their *compagnonnage* and to offer feasts to members in order to be allowed to work. Only those *compagnons*, servants and *valets* (*garçons*) approved by the *compagnonnage* could work in the city.[173]

In 1573 at Beauvais, the weavers, in reaction to their low salaries, banded together and went about the streets robbing people, or so the authorities said. Some of these rioters were arrested and imprisoned in the episcopal prison. They were liberated by an armed uprising led by a weaver, Nicolas Pelerin. In the course of the upheaval, the homes of the master drapers were attacked.[174]

At Dijon *compagnonnage* was strongly entrenched by 1579 among the

---

[166] *Commentaire sur l'édit du roi Charles Neufieme, roi*, p. 4. See BN MS Fr. 21800, fo. 28r.
[167] Boissonade, *Le socialisme d'etat*, p. 141.
[168] Hauser, *Ouvriers du temps passé*, pp. 210–30.
[169] Coornaert, *Les corporations en France*, p. 111. See also BN MS Fr. 8613, fo. 233r.–v.
[170] Coornaert, *Les corporations en France*, p. 111.
[171] Ibid.
[172] Lalourcé and Duval, *Recueil des cahiers généraux des trois ordres aux états généraux* (Paris, 1789), II, 349.
[173] Hippolyte Boyer, *L'ancien compagnonnage à Bourges* (Bourges, 1891), p. 29.
[174] *Documents pour servir à l'histoire de Beauvais et du Beauvaisis*, ed. V. LeBlond, p. 3; Charles Fauqueux, *L'industrie textile à Beauvais* (Beauvais, 1974), p. 9.

cabinetmakers and probably well established among the locksmiths, tailors and shoemakers before the end of the century. In December 1579 the municipal council was dismayed by the news that the journeymen cabinetmakers had drawn up laws and statutes and had elected officers to govern their organization. They banished the captain and treasurer and confiscated the treasury and roll book. Finally, they prohibited all such *compagnonnages*.[175] Despite this prohibition the authorities found it necessary to enjoin all *compagnon* cabinetmakers, shoemakers and locksmiths from entering, leaving or assembling in the town in groups larger than two.[176]

At the national level the prohibition of confraternities of 1561 was reiterated in 1566, 1577 and 1579. At the same time the teachings of the Counter-Reformation Church were marshalled against these organizations. In 1578 René Benoist published *De l'institution et de l'abus survenu es confreries populaires, avec la reformation necessaire en icelles.*[177] In this work, Benoist argues that those charitable confraternities which were not worldly, carnal, or involved attempted combinations were approved of by both the Old and New Testament.[178] The confraternities of the rude and ignorant, however, must be sanctioned by the Church hierarchy.[179] But their practice of holding Masses involving the dispersion of holy water and the dispensing of holy bread on Sundays and holy days represents a challenge to the power of ecclesiastical pastors.[180] They collect offerings and oblations which by right belong to priests. Indeed, they even dare to take up collections during parochial Masses.[181] Those among the populace who participate in the ceremonies of the confraternities do not go to hear parochial Masses and are deprived of sermons heard there. Accordingly, they are not instructed properly, especially about working faithfully in one's estate, which is very important with respect to proper police.[182] Popular confraternities organize combinations to control labour, use the batons of their associations to commit all manner of abuses, and are noxious to both religion and economy.[183] The dissipation encouraged by the confraternities leads to the waste of money in taverns and festivities, while wives and children are left in necessity.[184]

---

175 James Richard Farr, *Hands of Honor: Artisans and Their World in Dijon, 1550–1650* (Ithaca, 1988), pp. 68–9.
176 Hauser, *Les compagnonnages d'arts et métiers à Dijon aux XVIIe et XVIIIe siècles* (Dijon, 1907; Marseilles, 1979), p. 13.
177 (Paris, 1578). On Benoist see Emile Pasquier, *Un curé de Paris pendant les guerres de religion. René Benoist, le pape des Halles: 1521–1608* (Angers, 1913; Geneva, 1970).
178 Benoist, *De l'institution*, fo. 6r.
179 Ibid., fo. 9v.
180 Ibid., fo. 10r.
181 Ibid., fo.10r.–v.
182 Ibid., fo. 10v.
183 Ibid., fo. 11r.–v.
184 Ibid., fo. 11v.

Proper confraternities like those of the Holy Sacrament, of the Psalter, of the Immaculate Glorious Virgin Mary are not given to monopolies, but accept people from all estates. The archbishop of Paris has recently issued statutes which have been attacked and condemned by the ignorant and unlearned. These prohibit the saying of Mass or other ceremonies by confraternities on Sundays and feast-days and prohibit the removal of the batons of confraternities from the churches to prevent the scandals and mockeries which occur around them.[185] This last measure no doubt was designed to castrate the confraternities by depriving them of their central symbols during their customary processions and feasts.

The threat of the confraternities was such as to mobilize the pen, once again, of Philibert Bugnyon. Hitherto he had aimed his fire at domestic servants. But such was the threat that in 1585 he brought out his *Commentaire sur les edicts et ordonnances du Roy contenans les inhibitions et defenses des confrairies monopolaires et les causes pourquoy.*[186] Bugnyon recapitulates many of the arguments of Benoist against popular confraternities. He cleverly adapts the religious arguments of the latter to make his points. Thus, he approves the banning of the consecrated wafer from the processions of the confraternities because it is being reserved for those who belong to the confraternities rather than being democratically made available to all on Sundays at parochial Mass.[187] On the other hand, he argues that the banning of the confraternities is justified, given their dissipation in times which are very difficult.[188] Finally, he invokes the authority of Bodin, citing his argument that the monopolies of merchants, artisans and workers are a factor in the rise in prices.[189] Monopolies of artisans, he concludes, could be prevented by dispersing the artisans into different quarters of the city, as is done in towns in Africa and elsewhere in Europe.[190]

Bugnyon need not have worried. Economic regression and a growing supply of labour from expropriated peasants undermined all attempts on the part of workers to improve their wages during the religious wars. Repression by royal and municipal officials did the rest. The inability of workers to improve their living standards in part explains the failure of the continuing interest in technology to turn into major investment in mechanical innovations during this period. For, if workers' wages fall too far behind the level of surplus value they have created, as seems to have been the case, a major incentive towards the improvement of productivity through technological improvements is absent. Contrast this situation in France with that in Holland, where a high wage economy promoted constant technological innovation.[191] The other reason for the lack of interest in technolo-

---

[185] Ibid., fo. 17r.
[186] (Lyons, 1585).
[187] Bugnyon, *Commentaire sur les edicts du roy*, p. 9.
[188] Ibid., p. 12.
[189] Ibid., p. 28.
[190] Ibid., p. 32.
[191] See Jonathan I. Israel, *Dutch Primacy in World Trade, 1580–1740* (Oxford, 1989), p. 356.

gical investment was the relationship between such investment and profits. In the final analysis, capital investments, including investment in new technology, is a function of profit expectations, which depend on the market-place. If, in most sectors, the market is stagnant or regressing, the incentive to make such capital investments simply is not present. Such was the case for the duration of the French wars of religion.

6

The Bourbon economic restoration

... we are in our lands more ingenious and subtle in all things since the greatest part of the arts ... have either been invented or brought to their perfection here.

Nicholas Briot, *Response* ... (1617)

In 1595 the wars of religion came to an end. France embarked on the road to recovery under Henri IV and his minister Maximilien de Sully. The limits and extent of this economic revival at the end of the sixteenth and beginning of the seventeenth century are suggested by a study of the textile industry in the north of the kingdom by Pierre Deyon.[1] According to Deyon, a recovery began at the end of the 1590s which quickly brought the level of production back to the highest points of the sixteenth century. Expansion, although more irregular after 1600, continued until 1628. Agrarian crises in 1617–18 and 1625 interrupted production, as did a brutal commercial collapse in 1614 which was linked to a Europe-wide crisis. But growth, however interrupted, continued until the late 1620s, when a definitive tendency towards decline set in.[2]

Deyon's view is reinforced by Pierre Jeannin's study of the mining industry in the southern Vosges.[3] A vigorous economic revival is visible there during the closing years of the sixteenth century. This trend continued until the end of the reign of Henri IV and then faltered, petering out in the course of the 1620s. The prosperity of mining under Henri IV appears to be matched by metallurgy. A study of iron manufacture around 1600 in the Nivernais reflects an annual return on invested capital of over 50 per cent.[4] The cost of labour was only between 13 and 15 per cent of net costs.

The rest of the seventeenth century, from the 1620s or possibly from as late as the 1640s, in France at least, was marked by slow growth. During the reign of Louis XIV there were phases of actual economic decline. Certain areas like the

---

[1] 'Variations de la production textile aux XVIe et XVIIe siècles: sources et premiers resultats', *Annales: ESC* 18 (1963), 921–55.

[2] Deyon, 'Variations de la production textile', pp. 947–50; Israel, *Dutch Primacy*, p. 121.

[3] 'Conjoncture et production du cuivre dans les Vosges méridionale à la fin du XVIe et au début du XVIIe siècle' in *Conjoncture économique, structures sociales. Hommage à Ernest Labrousse* (Paris, 1974), pp. 121–38.

[4] Guy Thuillier, 'Forges et fourneaux en Nivernais vers 1600', *Bulletin philologique et historique (jusqu'à 1715) du comité des travaux historiques* (1957), pp. 463–70.

northeast affirmed their superiority over the rest of the kingdom. On the other hand, it is by no means clear that the Mediterranean region suffered the regression that had once been thought to have occurred.[5]

In the meantime the return of internal peace provided the foundation for a demographic recovery in the reign of Henri IV based on an increase in marriages, a higher birthrate and a lower mortality rate. All these positive trends in turn were rooted in a period of generally abundant harvests and relatively low labour costs which lasted until the mid-1620s.[6] The reign of Henri IV saw a major effort to revive the economy of France based on state intervention. Broadening and developing the public and private initiatives taken during the wars of religion, Henri IV's government attempted to revive agriculture, stimulate and protect industry, lower interest rates, foster invention and science, and lay down an infrastructure of roads and bridges. The question of direct state support for industry based on protectionism was passionately debated at the highest levels of policy. The transformation of the displaced rural population into a disciplined wage-earning proletariat became a priority at the local and national level. State support helped the impulse towards empirical science to grow stronger. But the further growth of state bureaucracy and a renewal of economic stagnation weakened the drive towards economic and technological innovation following the death of Henri IV.

AGRICULTURAL RENEWAL

The importance of agriculture to the French economy was set out in a royal edict of 1599 which was concerned with the draining of swamp and marsh land. In the preface to this Act, Henri IV asserts, in classic mercantilist style, that the strength of princes lies in the numbers and wealth of their subjects. It is agriculture, furthermore, that is the basis of the wealth of all nations, including the French. Not only does agriculture make it possible for people to live, but it makes trade possible and allows the kingdom to acquire precious metals from nations which have them in greater abundance. Accordingly, as peace has arrived, the king has resolved on measures to improve agriculture.[7]

The English observer George Carew noted the fundamental importance of agriculture to the French economy:

The fertility of the soil is so great, as besides, that it furnisheth abundantly to the inhabitants all necessary commodities for the use of man's life, it uttereth also to strangers so great quantity of the same, as without labouring in any mines of their own ... in recompense of the said commodities offered, they draw into their country greater store of

---

5   *Histoire économique et sociale de la France*, ed. Chaunu and Gascon, Part I, vol. I, 334–5; Jean-Pierre Poussou, 'Manufactures', *Dictionnaire du grand siècle*, ed. François Bluche (Paris, 1990), p. 752.

6   *Histoire de la France rurale*, II, ed. Neveux, Jacquart and Le Roy Ladurie, p. 190.

7   Isambert, *Recueil générale*, XV, 213.

silver and gold, than cometh into any region in Christendom comparing quantity for quantity.[8]

Indeed, there can be little doubt of the importance of agriculture in making possible the recovery of the economy under Henri IV. The re-establishment of agriculture was facilitated, above all, by the restoration of internal peace. But the cancellation of arrears on taxes, the reduction of direct taxation and a lowering of the rate of interest helped as well.[9]

Henri IV and Sully were deeply interested in everything that could possibly stimulate agricultural production. In 1598 a M. Fabry and his sons were given royal letters-patent to produce a new and improved plough, to develop a device for moving the plough more easily, and to establish a new kind of grain mill based on those in use in Provence.[10] In 1604 the crown issued a patent for a machine which could clear land for agriculture by ridding it of stone and slate.[11] The monarchy likewise showed a renewed interest in developing rice at the expense of grain, recognizing its higher caloric value.[12]

An anonymous memorandum drawn up for the king in 1597 regarding a pump invented by a certain gentleman from Metz, the Sire Travah, reflects just how enlightened the thinking of Henri's entourage was on the subject of agriculture. The pump, according to the author of the report, was held to be inexpensive to build and could last thirty or forty years. It could be used, in the first instance, to irrigate otherwise infertile land or to drain marshes and transform them into arable land. More to the point, argues the memorandum, such a pump would allow the creation of water meadows which would allow an increase in forage of between 50 and 66 per cent. The resultant augmentation in livestock would provide a great increase in manure, allowing a growth in agricultural output, especially grain.[13]

The apparent recognition of the importance of water meadows to improved agricultural output in this report – seen as critical, for example, to the English Agricultural Revolution – reflects the sophisticated approach to the problems of agriculture among the advisers of Henri IV.[14]

By the edict of 1599 noted above, Henri IV initiated a programme of draining marshes and swamps in an effort to increase the area of cultivable land. In order to

8   George Carew, 'A Relation of the State of France ...' in Thomas Birch, *An Historical View of the Negotiations between the Courts of England, France and Brussels* (London, 1749), p. 430.
9   Collins, *Fiscal Limits*, p. 88; Mark Greengrass, *France in the Age of Henri IV: The Struggle for Stability* (London, 1984), pp. 84–5, 131; Ernest Lavisse, *Histoire de la France depuis les origines jusqu'à la Révolution*, vol. IV, pt II: *Henri IV – Louis XIII (1598–1643)*, ed. H. Mariéjol (Paris, 1911), pp. 2, 71.
10 AN Coll. Lenain MS 63, fo. 648.
11 Ibid., fos. 128–9.
12 *Documents historiques inédits, tirés des collections manuscrits de la Bibliothèque royale et des archives ou des bibliothèques des départements*, ed. Jacques Joseph Champollion-Figeac (Paris, 1841–8), IV, 102–4.
13 BN MS Fr. 16739, fo. 232 r.–v.
14 Eric Kerridge, *The Agricultural Revolution* (New York, 1968), p. 40.

facilitate this undertaking, Henri conceded a fifteen-year privilege to Humphrey Bradley and his company of Brabanters.[15] In a memoir to the king drawn up at the time that the privilege was renewed, Bradley held out the prospect that the draining of marshes in the kingdom would ultimately provide a living through agriculture and other kinds of employment for some 300,000–400,000 households. The roads built across the marshes, he promised, would improve communications throughout the kingdom. The draining of these potentially highly fertile lands would enable France to produce much more grain, livestock and other commodities, a good portion of which could be exported.[16] Over the period 1600 to 1630, Flemish entrepreneurs, engineers and labourers drained marshland in Picardy, Normandy, Vendée and Poitou, Bordelais, Provence and Languedoc.[17]

In the Midi a veritable school of hydraulics had been created in the wake of the work of Adam de Crapponne which busied itself, among other things, with draining the marshes between the canal of the Crau and Marseilles. In Languedoc, between 1558 and 1585, the Narbonnaise had occupied themselves in draining the swamp around their town. In 1592 a syndicate headed by an engineer, a lawyer and a *bourgeois gentilhomme*, undertook to drain the swamp at Launac (Gard), extending their operation to other marshes at Taraillon and Pérignan near Narbonne, while still another syndicate carried through the drainage of the muddy plain of Livière nearby. With the return of peace at the beginning of the seventeenth century, the public authorities in Languedoc and Provence called the Flemings and Dutch into the region to undertake further drainage operations.[18]

SULLY VERSUS LAFFEMAS

In discussing the reign of Henri IV, it is common to consider its economic policies in terms of the opposition between Maximilien de Sully and Barthélemy de Laffemas. Sully, it is said, favoured agriculture, while Laffemas was the champion of manufacture. But as two recent biographies of Sully, those of David Buisseret and Bernard Barbiche, have made clear, this is too simple a view.[19] Although Buisseret admits that Sully seems to have opposed the protection and development of manufacturing in 1598, by 1603, he argues, he was actively promoting industry, including the establishment of silk manufacturing.[20] Barbiche, on the other hand, categorically insists that Sully shared Laffemas' enthusiasm for

---

15 Isambert, *Recueil général*, XV, 214–22.
16 BN MS Fr. 16740, fo. 38r.
17 Dienne, *Histoire du dessèchement* (Paris, 1891), pp. 80, 91, 150, 161, 175; Henri Enjalbert, 'Le commerce de Bordeaux et la vie économique dans le Bassin Aquitaine au XVIIe siècle', *Annales du Midi* 62 (1950), 28.
18 Le Roy Ladurie, *Les paysans de Languedoc*, I, 442–3.
19 Buisseret, *Sully and the Growth of Centralized Government in France, 1598–1610* (London, 1968); Bernard Barbiche, *Sully* (Paris, 1978).
20 Buisseret, *Sully and the Growth of Centralized Government*, pp. 171–2.

manufacturing.[21] Buisseret, it seems, is closer to the truth, but even his views require a certain qualification and elaboration.

Buisseret would have it that by 1603 Sully had become an enthusiastic supporter of a French silk industry, to say nothing of the development of industry in general. Yet, in his memoirs, Sully recalls that in 1603 he had a bitter quarrel with the king on the subject of the silk industry and on the establishment of new industries. The king, he reminisces, was determined to establish the cultivation of the mulberry, the manufacture of silk and all manner of foreign manufactures in the kingdom. Moreover, he was prepared to import foreign workers and to have large buildings constructed to house these manufactures at great expense. Sully notes that he did everything he could to block these projects.[22] Given the evidence of this text, it cannot be denied that Sully opposed Laffemas' proposals for the establishment of silk and other new manufactures as late as 1603. Moreover, although the king confronted Sully in a face-to-face showdown and forced him to give way, Sully claims that he continued to maintain his opposition, saying that 'since you say that it is your absolute will, I will no longer speak of it. Time and practice will teach you that France is not ready for such baubles.'[23]

How, then, can we continue to maintain, alongside Buisseret and Barbiche, that Sully encouraged industry as much as agriculture? We can do this by recognizing, in the first place, that, after the king had commanded, Sully, as his loyal servant, faithfully executed the royal will. At the same time, we have to try to understand Sully's policy towards manufacturing by carefully analysing his viewpoint and putting it in its correct historical context. He argues an early modern version of comparative advantage, explaining that each region and kingdom of the world produces certain things better than others. France should try to produce those things which it produces well and avoid trying to produce things its climate, geography and the character of its people are contrary to. It should then trade the things it produces efficiently for the exports it requires. Among the things that Sully believed France produced better than any other nation were grains, vegetables, salt, wines, pastels, oils, ciders, wool, sheep, pigs and mules. But his list goes well beyond such primary agricultural products and includes well-established manufactures like cloth, linen and canvas as well. In other words, according to Sully, there were certain well-founded industries in France like cloth, linen and canvas production which were partly based on agriculture and complementary to it that he approved of without reservation.

Sully supported this kind of economic activity for the additional reason that it required rural workers (*gens de peine et du travail*), who, according to him, made the best soldiers. On the other hand, silk manufacturing tended to produce men who were meditative, idle and sedentary, and so unfit to be soldiers. In addition,

---

[21] Barbiche, *Sully*, p. 198.
[22] *Mémoires de Sully*, ed. Louis-Raymond Lefèvre (Paris, 1942), p. 285.
[23] Ibid., p. 287.

given France's climate, it would be impossible to guarantee an adequate supply of mulberry leaves which the silkworms required.

Sully's notion of encouraging an economy that produced a rural population made strong and virtuous by agricultural work recalls the ideas of Roman republican thinkers. But his economic conceptions seem also rooted in Calvinist ideas, with their emphasis on thrift and accumulation as against waste and consumption. According to Sully, the establishment of luxury manufactures will lead to the ruin of the state because they will encourage wastefulness, weakness and excessive consumption, above all among the bourgeoisie.[24] As to the argument that such manufactures are necessary to prevent the haemorrhage of gold and silver from the kingdom, he argues that the answer to this threat is strict sumptuary regulation, especially with regard to the bourgeoisie.[25]

Sully's preoccupation with the extravagance of consumption is reflected in the so-called *Project et memoires de M. de Rosny touchant les finances.*[26] In this remarkable document, which resembles a national economic account, he estimates the amount of the surplus product of the kingdom spent or forgone as a result of expenditure on the maintenance of the Catholic Church, the collection of tithes, purchase of exemptions and offices, costs of justice, taxation, holy days, feasting and merry-making. The total spent on such consumption, according to Sully, amounted to the extraordinary figure of 239,500,000 *livres*, or almost twice the accumulated royal deficit. The clear implication of this estimate is that a large fraction of this consumption or waste could be saved and invested for productive purposes.[27]

Sully's economic arguments against manufacturing, especially luxury manufacturing, made a certain amount of sense. So, too, did his strictures against consumption as against productive investment. To be sure, they did not answer the king's counter-argument that the bourgeoisie, whose presence was increasingly felt, would rebel against such attempted restrictions on their expenditure.[28] Indeed, Sully does not at all address the relationship of the bourgeois thirst for conspicuous consumption to their envy of the nobility.

Buisseret is rather dismissive of Sully's supposed commitment to free trade.[29] Indeed, one may question the degree of his dedication to the expansion of trade altogether. Despite his espousal of a kind of concept of comparative advantage, there is an underlying conservative principle to his thinking based

---

[24] Ibid., pp. 286–7.
[25] Ibid., p. 286.
[26] *Les œconomies royales de Sully*, ed. Buisseret and Barbiche (Paris, 1970–88), II, 268–70; François Véron des Forbonnais, *Recherches et considérations sur les finances de France depuis l'année 1595 jusqu'à l'année 1721* (Basle, 1758), I, 104–5.
[27] For more details on Sully's economic conceptions see C. Turgeon, 'Les idées économiques de Sully', *Revue d'histoire économique et sociale* 11 (1923), 249–69.
[28] *Mémoires de Sully*, p. 285.
[29] Buisseret, *Sully and the Growth of Centralized Government*, p. 172.

on the notion that human needs should be limited and that the land is the source of value. On the other hand, his thought does entail a sense of the necessity for specialization and interdependence which implies some need for trade between nations.

The whole question of free trade and protectionism during the reign of Henri IV needs to be understood in its context. Sully opposed the protectionist schemes of Laffemas when they were first raised shortly before the meeting of the Assembly of Notables of 1596.[30] As a political issue, the matter was posed in the form of a struggle between the cities of Tours and of Lyons. In a *cahier* drawn up for this assembly, the municipal government of Tours demanded the prohibition of foreign silk and support for the restoration of the industry at Tours. According to the *cahier*, prior to the civil wars there were some 800 master silk workers in Tours. In contrast, at present there were only one-quarter as many masters and many of these were forced to work for others.[31]

Laffemas became the defender of the Tourangeaux using the opportunity to advance his own protectionist schemes in the course of doing so.[32] Meanwhile, the city of Lyons, a trading and banking city, represented itself as the champion of free trade. In the first part of the century, Lyons had been the focal point of French banking, commerce and industry.[33] Largely dominated by Italian bankers and merchants, the city had promoted the idea of reducing trade barriers. The influence of these Italian capitalists from Lyons had reached its peak in the reign of Henri II. Indeed, Laffemas linked the continued advocacy of free trade with those who wished unpatriotically to perpetuate Italian control over the French economy.[34] As a matter of fact, under the influence of these Lyonnaise Italians and in an atmosphere of commercial prosperity France had never pursued a policy of free trade, but, as Richard Gascon puts it, had followed a policy of 'mitigated nationalism'.[35] With the onset of the religious wars, and especially from the 1570s, there developed a 'nationalism of crisis', entailing the exclusion of foreign manufactures. The programme of Laffemas, finally, embodied a programme based on a 'nationalism of reconstruction'.[36]

The Lyonnaise on this occasion argued that, given the comparative costs of silk production, the French would lose money by attempting to produce silk cloth themselves, rather than importing it from Italy.[37] Despite the efforts of the Lyonnaise, Tours won this battle and importation of manufactured silk into

---

[30] Hauser, *Les débuts du capitalisme*, p. 188.
[31] Ibid., pp. 188–9.
[32] Ibid., p. 192.
[33] See Gascon, *Grand commerce et vie urbaine au XVIᵉ siècle: Lyon et ses marchands.*
[34] Laffemas, *Responce à messieurs de Lyon, lesquels veulent empescher, rompre le cours des marchandises d'Italie, avec le préjudice de leurs foires, et l'abus aux changes* (Paris, 1598), p. 10.
[35] *Histoire économique et sociale de la France*, ed. Chaunu and Gascon, Part I, vol. I, 346.
[36] Ibid.; see also Gaston Zeller, 'Aux origines de notre système douanier' in *Aspects de la politique française sous l'ancien régime* (Paris, 1964), pp. 316–18.
[37] Hauser, *Les débuts du capitalisme*, pp. 196–7.

France was banned.[38] Sully appears to have sided with the Lyonnaise interest against that of Tours. Indeed, we know that he spurned the efforts of the Tourangeux to win his favour from an entry in his memoirs for January 1599.[39] His reasons for resisting the demands of the Tourangeux for the protection of their industry at that time were the loss other cities would suffer as a result and the expense of the large enterprise they envisioned, involving 'a large establishment for the silk and for the drawing of the gold and silver thread'.[40]

Sully's immediate objections to these proposals were rooted in his attempts to bring down royal expenditure and deal with an enormous royal deficit. But they had their theoretical basis in his ideas on comparative advantage and hostility to luxury expenditure rather than productive investment. However, there is another aspect of his championing of the merchants of Lyons that deserves to be considered. The French state was effectively bankrupt in 1599 and was, accordingly, highly dependent on the credit made available by Lyonnaise-Italian bankers like the Gondis or Sébastien Zamet. Such was the state of the royal finances that Sully could not afford to offend these financiers. Indeed, it was precisely between 1599 and 1604 that he began, step by step, to free the finances of the monarchy from control of these Italian bankers. He leased the Cinq Grosses Fermes to a French syndicate in 1599 and the Aides Générales to a syndicate led by Jean de Moisset in 1604. The gabelles were likewise farmed out to French subjects. As a result of these measures, Henri IV and Sully shifted the financial centre of the kingdom away from the Italians of Lyons to Paris, where French bankers from Paris, Rouen and the Loire valley tended to dominate. Lyons remained a centre for the settlement of royal and commercial accounts, but after 1604 it was no longer in a position to dominate royal policy.[41]

It is in the light of this effort to free France from foreign financial control that the hostility of Sully to the manufacturing schemes of Laffemas has also to be seen. The issue was at its most intense between 1596 and 1603 at a time when Sully could hardly afford needlessly to alienate these Lyonnaise financial interests more than he was already doing. By 1603 the finances of the crown had improved somewhat and the degree of leverage over royal finances exercised by the Italians had diminished. Thus, while he continued to oppose Laffemas' programme in theory, he could afford to relent in practice in accord with the will of the king.

THE ATTACK ON FINANCIERS

An illuminating light is thrown on the economic situation of the time by a largely ignored treatise, Louis Turquet de Mayerne's *Traicté des négoces*

---

38 The ban against Italian silk manufactures was lifted in 1601. See Ernest Pariset, *Histoire de la fabrique lyonnaise, étude sur le régime social et économique de l'industrie de la soie à Lyon depuis le XVI* siècle (Paris, 1901), pp. 57–8.
39 *Les œconomies royales de Sully*, II, 368.
40 Ibid.
41 Collins, *Fiscal Limits*, pp. 77–9.

(1599).[42] Mayerne is best known for his *La monarchie aristodemocrate*, in which he called for abolition of the traditional aristocracy as a ruling class and the institution of a constitutional monarchy based on a landed and commercial elite.[43] In the *Traicté des négoces*, Mayerne contents himself with regretting that merchants, by which he means merchant capitalists, are ranged with the third estate, whereas, in fact, the state of merchant is an honourable one which ought to be pursued not only by the most eminent commoners but also by the nobility.[44]

Among the most striking features of the *Traicté des négoces* is Mayerne's attack on the Italian bankers, whom he accuses of corrupting French society at every level. Their control of interest rates has been extremely damaging to merchants, many of whom have left trade, finding that profits are higher and easier to obtain from lending money at interest.[45] The result has been the devastation of manufacturing and the loss of tax revenue.[46] There ought not to be any private lending to artisans, farmers or workers. Such lending should be done through special funds made available through public offices of charity.[47] Mayerne is here proposing that the municipal *bureaux des pauvres* perform the role of savings and loans associations based on the establishment of loan funds.

The monarchy ought to regulate usury by ordonnance, making the loan of money an accessory to commerce. In this way, credit would be used to facilitate rather than to destroy trade, as at present.[48] Indeed, Mayerne goes so far as to say that the profession of banker ought to be prohibited, forcing those with capital to invest in manufactures. Manufactures require large investments of capital. These funds should be attracted from all classes and orders of society by honouring those who invest in this way.[49]

The revival of manufactures was in Mayerne's view directly related to controlling interest rates and the activities of the Italian bankers. He coupled these propositions for the capitalization of industry with an appeal for protectionism to stimulate the production of cloth and books and to assist the establishment of a silk industry. His viewpoint largely coincides with that of Laffemas on these matters.[50] Mayerne admitted, that, at the moment he was writing, France lacked the raw silk and the manufacturing capacity to do without foreign silk. But

---

[42] *Traicté des négoces et traffiques ou contracts qui se font en choses meubles, reiglement et administration du bureau ou chambre politique des marchans ...* (Paris, 1599).

[43] See Roland Mousnier, 'L'opposition politique bourgeois à la fin du XVIe siècle et au début du XVIIe siècle', *Revue historique* 213 (1955), 1–20.

[44] Ibid., pp. 9–10.

[45] Ibid., p. 82.

[46] Ibid., pp. 82–3.

[47] Ibid., p. 82.

[48] Ibid., p. 85.

[49] Ibid., p. 91.

[50] Laffemas, *Responce à messieurs de Lyon*, p. 10.

mulberry trees could be grown in Provence and Languedoc which could nourish the silkworm. Indeed, he argued that the nobility should be encouraged and, if necessary, should be forced to plant mulberry trees on their lands. The royal domain should likewise be so planted.[51]

As in Laffemas' plan, Mayerne's proposals for the development of industry behind a wall of protectionism were designed to limit the outflow of gold and silver from the kingdom. But the notion of retaining bullion within the borders of the kingdom was linked in his mind with the need to stimulate the economy by increasing the amount of capital available for investment in manufacturing activity. The level of economic activity, and particularly the level of investment in industry, was related to the quantity of sound money in circulation. Indeed, no economic recovery was possible, according to Mayerne, without the re-establishment of a stable currency based on silver and gold.[52]

High interest rates ranging from 10 to 12 per cent had crippled the French economy for forty years. Henri IV's ordonnance of 1601, fixing the rate of interest at no more than $6\frac{1}{4}$ per cent, seems inspired by sentiments identical to those of Mayerne's. High interest rates, according to this decree, have ruined many noble families and crippled trade and commerce as well as manufacturing and agriculture. Many subjects prefer to live idly off their *rentes* in the city rather than to apply themselves to agriculture.[53] The rate of interest was being lowered to encourage trade and manufacture and to restore the estates of the nobility.[54]

The ordonnance of 1601 appears to have been inspired in large part by the ideas of Sully. Indeed, its stress on agriculture tends to reinforce the likelihood that this is so. Arbitrarily lowering interest rates in this way was one of the main elements in his campaign to transfer the finances of the state from Italian into French hands. Moreover, it could be argued that lowering interest rates was a far more effective way of stimulating economic recovery, including the recovery of manufacturing, than was a system of protectionist measures or expensive and direct state support of manufacturing.

Henri IV and Sully were intent on strengthening, rather than weakening, the nobility. What they feared was faction and violence on the part of both old and new nobles. According to the ordonnance of 1601, lower interest rates were designed to restore the estates of the nobility. The result of high interest rates had been to encourage the nobility to live in idleness in the towns. The effect of living on usury in this way was to stimulate faction and civil strife. In the view of the monarchy, the elites should devote themselves to the liberal arts and, notably, to the improvement of their estates.

[51]   Mayerne, *Traicté des négoces*, p. 92.
[52]   Ibid., pp. 107–8.
[53]   Veron de Forbonnais, *Recherches*, I, 49.
[54]   Ibid., I, 50.

The Bourbon economic restoration

It was to promote this end that Henri IV became the patron of Olivier de Serres' masterpiece *Le théâtre d'agriculture* (1600), making it for a time his after-dinner reading and recommending it to everyone he encountered. Serres dedicated a total of five editions to Henri prior to the latter's death. Serres' ideal was the restoration of the nobility based on its return to a virtuous and productive life in the countryside. His work holds out the prospect of the prosperous and comfortable life of the country gentleman. Disdaining the affectation and display of the town, he promoted the notion that the healthiest, most profitable and most agreeable existence for a gentleman was to be achieved through devoting himself to increasing the prosperity of his estates. Serres' work was dedicated to demonstrating how such an estate ought to be organized and managed.[55]

Serres' advice was directed at the old nobility in so far as they still had the means to reconstruct their estates. But, as Jean Babelon has perceptively written, it was directed still more at the new noblemen who had risen from the ranks of the bourgeois notables as a result of fighting in the wars and seizing the land of the peasants, ecclesiastics and old noble families.[56] Such newly ennobled men were determined to make their recently acquired estates as profitable as their commercial activities and offices had been. It was to men such as these, above all, that Serres' work was directed.

There are several published accounts of Serres' life and work which provide significant biographical details or insights into his agronomic achievement.[57] But by far the most revealing study of Serres' agronomy produced to date is to be found in André J. Bourde's *Agronomie et agronomes en France au XVIIIᵉ siècle*.[58] Although Bourde's work deals largely with the achievements of the agronomists of the Enlightenment, he reviews the agronomic literature of the sixteenth and seventeenth century as a prelude to his discussion of the agriculture of the eighteenth century. In his discussion of Serres he is thus able to appreciate his achievement in the light of the best work of the Enlightenment. It is consequently on his discussion of Serres' work that we shall mainly rely.

Serres' writings were based on forty years of agrarian experience. But, as he makes clear in his preface, agronomy cannot be based on empiricism, but must strive towards general rules and principles. In effect, he tried to realize Palissy's programme of introducing 'philosophy' into agriculture. Theory and practice must go hand in hand in striving towards an understanding of first

---

[55] Lavisse, *Histoire de la France*, pp. 71–2.

[56] Babelon, *Henri IV* (Paris, 1982), p. 783. In 1605 François Miron estimated that in the last few years more than half the land in the kingdom had been put up for sale.

[57] Henry Vaschalde, *Olivier de Serres, seigneur de Pradel, sa vie et ses travaux, documents inédits* (Paris, 1886); Fernand Lequenne, *Olivier de Serres, agronome et soldat de Dieu* (Paris, 1983). Marthe de Fels, *Olivier de Serres* (Paris, 1963); A.G. Keller, 'Olivier de Serres', *DSB* XII, 316–17.

[58] *Agronomie et agronomes en France* (Paris, 1967), I, 51–7.

principles in agriculture. Indeed, Serres explicitly refers to agronomy as a science.[59]

Offering advice which would not be matched until the mid-eighteenth century, Serres counsels the estate owner to set aside as much land as possible for permanent pasture, and devote the rest to different types of cultivation depending on the character of the soil. His advice on clearing the land for farming and cultivating different soils in ways that reinforce each other was unsurpassed for another 150 years. Serres' suggestions on the handling of seeds reached a level of expertise which also remained unmatched until the nineteenth century: meticulousness in the choice of seeds, steepage of seeds in manure to increase their yield, proper methods of planting, harrowing and rolling.

In his work, one discovers painstakingly detailed descriptions of the cultivation of a variety of grains and quite new observations on the growing of rice. He provides excellent advice on the winnowing, storing and sale of wheat. On this latter point, Serres advises the sale of grain at a time when it would bring a good return in the market. But he explicitly opposes hoarding at times of dearth as contrary to the public interest.[60] Serres' attitude is that of someone interested in profits through efficient production rather than through commercial speculation. His view is typical of sixteenth-century Calvinism in this respect.

Serres' point of view on the practice of agriculture fuses his economic and political outlook. He was opposed to the leasing out of the proprietor's estates to tenants, whom he regarded not only as generally untrustworthy but as likely to diminish rather than enhance the value of the land they exploited.[61] Instead, he called upon the estate owner to manage the land himself. Exploiting the land himself, the owner will realize more than the usual return.[62] Looking after his own affairs, each proprietor will ensure that his land is tilled with science and diligence and will oversee and encourage his workers directly. This, he observes, will be no less useful to the estate owner and to the public than the contrary practice has been damaging – the resultant lack of subsistence having given rise to sedition and plagues.[63] Here Serres is clearly referring to the calamities of the forty years of civil war. His appreciation of the link between food shortage and social turmoil reminds us of the insight of Palissy, that earlier Calvinist agronomist writing at the beginning, rather than at the end, of the religious wars.[64]

Serres affords the reader some remarkable insights into the utility of sowing artificial grasses and into the cultivation of alfalfa and sainfoin. He recommends

---

[59] Serres, *Théâtre d'agriculture* fo. sig. e ii r.–v. Interestingly, Laffemas uses the term *science* when referring to the techniques of craftsmen. See *Source de plusieurs abus et monopoles qui se sont glissez et coulez sur le peuple de France depuis trente ans ou environ à la ruyne de l'Estat* (n.p., 1596), p. 12.

[60] Serres, *Théâtre d'agriculture*, pp. 137–8.

[61] Ibid., p. 57.

[62] Ibid., p. 55.

[63] Ibid., p. 57.

[64] See above, p. 67.

dry leaves, turnips and acorns as supplements to the usual forage, a recommendation which would only be rediscovered at the end of the *ancien régime* during the great drought of 1785.

Serres' discussion of the choice of livestock, the adoption of different breeds for different kinds of pasture, and the techniques of animal husbandry would not be matched for another 150 years and then only through the observations and writings of a multitude of agronomists. It is rare among the writers of the Enlightenment to encounter a discussion of livestock as a source of energy or fertilizer or of meat or dairy products which is at the level of Serres' account. The writers of the Enlightenment would continue to be dependent on his description of sericulture. Despite his belief in the importance of agriculture, Serres did not share Sully's opposition to the development of a French silk industry. His discussion of silk in *Le théâtre d'agriculture* echoes that to be found in his pamphlet on the subject printed by order of Henri IV, designed to encourage the planting of mulberry trees, the raising of silkworms and the production of silk thread, which until then had largely been confined to the Midi.[65]

Serres interested himself in other industrial crops like saffron, flax, pastel, madder and weld, as well as the bark of the mulberry, on whose use he received a royal patent. Indeed, the terms of this patent, which was for a twenty-year period, make it clear that he understood the process of how to develop an industrial enterprise as well as any of his contemporaries.[66] He also introduced France to the use of hops and encouraged the cultivation of maize and potatoes.

Serres showed himself respectful of old usages and customs. Moreover, as we have seen in our discussion of the relationship between Serres and Besson, he had learned to be suspicious of experiments having to do with the use of new ploughshares. Indeed, he cautions that one should not indiscriminately give oneself up to enthusiasm for new inventions.[67] On the other hand, he does admit that there are useful new inventions. Moreover, he shows no hesitation in utilizing older technology in the best possible way. In discussing ploughing, for example, he notes that there is the problem of large clods of earth which are not broken up, and which have to be pulverized with spades and clubs. This procedure can be expensive, owing to the length of time it takes. In its place, he suggests the use of the roller, by means of which one man with one or two draught animals can do the work of ten working by hand.[68] What is interesting is not so much Serres' willingness to use an old and tried invention, but the careful way in which he estimates the worth of the mechanism in terms of its savings in labour.

Serres, we have noted earlier, was very interested in irrigation. In the *Théâtre*,

---

[65] *La cueillette de la soye par la nourriture des vers qui la font* (Paris, 1599).

[66] *La seconde richesse du meurier-blanc qui se treuve en son escorce, pour en faire des toiles de toutes sortes* (Paris, 1603); see also *Documents*, ed. Champollion-Figeac, IV, 113, 120.

[67] Serres, *Le théâtre d'agriculture*, pp. 81–2.

[68] Ibid., p. 57

he notes that at Pradel he had been inspired by Crapponne to divert a stream, not only to irrigate his land, but to turn his water-mills. Apparently, there were those of his neighbours who doubted the value of this experiment. However, he observes that in fact the practice of irrigation had turned out to be both useful and profitable.[69] Indeed, we know that he was in the process of writing a book on all sorts of mills, including water, wind and handmills, a work which has not survived.[70]

THE MANAGEMENT OF LABOUR

Serres, then, we can conclude, was by no means a Cato when it came to the development of industry and technology. Indeed, his interest in these matters helps us to see the degree to which the question of the development of industry in this period was related to the development of agriculture. But dwelling too much on his interest or lack of interest in technology, taken by itself, is really to miss the point. He saw the use of technology as one way in which labour could be saved, production might be increased, and profits and productivity raised. But of these matters, it was the questions of raising productivity and profits which were uppermost in his mind. In our world, which has been overrun by machines, we still almost automatically think of the introduction of new technology as the principal means of raising productivity. But even in our universe resort is had to other methods as well. Raising the rate of absolute exploitation by forcing people to work longer or more intensively or by cutting their salaries is one of them. Another approach is to increase the rate of relative exploitation by reorganizing the workforce and the process of production. Profits can also be increased by economies in the use of materials and by limiting expenses. Savings and accumulation can occur by paring down consumption as Sully's so-called national expenditure accounts suggest. Serres' commitment to technology has to be seen in the context of this array of alternatives for creating and accumulating wealth.

Serres' work has been studied more or less thoroughly as a work of agronomy. But his treatise is as much a work on how to manage an estate profitably and has to be studied from this perspective. Book I, in particular, is devoted to the art of effectively managing the estate, including the household, and above all to the proper organization of labour. Serres discusses the organization and management of the estate in chapter 6, entitled 'De l'office de père-de-famille envers ses domestiques et voisins'. *Père-de-famille* or *paterfamilias* is the term Serres invariably uses with reference to the proprietor who is head of a household made up of dependent wife, children, domestics, workers and tenants. The estate and household, like everything else in nature, according to Serres, must be based on order. Such order is established by Divine Providence, according to which each is

[69] Vaschalde, *Olivier de Serres*, p. 14.
[70] Serres, *Théâtre d'agriculture*, Book VII, ch. 1. See Lequenne, *Olivier de Serres*, p. 14.

held to his office, some having been given the knowledge to command, others to obey. His prose is infused with fundamental Calvinist notions. The wife of the *père-de-famille* is a gift of God, while his home is the Lord's domicile. The availability of labour at the time of harvest is an example of providential design.[71]

The *père-de-famille* must know how to command in order to make his estate profitable. A wise and virtuous wife is more valuable than all the rules of agriculture. Without a wife who is a proper manager, all the savings made by effective administration will be consumed and squandered. Hence, peace and concord between husband and wife is essential to the prosperity of the estate and the proper education and obedience of children. The wife thus plays an essential role in managing and limiting consumption and in the socialization of the young. Her role in controlling consumption, in Serres' experience, is all the more important because she has the onerous duty of feeding the workforce. Indeed, Serres suggests that she be relieved of this heavy duty by paying wages in kind or money.[72]

A household based on concord will make itself recognized as a house of the Lord which will inspire fear and obedience from subjects and servants and ensure the blessings of prosperity in this world. Children and servants should be instructed in the fear of God so that, based on the reverence that they owe their parents, they carry out their duties without complaint. On the other hand, the *père-de-famille* must be charitable to his workers and dependants, especially in periods of famine and dearth. The social and economic utility of inculcating ethical and religious norms is taken for granted by Serres. The *père-de-famille* should be truthful, continent, sober, patient, prudent, provident, economical, liberal, industrious and diligent. Of these, only truthfulness and liberality are qualities that can realistically be associated with the old nobility. The rest seem to be the characteristics of the early modern version of rational economic man.

Nothing should be taken from those who are subject which is not due from them. On the other hand, everything that is owing, including the smallest obligation, should be punctiliously collected. Feudal obligations, seigneurial rights, rents in kind or money are treated indistinguishably as income. It is better to lend than to borrow. Lending and commerce which is compatible with agriculture and which will reinforce the profitability of the estate should be pursued. The patriarch should not simply maintain his income by cultivating the land but strive to increase his income by soundly based investment.

Serres had over forty years of experience dealing with workers. His advice consists of a detailed study of how to control and manipulate them so as to get the greatest value from them. The qualities that he mentions as essential to the *père-de-famille* are, above all, useful in enabling him to command his workers and make them work willingly and without complaint. Workers have to be physically suited

[71] Ibid., pp. 128–9.
[72] Ibid., pp. 57–8.

to the tasks assigned to them and their individual psychology understood so that one knows how to motivate them by treating them roughly or gently as the case may be. They should be called by name, encouraged to become involved in the task, to be concerned as to how their fellow workers are carrying out their function, praised or blamed as necessary. Masters should involve workers in planning projects, feigning to follow their advice so they will work more willingly. The prospect of workers being able to establish themselves as independent proprietors ought to be held out as an eventual reward for diligence. Workers should not be either always rebuked or always praised but should be continually exhorted to improve.

Serres is under no illusions about those who work for wages. They must be constantly urged to the task, since a general brutishness characterizes all workers (*mercenaires*), making them all negligent, without conscience, shameless, friendless, heedless of anything except occasions for appropriating food and collecting their pay. It seems clear that such a view of the essential nature of these wage workers is based on years of struggling to make them work.

The *père-de-famille* should rise early so as to set an example of diligence for his employees. He should employ a foreman of middle age, between thirty and fifty years old. He should retain control of the principal matters of the estate, giving the foreman control of the rest of the details. On the other hand, the foreman should be required to render account frequently to the *père-de-famille*.

It is important to take good care of the means of production and the fixed capital assets of the estate. In the evenings, the workers and servants should be employed in making baskets, sieves, and other wooden objects, depending on the region and province. It would be shameful for a household to spend money on such things. In inclement weather or seasons, workers should be kept busy making or repairing tools and implements made of wood. Those of iron should be ordered at the blacksmith. It is important to have a reserve of at least 50 per cent of ploughs, ploughshares, hoes, spades, shovels and axes so that time is not lost during periods of work repairing, looking for, making or borrowing such implements. They should be stored in good order, the wooden tools separated from the iron in a locked cabinet. Priority should be given to the repair or installation of such indispensable things as mills or drainage, the harmful effects of whose disrepair can be counted in as little as a few hours. Less important repairs or improvements can be delayed, especially those designed merely to give pleasure.

Serres urges caution in dismissing workers, especially those who have skills that are required or whose work is indispensable at times like the harvest. Indeed, it is at such times, when labour is scarce and they have already earned some money, that workers are likely to leave their work. Workers should be paid on time and exactly what they are owed. They should never be paid in advance, as the prospect of their pay is essential to their sense of discipline. Workers hired by the day are marvels of industry at the beginning, coming malnourished as they do from their impoverished hovels. But such discipline is quickly dissipated after they have received some nourishment and earned some money. Their pace of work slows down to the point of being insupportable. Encouraged by the perverse attitude of the domestic servants, the hired hands get angry over the duration of the work-day. At the same time, they attempt to increase the number of days of work to be done, heedless of their duty and of giving their employer satisfaction. As an employer, Serres was totally disabused about the ruses of wage labour in trying to maximize their gains with the least effort. His advice consisted of ways of managing that would mitigate or overcome this resistance.

Work should be planned the evening before, so that the workers can be set to work at first light. They should be fed before dawn, so that they are ready to work at the break of day. The best way of carrying out large projects is to time them for long and fair days, at which time large numbers of day-labourers should be hired. Otherwise, a given job can cost up to one-third more to carry out. Despite the difficulties of having to hire such day-labour, it is on balance to be preferred to hiring workers by the year. It is the least expensive form of labour and can be always obtained in exchange for money, concludes Serres.

Serres understood the advantages of a system in which the employer has access to ready supplies of labour which can be hired and dismissed at will and for which he is otherwise not responsible (variable capital). Indeed, the advantages of this system were such as to strike him as divinely inspired. Serres remarks especially on the almost miraculous appearance of large numbers of mountain people in the grain-growing regions at harvest-time when a great deal of labour is required. Without their help, it would not be possible to take in the grain. While their labour is necessary to the harvest, the almost infinite number of such men, women and children who descend from the mountains in turn earn enough money to support themselves through the winter, not having enough work otherwise to sustain themselves. In this way, Serres marvels, God provides for the sustenance of the whole human race, based on the diverse vocations He has assigned to them.[73]

Serres' work was much read in the seventeenth century, as its many editions suggest. But it does not seem that many proprietors followed its recommendation to exploit their land directly. A retreat is already sounded in the writings of Antoine de Montchrétien. Having read Serres, he too champions the idea that proprietors should exploit their lands directly, but he despairs of their doing so. The common practice is leasing out the land. The best that he hopes for is that the crown will not place too great a burden of taxation on the *laboureurs* who are starved of capital.[74]

Serres' ideal for the development of agriculture on the basis of the direct

[73] Ibid., pp. 128–9.
[74] Montchrétien, *Traicté de l'œconomie politique*, pp. 42–3.

capitalist exploitation of large estates remained unrealized. Most of the arable land continued to be leased out to tenants or sharecroppers, who worked the land with the help of family and wage labour. But we should not therefore think that French agriculture, particularly in the north of the kingdom, was doomed to stagnate. Scattered farmland, combined with open fields, may, in fact, be regarded as combining some of the advantages of scale of large estates with the minimal loss of labour input which is characteristic of the small farm.[75] Indeed, in both northern France and the English Midlands such arrangements made possible more than respectable levels of agricultural productivity.[76]

Indeed, there is little doubt that the richer peasants who farmed many of these tenements exploited them for a profit and used wage labour to do so. Despite the persistence of a large stratum of subsistence producers, and the inordinate role of rents, taxes and seigneurial dues in the rural economy, an authentically capitalist element had nonetheless been added to the French rural economy whose importance in the long run was to grow.

Certainly dispossession of the poor peasantry and their transformation into a rural proletariat or semi-proletariat continued until the time of the Fronde. This process by itself does not appear to have provoked much effective protest. Rather, protest appears to have broken out where the interests of both rich and poor peasants in the countryside seemed jointly to be threatened. Such seems to have been the case with respect to the rising level of rural taxation in the first half of the seventeenth century. The alienation of the collective rights of villages over common lands into the hands of the bourgeoisie likewise provoked an outcry in the same period.[77]

DRAINAGE OF THE LAND

The drainage of marshland by developers seems to have been a particular sore point in the reign of Henri IV and in its immediate aftermath. One of the earliest projects of Humphrey Bradley's Société générale de dessèchement des marais et lacs du France unfolded in the wetlands of Saintonge near Rochefort. Bradley signed a contract with Jeanne de Saulx-Tavannes by which she ceded part of the land which was to be drained in return for the continued use of it with a nominal rent on the rest. The contract was ultimately transferred from Bradley to his associates Jérôme and Marc de Comans and François de la Planche. A host of workers were brought in from Flanders. Some 90,000 *livres* had been spent on the project by 1610. That year the peasants in the region rebelled and the

[75] See the ground-breaking article by Stefano Fenoaltea, 'Transaction Costs, Whig History, and the Common Fields', *Politics and Society* 16 (1988), 171–240.

[76] Goldstone, 'Regional Ecology and Agrarian Development', p. 322.

[77] *Histoire de la France rurale*, II, ed. Neveux, Jacquart and Le Roy Ladurie, pp. 294–6; Georges d'Avenel, *Paysans et ouvriers depuis sept cent ans* (Paris, 1899), pp. 60–1.

embankments which had been constructed were destroyed in several places. The Flemish pioneers themselves were attacked by the peasants, who claimed that immemorial rights of reed gathering, fishing and pasturage were being stripped away. Ultimately, part of the drained land had to be given to the peasants in recognition of their claims.[78]

In 1612 Marc de Comans arrived in Languedoc at the invitation of the authorities to begin large-scale drainage operations by undertaking a survey of marshes in Languedoc. He was heartily welcomed by the elites, but such was the hostile reaction of the peasants living near the marshes to this threat to their livelihood that Comans was forced to abandon his project.[79] In 1617 a syndicate of which Bradley was a part began the drainage of the swamp of Varnier at the mouth of the Seine. The next year the inhabitants of the region protested that they could no longer pasture their flocks and 'furthermore that there are an infinity of the poor who have no other means of livelihood except the swamp'.[80]

RENEWAL OF INDUSTRY

Barthélemy de Laffemas became the champion of the idea of creating a strong national industry. Born in 1545 at Beausemblant in Dauphiné, Laffemas became a merchant trafficking with other countries. In 1566 he became *tailleur-valet de chambre* of the young Henri de Navarre, and, ten years later, his *argentier*. Later he was named *valet de chambre* to the new king. At the Assembly of Notables of Rouen Laffemas outlined a comprehensive scheme for economic recovery based on state support for manufactures and the exclusion of foreign imports. In his *Sources de plusiers abus et monopoles* and *Reiglement general pour dresser les manufactures* published shortly afterwards, he presented this scheme as a way of setting the poor to work.[81] At the same time, he called for the close regulation of industry by the establishment in each town of a *chambre de métier* in each craft. These bodies were to assure the quality of products, while restoring workers to obedience, suppressing combinations and forcing the poor to work by threatening them with confinement in workhouses.[82]

Between 1598 and 1600 Laffemas headed an enquiry into necessary economic reforms based on reports from the principal guilds of Paris. At the same time, he carried on his lobbying and pamphleteering in favour of the establishment of a silk

[78] Dienne, *Histoire du dessèchement*, p. 80; Louis Papy, *L'homme et la mer sur la côte de la Loire à la Gironde, étude de géographie humaine* (Bordeaux, 1941), p. 386.
[79] Dienne, *Histoire du dessèchement*, p. 197.
[80] Ibid., p. 153. For similar struggles in Picardy see ibid., p. 163.
[81] The full title of the second work is *Reiglement général pour dresser les manufactures en ce royaume et couper les cours des draps de soye et aultres marchandises qui perdent et ruynent l'Etat* (Paris, 1597).
[82] *Source de plusieurs abus et monopoles*, pp. 12–13. On Laffemas' economic ideas see Hauser, 'Le système social de Barthélemy de Laffemas', *Revue bourguignonne* 19 (1908), 113–31; Charles Woolsey Cole, *French Mercantilist Doctrines Before Colbert* (New York, 1931, 1969), pp. 63–112.

industry and other manufactures. Fundamental to this effort was the claim that the establishment of such industries was required to eliminate English and other imports which were impoverishing the population of France.

In April 1601 the king established a commission to study Laffemas' proposals. The next year Laffemas was appointed Controller General of Commerce and assumed direction over this commission. During the next two years (1602–4), the commission met seventy-six times to consider a wide variety of proposals for the development of industry.[83]

In the fourteen years between the Assembly of Rouen and the death of the king (1596–1610) at least forty new enterprises were created with the help of royal monopolies usually accompanied by royal grants. It has been estimated that the crown spent between 800,000 and 900,000 *livres* in support of such enterprises during this period.[84] Paris alone saw the opening of at least fifteen new enterprises, including workshops for the manufacture of fustian, tapestries, silks, oriental carpets, gold-stamped leather, and steel and lead pipe. Sully and Laffemas co-operated in the assessment and patenting of about thirty-five new inventions or processes during the same period. These included five new kinds of grain mills, a mechanical thread spinner, water-pumps, derricks, mechanical treadmills, self-propelled cars, boats, clocks, presses and furnaces.

The economic applications which were envisaged for some of these innovations can be seen if we refer once more to the anonymous memorandum regarding the water-pump of the Sire Travah of Metz. This pump was seen by Henri's advisers as opening the door to – among other things – the widespread development of water meadows, the key to increasing both the amount of livestock and the productivity of agriculture. Useful to agriculture, the pump, it was held, would make it possible to do without water-mills. Such mills were, in many cases, an obstacle to navigation. Water-mills were also expensive to build because they used so much wood. The milling of grain at such mills, furthermore, might be an excessively costly business, because of their distant locations. The proposed pump would be powerful enough to supply a whole town. It would have enough pressure even to provide water to the upper storeys of houses. The applications envisaged for the pump in industry were notable: it could be used to get rid of ground-water accumulated in mines – the greatest single obstacle to mining operations; dyers, tanners, bleachers of canvas, cotton and fustian, all of whom require much water, would find the pump of value; finally, the pump could be employed to work bellows for all those, especially ironmasters, who employ fire in manufacturing.[85] In conclusion, the anonymous author of the memorandum adds the rather surprising observation that the action of the pump could be improved by seeking the advice of expert

---

83   The documents of this commission are collected in *Documents*, ed. Champollion-Figeac, IV.
84   Boissonade, *Le socialisme d'etat*, p. 185.
85   BN MS Fr. 16739, fos. 232r.–233r.

mathematicians and architects.[86] The connection between theoretical knowledge and practical application, contrary to a commonly held view in the history of science, thus appears to have been perfectly well understood.[87]

Interest in new machines may have been stimulated by a partial recovery of wages during the reign of Henri IV.[88] In any case, the notion of raising the productivity of labour was fundamental to the attraction of the new inventions. Thus in 1604 Laffemas published a *Recueil presentée au roy, de ce qui se passé en l'assemblée du commerce, au palais, à Paris*,[89] in which the question of productivity predominates. In this report to the king, Laffemas attempts to summarize the projects set up with the help of the commission over which he had presided during the last few years. One of these projects was an iron and copper rolling and slitting mill at Etampes which produced laminated metal pieces which previously had to be made by hand by a locksmith or brazier, or imported at great expense. In the new mill, in contrast, the output in one day was greater than that possible for a brazier in a month, and at much lower cost.[90] Another invention, signalled out by Laffemas, was a new flour sieve which could process more flour in an hour than normally could be handled in a day. Moreover, it required little or no physical labour, so that a child, blind man or crippled old man could earn his living operating it.[91] Laffemas noted a new mechanical spinner which could spin wool, cotton, linen and canvas thread and which could likewise be operated mechanically by those otherwise unemployable.[92] The notion of improving output per individual worker is similarly embedded in the royal patent issued for a press said to allow one man to do the work of forty.[93]

Regarding many of these new enterprises, Gaston Zeller makes the important point that they were fundamentally different from the older forms of manufacturing characteristic of the sixteenth century. The new industries established or proposed under Henri IV were for the most part large and concentrated enterprises.[94] Their outstanding characteristic was the attempt to speed up the turnover of capital and to raise productivity by concentrating workers under a single roof. But such an enterprise required a considerably higher investment of

---

[86] Ibid., fo. 233r.
[87] See Margaret C. Jacob, *The Cultural Meaning of the Scientific Revolution* (Philadelphia, 1988), p. 32.
[88] Denis Richet, 'Croissance et blocages en France du XVᵉ au XVIIIᵉ siècle', *Annales: ESC* 23 (1968), 766–7.
[89] See *Documents*, ed. Champollion-Figeac, IV, 282–301.
[90] Ibid., IV, 286–7.
[91] Ibid., IV, 288.
[92] Ibid., IV, 296.
[93] AN Coll. Lenain MS 63, fo. 804.
[94] Zeller, 'L'industrie en France avant Colbert' in *Aspects de la politique française*, pp. 321–3. The new large scale of enterprise is seen in the plans for a huge new silkworks in Paris which formed the basis for the construction of the Place Royale conceived initially as a manufacturing and commercial showcase. See Hilary Ballon, *The Paris of Henri IV: Architecture and Urbanism* (Cambridge, Mass. and London, 1991) pp. 59–77.

capital. Thus, for example, an entrepreneur, who wished to open eighteen silk manufactures in Provence, appealed to the crown for funds to build and equip these 'maisons', which had to be 'large and spacious'.[95] Likewise, the entrepreneurs who proposed to create a new manufacture for Bruges satin and damask silk at Troyes rented a 'maison' which could accommodate 400 looms, 200 of which were to be built at the expense of the entrepreneur.[96] The same large scale is manifest in a proposed tapestry works at Montreuil involving 100 looms, and a lace manufacture at Rouen requiring 150 looms.[97] In such enterprises the labouring process involved in manufacture was basically transformed, in that the producer, having lost all control of the means of production to the employer, was now completely at his mercy. Even without technological innovation involving further division of labour, such a reorganization of labour offered the possibility of real gains in productivity.

It is difficult to measure the success of the campaign to develop French manufactures under the first Bourbon king. Fagniez, for example, had his doubts about the success of Laffemas and Henri IV in developing the silk industry. At best, he believed, the picture was a mixed one at the end of the reign of Henri IV.[98] Nevertheless, one cannot but be impressed by the success of this effort if one looks, for example, at French exports to the Levant. Jonathan Israel has published a table comparing the growth of Dutch trade with the Levant to that of England, France and Venice between 1604 and 1613, the most profitable branch of this trade being silks. Dutch remittances in the nine-year interval more than tripled to 500,000 ducats. However, the Dutch were unable to exploit the silk trade, which was the most profitable part of this commerce. It was Venice and France which held the monopoly on this traffic. Moreover, whereas in 1603 the Venetian trade amounted to 1,250,000 ducats, it had fallen to 850,000 ducats in 1613. French trade, by contrast, had grown from 800,000 to 1,750,000 ducats, a figure which exceeded the Venetian, Dutch and English combined total.[99] Given the fact that the Mediterranean market was central to the whole of the European textile industry, the French commercial advantage only underlines the strength of French textile manufacturing.[100]

Experiments with new forms of industrial organization are especially apparent in the silk industry at Nîmes. There Antoine and Lois Bonfa tried to make their workshop into a real industrial enterprise by attracting outside investment. Through their connections with the fairs of Beaucaire, they borrowed funds from Italian and Lyonnaise bankers to capitalize their enterprise. They also tapped

---

95 *Documents*, ed. Champollion-Figeac, IV, 216, 218.
96 Ibid., IV, 226.
97 BN MS Fr. 16739, fos. 227v., 228v.
98 Fagniez, *L'économie sociale*, pp. 130–4.
99 Israel, *Dutch Primacy*, pp. 99–100.
100 Richard T. Rapp, 'The Unmaking of the Mediterranean Trade: International Trade Rivalry and the Commercial Revolution', *Journal of Economic History*, 35 (1975), 499–525.

other sources of credit through their connections with Auignon, the Comtat-Venaissin, as well as Paris. At the same time, breaking with long tradition, they actively sought out other partners in their business and employed workers by the piece, rather than by the day.[101]

The statutes of the Lyons silk spinners of 1601 reveals that mechanical silk spinning had made considerable progress. By that time, there were silk-spinning mills in at least eleven small towns around Lyons. Masters were limited in the number and size of the mills they could control: thus, no master could operate more than four mills and no mill could have more than eighteen spinning machines – still a large number of machines.[102]

The introduction of new products, or the improvement of the quality of manufactures, captured the imagination of the monarchy. Henri IV conceived the notion of establishing a conservatory of arts and crafts at the Louvre in which models of all kinds of new inventions were put on display for the purpose of public instruction.[103] Masters of painting, sculpture, cabinetmaking, jewellery manufacture, clock-making, armour-making, mechanical arts and engraving were installed in the Grand Galerie of the Louvre. These skilled masters were to train workers who, freed from the normal guild restrictions, were to establish themselves in towns throughout the kingdom, improving the whole level of manufacture.[104]

INVENTIONS AND PROGRESS

Contemporaries were increasingly conscious of the surge of invention taking place in France. Laffemas' son, Isaac, claimed that the commission over which his father presided had reawakened the mechanical sciences in France.[105] Palma Cayet, commenting on the large number of inventions patented during these years, noted that 'France seemed to wish to claim the rightful ownership of all kinds of arts and inventions as it is France which elaborates all of them'.[106] Laffemas himself was convinced of the inventive genius of the common people. Pointing to the fact that the son of an ordinary gardener had been able to discover a more effective way of spinning silk thread, he asserted that there was every reason to believe that other rustics could discover better ways of producing silk if they were given the opportunity to do so.[107]

[101] Teisseyre, 'L'industrie lainière à Nîmes', p. 397.

[102] H. Baret, *Histoire du travail dans l'ancienne généralité de Lyon: Lyonnais, Forez, Beaujolais* (Saint-Etienne, 1939), pp. 37, 40.

[103] Lespinasse, *Les métiers et corporations*, I, 107; Fagniez, *L'économie sociale*, pp. 101–2.

[104] Boissonade, *Le socialisme d'état*, p. 177.

[105] *L'histoire du commerce de France* (Paris, 1606), p. 45. See *Archives curieuses de l'histoire de France*, XIV, 415.

[106] Palma Cayet, *Chronologie novenaire contenant l'histoire de la guerre sous le règne de très chrétien roy de France et de Navarre* in *Nouvelle collection des mémoires pour servir à l'histoire de France*, ed. J.F. Michaud and B. Poujoulat, vol. XII (Paris, 1836–9), Book VI, p. 259.

[107] *Lettres ... de feu la royne mère*, pp. 10–11.

The increasing awareness of innovation can be seen in the works of Guido Panciroli. In the first volume of his work on discoveries and inventions, published for the first time in the French vernacular shortly after the reign of Henri IV, Panciroli attributed most inventions to Antiquity.[108] Inventions which might have been seen as innovations were considered in this first volume as having been lost in the past and as having been subsequently recovered. But in the second volume of this work, Panciroli felt obliged to devote a special section to 'things newly invented and previously unknown'. Included in this new category was the discovery of the New World with its hitherto unknown fauna and flora, as well as porcelains, brass, sulphuric acid, whisky, compasses, printing, maps, domed architecture and telescopes.[109]

But perhaps the most striking expression of the growing consciousness of the new material possibilities of technology can be found in the writings of Nicolas Briot. Briot, a Calvinist who had worked in Germany for many years, had invented a new machine for minting coins. He entered into a dispute with the officers of the Cour des monnaies and the workers in the Paris mint which went on for years. In his *Response* (1617) Briot attempted to answer the objections raised by opponents to his machine.[110] One of these objections was that non-European monarchies, including the kingdom of China, considered the most well-governed and inventive state in the world, did not use machines to coin their money. Briot's answer was a startling assertion of Western superiority. He noted that Europeans were completely different from these non-Europeans in religion, government, culture, manufacture and technology, including

an infinitude of other beautiful and good inventions which not long since were unknown to us and of which we now make good use and of which the great part of which are not used by these barbarians and nations. But it is enough to call them barbarians to avoid taking their practice as example. Of necessity one must believe that we are in our lands more ingenious and subtle in all things since the greatest part of the arts alleged above have been either invented or brought to their perfection here.[111]

Among the most important inventions of the period was the silk loom invented by Claude Dangon which helped revitalize the French silk industry.[112] Prior to the religious wars, the number of looms in Lyons had peaked at 7,000, falling to a mere 1,600 looms at the conclusion of the conflict. Dangon's loom was not only

108 *Livre premier des antiquitez perdues, et si vif représentées par la plume de … G. Panacrol* (Lyons, 1617). Panacroli's model for this first volume seems to have been Polydor Vergil's *De inventoribus rerum*, one of the most popular books of the sixteenth century.
109 *Livre second des choses nouvellement inventees, & auparavant incognues* (Lyons, 1617), preface.
110 *Response faite par Nicolas Briot, … aux remonstrances de la Cour des monnayes et des prévosts, ouvriers et monnayers, tant de la monnaye de Paris que des autres monnayes de France* (Paris, 1617).
111 Ibid., p. 23.
112 Arthur Jean Kleinclausz, *Histoire de Lyons* (Lyons, 1939–50), II, 4, 14–16; Henri Hennezel, *Claude Dangon. Essai sur l'introduction des soieries faconnées en France d'après des documents inédits, 1605–13* (Lyons, 1926).

easier to operate but was able to produce highly competitive velvets and taffetas in multiple colours. By 1611, with the help of the monarchy and city officials, Dangon had established nineteen looms in his own workshop and seven more with other masters. Beside the *compagnons* and apprentices in his employ he was providing work for scores of others in preparing and mounting the thread on the loom, maintaining the looms and finishing the cloth.[113] In 1611 he proposed to establish, with the help of the municipality, 200 looms throughout the city and to supply apprentices at the rate of six every six months to those who would follow his example by installing his machines. The Italian silk importers in Lyons conspired against him, stirring up other silkmasters to oppose Dangon. They tried to steal his designers, workers and customers. His workers were incited to threaten him and sabotage his machines.[114] According to the analysis of Salvatore Ciriacono, despite the long-term importance of his machine for the competitiveness of the French silk industry, Dangon's efforts were defeated by the rigidity of the Lyonnaise guild system.[115] Ciriacono is mistaken on this point, since, in fact, Lyons had only recently, once again, rejected the establishment of such a guild system.[116] Rather, as we have seen, he was defeated by the continuing domination of Italian importers of manufactured silk, a fact which ultimately made the fortune of the rival manufacturing centre of Tours.[117]

Royal patents for new inventions continued to be issued after the death of Henri IV. In 1614 patents were granted for a new pumping system,[118] furnace,[119] horseless carriage,[120] and chimney flue.[121] The next year a patent was issued to a Fleming for an anti-rust compound.[122] But the failure of the monarchy adequately to support the development of new inventions and their application to manufacturing is particularly noticeable. Indeed, even the pace of invention seems perceptibly to slow in the decades following Henri IV's death.

One of the most important initiatives Henri IV took was to invite foreign entrepreneurs and workers to emigrate to France. In so doing, he attempted to reverse the drain of skills and capital that had occurred during the wars of religion. There was a notable influx of Italian, German, Flemish and Dutch entrepreneurs and skilled workers, who helped to invigorate land drainage, silk-making, tapestry-making, lace-making, and metallurgical, glass-making and mining indus-

---

[113] Hennezel, *Claude Dangon*, p. 25.
[114] Ibid., p. 32.
[115] Salvatore Ciriacono, 'Silk Manufacturing in France and Italy in the Seventeenth Century: Two Models Compared', *Journal of European Economic History* 10 (1982), 171–3.
[116] Justin Godart, *L'ouvrier en soie. Monographie du tisseur lyonnais, étude historique, économique et sociale* (Lyons, 1879; Geneva, 1976), p. 80.
[117] Boissonade, *Le socialisme d'état*, pp. 249–50.
[118] An Coll. Lenain MS 63, fo. 130.
[119] Ibid., fo. 38.
[120] Ibid., fo. 50.
[121] Ibid. fo. 107.
[122] Alexandre Tuetey, *Inventaire analytique*, I, no. 3426.

tries. One such inventive immigrant was the Englishman Richard Lee, the inventor of the stocking frame.[123] In 1589 Lee held a living as curate or incumbent at Calverton, Nottinghamshire, having graduated from the University of Cambridge. Tradition has it that he was inspired to invent the stocking frame owing to the indifference shown towards him by a young woman whom he was attempting to court who was preoccupied by her knitting. Attempts to interest Queen Elizabeth and James I having failed, Henri IV invited Lee to France, where he was promised royal support. Lee, his brother and nine English workers established themselves in a workshop in Rouen. The death of Henri IV and the subsequent confusion cut off further prospects of royal support. Lee died a broken man in Paris in 1610 or soon after. Seven of his workmen returned to England and, together with an ex-apprentice of the inventor, Aston of Calverton, laid the foundation of the stocking-frame knitting industry in England.

The failure of Dangon's silk loom in Lyons and Lee's stocking frame in Rouen is matched by that of Briot's coining machine. Born in 1579 at Dumblain in Bassigny, then part of the duchy of Bar, Briot learned the basics of coining and engraving from his father.[124] In 1605 he was appointed *tailleur général des monnaies de France*. Work in Lorraine and visits to Germany brought him into contact with the latest technological developments in the practice of minting. By 1609 he had invented a new minting machine which consisted of a mechanical scissor, laminator and stamper. Briot claimed that his machine would allow one man to produce daily as much as twenty men working by hand. According to him, his machine abridged seventeen steps in the manufacture of coin by the traditional hand manufacture. On the basis of his new machine, he proposed to produce a uniform and standardized coinage for France.[125]

Briot was opposed by the personnel of the Paris mint. The objections of the craftsmen of the mint are known to us because they are included in Briot's defence. The remonstrances of the artisans and Briot's rejoinders provide an interesting insight into the whole question of the introduction of new machines at this juncture. In the first place, Briot's opponents were at pains to make it clear

---

[123] Gravenor Henson, *History of the Framework Knitters*, introd. Stanley D. Chapman (Nottingham, 1831; New York, 1970), pp. 39–53; Abbot Paysan Usher, *A History of Mechanical Inventions* rev. edn (Cambridge, Mass., 1954), pp. 277–81; Milton and Ann Gross, *Stockings for a Queen: The Life of the Rev. William Lee, the Elizabethan Inventor* (London, 1967), pp. 126–49; Thirsk, 'The Fantastical Folly of Fashion: The English Stocking Knitting Industry, 1500–1700' in *Textile History and Economic History*, ed. N.B. Harte and K.G. Ponting (Manchester, 1973), pp. 68–71; *DNB* XI, 823–4.

[124] Henri Lepage, *Nicolas Briot, graveur de monnaies du duc de Lorraine Henri II* (Nancy, 1858); Fernand Mazerolle, *Nicolas Briot, medailleur et mécanicien (1580–1646)* (Brussels, 1891); *DBF* VII, 338; *DNB* II, 1259–60.

[125] Briot, *Raisons et moyens proposés au Roi et à messeigneurs de son Conseil … pour rendre et faire toutes les monnayes de ce royaume à l'avenir uniformes et semblables, et faire cesser toutes les falsifications, déguisemens, rognemens et affaiblissémens des monnoyes* (n.p., n.d.), p. 2. Further extensive documentation in Mazerolle, *Les médailleurs françaises du XVᵉ siècle au milieu du XVIIIᵉ* (Paris, 1902), II, 298–485.

that they were not in principle against innovation. 'We do esteem that it is wrong to reject new inventions because they are novelties. We well know that many good things have been received into the world which were new in their time.'[126] It is interesting that Briot's enemies felt it necessary to make their own openness to invention clear at this point. Evidently a certain receptivity to invention had developed among members of the educated middle class to whom their petition was addressed. Briot's opponents thus chose to dwell not upon their opposition to mechanization as such but rather upon the failed experiment with the mechanical milling of coins under Henri II. Briot's answer was to allow that those machines had been technically imperfect, but that it should not be assumed that his invention had the same problem.

Briot's opponents argued that it was not necessary to introduce machine coining since France had done without it until that point. Briot argued that if states only introduced those inventions which were necessary very few would be introduced. His invention was at one and the same time necessary as well as useful and even pleasurable. The fact that France had survived without such an invention until now was no argument against its introduction.[127]

The opponents of Briot warned that such a machine would lead to counterfeiting, given that three or four men could quickly and noiselessly produce a large amount of coin. He responded by pointing out that at the present time the number of mints where coining by hammer was carried on was already large. These mints were inefficient and wasteful. The possibilities of a breach in security under such circumstances, Briot appears to be suggesting, were evident. The construction of his machine and its use, on the other hand, required great skill, which is the product of long experience. A counterfeiter would have difficulty in carrying out such a project. In contrast, the existing system of coining by hammer was easy to learn and produced defective coins which were easy to counterfeit.[128] Fewer workers would be required for his machines but they would have to have a higher level of skill, which cannot easily be imitated.

In 1624 Briot took the farm of the Paris mint, but ultimately became discouraged by further bureaucratic obstruction and moved to England. Charles I named him engraver of the English coinage and in 1628 he became a nationalized Englishman. His machine played an important part in the standardization of the English coinage. During the civil wars, he loyally followed the royalist cause. The lesson of Briot's experience seems obvious. He was defeated not by strong government, but by a weak and confused regime which lacked a sense of direction when it came to economic matters. Under stronger regimes like Henri IV's or even Charles I's government, which, all things being equal, had a more positive approach to economic affairs, men like Briot flourished.

---

[126] Briot, *Response fait par Nicolas Briot, ... aux remonstrances de la Cour des monnoyes ...*, p. 2.
[127] Ibid., p. 5.
[128] Ibid., p. 6.

DISCIPLINING THE WORKFORCE

The regime of Henri IV sought to impose a strict discipline over workers. In 1597 Laffemas complained that 'the civil wars are in part the cause of the lack of respect and honour shown by servants, workers and others towards their masters by reason of which merchandise and manufactures are not made as they should be'.[129] In order to remedy this abuse, among others, the edict of 1597 sought to extend the regime of guilds to industries in all French towns. This edict was no more successful in doing so than the earlier one passed under Henri III.[130] Attempts to install a system of guilds in Lyons, for example, failed. In 1603 the traditional freedom of work in the city was affirmed. Among the reasons alleged for the continuation of this regime of economic liberty was the idea that Lyons could not sustain its population on the basis of its rather poor hinterland. Its population, it was alleged, could only maintain itself by a commerce which allowed freedom to all manner of workers and artisans.[131] Only an urban regime based on freedom of commerce and industry could provide a strong enough economic base to support its population. The majority of other French towns and the countryside, it should be noted, remained free of the guilds as well.[132]

The indiscipline of workers continued to be a worry. In 1597 the grain stevedores on the Paris docks were put on trial for combining to extort higher wages.[133] In 1601 a *compagnon* shoemaker was assaulted in Paris by other shoemakers for refusal to pay dues to the *compagnonnage*.[134] That same year, the Paris Parlement forbade the *compagnon* shoemakers, cobblers and tailors to leave their masters before the expiration of their contracts of employment, to congregate in taverns and to meet together in groups larger than three.[135] At Dijon in 1608 the *compagnon* shoemakers were denounced for trying to organize and combine over wages.[136]

A major effort to restore the mining industry was launched under Henri IV:[137] notable were the surveys of the mines of the kingdom by Jean de Malus and Jean du Chatelet, baron de Beausoleil.[138] More remarkable was the

---

[129] Laffemas, *Reiglement général pour dresser les manufactures et ouvrages en ce royaume*, p. 12.

[130] Lavisse, *Histoire de France*, VI, pt II, 73.

[131] Godart, *L'ouvrier en soie*, p. 80.

[132] The corporatist regime did not finally triumph until Colbert. See Hauser, *Les débuts du capitalisme*, p. 160.

[133] BN MS Fr. 8609, fo. 289r.–v.

[134] Hauser, *La modernité au XVIᵉ siècle* (Paris, 1963), p. 101; Coll. Lamoignon, x, fos. 178r.–181v.

[135] Coll. Lamoignon, x, fos. 178r.–181v., 198r.–200v., 237r.–240r.; BN MS Fr. 8085, fos. 283r.–286r, 307r.–310r.

[136] Hauser, *Les compagnonnages d'arts et metiers à Dijon au XVIIᵉ et XVIIIᵉ siècles* (Paris, 1907), p. 74.

[137] Boissonade, *Le socialisme d'état*, pp. 210–25.

[138] See Jean Du Puy, *La recherche et descouvert des mines pyrenées* in Gobet, *Les anciens minéralogistes*, pp. 75–147; Martine de Bertereau, *La restitution de Pluton* (Paris, 1640); Roman d'Amat 'Jean Du Chatelet', *DBF* XI, 1203.

appearance of the first female mining engineer, Martine de Bertereau, whose career, largely of her own making, symbolizes the innovative character of the period.[139] Although the opening of mines was seen as a way of providing work for the unemployed, in fact the problem seems to have been to try to keep men at work in the mines that were opened. Jean de Malus, who explored the mines of the Pyrenees in 1600, had, in effect, to 'disenchant' the mines by entering them in the face of the local population's fear of evil spirits.[140] Miners were not only superstitious but given to blasphemy, gambling and quarrelling amongst themselves.[141] The work was hard and labour turnover high. An *arrêt* of 1604 attempted to prevent miners from leaving without permission of the *lieutenant* of the grand master of the mines.[142] By the same *arrêt*, miners were to be supplied with physicians and priests to look after their bodies and souls, but they were also to be threatened with torture for indiscipline.[143] According to J.A. de Thou, the attempt to restore mining ultimately failed because French workers would not put up with the low wages and poor and dangerous working conditions in the mines.[144]

An unmistakable tendency to regard workers as criminals is manifest in the *cahiers* prepared for the Estates-General of 1614. One such *cahier* called for a crackdown on migrant workers, many of whom, it was alleged, were involved in criminal activity. Internal passports controlled by the parish priest and two or three upstanding and respectable members of a parish should be required of those workers who must travel. Each bishop should have a seal with the inscription 'police du diocèse de ...' and the bishops should make stamps of this seal, distributing them to each parish. As things stand now, those workers who travel about the towns and cities seeking masters, not having such certificates, are suspect, standing about on the pavement mingling with beggars as they do. Not only should they be required to carry passports, but their wages, which are too high, and their clothes, which are too pretentious, should be regulated and controlled.[145]

Despite Serres' preference for agricultural workers employed on the basis of a daily wage, he was concerned about the disorderly attitudes of such employees. Many such workers, he noted, had seen service in the religious wars and had become proud and arrogant as a result. A restoration of discipline was absolutely

---

[139] See Alexis Chermette, 'Martine de Bertereau 1590–1643: une femme ingenieur des mines au XVIIᵉ siècle', *Mémoires de l'academie des sciences, belles-lettres et arts de Lyon* 3rd series, 40 (1986), 46–57.

[140] Du Puy, *La recherche et descouvert des mines*, pp. 120, 130.

[141] Fleury, *De la législation minérale*, p. 88.

[142] BN MS Fr. 10718, fo. 31r.–v.

[143] *Inventaire des arrêts du Conseil d'Etat (règne de Henri IV)*, ed. Noël Valois (Paris, 1886–93), no. 8310.

[144] Cited in Fagniez, *L'économie rurale de la France sous Henri IV: 1589–1610* (Paris, 1894), p. 26.

[145] *Documents relatifs aux états généraux de 1614*, ed. Georges Marie René Picot and Paul Guérin (Paris, n.d.), pp. 192–3.

indispensable.[146] Appeal was made to the pope in 1599 to limit the number of feast-days, which were leading workers into dissipation and preventing the land from being worked as it should be.[147] A *règlement* of 1601 which attempted to fix wages and impose discipline on agricultural workers in the Ile-de-France likewise reflects this state of mind among employers and magistrates. Echoing the remonstrances of the 1570s, it complains of combinations by the workers which are driving up wages, to the ruin of both farmers and landlords, threatening the concept of property itself. The *règlement* limits the wages of all categories of agricultural workers, including teamsters, shepherds, reapers, grain threshers, vine-dressers and gardeners. It reimposes sumptuary regulation, prohibiting rural workers from wearing black or coloured capes. It forbids them to visit cabarets, to leave the presence of their masters on Sundays and feast-days, or to leave their employment without written permission.[148] This measure certainly did not put an end to the matter, as can be seen from a *cahier* to the Estates-General (1614) which complained that rural workers were stealing the tools of their masters, rustling livestock, or using their masters' horses to work other people's property.[149]

The expropriation of poor peasants and the harsh conditions of labour in the countryside evidently caused a constant exodus of the poor towards Paris and the other principal towns. The resultant shortage of labour in the countryside was reflected in the deliberations of the Paris Parlement. In April 1597, for example, the *procureur-général* reported that there was a scarcity of rural workers. But, at the same time, he noted the presence of an 'infinity' of poor who were perfectly able to work in the capital. The court ordered these poor to return to the villages and small towns they came from.[150] Expulsions of the poor from the cities into the countryside were again ordered in 1603 and 1612.[151]

The growing number of the poor flocking to the towns is attested to in the complaints of scores of contemporaries. The volume of such complaints appears to have risen throughout the civil wars, reaching a peak, apparently, at the beginning of the new century. Partly, no doubt, the movement of the poor towards the town reflects the violence, poverty and disorder in the countryside due directly to the war. More fundamentally, it is a reflection of rural foreclosures and expropriations, which, we have noted, continued right through the reign of Henri IV.

---

[146] Serres, *Théâtre d'agriculture*, p. 39.
[147] J. Martin Ultee, 'The Suppression of Fetes in France, 1666', *Catholic Historical Review* 62 (1976), 182.
[148] This piece is reproduced in A. Miron de l'Espinay, *François Miron et l'administration municipale de Paris ... de 1604–6* (Paris, 1885), pp. 352–6; see Jacquart, *La crise rurale en Ile-de-France*, pp. 266–7.
[149] *Documents relatifs aux états généraux de 1614*, ed. Picot and Guérin, p. 192.
[150] BN MS Fr. 8609, fo. 195r.–v.
[151] BN MS Fr. 21902, fos. 28v.–49r.

During the reign of Henri IV the rural cloth industry prospered. The drapers of Paris were to claim in 1614 that one-third of the French population depended on the manufacture of cloth for a livelihood.[152] Boissonade's estimate is more moderate, calculating that about one-tenth of the population, or between 1.5 and 2 million people, were involved in cloth production.[153] But even Boissonade's more modest figures, which are not necessarily more accurate, reflect a remarkable degree of rural proto-industrialization. Indeed, there were complaints that the development of the putting-out industry was taking manpower away from agriculture. Thus, the *cahier* to the Estates-General of 1614 of the nobility of the important proto-industrial centre of the Orléannais complained that the manufacture of silk stockings in the rural areas had led to the abandonment of agriculture owing to a shortage of labour. Only the sick, old and children ought to be allowed such work according to this *cahier*.[154] An anonymous complaint of the same period develops this point further, arguing that the putting-out industry should be banned from the small towns and villages. In particular, males should be prohibited from pursuing such occupations. Instead of being available to cultivate the land and for other 'virile' occupations, men spend their time knitting in the sun. Meanwhile, the *laboureurs* and their wives and children, deprived of this wage labour, must sweat and labour with great difficulty.[155] On the other hand, the drapers of Paris complained that the young men of the villages were taking service with the nobility in the towns, owing to which there was a shortage of labour.[156]

The draining of marshes as well as the vast building and construction programmes undertaken by Sully and Henri IV were designed to provide work, especially in the rural areas. The edict of 1599 on the draining of marshes explicitly mentions how such projects can help the 'infinitude of poor who have been destroyed by the wars to work and earn their livelihood and little-by-little re-establish themselves and raise themselves from misery'.[157] The extensive road-, canal- and bridge-building programmes of Sully were aimed, as contemporaries noted, not only at improving the infrastructure of the country, but also at providing employment for thousands of the otherwise unemployed.[158] Such public expenditure was especially notable in the *pays d'élection*.[159] The greater

---

[152] AN K 675, no. 151.

[153] Boissonade, *Le socialisme d'état*, p. 254. Modern estimates are that 22 per cent of the rural workforce in France was engaged in industry at the beginning of the seventeenth century. See Jordan Goodman and Katrina Honeyman, *Gainful Pursuits: The Making of Industrial Europe: 1600–1914* (London, 1988), p. 105.

[154] Geneviève Aclocque, *Les corporations, l'industrie et le commerce à Chartres du XIᵉ siècle à la Revolution* (Paris, 1917), p. 152.

[155] *Documents relatifs aux états généraux de 1614*, ed. Picot and Guérin, p. 104.

[156] AN K 676, no. 20.

[157] Isambert, *Recueil général*, XV, 213; Dienne, *Histoire du dessèchement*, p. 221.

[158] Buisseret, *Sully and the Growth of Centralized Government*, pp. 107–8; Verbon de Forbonnais, *Recherches*, p. 67.

[159] Buisseret, *Sully and the Growth of Centralized Government*, p. 112.

part of expenditure on public works was made in the countryside, designed to keep unemployed workers away from the towns. But, as everyone knows, the reign of Henri IV saw an immense expenditure on the reconstruction of Paris itself. In the capital the most spectacular undertakings were the work on the Louvre, Tuileries, Pont Neuf, Place Royale and Place Dauphine. But, under the leadership of the *prévôt des marchands* François de Miron, work was also carried out on paving the streets, building bridges, quays, aqueducts, sewers and fountains.[160] These extensive construction projects helped to absorb some of the flood of poor migrants who threatened to inundate the city.

Intolerance towards these poor migrants had been growing throughout the sixteenth century.[161] But this impatience appears to have reached its zenith at the turn of the century. More or less typical is the attitude in Montaigne's *La police des pauvres*.[162] In this description of the Parisian Bureau des Pauvres, Montaigne laments that the number and incorrigibility of the poor had grown so great that neither charity nor beating and imprisonment appeared to be able to control them or force them to work.[163]

The solution to the problem, a solution to which many writers of the period came to subscribe, was to transform these great numbers of impoverished subjects from being a burden into an opportunity. Among those who put the case most forcefully was Montchrétien. According to him, there is no animal born into the world who is more imbecilic than is man. However, in a few years, he can be rendered capable of great service. Those who know how to make use of this living tool, of this moving instrument, can claim to have arrived at the highest point of economy. The northern nations, i.e. England, Holland, have a better understanding of how to do this than the French. The result is that many Frenchmen seek work in Germany, England and Flanders, while still others, although robust, live in idleness at home.

France does not allow slavery. The serf, even if he belongs to someone from another nation, is set free on French soil. But although servitude has been abolished for good and Christian reasons, it is, nevertheless, the case that the public ought to take care to employ men at works and artifices which unite individual profit to common utility. The government of the ruler who prevents brigandage and thievery by providing work is to be preferred to the government

---

160 Henri de Carsalade Du Pont, *La municipalité parisienne à l'époque d'Henri IV* (Paris, 1971), p. 222; Ballon, *The Paris of Henri IV*, *passim*.

161 For a history of sixteenth-century attempts to deal with the Paris poor see Richard Francis Elmore, 'The Origins of the Hôpital-General of Paris' (University of Notre Dame, Ph.D. Dissertation, 1975), pp. 24–46; Jacques Depauw, 'L'assistance à Paris à la fin du XVIᵉ siècle', *Société française des hôpitaux* no. 59 (1989), 10–21.

162 (n.p., 1600).

163 Montaigne, *La police des pauvres*, fo. sig. D iv.

of a sovereign who only represses such criminal acts. Those who do not voluntarily work should be forced to do so.[164]

Montchrétien, like others, had the idea of transforming the unproductive poor into a productive working class by forcing them to work for wages. He advanced the concept that the mass of the poor, transformed into proletarians, could become the basis of a national industry. Fundamental to this idea was that the poor have no right to deprive the nation of their work. Likewise basic to this concept was the premise that those poor who could not work in industry ought to find employment in public works. Above all, it entailed the conception that the establishment of manufactures was less to provide work for the poor than to provide cheap labour for the construction of a national economy. Foreign imports, especially those of the Italian, Dutch and English, had undermined French industry. It was incumbent on the state to exclude these imports while encouraging the development of French industry. It was necessary to set the poor to work, control salaries and discipline the workforce in order to carry out this programme.[165] It seems that one of the principal problems in the way of such a project was the existence of a demoralized mass of expropriated migrants to the towns who had lost interest in productive activity, just as in the Third World and now even in the cities of many developed Western countries there are vast numbers of such discouraged individuals. Certainly, at the beginning of the seventeenth century in France, a kind of culture of poverty had developed in which the idea of working for mere subsistence could find no place. There was no question of raising wages above the level of subsistence which in modern times has been the key to the resolution of this problem. Rather, contemporaries, particularly from the middle class, complained that the destitute had become habituated to charity and to criminal behaviour. The answer to this problem for many of these critics was the separation of the poor from the rest of society in workhouses where they would be forced to work. The threat such elements posed to property and public order could be eliminated by confinement. At the same time, by a process of coercion such people could be transformed into wage labour.[166]

In Paris the enclosure of the poor was initiated in 1611. Two years later Rouen followed the lead of Paris and in 1614 Lyons followed suit.[167] In Paris the round-ups by the authorities were resisted not only by the poor themselves but by pages,

[164] Montchrétien, *Traicté de l'œconomie politique*, pp. 25–8. For Montchrétien's economic teaching see Cole, pp. 113–61; Paul Dessaix, *Montchrétien et l'économie politique nationale* (Paris, 1901; Geneva, 1970); Jules Duval, *Mémoire sur Antoine de Montchrétien, sire de Vateville* (Paris, 1868; Geneva, 1971); Gianfranco Brazzini, *Dall'economica aristotelica all'economica politica. Saggio sul 'Traicte' di Monchrétien* (Pisa, 1988); Nicola Panichi, *Antoine de Montchrétien. Il circolo dello stato* (Milan, 1988).

[165] Jean-Pierre Gutton, 'A l'aube du XVIIe siècle: idées nouvelles sur les pauvres', *Cahiers d'histoire* 10 (1965), 87–97.

[166] Gutton, *La société et les pauvres*, pp. 303–26.

[167] Ibid., p. 298.

lackeys, stable hands, kitchen workers, *manœuvriers*, and other unskilled and vulnerable workers, who fought the police carrying out the manhunts, asserting that to enclose the poor was an offence to God.[168]

The object of harsh confinement was in part to force a change of mentality on the poor. One of the magistrates responsible for the round-up of the Parisian poor, defending his actions, argued that the purpose of such arrests was not to hunt the poor down, but on the contrary to detain, embrace and nourish them, having care for the saving of their souls.[169] In reality, part of the motivation behind these arrests and imprisonment was to inspire the poor with fear so that they would flee the towns.[170] Indeed, of the 8,000–10,000 poor who were normally to be found in the centre of Paris, the police were initially able to find only ninety-one to round up for confinement.[171]

The statutes of the hospitals in which they were enclosed called for sexual segregation and forced labour for both men and women.[172] A considerable literature appeared in the next twenty years detailing how to manage these workhouses and, above all, how to transform their inhabitants into productive workers. Heavy doses of religious instruction and manual labour were seen as essential to most of these schemes.[173]

One of the last and most elaborate of the many such plans was drawn up anonymously in 1622, referred to as the Maison royale de Monhuat.[174] The premise of this work is that the hospitals established for the poor so far had failed, because they were too expensive to maintain and failed to enforce a sufficiently rigorous discipline on the poor confined in them.[175]

The Maison royale in this proposal, to be located roughly where Trocadero now stands, was to be an immense complex of factories and residences in which every kind of manufacturing was to be carried on with the help of water power. This industrial dystopia of truly baroque proportions was to be self-sustaining and almost self-sufficient. Almost every detail of this 'petite republique' was laid out, down to housing, clothing, food and religious instruction.[176]

The residents were to be lodged in cells with room for eight inmates, one of whom, called the 'prudent', would oversee the others. Failure to pray, work or behave properly was to be reported to the bourgeoisie appointed to manage the establishment, who would then isolate the reprobate in a fasting chamber. The daily visit of the bourgeois supervisors was necessary to maintain the inmates in 'a

---

[168] *Mémoires concernans les pauvres que l'on appelle enfermez* in *Archives curieuses de l'histoire de France*, XIV, 249.
[169] Ibid.
[170] Ibid., p. 252.
[171] Ibid., p. 253.
[172] *Status pour les hospitaux des pauvres enfermez* (Paris, 1611) in ibid., XV, 271–84.
[173] Gutton, *La société et les pauvres*, pp. 309–19.
[174] 'Projet de dépôt de mendicité sous Louis XIII', *Revue retrospective* 8th series, 2 (1835), 207–86.
[175] Ibid., p. 280.
[176] Ibid., p. 281.

marvellous fear and respect however wicked and criminal they were, which will force them to surrender their bad attitudes and teach them to work'.[177] The objective of this severe treatment, according to the anonymous author of this project, was to force the poor either to find work or to leave the city as an alternative to the harshness of penal confinement.[178]

It is difficult to assess the success of the attempt of the state to foster economic activity under Henri IV. One can point to the incontestable success of its efforts to foster such industries as glass-making, embroidery, linen, canvas, lace, cotton and above all silk manufacturing. Indeed, although efforts to implant silk manufacturing north of the Loire failed, without a doubt it took root in the Touraine, Lyonnaise, Languedoc, Provence and Dauphiné. Most important was the policy of state protectionism codified under Henri IV which assured these industries a national market for their products that otherwise would not have been available. Some contemporaries complained, as we have seen, that the spread of such industries into the countryside was to the detriment of the agricultural economy, which had to compete with industry for labour. I would argue that, on the contrary, the development of rural industry, which would intensify in the seventeenth century, was indispensable to the further development of a wage-based agriculture.

Probably the least successful part of Henri's economic policy was that of direct financial support for new enterprises. But too little is known about the subsequent history of these enterprises to draw definitive conclusions about this aspect of royal policy. On the other hand, there is no question that Sully's attempts to provide a stronger infrastructure to the French economy in the form of roads, bridges and canals was highly successful.[179] Likewise bearing fruit for the future of the economy was Sully's creation of a permanent corps of state engineers.[180]

Clearly, state intervention, especially in the form of protectionism, was indispensable to all successful economies in the early modern period. Protectionism was all the more important to post-civil-war France, whose economy, which had lost ground to England and Holland in the international marketplace, it was at pains to recover. All the more so as the positive aspects of state intervention tended to be vitiated by the increasing bureaucratization of French society dictated largely by fiscal and political considerations. The accompanying policies of foreign wars and heavy taxation which came to predominate in the following reign of Louis XIII must likewise be seen as nugatory from an economic point of view.

---

[177] Ibid., p. 236.
[178] Ibid., p. 284.
[179] Boissonade, 'Les voies de communications terrestres et fluviales en Poitou sous le règne de Henri IV', *Revue Henri IV* 2 (1907–8), 193–228, 295–311, and 3 (1909), 64–102; Buisseret, 'The Communications of France during the Reconstruction of Henri IV', *Economic History Review*, 2nd series, 19 (1965), 43–53.
[180] Buisseret, 'Les ingénieurs du roy de Henri IV', *Bulletin de géographie* 77 (1964), 13–84.

THE EMERGENCE OF THE NEW SCIENCE

The growing influence of Paracelsus is the most evident trend in French scientific circles towards the end of the sixteenth century. Huguenot doctors of medicine like Roch Le Baillif, Joseph Duchesne and Théodore de Turquet de Mayerne promoted the principles of Paracelsian medicine in Paris in the teeth of the fierce resistance of the stubbornly Galenic medical faculty of the University.[181] In the south of France the physician Antoine Constantin countered the increasing power of an elitist medicine by promoting Paracelsian notions of empirical healing and folk medication.[182] At the beginning of the new century Jean Beguin attracted large audiences in Paris to his lectures on Paracelsian chemistry, ran chemical experiments in a newly created laboratory and published a textbook on the subject which dominated the field for nearly a hundred years.[183]

Mayerne had received his medical training at Montpellier, where Paracelsus' views were widely accepted. The most impressive figure there at the end of the sixteenth century was Pierre Richer de Belleval, who created the first authentic botanical garden in the kingdom.[184] Belleval first came to Montpellier to study medicine in 1584, but it was at Avignon that he received his medical degree (1587). He practised at Avignon and then at Pezenas, where he came under the protection of the governor of Languedoc, Henri de Montmorency. In 1593 he was appointed to the new royal chair of anatomy and botanical studies of Montpellier. Two years later he received a doctorate there.

In the meantime, Belleval began to create his botanical garden based on royal patronage. It was made up of the King's Garden (medicinal plants), the Queen's Garden (mountain plants from Languedoc and elsewhere) and the King's Square (plants of purely botanical interest). The object of the garden was to carry on experiments of interest to both medicine and agriculture. The establishment of Belleval's royal chair of anatomy and botany was paralleled by the creation of a royal chair of pharmacy and surgery. The establishment of this chair at

---

[181] Debus, *The Chemical Philosophy*, I, 148–61; A.G. Chevalier, 'The Antimony War – A Dispute Between Montpellier and Paris', *CIBA Symposium* 2 (1940), 420–1.

[182] See *Brief traicte de la Pharmacie Provencale suivant laquelle la medecine peut estre faicte des remedes qui se trouvent en chasque province, sans qu'on soit contraint les aller mandier ailleurs* (Lyons, 1597). On the growing academic attack on folk medicine see Alison K. Linge, 'Empirics and Charlatans in Early Modern France: The Genesis of the Classification of "Other" in Medical Practice', *Journal of Social History* 19 (1985–6), 583–604.

[183] P.M. Rattansi, 'Jean Beguin', *DSB* I, 571–2; T.S. Patterson, 'Jean Beguin and his *Tyrocinium Chymicum*', *Annals of Science* 2 (1937) 243–98; James Riddick Partington, *A History of Chemistry* (London, 1962), III, 1–4; Hélène Metzger, *Les doctrines chimiques en France du début du XVIIᵉ siècle à la fin du XVIIIᵉ siècle* (Paris, 1969), pp. 36–44.

[184] Roman D'Amat, 'Pierre Richer de Belleval', *DBF*, V, 1342–3; Louis Dulieu, 'Pierre Richer de Belleval', *DSB* II, 592; Dulieu, 'Pierre Richer de Belleval', *Monspeliensis Hippocrates* (1968), 1–18; Louise Guiraud, *Le premier jardin des plantes de France: étude historique et documents* (Montpellier, 1911); Reed, *Botany in Medieval and Renaissance Universities*, pp. 80–90.

Montpellier represented the culmination of a century of effort on the part of apothecaries and surgeons to have an education equal to that of physicians.[185] Belleval's garden was destroyed by civil strife. He died before he could publish his planned herbarium of Languedoc.

Belleval's botanical activity at Montpellier paved the way for the work of Guy de La Brosse, the founder of the Parisian Jardin des Plantes.[186] The bulk of La Brosse's activity took place in the reign of Louis XIII. Nevertheless, it is worth underlining the presence in his thought of the same blend of Paracelsianism and empiricism which characterized Duchesne and Beguin. In the case of La Brosse, however, it is empiricism which has the upper hand. His strong interest in the application of botanical and chemical knowledge to agriculture is also noteworthy. Samuel Hartlib considered him a pioneer in this respect.[187]

The empirical bent of French science is nowhere better exemplified than in the activity of Nicolas Claude Fabri de Peiresc.[188] Peiresc was a great amateur and collector who amassed a vast collection of antiquities, curiosities, books and manuscripts. His gardens at Belgentier in Provence were in their day the third largest in the kingdom after those of the king in Paris and Belleval in Montpellier. His cosmopolitanism is reflected in his vast correspondence at home and abroad, while his patronage and support of scientific endeavour played an important role in the establishment of the new philosophy, paving the way for Mersenne and Gassendi.

Peiresc was born in 1580. His father was a *conseiller* in the Parlement of Provence. He began his education at Aix and Avignon and continued it at the Jesuit College of Tournon where he began to study astronomy for the first time. In 1599 he went to Padua, where he met the learned antiquarian,

---

[185] Dulieu, *La pharmacie à Montpellier de ses origines à nos jours* (Lamalou-les-Bains (Hérault), 1973), p. 59.

[186] Henry Guerlac, 'Guy de la Brosse', *DSB*, II, 536–9; Guerlac, 'Guy de la Brosse and the French Paracelsians' in *Science, Medicine and Society in the Renaissance: Essays to Honor Walter Pagel*, ed. Debus (New York, 1972), I, 177–99; Rio C. Howard, 'Guy de la Brosse and the *Jardin des plantes* in Paris' in *The Analytic Spirit: Essays in the History of Science*, ed. Harry Woolf (Ithaca, 1981), pp. 195–224; Howard, 'Guy de la Brosse: The Founder of the *Jardin des plantes*' (Cornell University, Ph.D. Dissertation, 1974).

[187] Rio Howard, *La bibliothèque et la laboratoire de Guy de la Brosse au Jardin des plantes à Paris* (Geneva, 1983), p. 14.

[188] Harcourt Brown, 'Nicolas Claude Fabri de Peiresc', *DSB* X, 488–92; Seymour L. Chapin, 'Astronomical Activities of Nicholas Claude Fabri de Peiresc', *Isis* 48 (1957), 13–29; Jean Bernhardt, 'Les activités scientifiques de Nicolas Claude Fabri de Peiresc', *Nouvelles de la République des lettres* 11 (1981), 165–84; Jonathan L. Pearl, 'Peiresc and the Search for Criteria of Scientific Knowledge', *Proceedings of the Sixth Annual Meeting of the Western Society for French History* 6 (1978), 110–19; Pearl, 'The Role of Personal Correspondence in the Exchange of Scientific Information in Early Modern France', *Renaissance and Reformation* 8 (1984), 106–13; P. Costabel, 'Les satellites de Jupiter de Galilée à Newton', in *Peiresc ou la passion de connaître: actes du colloque de Carpentras 5–7 novembre, 1987* (Paris, 1990), pp. 91–108; A. Beaulieu, 'Mersenne, rival de Peiresc', in *Peiresc*, pp. 23–46; F.J. Baumgartner, 'The Origins of the Provençal School of Astronomy', *Physis* 28 (1991), 291–304.

numismatist and lawyer Giovanni Vincenzo Pinelli. There he met Galileo, too, then a professor at the university. During 1600 he travelled in Italy, Switzerland and France, visiting libraries and galleries, while being received into the homes of distinguished men. He then enrolled in the law faculty of the University of Montpellier, taking the learned Huguenot jurist Julius Pacius as his mentor.

From Pinelli and Pacius he acquired an insatiable interest in Antiquity, the arts and the wonders of the natural world. Having completed his legal training, Peiresc was appointed *conseiller* in the Parlement of Provence. In the next few years, he served as secretary to Guillaume du Vair, president of the Parlement of Provence, accompanied the embassy of Le Fèvre de la Broderie to England and visited the Netherlands, where he met L'Obel and L'Ecluse.

During these years, Peiresc maintained his earlier enthusiasm for astronomy. But his interest was greatly intensified by the news of Galileo's discovery of the moons of Jupiter (7 January 1610). This discovery, made possible by the invention of the telescope, powerfully reinforced the Copernican world-view, while opening the way to new vistas for observational astronomy. In the next months, Peiresc ordered five telescopes to be constructed and sent to him from Paris. On 25 November he was able to sight Jupiter's moons through one of these instruments.

Peiresc corresponded with Francis Bacon, sharing with him a strongly empirical approach as well as a commitment to the utilitarian purposes of scientific enquiry. This is seen in the fact that from 1610 to 1612 Peiresc continued his observations of the moons of Jupiter in order to create tables which he hoped, mistakenly as it turned out, could serve as the basis for the determination of longitude. In 1611 he even sent an assistant, Jean Lombard, to Malta, Cyprus and Lebanon to record the position of the moon in local time as part of this effort.

Another contemporary influenced by Galileo was the canon theological of Sarlat, Jean Tarde.[189] Tarde received a doctorate in law from the University of Cahors and then continued his studies at the Sorbonne. In 1606 he undertook a topographical survey of the diocese of Cahors. In carrying out this survey, he used a small quadrant equipped with a compass needle and attached to a sundial, which he described in *Les usages du quadrant à l'esquille aymantie* (1621). During a trip to Italy, he visited Galileo and reported the substance of his conversations with him in *Borbonia sideria* (1620), translated two years later into French as *Les astres de Bourbon*. In this work, he put forward the mistaken

---

189 Edward Rosen, 'Jean Tarde', *DSB*, XIII, 256–7; Jean Tarde, *A la recontre de Galilée: deux voyages en Italie*, ed. François Moureau and Marcel Tetel (Geneva, Slatkine, 1984); Antonio Favaro, 'Di Giovanni Tarde e di una sua visita a Galileo dal 12 al 15 novembre 1614', *Bolletino di bibliografia e storia delle scienze matematiche e fisiche* 20 (1887), 345–71; Gabriel Tarde, 'Observations au sujet des astres de Bourbon du chanoine Tarde', *Bulletin de la société d'histoire et d'archéologie du Périgord* 4 (1877), 169–73.

idea, based on his observations, that sunspots were really planetary bodies. Tarde praised the Copernican hypothesis being championed by Galileo, but did not commit himself to its truth or falsity.[190] The first really whole-hearted French supporter of Galileo's Copernicanism was Elia Diodati, a member of the Parlement of Paris, who came from an Italian Protestant family exiled in Geneva. In 1620 he met with Galileo, offering to arrange for the publication of the *Sidereal Messenger* and any other of Galileo's works in France in case of censorship in Italy.[191]

Tarde's and Peiresc's observations were vitiated by the false theoretical premises on which they were based. Nevertheless, their works testify to the strongly empirical cast of French science of the time and mark the foundation of observational astronomy in that country. Indeed, it seems that French science in the late sixteenth and early seventeenth centuries must be seen as largely marked by what Thomas Kuhn has called its experimental rather than classical approach.[192] According to Kuhn, disciplines like geometry, astronomy, statics, harmonics and optics had developed from Antiquity a mathematically based set of techniques and concepts which he defines as classical science. In contrast, there emerged a new current of scientific enquiry in the seventeenth century, embodied above all in the work of Bacon, which Kuhn calls experimental. Theory was played down by this school and its empirical approach was apparent in its desire to base knowledge on a radically new engagement with nature. Our review of French science helps to make it clear that this new approach had already begun to emerge in France in the midst of the religious wars.

There were some in France, nevertheless, who were pushing their enquiries in the direction of a more classical approach to nature. Thus, a distiller by the name of Jean Brouaut who died in 1603 or 1604 undertook a series of experiments in hydrostatics that anticipate Galileo's hydrostatic experiments published in his *Discorsi*.[193] In 1613 Jacques Aleaume, as head of a circle of Parisian savants, carried out a further series of experiments which likewise confirmed Galileo's hydrostatic conclusions.[194] But it was François Viète (1540–1603) who, beyond all

---

[190] Baumgartner, 'Sunspots or Sun's Planets: Jean Tarde and the Sunspot Controversy of the Early Seventeenth Century', *Journal of the History of Astronomy* 18 (1987), 50.

[191] Baumgartner, 'Galileo's French Correspondents', *Annals of Science* 45 (1988), 175.

[192] Thomas S. Kuhn, 'Mathematical versus Experimental Traditions in the Development of Physical Science', *Journal of Inter-Disciplinary History* 7 (1976), 1–31; Antonio Pérez-Ramos, *Francis Bacon's Idea of Science and the Master's Knowledge Tradition* (Oxford, 1988), pp. 33–5.

[193] Suzanne Colart-Bodet, 'Un distillateur français, médecin et fabricant de remèdes, précurseur de Galilée? ou du rôle meconnu des distillateurs dans la transition entre la scolastique et la science moderne', *Vorträge der Hauptsversammlung der Internationalen Gesellschaft für Geschichte der Pharmacie* (Stuttgart, 1975), pp. 11–20. For further details on Brouaut see Colart-Bodet, *Le code alchimique dévoilé: distillateurs, alchimistes et symbolistes* (Paris, 1989), pp. 10, 14–15, 22–3 and passim.

[194] Baumgartner, 'Galileo's French Correspondents', p. 173.

his contemporaries, anticipated the classical direction that French science would take.[195] Viète developed his mathematical ideas in close association with his interest in cosmological and astronomical matters. Evidently he saw his algebra as a way of resolving problems of astronomy as well as mathematics.[196] Indeed in the conclusion of his treatise *In artem analyticem isagoge* (1591), he notes: 'Finally, the analytical art ... appropriates to itself by right the proud problem, which is: TO LEAVE NO PROBLEM UNSOLVED.'[197] Viète apparently well understood that his systematic and abstract algebra, whose equations rise above all connection with geometric magnitude, figure and proportion, would be a powerful new instrument at the disposition of mathematicians and philosophers of the next generation. Indeed, a contemporary of Viète, the mathematician Henri de Monantheuil, who years earlier had already hailed the growing interest in technology, seems to announce the new century when, a few years later, in a commentary on Aristotle's *Mechanical Questions*, he asserts that Plato had enunciated only part of the truth in conceiving God as a geometer. God is in the first place a mechanic, because His world is a machine of which He is the builder and architect.[198]

[195] Viète's algebra represents a reaction by an intellectual and social elite to the excessively practical bent of existing French mathematics. See Cifoletti, 'Mathematics and Rhetoric', pp. 63, 99–100, 288–91; H.L.L. Busard, 'François Viète', *DSB* XIV, 18–25; Jacob Klein, *Greek Mathematical Thought and the Origin of Algebra*, tr. Eva Braun (Cambridge, Mass., 1968), pp. 150–85, 313–53; John S. Morse, 'The Reception of Diophantus's Arithmetic in the Renaissance' (Princeton University, Ph.D. Dissertation, 1981), pp. 117–86; Richard Ferrie, 'Two Exegetical Treatises of François Viète' (Indiana University, Ph.D. Dissertation, 1980); Michael Sean Mahoney, *The Mathematical Career of Pierre de Fermat: 1601–1665* (Princeton, 1973), pp. 26–71.

[196] Morse, 'The Reception of Diophantus' Arithmetic', p. 269.

[197] *Introduction to the Analytical Art*, tr. J. Winfree Smith in Klein, *Greek Mathematical Thought*, p. 353.

[198] Rossi, *Philosophy, Technology and the Arts*, p. 143.

7

Braudel, Le Roy Ladurie and the inertia of history

E pur si muove.

In summarizing the results of this enquiry into French science, technology and economic life from the beginning of the sixteenth century until the time of Richelieu, emphasis has to be laid on the importance of two interrelated rural phenomena: proto-industrialization and primitive accumulation. During the first part of the sixteenth century, there was a great expansion of rural manufacture based on more extensive employment of wind and water power, and the use of the forests as a source of both energy supplies and raw materials. Mining, quarrying, iron, glass and ceramic manufacture all developed. At the same time, the countryside saw a great expansion of textile manufacturing extending beyond the manufacture of wool cloth to linen and canvas as well as silk. The introduction of new techniques certainly played a part – silk-spinning machines, improvements in the printing press, new tools in mining – but the essential gains came from the development of a relatively new labour process, namely the systematic exploitation of rural labour by merchant capitalists.

The economic expansion of the first part of the century came to an end with the outbreak of the wars of religion in the 1560s. The crisis which came to a head in that decade was the product of deep-seated problems in French economic life. The benefits of economic expansion had gone to fewer and fewer people as the century progressed. Court nobles, ecclesiastics, town notables and great merchants skimmed off the greater part of economic surplus, leaving the mass of urban and rural producers – including craftsmen and unskilled labourers – with less and less. The result was a gradual choking off of demand, while at the same time manufacturers and merchants found that rising food prices and higher taxes were reducing profit margins and driving up labour costs. In the meantime, the surpluses that were available were not invested productively, but instead were wasted in conspicuous consumption. The inadequate level of investment in the agricultural sector was particularly serious.

The consequences of these processes were economic and financial crises which left the state without the resources to control the kingdom politically and, in particular, to deal with an increasingly unruly nobility. The result was the outbreak of the wars of religion, which were not only a revolt led by the noble class against the authority of the state, but a feudal reaction against the upstart bourgeoisie and the commoners.

During the next three decades France was split into Catholic and Huguenot factions, both led by noble chieftains who wreaked havoc on the population and caused a steep decline in economic activity. Despite these misfortunes and in the midst of the apparent archaism of feudal reaction, the most astonishing feature of this period of civil wars was the continuing advance of the middle class. In response to the economic crisis artisans, engineers, architects, naturalists and entrepreneurs advanced ideas or put forward projects to improve agricultural output or to produce manufactures more efficiently or more cheaply. While the prospects for the success of many of these proposals was dubious in the context of the religious wars, there seems little doubt that many of these individuals understood that the essential problem of the French economy was to increase the productivity of labour – a quintessentially modern idea. While this notion of augmenting what Marxists refer to as relative surplus value as a way of improving profitability gained increasing attention, more and more voices began to be raised in favour of a reform of science in the direction of greater practicality and empiricism. The ideas of Ramus and Paracelsus were critical in this respect, but the botanists and naturalists associated with the University of Montpellier were also very important. Heightened interest in new technology and in a more empirical and practical science was an expression of the growing strength of the middle class in French society, despite economic decline and feudal reaction.

The essential reason for the continued progress of the middle class during the religious wars was the onset of significant primitive accumulation in the French countryside. In the first part of the sixteenth century the phenomenon of growing dependence on wage labour was an essential complement to proto-industrialization in the countryside and the expansion of the urban economy. But the violence, pillaging, destruction and crushing debt of the religious wars greatly increased the rate of expropriation of the less well-off peasantry largely to the benefit of both the rural and urban bourgeoisie. The urban bourgeoisie, in particular, was able to buy up a considerable portion of the land abandoned by insolvent peasants. At the same time, the more prosperous peasants were given access to this expropriated land through the extension of leasing and sharecropping opportunities. Meanwhile, the increase in the number of the landless, or the nearly landless, helped to offset whatever decline in the labour supply resulted from the ravages of war and plague. One of the surprising results of recent research on the economy of Normandy, Dauphiné and even the Ile-de-France is evidence that both rural industry, especially wool cloth, linen and canvas manufacture, and agricultural productivity continued to advance during the religious wars. It appears likely that the development of the rural wool cloth industry in Beauvaisis dates from the period of the religious wars as well. These results can be complemented by what we know of the progress of silk and silk stocking manufacture in Languedoc, Hurepoix and Beauce in the same period.

The reign of Henri IV saw the return of peace, the revival of profits and a renewal of economic expansion. The process of primitive accumulation which had begun during the religious wars continued during Henri's reign and right down until the beginning of the reign of Louis XIV. Agricultural rent, which had declined during the religious wars, began to rise once again. But in the north of France, for example, ample room existed for profits, since rents did not reach the level of 1560 again until 1620. Meanwhile, there was plenty of opportunity for rural entrepreneurs to reap substantial profits. Indeed, *fermiers* and *laboureurs* were able to sustain profit margins by holding wages down while proceeding to consolidate their holdings. The effects of rent increases were further offset by improvements in agricultural techniques, specialization and the further commercialization of agriculture as a result of expanding markets in the towns.[1]

Interest in science and technology if anything expanded in the reign of Henri IV. Most of all the monarchy became committed as never before to trying to stimulate science, technology and economic activity. It patronized the Paracelsians and the naturalists. Resuming the initiatives of Charles IX on a larger scale, it patented and supported all sorts of new inventions and infant industrial enterprises. A programme of public works designed to bolster the prestige of the monarchy and to provide a stronger infrastructure of roads, bridges and canals was carried out under the direction of Sully. The ideas of Laffemas, which called for a great expansion of industry behind a protective wall of tariffs, were implemented. The poor and unskilled labour force was brought under unprecedented control, with the idea of transforming it into an inexpensive and compliant workforce. At the same time, the monarchy attempted to strengthen the hand of capitalists over skilled labour and to improve the reputation of French manufactures by strengthening the authority of the guilds.

THE INERTIA OF THE *ANNALES*

The results of our investigation should now be brought to bear on current views of the *ancien régime*, dominated as they are by the *Annales* school. This is necessary because the picture of early modern France I have painted is so greatly at variance with that drawn by the current generation of *Annales* historians, whose influence, as is well known, extends well beyond the borders of that country. The advance of science, technology, proletarianization and rural industrialization plays almost no part in their view of sixteenth- and seventeenth-century France. The labours of the *Annales* school, as everyone knows, have led to an enormous enlargement of our understanding of the historical process, especially in the medieval and early

---

[1]   Jacquart, *Paris et Ile-de-France aux temps des paysans*, pp. 68–9, 196.

modern period. Its stress on regional history studied in depth and using, as far as possible, sources that are quantifiable has set a standard for all future historical investigation. Its commitment to a global or total kind of history which freely borrows the techniques and insights of sociology, anthropology, demography, geography, psychology and linguistics has made possible a far greater profundity of historical analysis. It is also fair to say at the outset that the *Annales* cannot be identified with a single ideological point of view. It made a point of including within its ranks a diverse group of historians ranging from Marxists like Ernest Labrousse and Pierre Vilar to those hostile to Marxism like Pierre Chaunu and François Furet.

In analysing the perspective of the *Annales* school on the *ancien régime*, I am going to explore the views primarily of Le Roy Ladurie and Braudel. Not only have they been perhaps the most prolific, celebrated and powerfully entrenched historians of this school, but they have been largely responsible for shaping this generation's sense of the *ancien régime*. Braudel has produced a monumental study of the Mediterranean as well as a history of capitalism.[2] Le Roy Ladurie has devoted himself almost exclusively to the study of the *ancien régime* and his work has had an even more direct and profound impact on our conception of this period.[3]

It has been the singular achievement of these two historians, who were for many years in the relationship of master and protégé, to present to us a profoundly conservative view of pre-revolutionary French history in the guise of a new kind of history. The approach to the *ancien régime* championed by Braudel and elaborated by Le Roy Ladurie entailed a devaluation of the importance of politics and social conflict in favour of a stress on climate, geography, demography, technology and popular culture. Politics and class conflict were relegated to tertiary or secondary levels or to the realm of event and conjuncture. The profound level or level of structure – demography, geography, climate, popular culture – was seen to be determinative.[4] Given this emphasis on such relatively intractable factors as climate, geography and popular culture, the emphasis was put on continuing structures, recurrent patterns or long-term processes (*la longue durée*) rather than on political or social change.

The *ancien régime* was seen by Braudel and Le Roy Ladurie as the archetype of such a structure. We can form an idea of how they approached it from Le Roy

---

2   *La Méditerranée et le monde méditerranéen à l'époque de Philippe II* (Paris, 1949), 2nd edn, 2 vols. (Paris, 1966); tr. Sian Reynolds, 2 vols. (New York, 1972–3); *Civilisation materielle et capitalisme (XV–XVIIIe siècles)*, 3 vols. (Paris, 1967–79), tr. Miriam Kochan, 3 vols. (London, 1981–4).

3   *Les paysans de Languedoc, histoire du climat depuis l'an mil* (Paris, 1967), tr. Barbara Bray (London, 1972); *Montaillou: village occitan de 1294 à 1324* (Paris, 1975), tr. Bray (New York, 1978); *Prestations paysannes, dîmes, rente foncière préindustrielle*, ed. Le Roy Ladurie and Joseph Goy, 2 vols. (Paris, 1982), tr. Susan Burke (New York, Paris, 1982).

4   Lynn Hunt, 'French History in the Last Twenty Years: The Rise and Fall of the Annales Paradigm', *Journal of Contemporary History* 21 (1986), 212.

Ladurie's inaugural address upon his entry into the Collège de France in 1973, entitled 'L'histoire immobile'.[5] Coming a few years after the publication of his great thesis *Les paysans de Languedoc*, as well as the events of May 1968, this lecture embodies an outlook which has remained more or less intact since then. It informs Le Roy Ladurie's contribution to the prestigious *Histoire économique et sociale de la France*, edited by Braudel and subsequently translated into English under the title *The French Peasantry, 1450–1660*.[6]

Almost from the beginning of this lecture Le Roy Ladurie attempts to differentiate his perspective from that of Marx:

from the fading cry of Marxism we retain a lesson which there is only in part to be found, namely, that in the last analysis it is in the economy, in social relations and more fundamentally in biological facts rather than in the struggle of classes that it is necessary to seek the motor of the history of the masses at least during the period which I study.[7]

The curious aspect of this proclamation is that, far from this approach providing Le Roy Ladurie with a sense of the dynamic of what he refers to as really significant history (i.e., a history, as he himself defines it, of the mass of humanity), it gives him a sense of the inertness of that mass. Like Marx, Le Roy Ladurie has been preoccupied with the social and economic determinants of history. But unlike him, he has insisted on the importance of the biological or demographic factors as well. As a consequence, he has been able to lay stress on historical continuity and the long historical run rather than on the Marxist themes of change, rupture and discontinuity.[8] It was this neo-Malthusian perspective which led him to the conclusion that the period 1300–1730 must be seen as a period without a motor or, in other words, as static and immobile.

The history of the *ancien régime*, according to Le Roy Ladurie, should be seen as a stable ecosystem in which the level of technology remained more or less unchanged. In consequence the level of agricultural productivity and therefore the ceiling on population remain fixed.[9] According to him, 'whatever changes took place between 1300 and 1720, they did not alter the characteristics of the mode of production ... which from one end to the other of the period continued to dominate our agrarian world'.[10] This world of stagnant productivity was subject

---

[5]   *Annales: ECS* 29 (1974), 673–92, republished in *Le territoire de l'historien* (Paris, 1978), II, 7–34; *The Mind and Method of the Historian*, tr. Sian and Ben Reynolds (Chicago, 1981), pp. 1–27. The viewpoint in this article is reiterated in the more recent 'L'historiographie rurale en France XIVe–XVIIIe siècles: essai d'histoire systématique ou 'eco-systématique' in *Marc Bloch aujourd'hui: histoire comparée et sciences sociales*, ed. Hartmut Atsma and André Burguière (Paris, 1990), pp. 223–52.

[6]   Tr. Alan Sheridan (Berkeley, 1987).

[7]   Le Roy Ladurie, 'L'histoire immobile', II, 9.

[8]   Hunt, 'French History in the Last Twenty Years', p. 214.

[9]   Le Roy Ladurie, 'L'histoire immobile', II, 16, 28.

[10] Ibid., p. 29.

to what Le Roy Ladurie characterized as a Ricardian cycle which based itself on the ratio of rent, salaries and population. At the beginning of the fourteenth century when the population of the French kingdom was unprecedentedly high (17 million), rents were high, salaries were low and the land was divided up into small plots. As a result of plague and war, the population fell to 9 million in 1440 and led to a reversal in the ratio of rent, salary and land. Rent levels declined, salaries rose and those peasants who survived the wars and plague had access to much larger plots of land. At this point (1440), a new cycle began, characterized by increasing population (17 million once more by 1550), rising rents, declining salaries and rural pauperization. Once again war and plague intervened towards the end of the sixteenth century, leading to a stabilization of rents, salaries and land holdings.[11]

Only in the eighteenth century was this cyclical pattern broken, when technological change and increases in agricultural productivity allowed a 'vast' demographic expansion from 19 to 27 million.[12]

For three centuries the limits of technique fixed natural limits beyond which humankind was unable to move. The amount of land available being limited, the human population was forced to adjust itself accordingly. There were ups and downs, but over the long term, the system was in a stable state within its fixed ecological limits.

MALTHUSIANISM VERSUS PROTO-INDUSTRIALIZATION

Looking over this perspective laid out by Le Roy Ladurie, we immediately notice a significant discrepancy in his numbers. In particular, Le Roy Ladurie has exaggerated the demographic breakthrough which occurred in the eighteenth century. Thus he characterizes the increase from 19 to 27 million during the eighteenth century as 'vast'. But if this increase of approximately a third is considered vast, what shall we make of an increase of nearly 100 per cent, from 9 to 17 million between 1440 and 1550? Indeed, the increase during this earlier period is well over 100 per cent if we substitute for the 17 million figure the more likely figure of 19 or 20 million which most historians accept.[13] This discrepancy is all the more serious when we realize that there was no demographic decline in the late sixteenth and seventeenth centuries comparable to the collapse of the late Middle Ages. The wars and plagues of this period did have an impact, but only in stabilizing the population at between 19 and 20 million. Despite the difficulties of the late sixteenth and seventeenth centuries there was no repetition of the downward cycle of the late Middle Ages.

[11] Ibid., pp. 19, 29.
[12] Ibid., p. 24.
[13] Le Roy Ladurie corrects himself in 'Demographie et histoire rurale en perspective' in *Histoire de la population française*, ed. Jacques Dupâquier *et al.* (Paris, 1988), I, 515.

Clearly, like causes should produce like effects. Fixed amounts of land, stagnant productivity and population increase should have led to a demographic regression but did not. Some new factor intervened which put a barrier in the way of such a catastrophe and as such puts into question Le Roy Ladurie's model of a stable ecosystem based on a cycle. It is curious that he did not recognize this new element placed in the way of demographic collapse since it is an integral part of his own *Les paysans de Languedoc*. One of the most striking episodes in this work is the fate of the peasants of the mountainous uplands of the Cevennes who, as Le Roy Ladurie tells their story, reached the ecological limits of subsistence by the first quarter of the sixteenth century. They were rescued from the threshold of demographic catastrophe by the spread of the chestnut throughout the region, and by silk production, mining and milling, more often than not under the auspices of the merchants of Nîmes.[14]

Le Roy Ladurie's treatment of the subsequent development of proto-industrialization in Languedoc is, indeed, a curious one. Thus, he does note the further expansion of the rural silk industry in the province in the midst of the religious wars and makes mention of the subsequent efforts of Laffemas to extend it further during the reign of Henri IV.[15] Yet he tends to play down the significance of this effort even though its impact on international trade was of major importance, as we have noted. Moreover, he sees no further progress in the secondary sector of the economy beyond this particular industry. But far from progress being confined to the silk industry, as Le Roy Ladurie insists, it seems that wool cloth production in Languedoc recovered after the religious wars, centred on the small towns in the foothills of Languedoc.[16] The availability of water-power as well as lower labour costs played an important role in the migration of industry to these regions. Likewise we ought to take notice of the development of ribbon- and lace-making in the rural Velay in the first half of the seventeenth century.[17] Indeed, the seventeenth century was to see an enormous expansion of rural industry in Languedoc. So much was this the case that the most recent student of the phenomenon does not hesitate to assert that Languedoc became early modern Europe's most important proto-industrial centre.[18]

The development of rural industry and attendant rural commercialization obviously opened up opportunities for alternative or secondary employment for rural producers in Languedoc and elsewhere in France. Proto-industrial activity

14 *Les paysans de Languedoc*, I, 211–20.
15 Ibid., I, 439–42.
16 J.K.J. Thomson, *Clermont-de-Lodève, 1633–1789: Fluctuations in the Prosperity of a Languedocian Cloth-Making Town* (Cambridge, New York, 1982), p. 38.
17 Germain Martin, *Le tissage du ruban à domicile*, p. 30; Martin, *L'industrie et le commerce du Velay aux XVIIᵉ et XVIIIᵉ siècles* (Le Puy, 1900), p. 24; Louis Lavastre, *Dentellières et dentelles du Puy* (Le Puy, 1911), p. 5.
18 Thomson, 'Variations in Industrial Structure in Pre-Industrial Languedoc' in *Manufacture in Town and Country before the Factory*, ed. Maxine Berg, Pat Hudson and Michael Sonenscher (Cambridge, 1983), p. 62.

made possible a fuller mobilization of the surplus labour capacity of the rural population, including men, women and children, offering families much-needed supplementary resources.[19] The importance of rural industry in this respect was indeed glimpsed by Denis Richet at a time when some of the *Annales* historians were still not prepared to turn their backs on Marxism. Writing in 1968 on the occasion of a meeting of French and Hungarian historians, Richet stressed the importance of industry to the fate of the mass of the French population: 'Incontestably', he wrote, 'and without underestimating a technical progress which was undoubtedly substantial, industrial growth in the sixteenth century was not only a recuperation but an absolute advance. It allowed us to escape the nightmare of the "Malthusian cycle" and to recover the problematic of progress of which Marx has been the herald.'[20] The industrial and commercial progress which continued in the seventeenth century was all the more important, according to Richet, considering the stagnation of agriculture during the period.[21]

The key role of rural industry in sustaining the population was missed by Le Roy Ladurie, apparently because of a conceptual blindness to the importance of the notion of class to the historical process. Yet it was precisely the development of the middle class during the period 1440–1560 which made an alternative to subsistence agriculture possible, providing critically important additional resources to the increasingly hard-pressed rural population. Thus, in an earlier chapter of this work, we noted how Le Roy Ladurie had conceded the development of a rural capitalism in Languedoc. But we also observed that he tried to qualify this concession by stressing the mass of pauperized rural producers which came to coexist with the emergent class of rural capitalists, the latter only interested in the extraction of absolute surplus value rather than the more economically progressive relative surplus value from this increasingly wretched semi-proletariat.

In response to this position we should recall first of all that the agriculture of sixteenth-century Languedoc was far from inert, serving as the seedbed for the introduction into the French kingdom of a great variety of new plants and foods.[22] In the middle of the sixteenth century, new irrigation canals and drainage systems

---

[19] Jean-Claude Debeir, Jean-Paul Deléage, Daniel Hémery, *Les servitudes de la puissance: une histoire de l'énergie* (Paris, 1986), p. 146.

[20] Richet, 'Croissance et blocages en France du XVe au XVIIIe siècles', *Annales: ESC* 23 (1968), 781. For a critique of the whole notion of a Malthusian trap see Julian L. Simon, 'Demographic Causes and Consequences of the Industrial Revolution' in *Population and Development in Poor Countries*, ed. Simon (Princeton, 1992), pp. 24–40.

[21] Richet, 'Croissance et blocages', pp. 781–2. The importance of rural industry or commercialization in sustaining the population has been noted by Bois, *The Crisis of Feudalism*, pp. 382, 389, Alain Croix, *La Bretagne aux 16e et 17e siècles: la vie, la mort, la foi* (Paris, 1981), I, 218, Guy Lemarchand, *La fin du féodalisme dans le pays de Caux* (Paris, 1989), pp. 125, 190, 281. For a critique of the neo-Malthusian view in the light of early modern industrialization see Goodman and Honeyman, *Gainful Pursuits*, pp. 13–14.

[22] Le Roy Ladurie, *Les paysans de Languedoc*, I, 55, 60–76.

were installed around Narbonne. In certain areas of Languedoc the more efficient scythe replaced the traditional sickle. There was a widespread adaptation of the plough known as the *charrue mousse* with moulder board, replacing the age-old *araire*.[23]

Thus there was no shortage of attempts to increase the productivity of rural agricultural labour. Indeed, as we have attempted to demonstrate, there was widespread consciousness of the need to augment labour productivity in both industry and agriculture. If this effort fell short of the mark – and it is not entirely clear that it did – the primary reason would appear to be that good profits were possible in both agriculture and industry through the extraction of absolute surplus at minimal risk from a population increasingly dependent on wage labour. Wretched semi-proletarians were, in fact, the ideal basis for the further development of rural commercialization and industrialization. So far as the manufacturing sector was concerned, this was especially the case with the putting-out cloth industry.

In the previous chapter I rather sardonically noted Olivier de Serres' perspective which stressed the providential nature of the rural labour market which furnished wages to the impoverished mountain people of the Vivarais while supplying crucially important supplies of labour to employers at the time of harvest.[24] But perhaps the last laugh must be left to Serres, who apparently understood the relationship between demographic survival and the availability of wage labour to a working population. Capitalist entrepreneurs offering wages do, after all, represent an escape from feudal landlords collecting labour as rent or subsistence producers attempting to reproduce themselves on micro-plots. While it would be quite incorrect to suggest that consolidation of land into large farms or estates became the rule in Languedoc or elsewhere, it is also true that no process of subdivision of the land occurred between 1560 and 1720, as had happened in the late medieval crisis. Land ownership remained largely in the hands of the nobility, clergy and, increasingly, the urban bourgeoisie. Their large or medium-sized holdings were not divided up, but rather were rented or sharecropped by prosperous peasants who hired wage labour when necessary to work the land. If there was land redistribution in this period, it was not in favour of the small or medium-sized producer as had been the case in the late middle ages, but rather in favour of the well-to-do.

Le Roy Ladurie makes it appear that the population of Languedoc was haunted during the seventeenth century by the spectre of scarcity. Actually, what is striking alongside a buoyant industrial economy is the commercialization of agriculture which helped to cushion the population against scarcity. The olive oil, wine, almonds and wheat of the plains and foothills of lower Languedoc were exchanged for the timber, chestnuts, livestock, industrial raw materials and milk

23 Ibid., I, 80, 83, 86–7.
24 See above, p. 173.

products of the mountains, while surplus grain was drawn from the wheat-growing plains of upper Languedoc. The relatively high and stable prices that characterized the grain markets indicate that the province avoided the disasters of scarcity or abundance which caused sharp price fluctuations elsewhere.[25]

CAPITALISM WITHOUT WORKERS

Le Roy Ladurie's neglect of rural industry made him belittle the significance of the capitalism that emerged under the *ancien régime*. But capitalism is still capitalism whether it is based on a regime of intensive or extensive growth. France, unlike Holland, was a country of low wages, where the introduction of machinery to replace human labour did not make economic sense in terms of enhancing profitability. This did not block either the commercialization of a considerable proportion of its agriculture or the progress of rural industrialization. But these failings of Le Roy Ladurie are relatively minor compared to the distortion of the understanding of capitalism practised by his master Braudel. According to Braudel, capitalism is to be understood as the third or highest level of a cake which is supported on larger and more substantial lower layers which, in turn, represent material life and market exchange. In the pre-industrial period capitalism in the sense of exchange for profit (profits → commodities → profits) played a relatively minor role compared to the exchange of commodities in the market and the brute reality of material life. In this schema, capitalism – which, according to Braudel, has been at least potentially present since Antiquity – is comparable to the political order, while market exchange is to be understood on the analogy of conjuncture. Such phenomena cannot be compared to the fundamental factors or deep structures of material life such as geography, natural resources, energy reserves, demography, climate, technology and *mentalité*.[26]

Braudel fails to see that capitalism is not simply to be understood as a particular use of the market, but is, in fact, a relationship between profit-seeking market activity and the exploitation of wage labour. Thus he appears to have little sense of the impact of proto-industrial activity or primitive accumulation on the material life he describes.[27] In so far as these do entail processes of expropriation and more intensive use of land and resources, they necessarily profoundly affect such so-called structural factors as demography, energy and raw material reserves, technology and even geography. The depletion of the forests, the draining of marshland, water pollution, the loss of fish and game, chronic problems of erosion and flooding, terracing of the landscape, problems of subsistence, and the

25 Thomson, 'Variations in Industrial Structure in Pre-Industrial Languedoc', pp. 64–5.
26 Dosse, *L'histoire en miettes*, pp. 146–7; Immanuel Wallerstein, 'Braudel on Capitalism, or Everything Upside Down', *Journal of Modern History* 63 (1991), 354–61.
27 William Hagen, 'Capitalism and the Countryside in Early Modern Europe: Interpretations, Models, Debates', *Agricultural History* 62 (1988), 26; Samuel Kinser, '*Annaliste* Paradigm? The Geological Structuralism of Fernand Braudel', *American Historical Review* 86 (1981), 75–6.

disappearance in many places of the hamlets of marginal farmers are what most immediately come to mind.

Rural proto-industrialization did have its limits, as has every subsequent phase of the history of capitalism. Indeed, Pierre Deyon and Pierre Jeannin have pointed out how in the eighteenth century proto-industrialization led to over-population and immiseration which could only be overcome by industrial and agricultural revolution. Nevertheless, during its phase of development, they also note that proto-industrialization was undoubtedly progressive, helping to stabilize the population during the seventeenth century and facilitating capital accumulation, intensification of markets and the spread of technical know-how in the countryside.[28]

THE AVOIDANCE OF CLASS

If Le Roy Ladurie tends to minimize the importance of the concept of class, he is positively dismissive of the notion of class conflict. In his account the crisis of the religious wars breaks out at a point when the build-up of population reaches an unsustainable level reflected in low salaries, food shortages and plagues.[29] But if we ask the question of whether class conflict had anything to do with it we get a dismissive response. Le Roy Ladurie does admit that during the late medieval crisis the nobility behaved like 'gangsters', but by the time of the outbreak of the religious wars he considers the nobility to be irrelevant.[30] The inflation of the sixteenth century had destroyed the economic basis of the seigneurie. The bourgeoisie was pushing against an open door. It is strange and inexplicable, then, that the seigneurie in his work reappears in the eighteenth century as more powerful than ever and, indeed, as a progressive force at that, in the forefront of the advance towards capitalism.[31] This incongruity is not accounted for in his work.

The discrepancy is the product of the neglect, I would suggest, of the factor of class conflict in favour of an unfortunate economism. In a work that I published in 1991 I cited the testimony of the Baron Raymond de Fourquevaux, who in 1573 was governor of Narbonne.[32] According to his account, the religious wars in Languedoc were the result of the hostility of the nobility to the economic advance of the bourgeoisie. The principal area of conflict was over the land, a conflict into which the peasants were drawn on the side of the bourgeoisie. The reaction of the nobility was to abandon the peasantry to the violence of the wars. To this key

[28] 'La proto-industrialisation: développement ou impasse?' *Annales: ESC* 35 (1980), 52–65; see also Deyon, 'L'enjeu des discussions autour du concept de proto-industrialisation', *Revue du Nord* 61 (1979), 9–15.

[29] Le Roy Ladurie, 'L'histoire immobile', II, 29.

[30] *Histoire de Languedoc*, ed. Philippe Wolf (Toulouse, 1988), pp. 293–5.

[31] Le Roy Ladurie, 'De la crise ultime à la vraie croissance, 1660–1789' in *Histoire de la France rurale*, II, ed. Neveux, Jacquart and Le Roy Ladurie, p. 431.

[32] *Iron and Blood*, pp. 60–1.

piece of evidence I added a considerable number of other contemporary accounts from both inside and outside Languedoc which likewise testified to the link between aristocratic reaction and the wars.[33] It is possible that this evidence is in some way misleading and that class conflict was not an essential cause of the wars of religion. But how is it possible in the end to write about the peasants of Languedoc without writing about the nobility? One would think that Le Roy Ladurie as the historian of Languedoc would acknowledge the existence of this kind of evidence and pass judgement on this problem instead of ignoring it in favour of more 'deep-seated' causes. Not that one doubts for a moment that demography, technology and economic productivity are important. But in this case they become an evasion because they are given primacy and are not integrated with conjunctural factors, in this case the question of class conflict.

All the more is this the case since I reject the notion that the period of the religious wars and the seventeenth century which follows are just the downswing of a Ricardian cycle or an illustration of a history without a motor. As I have attempted to point out, little if any demographic decline or redivision of the land occurred during this period. The view that the history of the period 1300–1720 is one of static equilibrium or of a history without a motor is not sustainable. In place of this perspective, I reassert a view based on the importance of class conflict in which the fourteenth and fifteenth centuries are rightly conceived of as the period of the decline, if not the fall, of feudalism and the later period, the sixteenth and seventeenth centuries, especially from 1500 to 1620, is one of continuing bourgeois advance. This advance is indisputable with respect to the first part of the sixteenth century, but is no less true of the period 1560–1620.

But suppose that for the moment we allow that population, if not declining in the seventeenth century, was at least stagnant, and the more dubious claim that productivity, including industrial productivity, was also stagnant. Is Le Roy Ladurie justified in reducing the sources of important change to the economic or demographic? Ought not an enlargement of the state structure, a re-equilibration process between the classes, the development of philosophical rationalism and the Scientific Revolution, to be seen as at least as important to the future as economics or demography? Is not the economic and demographic future itself, in part at least, a product of these factors? How can one seriously maintain a view of the *ancien régime* based on the concept of an ecosystem which ignores these non-structural factors?

SOCIETY AND BIOLOGICAL METAPHORS

But even more to the point, we may ask what, after all, Le Roy Ladurie has in mind in referring to the *ancien régime* as an ecosystem. Clearly part of the strategy

[33] Ibid., pp. 61–5.

in deploying such a term is to play on its fashionableness. In any case the term has at least two meanings, which are quite distinct. In the first it refers to a relatively closed interdependent biological system. Given his stress on the biological constraints on the society of the *ancien régime*, Le Roy Ladurie would seem to be referring to this kind of ecosystem. But most ecologists and anthropologists who use the term when speaking of the relationship between society and nature employ it in a completely different sense. Ecosystem in this signification refers to the interaction between a human environment and a natural system. In this sense the France of the TGV is as much an ecosystem as is the France of the seventeenth century. Moreover, this meaning of ecosystem entails not simply the unilateral action of nature on society but their mutual interaction. Nature is as much acted upon as it acts upon society. Such an understanding of ecosystem has nothing in common with Le Roy Ladurie's concept of a natural system in which no real growth or innovation occurs. Indeed, it is highly unlikely that such a stagnant society has ever existed.[34]

THE FLIGHT FROM POLITICS

But the methodological problems of Braudel and Le Roy Ladurie are not confined to a disregard of the factor of class or to an improper definition of society. Equally difficult for them has been the whole question of politics, especially in relation to pre-revolutionary French history. Our study would appear to confirm once again the centrality of the state to the development of French capitalism. Indeed, the character of the state which did emerge from this period of disorder, committed as it was to curbing the anarchic violence of the nobility, opening careers to members of the bourgeoisie and to a conscious policy of fostering economic growth, science and technology, must be seen as an important indicator of bourgeois advance. But more to the point, the tariff and labour policies, infrastructural initiatives, patents and subsidies, patronage of luxury and armaments industries, and policies with respect to taxation, recruitment of personnel, foreign trade and colonies were absolutely critical to the development of the French economy in both a negative as well as a positive sense. Yet in Braudel's work politics is regarded as epiphenomenal.[35] The *Histoire économique et sociale de la France*, the great collaborative enterprise of the *Annales* published in the late 1970s under the editorship of Braudel, hardly does better. Obviously, the editor felt that the importance of the state to French economic and social history could not be ignored. In consequence, we have a long introductory essay by Pierre Chaunu in the first volume.[36] But despite the quality of this contribution, it is detached from

---

[34] Jones, *Growth Recurring*, pp. 6, 29.
[35] Dosse, *L'histoire en miettes*, pp. 112–13.
[36] See *Histoire ééonomique et sociale de la France*, Part 1: *De 1450 à 1660*, vol. 1, pt 1, 'L'état', pp. 11–228.

the rest of the text, which is made up of essays by Le Roy Ladurie, Richard Gascon and Michel Morinneau dealing with the history of the French economy but with little reference to the role of the state.

It is fascinating, therefore, to observe the way the problem of the state is approached in Le Roy Ladurie's recent history of the French monarchy, *L'état royal*.[37] In this in some ways excellent treatment the state, as one would expect, is conceived of as largely a mirror or an expression of what are regarded as deeper historical factors. On the other hand, confronted by the massive reality of the state, Le Roy Ladurie is forced to concede, relative to the formation of a rural bourgeoisie in the Paris basin: 'In view of such phenomena the concept of the classical monarchy ought to incorporate the induced effects that it engenders outside its own domain and in the economic and social realm.'[38] This point is conceded in passing, but is not further developed. Yet as a matter of fact the role of the state fiscal apparatus to the process of primitive accumulation under the *ancien régime* can hardly be overstated. The process of expropriation from the land, development of wage labour and strengthening of the bourgeoisie was as much a political as an economic process.

Even Pierre Goubert, an *Annaliste* who cannot be accused of ignoring questions of class or politics, nevertheless feels called upon to belittle the significance of the state in his recent history of the *ancien régime*:

the institutions of the state are only institutions among other institutions: their only originality is in wishing to dominate the others, and, possessing the means of force, to more and more succeed in doing so. It is certain that the history of this conquest, uneven albeit progressive, incomplete and unpopular, constitutes one of the 'keys' to the comprehension of the pre-Revolutionary centuries: it is surely not the only one.[39]

Goubert envisages the state as somehow conquering the rest of society that is already organized in the form of a multiplicity of institutions. But his view does not give sufficient weight to the activity of the monarchy in shaping the rest of society in the form of estates, orders and corporations owing their personalities to such legal recognition. In short, the historians of the *Annales* have tended to minimize the importance of the political and legal power of the state to the organization and maintenance of a hierarchically and corporatively organized society like that of the *ancien régime*. In part, the antipathy of the *Annales* towards the political stems from an understandable reaction against traditional historiography's stress on politics as the essence of the historical. But this is a battle which has long since been won. Today it is the state as an institution and the political as

---

[37] (Paris, 1987).

[38] Ibid., p. 34. Charles Tilly emphasizes the role of the fiscal pressure of the French state in stimulating the process of primitive accumulation and the development of a rural bourgeoisie. See 'How One Kind of Struggle – War – Reshaped All Other Kinds of Struggle in Seventeenth Century France', Ann Arbor, CRSO Working Paper No. 241 (1981).

[39] Pierre Goubert and Daniel Roche, *Les Français et l'ancien régime* (Paris, 1984), I, 189–90.

a special form of behaviour that should command our attention. Despite his hopeless idealism, Roland Mousnier's emphasis on understanding the *ancien régime* as a society of orders based on the monarchy better approximates the close relationship which existed between the society and the state prior to the Revolution than does the approach of the *Annales*.[40] Mousnier posited the *ancien régime* as a society constituted on the basis of judicial orders of clergy, nobility and commoners which were at one and the same time social and political categories. Although he mainly denied the strength of those deeper forces which threatened to upset the equilibrium of the society of orders, he did at least recognize the close dependence of this structure on state political power. In this respect the recent volume *L'état et les pouvoirs*, published by Robert Descimon, Alain Guery and Jacques Le Goff, with its stress on the political structures of the *ancien régime*, marks a definite advance by a younger generation of *Annalistes*.[41] The essential nature of the *ancien régime* was its political character. Attempts to characterize the *ancien régime* in non-political terms such as an ecosystem or as a mere reflection of deeper structures are fundamentally misconceived.

Failure to deal adequately with the political realm is manifest in Braudel's treatment of the decline of the Mediterranean and the triumph of the Atlantic economies. For him the decline of the Italians and the triumph of the Dutch is the product of the structural superiority of the economy of northern as against southern Europe.[42] The abundant grain, forest products and fish to which the Dutch had access supposedly guaranteed their triumph over the Italians. Yet Jonathan Israel, a leading historian of the seventeenth-century Dutch economy, while not wholly rejecting Braudel's view, nevertheless insists that equal stress must be laid on the importance of the control of the rich or luxury trades. Such control was not the product of a structural economic superiority, but was essentially the result of the will of a strong state which was prepared to assume the costs for the fleets, armies and navies required to achieve and maintain economic superiority.[43]

The flight from the political characteristic of the *Annales* is nowhere better exemplified than in the last and posthumous work of Braudel, *L'identité de la France*.[44] This work, meant to be an expression of the master's lifelong passion for France, takes the idea of motionless history to the point of stasis. In this work the concept of the inertness of the *ancien régime* is extended to the twentieth century. Until 1945, we are informed by Braudel, France was a country essentially bypassed by capitalism. Moreover, it was a France whose essential identity was formed

---

[40] See *Les institutions de la France sous la monarchie absolue: 1598–1789*, 2 vols. (Paris, 1974–80), tr. Brian Pearce (Chicago, 1979–84).
[41] (Paris, 1989).
[42] Braudel, *La Méditerranée et le monde méditerranéan*, 2nd edn, I, 573–6.
[43] Israel, *Dutch Primacy*, pp. 8–11. 122–5 and especially 408–9. See also Israel, *Empires and Entrepots: The Dutch, the Spanish Monarchy and the Jews, 1585–1713* (London, 1990), pp. 135–43, 190–1.
[44] 2 vols. in 3 (Paris, 1986).

before the Franks and even the Romans arrived on Gallic soil. Finally, to complete this dubious still life of an unchanging, indeed eternal, France, Braudel pictures a nation whose supposedly distinctive quality – variety – was essentially the product of geography. The trouble is that this supposedly unique national quality of variety is also claimed with considerable justification by France's next-door neighbour Germany. Indeed, Perry Anderson has pointed out how rooted is Braudel's insistence on variety as the distinctive French attribute in a reaction against what is really distinctively French, namely, precocious political centralization.[45]

THE DISTANT AND SAVAGE PAST

The idea of sudden, violent and profound change is equally at odds with the underlying assumptions of Braudel and Le Roy Ladurie. Accordingly, the focus on the long term, whatever else it might have meant, signified a reorientation of French historiography away from stress on the Revolution.[46] In the work of Braudel and Le Roy Ladurie social conflict, whether it is a question of the outbreak of the religious wars or revolts in Spain and Italy, is always seen as influenced in its results by deeper structures which determine the outcome. Invariably revolt proves to be futile for those who pursue this path.[47]

Le Roy Ladurie's *Le carnaval de Romans*, which is his most extended consideration of social conflict, exemplifies this approach.[48] In it he does acknowledge that the conflict at Romans was part of a struggle throughout Dauphiné against the nobility.[49] He likewise connects this conflict with a sense of the general advance of the bourgeoisie in Dauphiné in the sixteenth century.[50] But the overall effect is to underline the impotence of the artisans and peasantry faced with the immobility of the *ancien régime*. Indeed, the story-like narrative developed by Le Roy Ladurie which stresses the archaism of the *mentalité* of those involved in the conflict leaves the impression of a struggle based on a culture long since lost, and to which a contemporary Frenchman has no connection.

The effect of distance between the reader and sixteenth-century French society is made the greater because the author chooses to dress up his protagonists – the

---

[45] 'Nation-States and National Identity' review of *The Identity of France*, vol. II: *People and Production*, tr. Sian Reynolds (London, 1990), *London Review of Books* 13, no. 9 (9 May 1991), 3–8.

[46] Furet, 'Beyond the *Annales*'. *Journal of Modern History* 55 (1983), 399.

[47] In *Les paysans de Languedoc* Le Roy Ladurie pictures the Calvinists as reacting to the looming Malthusian crisis not as bent on breaking out of its limits and overcoming it. See ibid., I, 331–71. Braudel notes the frequency of social revolt in the Mediterranean but considers it as dependent a variable as the frequency of car accidents in modern society. See Braudel, *La Mediterranée*, I, 76–80.

[48] *Le carnaval de Romans: de la chandeleur au mercredi des cendres, 1579–1580* (Paris, 1979), tr. Mary Feeney (New York, 1989).

[49] See especially *Carnival in Romans*, tr. Feeney, pp. 108, 122, 127–8.

[50] See Chapter 14: 'Forerunners of equality', in ibid., pp. 339–70.

plebeians and patricians – in the festive garb of the carnival. Like the European reader of the nineteenth century who breathlessly absorbed the description by the intrepid explorer of savage and murderous rituals in exotic lands, we are treated to the spectacle of a carnival that is transformed into a massacre in a historically remote epoch.

The rival factions of patricians and plebeians were led by carnival kings who identified themselves with totem animals–the rich identifying themselves with symbols of sexual potency and dominance – the rooster, the eagle and the partridge – while the poor men's animals – sheep, hare, capon and donkey – were mainly castrated, mismatched or were bad omens. If we are to believe Le Roy Ladurie, the plebeians unquestioningly accepted the inferiority of their totems. True, he does note the centrality of the bear as a plebeian totem, but he stresses that it embodied the idea of a savage animality and of general violation.[51] It is unfortunate that he overlooks the fact that the bear – whose skin the plebeian leader chose to wear – was seen everywhere in France as associated with *mardi gras* and as such as the powerful master of future events.[52] Indeed, the bear was also seen as a panacea against all sorts of evils and as a sign of good luck, the following or riding of which preserved one from fear.[53]

Rather than stressing the struggle at Romans as the focal point of a province-wide advance of the bourgeoisie played out over half a century, Le Roy Ladurie chooses to emphasize the event as the unfolding of a ritualized drama based on an archaic *mentalité*. *Mentalité*, unlike political or social struggle, has an intractable and enduring quality which is comparable, if not quite so unyielding, as that of climate and geography.[54] Its elements can be understood by reference to the totemic and symbolical systems of thought familiar to the anthropologists. Referring to the use of anthropology by the *Annales*, Bernard Cohn notes 'that the anthropology projected by these historians is concerned with stability, structure, regularity, the local, the common, the small scale, and the expressive, symbolical and magical'.[55] But it is precisely this kind of unreflective anthropology, preoccupied with the study of supposedly unchanging micro-societies set apart in isolation from the effects of the state, colonialism and imperialism, which is increasingly in question.[56]

---

51 Ibid., pp. 214–15.
52 Paul Sébillot, *Le folk-lore de la France* (Paris, 1907, 1968), III, 22, 46–7.
53 Arnold van Gennep, *Manuel de folklore français contemporain* (Paris, 1947), I, pt III, p. 911.
54 See Stuart Clark, 'French Historians and Early Modern Popular Culture', *Past and Present* 100 (1983), 68, Robert Darnton, 'The History of *Mentalités*: Recent Writings on Revolution, Criminality and Death in France' in *Structure, Consciousness and History*, ed. Richard Harney and Stanford M. Layman (Cambridge, 1978), p. 133.
55 Bernard S. Cohn, 'Anthropology and History in the 1980s', *Journal of Inter-Disciplinary History* 12 (1981), 243.
56 Eric Wolf and John W. Cole, *The Hidden Frontier: Ecology and Ethnicity in an Alpine Valley* (New York, 1974), pp. 1–4; William Roseberry, *Anthropologies and Histories: Essays in Culture, History and Political Economy* (New Brunswick and London, 1989), pp. 10–13, 38–49, 125–44.

True enough, Le Roy Ladurie points out in passing that the carnival was in fact a product of late medieval culture and therefore was a recent creation.[57] But he trades on the authority of ethnography to leave an impression with the reader that he is not in the presence of something relatively new, a vehicle of plebeian social resistance, but of something remote and, indeed, primeval. Meanwhile, without rejecting the archaic character of aspects of popular *mentalité* my research has highlighted the importance of the craft tradition and even folk concepts of medicine to the creation of the new scientific empiricism of the early seventeenth century. Indeed, our investigation confirms the presence in the countryside of an energetic stratum of rural producers who were regarded by contemporaries as perfectly capable of economic innovation under the right circumstances.

The effect of cultural remoteness is reinforced by the conclusion to Le Roy Ladurie's work, in which he assimilates the struggle at Romans to the history of the earth itself. He tells us:

The Carnival of Romans makes me think of the grand canyon of the Colorado. A furrow of narrative sinks in a structural stratigraphy. It allows one to see as in a cross-section the social and mental layers of which are composed a very Old Regime. At the evening of the Renaissance it reveals a highly coloured and tortured geology.[58]

The futility of the political and social struggle of the plebeians of Romans is used as an example to demonstrate the durability and longevity of the overall system. The concluding geological metaphor, like the use of the term 'ecosystem', is meant to reflect Le Roy Ladurie's view of the *ancien régime* as embedded in nature and changing at the speed of the geology of the earth.

SOCIETY AS ORGANISM

The environmental determinism implicit in this view is especially characteristic of the work of Braudel. The metaphors he used constantly tend to sink the social back into the natural. Thus, it is not enough for him to suggest the diversity of the regions, societies and civilizations of Europe. He describes them in such a way as to suggest that these entities are organisms which are attracted to the Mediterranean by some kind of vital biological force: 'They have neither the same colours, nor the same age and they feel the force of the Mediterranean to different degrees.'[59] The nomadism of the peoples near the Mediterranean takes on the character of the tidal movements of the sea itself: 'This grand movement which impels the nomads of the steppe towards the sea, then from the sea toward the desert, how could it not be one of the great boundaries of the history of the

[57] *Carnival in Romans*, pp. 303–4.
[58] Ibid., p. 370. I have modified the quotation to bring it closer to the original French.
[59] Braudel, *La Mediterranée*, I, 175.

Mediterranean, or if one prefers, one of its rhythms?'[60] Mediterranean culture assumes the quality of a natural force in the following description of the extent of its influence:

But, according to the exigencies of history, the Mediterranean cannot but be a zone of density which regularly moves beyond its banks and in all directions at the same time. Allowing our images free play it evokes a field of forces, magnetic or electric or more simply an illuminated home whose light is progressively dispersed without one being able to mark exactly the division between darkness and light.[61]

One could argue that these biological, naturalistic and vitalistic images which abound in Braudel's work are nothing more than metaphorical language. But as a matter of fact they are used to reinforce, emotionally, a kind of geographic and environmental determinism.[62]

SUPPRESSING CONFLICT

The extent of the process of distancing from social conflict among the *Annales* school is manifest in a new study of conflict in French history produced under the aegis of Le Roy Ladurie and to which he is a contributor.[63] The tone of this volume is suggested in the preface by Jacques Julliard, director of studies at the Ecole des hautes études en sciences sociales. While admitting that France like no other country has been formed by conflict, he rhetorically poses the question 'however in considering the evolution of a country like France, one may ask at this point at the end of the century and millennium, if "the civilization" of classical conflicts inherited from the *ancien régime*, reformulated by the Revolution, appears today on the brink of exhaustion.'[64] In other words, we are dealing with a phenomenon which is more dead than alive. From this perspective the editors have produced a volume in which conflict and revolt are treated as more a question of style and culture than of anything else: 'One witnesses a ritualization and progressive institutionalization of conflicts which gives the history of France its dramatic character.'[65] In this theatre of stylized conflicts there is no longer any need to tie the revolts of the *ancien régime* to those of the Revolution. Conjunctural events do not lead to any result. At best they are used to illustrate the durability of the system. In this 'history as spectacle' the Jansenist controversy is considered to have the same weight as the Commune of Paris. Conflict, it is held, is a part of the 'identity of France', characterized 'as not taking the form of a final struggle but rather of an ordered confrontation in which the parties involved leave the

---

[60] Ibid., I, 162.
[61] Ibid., I, 155.
[62] Kinser, '*Annaliste* Paradigm?', pp. 69, 73.
[63] Jacques Julien et al., *L'état et les conflits* (Paris, 1990).
[64] Ibid., p. 14.
[65] Ibid., p. 12.

impression of not pushing their momentary superiority to the limit'.[66] It is in this spirit of consensus that the nation of the Albigensian Crusade, the Vaudois Massacre, the Saint Bartholomew's Day Massacre, the Year II, the June Days and the Commune is represented to us.

STRUCTURALISM AND HISTORICAL PETRIFACTION

Braudel and Le Roy Ladurie have devalued the historical weight of social conflict. But in the case of Le Roy Ladurie an underlying antipathy to social change has led him to the point of denying even the creative possibilities of literary self-expression. His attempt to demonstrate the immobility of the *ancien régime* is carried into the realm of culture in his experiment with literary and anthropological structuralism, *Love, Death and Money in the Pays d'Oc*.[67] This work places under the structuralist microscope more than sixty pieces of popular vernacular produced in the Midi between 1575 and 1789. The analysis of *mentalité* in this work is meant to complement Le Roy Ladurie's economic and social investigation of the peasants of Languedoc. Rejecting his master Braudel's strictures against a structuralism abstracted from its connection with socio-historical reality, Le Roy Ladurie in this work seeks analytically to penetrate to the essential motifs of Occitanian literature.[68]

Employing a structural approach, he attempts to demonstrate that the culture of the Midi was as stagnant and congealed as (in his view) was its economic and social life. The personal identity or the social experience of the writers of this popular fiction are dismissed. The ability of these authors to reflect or represent the experience or social aspirations of the Languedoc is disregarded. According to Le Roy Ladurie, we have to understand that the pays d'oc of the *ancien régime* was a society of 'limited good', in which economic growth, social mobility and political change were largely foreclosed. One man's gain was another man's loss. Accordingly, the literature produced in the confined space of this traditional society was based on a single literary motif, the so-called 'love square', consisting of the enterprising hero, the passive heroine, the dominating father of the heroine and the male rivals of the hero. The whole body of this popular Occitanian literature, no matter what its ostensible subject, explores the narrative possibilities of the four corners of this square. This structure is an indirect reflection of the problems of marriage, property and love among the bourgeoisie and peasantry of the Midi.

As a matter of fact, the plots of the fictions, such as Le Roy Ladurie presents them in appearance at least, explore a wide variety of personality types and narrative possibilities. By invoking a structuralist machine involving an exhaustive and tortuous dissection of internal narrative structures and symbolical and

---

[66] Ibid., p. 12.
[67] *L'argent, l'amour et la mort en pays d'oc* (Paris, 1980), tr. Alan Sheridan (New York, 1982).
[68] Kinser, p. 83.

mythological comparison, Le Roy Ladurie succeeds in convincing himself that the plots and characters in these stories are not what they seem, but, in fact, all deal with a single narrative with a restricted cast of characters, his so-called 'love square'.

This work of structuralist reductionism then allows him to claim that this literature is a reflection of the problems of property, marriage and love in a static or inert society. But, as we have noted previously, Le Roy Ladurie has misunderstood the notion of limited good as applying to the attitudes of what he calls a static society, when, in fact, it refers to the reactions of peasants to what they regard as the threat from the encroachment of capitalist social relations. It is doubtful whether the peasants of Languedoc or anywhere else were hostile to the production of more wealth within the peasant domestic economy. Moreover, it is by no means clear that Languedoc in the sixteenth, seventeenth or eighteenth centuries was economically stagnant. Indeed, the notion of limited good, properly understood as a defensive reaction to an encroaching capitalism, could usefully be applied to a study of popular Occitanian culture. It is notable that at one point Le Roy Ladurie himself alludes to the relationship between the sudden appearance of this kind of literature and the appearance of capitalist economic relations, but only to dismiss it.[69] Instead, what we have been given is a study of popular literature based on the assumption that those who created it were incapable of imagining anything but a single literary motif. Indeed, it is difficult to avoid concluding that Le Roy Ladurie's study of *mentalité* based on an obsessive structuralist logic ends in an impasse.

THE EXHAUSTION OF THE *ANNALES*

One has the sense, indeed, that the approach of Braudel and Le Roy Ladurie, which in the name of structuralism has removed humanity from the centre of historical focus and which has transformed the study of history from a study of change to the investigation of stasis, has in effect exhausted itself.[70] One of the morbid symptoms of this exhaustion is the sudden rise of a post-modernist historiography which explicitly rejects the privileging of the economic and social order over the political or psychological. This approach, elaborated at the outset of the greatest economic crisis the world has seen since the 1930s, no longer seeks the causes for historical events in the economic or social realm, but seeks to transform the level of the political and cultural into a text out of which meanings can be read in hermeneutical fashion.[71] Undoubtedly these developments are

[69] Le Roy Ladurie, *Love, Death and Money*, p. 152.
[70] 'Nous sommes au bout de quelque chose ... J'ai la sentiment d'un essoufflement', George Duby in *Magazine litteraire*, no. 248, December 1987, cited in *L'histoire en France*, ed. Thierry Paquot (Paris, 1990), p. 25.
[71] This turn is investigated in David Harvey, *The Condition of Post-Modernity* (Oxford, 1989); Bryan D. Palmer, *Descent into Discourse* (Philadelphia, 1990).

related to the general turning away from Marxism which has marked the 1970s and 1980s in France and elsewhere.[72] But the extreme determinism of the leaders of the *Annales* must bear part of the responsibility for these aberrations.[73] The disarming of history by such historiographical fads is all the more to be regretted at a time when a materialist approach has never been more urgently required. Given the economic and ecological crisis which today haunts humanity, the need for a properly historical perspective which respects the social and economic, but does not reify them has never more urgently been needed.

In attacking the structuralism of Braudel and Le Roy Ladurie I do not by any means wish to deny that there are, indeed, historical structures and systems. Certainly, the *ancien régime* is one such historical structure. But the understanding of this structure requires the use of a much more interactive model of history than the one used by Braudel and Le Roy Ladurie. Moreover, the understanding of such structures demands a sense of more than their repetitive structural patterns and rhythms. Historical systems have their points of origin as well as their endpoints. An understanding of their evolution in time from their beginnings to their termination is as important as understanding the elements of their structure.[74] The origins of the *ancien régime*, its successive phases and the reasons for its overthrow, all need to be investigated. Attempts to understand it without relation to the forces which determined its evolution and brought it to its end are as hopelessly inadequate as those which would attempt to understand the Revolution without reference to the society which preceded it.

The conception of the *ancien régime* as a stable ecosystem I regard as an untenable one. Rather I prefer to see it as a structured part of an evolving system of European class relations marked by conflict on an international scale. Certainly the notion of a stable ecosystem hardly describes the rapidly expanding French economy of the eighteenth century. Recent research makes it clear that France was a serious economic rival of England in the century prior to the Revolution.[75] Indeed, Le Roy Ladurie himself has stressed the dynamism of this period. At the other end of the period, the fourteenth and fifteenth centuries, which saw the irreversible decline of a politically independent feudal class and Church as well as the irrevocable emergence of a middle class and territorial state, can hardly be considered a part of a stable system. Indeed, Le Roy Ladurie's *ancien régime* as a stable ecosystem reduces itself at best to a 200-year period, 1500–1700. But we

---

72 See Lemarchand, 'Les grands tendances de l'historiographie française', *Cahiers d'histoire de l'institut de recherches marxistes* 31 (1987), 31–2, 43; George Ross, 'Intellectuals against the Left: The Case of France', *Socialist Register* 1990, pp. 201–29.

73 Hunt's article on the *Annales* ('French History in the Last Twenty Years') marks the leap from *Annaliste* determinism to post-modern voluntarism. See Hunt, *Politics, Culture and Class in the French Revolution* (Berkeley, 1984); *The New Cultural History: Essays*, ed. and introd. Hunt (Berkeley, 1989).

74 Wallerstein, 'Beyond Annales?' *Radical History Review* 49 (1991), 7–15.

75 Cf. Jean-Pierre Poussou, 'Le dynamisme de l'économie française sous Louis XVIᵉ', *Revue économique* 40 (1989), 965–84.

have tried to demonstrate that the sixteenth and early seventeenth centuries, marked as they were by continuing bourgeois advance, the growth in rural industry as well as the penetration of capitalist relations in agriculture, including a partial proletarianization of the peasants, to say nothing of the state's growing interest in science and technology, can hardly be regarded as stagnant. The typical French peasant in the *ancien régime* was certainly less well-off than the average English yeoman or Dutch burgher. But current historical investigation has established that in aggregate the vast French economy of the seventeenth and especially of the eighteenth century carried considerable weight relative to the other nations of Europe. It certainly cannot be dismissed as moribund. Is it really to be stagnant to have the third most powerful economy in Europe? And, if France was less dynamic than England or Holland, should we not explain this rather through an exploration of the role of the state, social classes and the international economic and state system, rather than invoking a geographical, environmental or cultural determinism?

The seventeenth century in France certainly had some regressive characteristics: agricultural and demographic stagnation, the treason of the bourgeoisie, bureaucratization and the triumph of a state religion. On the other hand, the problem of noble anarchy was resolved once and for all. Industry appears to have continued to make progress, as did the development of a national market. Science and philosophy, building on the achievements of the Renaissance, transformed the culture of the political and social elite. The splendid century has to be seen as a period of rationalization and re-equilibration. It certainly cannot be understood as the regressive turn of an inexorable cycle. In short, the *ancien régime* ought to continue to be understood as a progressive period in history, as it has customarily been regarded. All the more remarkably so given the burden of aristocracy and bureaucracy which it was required to continue to bear.

Le Roy Ladurie, we have seen, defines what he has called 'really significant history' to be the history of the masses of humanity. According to him, in the early modern period this is a history of inertia rather than movement. True enough, one cannot understand 'really significant history' without taking the great bulk of humanity into consideration. It is the major accomplishment of this last generation to have taken this challenge seriously. On the other hand, we may earnestly question whether the history of the masses alone is truly 'really significant history'. 'Really significant history' is the history of a process based on a relationship between these masses and their rulers. It is the study of the evolution of this relationship which must be the focal point of historical study. Considered as such this is a history of movement rather than inertia.

Bibliography

MANUSCRIPTS

ARCHIVES DE LA PREFECTURE DE LA POLICE DE PARIS
Collection Lamoignon

ARCHIVES NATIONALES
Barbiche, Bernard, *Ordonnances enregistrées au parlement de Paris sous le règne de Charles IX*
    MS 1967
Collection Lenain MS 63
F^{14}9774
F^{14}9776
K 675, no. 151
K 676, no. 20
K 955, no. 39
U448
X^{1a}1568
X^{1a}8625
X^{1a}8629
X^{1a}8630
Z^{14}567

MINUTIER CENTRALE
étude iii, 117
étude ix, 129, 130
étude xix, 60, 65, 267
étude xx, 34
étude xxxvi, 9
étude lxxxvi, 91

BIBLIOTHEQUE DE L'HISTOIRE DE LA VILLE DE PARIS
MS CP5168

.BIBLIOTHEQUE NATIONALE
MS fr. 8066
MS fr. 8067
MS fr. 8068

Bibliography

MS fr. 8075
MS fr. 8080
MS fr. 8081
MS fr. 8085
MS fr. 8607
MS fr. 8609
MS fr. 10718
MS fr. 11595
MS fr. 16739
MS fr. 16740
MS fr. 16744
MS fr. 18780
MS fr. 21225
MS fr. 21789
MS fr. 21800
MS fr. 21902
MS Collection Joly de Fleury 1422

PRINTED SOURCES

Articles et propositions lesquelles le roy a voulu estre deliberées par les princes et officiers de son conseil qui se sont trouvez en l'assemblée pour ce faicte à Saint-Germain-en-Laye au mois de novembre, mil cinq cens quatre vingts et trois 1583. BNL1[34]220.

Belon, Pierre, *Les remonstrances sur le default du labour et culture des plantes* (Paris, 1558).

Benoist, René, *De l'institution et de l'abus survenu es confreries populaires, avec la reformation necessaire en icelles* (Paris, 1578).

Bertereau, Martine, *La restitution de Pluton* (Paris, 1640).

Bessard, Toussaints du, *L'aigle compas* (Paris, 1572).

Besson, Jacques, *Le cosmolabe, ou instrument universel concernant toutes observations qui se peuvent faire par les sciences mathématiques, tant au ciel, en la terre, comme en la mer* (Paris, 1567).

 L'art et science, de trouver les eaux et fontaines cachées soubs terre, autrement que par les moyens vulgaires des agriculteurs et architectes (Orléans, 1569).

 Théâtre des instrumens mathématiques et mechaniques (Lyons, 1578; Geneva, 1594).

Bigottier, Claude, *Rapina, seu raporium encomium* (1540), ed. Joseph Bressard (Bourg-en-Bresse,1891).

Blanchard, Guillaume, *Compilation chronologique contenant un recueil en abregé des ordonnances, edits, declarations et lettres patentes des rois de France*, 2 vols. (Paris, 1715).

Bodin, Jean, *La response de Jean Bodin à monsieur de Malestroit*, ed. H. Hauser (Paris, 1932).

 The Six Books of A Commonweale, ed. Kenneth Douglas McRae (Cambridge, 1962).

Boillot, Joseph, *Modeles, artifices de feu et divers instruments de guerre avec les moyens de s'en prevaloir pour assieger, suprendre et deffendre toutes places* (Chaumont, 1598).

Bonnardot, François *et al.*, *Registres des délibérations du Bureau de la ville de Paris. Histoire générale de Paris.* vols. 1–7 (Paris, 1883–93).

Bordeaux, Christophe de, *Discours lamentable et pitoyable sur la calamité, cherté et necessité du temps present . . .* (Bordeaux, 1586).

Varlet à louer à tout faire. Recueil des poésies françoises, ed. Montaiglon (1855–78), I, 73–88.

Chambrière à louer à tout faire. Recueil des poésies françoises, ed. Montaiglon (1855–78), I, 89–108.

Breton, Robert, *Agriculturae encomium* (Paris, 1539).

Briot, Nicholas, *Raisons et moyens proposés au Roi et à Messeigneurs de son Conseil ... pour rendre et faire toutes les monnayes de ce royaume à l'avenir uniformes et semblables, et faire cesser toutes les falsifications, déguisemens, rognemens et affaiblissémens des monnayes* (n.p., n.d.).

Response faite ... aux remonstrances de la cour des monnayes et des prevosts, ouvriers et monnayers, tant de la monnaye de Paris que des autres monnayes de France (Paris, 1617).

Bugnyon, Philibert, *Commentaire sur l'edit du roi Charles Neufieme, roi de France, donné à Tholose, pour contenir les serviteurs et servantes en leurs devoirs et charges* (Lyons, 1572).

Commentaire sur les edicts et ordonnances du Roy contenans les inhibitions et defenses des confraires monopolaires et les causes pourquoy (Lyons, 1585).

Bullant, Jean, *Reigle generalle d'architechture des cinq manieres de colonnes* (Paris, 1560).

Recueil d'horlogiographie, contenant la description, fabrication et usage des horloges solaires (Paris, 1561).

Petite traicte de geometrie et d'horlogiographie pratique (Paris, 1562).

Carew, George, *A Relation of the State of France ...* in Thomas Birch, *An Historical View of the Negotiations Between the Courts of England, France and Brussels* (London, 1749).

Catalogue des Actes de François II, ed. Marie Thérèse de Martel 2 vols. (Paris, 1991).

Cayet, Pierre Victor Palma, *Chronologie novenaire contenant l'histoire de la guerre sous le règne de très chrétien roy de France et de Navarre* in *Nouvelle collection des mémoires pour servir à l'histoire de France*, ed. J.F. Michaud and B. Poujoulat, vol. XII (Paris, 1836–9).

Charron, Pierre, *Œuvres*, 2 vols. (Paris, 1635; Geneva, 1970).

Chauvet, Jacques, *Instruction et usage du cosmomètre, ou instrument universel pour les dimensions, tant géometrique que optiques, astronomiques et géographiques* (Paris, 1585).

La pratique universelle de l'arpenterie ... contenant l'explication de parfaictement mesurer, arpenter, toiser, aulner et prendre le plant de la superficie de tous corps et figures de telles formes qu'ils soient (Paris, 1585).

Condé, Louis Ier, *Mémoires*, (London, 1740).

Constantin, Antoine, *Bref traicte de la Pharmacie Provençale suivant laquelle la medecine peut estre faicte des remedes qui se trouvent en chasque province, sans qu'on soit contraint les aller mandier ailleurs* (Lyons, 1597).

Opus medicae prognoseos ... (Lyons, 1613).

Coquille, Guy, *Histoire du pays et duché de Nivernais* (Paris, 1612).

Coyecque, Ernest, *Recueil d'actes notaries relatifs à l'histoire de Paris et de ses environs au xvie siècle*, 2 vols. (Paris, 1905).

Danfrie, Philippe, *Declaration de l'usage du graphomètre, par la pratique du quel l'on peut mesurer toutes distances ... et pour arpenter terres, bois, prez, et faire plans de villes et fortresses, cartes géographiques* (Paris, 1597).

De l'Orme, Philibert, *Œuvres* (Rouen, 1648; Ridgewood, N.J. 1964).

Denorry, Miles, *L'usage de compas optique* (Paris, 1588).

Documents historiques inédits, tirés des collections manuscrits de la Bibliothèque royale et des archives ou des bibliothèques des départements, ed. Jacques Joseph Champollion-Figeac, vol. IV (Paris, 1841–8).

Documents pour servir à l'histoire de Beauvais et du Beauvaisis, ed. Victor Leblond (Paris, 1909).

Documents relatifs aux états généraux de 1614, ed. Georges Marie René Picot and Paul Guérin (Paris, n.d.).

Dubois, Jacques, *Conseil tres utile contre la famine* (Paris, 1546).

Du Cerceau, Jacques Androuet, *Livre d'architecture* (Paris, 1559).

Du Choul, Jean, *De varia quercvs historia accessit Pylati Montis Descriptio* (Lyons, 1555). *Description du Mont Pilat*, tr. E. Muslant (Lyons, 1868).

Dupont, Pierre, *La stromatourgie*, ed. Alfred Darcel and Jules Guiffrey (Paris, 1832).

Du Puy, Jean, *La recherche et descouverte des mines des montagnes Pyrénées, faicte en l'an mil six cens* in Gobet, Nicolas, *Les anciens minéralogistes du royaume de France* (Paris, 1779), I, 78–147.

Duvet, Jean, *L'Apocalypse figurée* (Lyons, 1561).

Edict du roy touchant les defenses de ne plus bâtir es faux-bourgs de la ville de Paris (Paris, 1549).

Edict et ordonnance du roy touchant les usures (Rennes, 1567).

Edict et reglement du roy sur les abus qui se commettent es manufacturers de lin ... (Paris, 1586).

Errard, Jean, *Le premier livre des instruments mathématiques mechaniques* (Nancy, 1584). *La géometrie et la pratique générale d'icelle* (Paris, 1594).

Estienne, Charles and Liebault, Jean, *L'agriculture et maison rustique* (Paris, 1572).

Estienne, Henri, *Introduction au traicte de la conformité des merveilles anciens avec les modernes* (Antwerp [Lyons], 1568).

The Frankfurt Book Fair. The Franco-fordiense Emporium, ed. and tr. J.W. Thompson (New York, 1911, 1968).

Estienne, Robert, *Les edicts et les ordonnances du roy très chrétien Charles IX de ce nom* (Paris, 1568).

'Etat de Paris au XVIe siècle', ed. J. Cousin, *MSHP* I (1875), 71–112.

Félibien, Dom Michel, *Histoire de la ville de Paris*, 5 vols. (Paris, 1725).

Felix et Thomas Platter à Montpellier, 1552–1559, 1595–1599 (notes de voyage de deux étudiants bâlois) (Montpellier, 1892).

Finé, Oronce, *La composition et usage du quarré géometrique* (Paris, 1556).

Fontanon, Antoine, *Les edicts et ordonnances depuis S. Loys jusques à present* (Paris, 1585).

Foulon, Abel, *Usaige et description de l'holomètre pour scavoir mesurer toutes choses qui sont soubs l'estandue de l'œil* (Paris, 1555).

Garrault, François, *Des mines d'argent trouvée en France, ouvrage et police d'icelles* (Paris, 1579).

Gesner, Conrad, *Vingt lettres à Jean Bauhin fils (1563–65)*, ed. Claude Longeon (Saint-Etienne, 1976).

Gohory, Jacques, *Devis sur la vigne, vin et vendanges d'Orl, de Suave, auquel la façon ancienne du plant, labour et garder este descouverte et reduicte au present usage* (Paris, 1550).

Gouberville, Gilles de, *Journal manuscrit d'un sire de Gouberville et du Mesnil au Val, gentilhomme campagnard du Cotentin de 1558 à 1562*, 2nd edn (Rennes, 1879; La Haye, 1972).

Journal manuscript d'un sire de Gouberville et du Mesnil au Val gentilhomme campagnard du Cotentin de 1558 à 1562, 2nd edn (Rennes, 1879; La Haye, 1972).

Haton, Claude, *Mémoires*, ed. F. Bourquelet, 2 vols. (Paris, 1857).

Herminjard, A.-L., *Correspondence des réformateurs dans les pays de langue française* 9 vols. (Geneva, 1866–97).

Institution des enfants de l'hospital de la trinité (Paris, 1553), BN Rés. Recueil Fontanon 270.

Inventaire des registres des insinuations du Châtelet de Paris, règnes de Francois Ier et de Henri II, ed. Emile Carpardon and Alexandre Tuetey (Paris, 1906).

Isambert, François André, *Recueil général des anciennes lois françaises*, 29 vols. (Paris, 1821–33; Ridgewood, N.J., 1964–6).

Joubert, Laurent, *Erreurs populaires et propos vulgaires touchant la medecine . . .* (Bordeaux, 1578).

    Segond partie des Erreurs populaires et propos vulgaires touchant la medecine . . . (Paris, 1580).

    Operum latinorum tomus primus . . . cui subjectus est tomus secundus, hunc primum in lucem proditus, 2 vols. (Lyons, 1582).

Lafaille, Germain de, *Annales de la ville de Toulouse*, 2 vols. (Paris, 1687–1701).

Laffemas, Barthélemy de, *Source de plusieurs abus et monopoles qui se sont glissez et coulez sur le peuple de France depuis trente ans ou environ à la ruyne de 'Estat* (n.p., 1596).

    Reiglement général pour dresser les manufactures en ce royaume et couper les cours des draps de soye et autres marchandises qui perdent et ruynent l'Etat (Paris, 1597).

    Responce à messieurs de Lyon, lesquels veulent empescher, rompre le cours des marchandises d'Italie, avec le prejudice de leurs foires, et l'abus aux changes (Paris, 1598).

    Lettres et exemples de feu la reine mere, comme elle faisoit travailler aux manufactures et fournissoit aux ouvriers de ses propres deniers (Paris, 1602).

Laffemas, Isaac, *L'histoire de commerce de France* (Paris, 1606).

    L'histoire du commerce de France in *Archives curieuses de l'histoire de France*, ed. L. Cimber and F. Danjou (Paris, 1834–41), XIV, 409–30.

Lalourcé and Duval, *Recueil des cahiers généraux des trois ordres aux états généraux* (Paris, 1789).

La Mare, Nicolas de, *Traité de la police*, 4 vols. (Paris, 1705–38).

Lapellinière, Henri, *L'Amiral de France* (Paris, 1584).

Le Boulenger, Louis, *Le projet et calcul faict par commandement du roy, de la grandeur, longeur et largeur de son royaume pays terres et seigneuries (1566)* in *Archives curieuses de l'histoire de France*, VI, 345–9.

Le Choyslet, Prudent, *Discours economiques, non moins utile que recreatif, monstrant comme, par le mesnagement de pouilles, de cinq cens livres, pour une fois employees, l'on peut tirer par an quatre mil cinq cens livres de proffit honneste* (Paris, 1572).

    A Discourse Upon Husbandry, tr. Richard Eden (London, 1580; Reading, 1951).

Le journal de Guillaume Paradin ou le vie en Beaujolais au temps de la renaissance (vers 1510–1589), ed. Mathieu Méras (Geneva, 1986).

Lescornay, Jacques, *Mémoires de la ville de Dourdan* (Paris, 1624).

Les cris de Paris qu'on crie journellement par les rues de ladicte ville avec ce, le contenue de la despense qui se faict par chacun jour (Paris, 1584).

Lespinasse, René de, *Les métiers et corporations de la ville de Paris*, 3 vols. (Paris, 1879–97).

Bibliography

Lettres de privilege du roy pour l'elevation des eaues et autres belles et utiles inventions (Paris, 1585).

Libavius, Andreas, *Praxis Alchymiae* (Frankfurt, 1604).

Livre de Podio ou chroniques d'Etienne Médicis bourgeois du Puy 1475–1565, ed. A. Chassaing, 2 vols. (Le Puy, 1869).

Machiavelli, Niccolo, *Le premier livre des Discours de l'estat de paix et de guerre . . .* (Paris, 1544).

Mémoires concernans les pauvres que l'on appelle enfermez, Archives curieuses de l'histoire de France, XV, 241–70.

Merliers, Jean de, *L'usage du quarré géometrique amplement descrit et demonstré* (Paris, 1573).

Mesmes, Jean Pierre de, *Les institutions astronomiques* (Paris, 1557).

Montaiglon, Anatole de Courde de, *Recueil des poésies françoises des XVe et XVIe siècles* (Paris, 1855–78).

Montaigne, G., *La police des pauvres* (n.p., 1600).

Montaigne, Michel de, *Œuvres complètes*, ed. Maurice Rat (Paris, 1962).

Montchrétien, Antoine de, *Traicté de l'œconomie politique*, ed. Th. Funck-Brentano (Paris, 1889).

Nicolay, Nicolas de, *Description générale de la ville de Lyon et des anciennes provinces du Lyonnais et du Beaujolais*, ed. Victor Advielle (Lyons, 1881).

Palissy, Bernard, *Les œuvres*, ed. Anatole France (Paris, 1880; Geneva, 1969).

Recepte veritable, ed. Keith Cameron (Geneva, 1988).

Panciroli, Guido, *Livre premier des antiquitez perdues, et si vif representées par la plume de . . . G. Panacrol* (Lyons, 1617).

Livre second des choses nouvellement inventees, [et] auparavant incognues (Lyons, 1617).

Paré, Ambroise, *Dix livres de la chirurgie avec le magasin des instrumens necessaires à icelle* (Paris, 1564).

Œuvres complètes, ed. J.F. Malgaigne, 3 vols. (Paris, 1840–1).

Des monstres et prodiges, ed. Jean Céard (Geneva, 1971).

Peletier du Mans, Jacques, *L'arithemetique* (Poitiers, 1549; Geneva, 1969).

De l'usage de geometrie (Paris, 1573).

Pena, Pierre and De l'Obel, Mathieu, *Stirpium adversia nova* (London, 1570).

Pigafetta, Filipo, 'Relation du siège de Paris', *MSHP* 2 (1876), 11–105.

Plaidorie pour la reformation de l'imprimerie (Paris, 1572). Bibliothèque Ste. Genevieve, Rés. E.8° 919R.

Plan de Paris sous le règne de Henri II par Olivier Truschet et Germain Hayau, ed. Jules Cousin, F. Hoffbauer and Louis Sieber (Paris, 1877).

Plan de Paris sous Louis XIII, 1615, ed. Mathieu Merian, *Extrait des études archéologiques sur les anciens plans de Paris*, ed. A. Bonnandet (Paris, 1880).

Plan de Saint Victor attribué à J.-A. Du Cerceau, copié et engravé par Dheulland en 1756 (Paris, 1880).

Platter, Thomas, *Description de Paris*, tr. Louis Sieber (Nogent-le-Routrou, 1896).

Beschreibung der Reisen durch Frankreich, Spanien, England und die Niederlande: 1595–1600, ed. Rut Keiser, 2 vols. (Basle, Stuttgart, 1968).

Prix des céréales et extraits de la mercuriale de Paris: 1520–1698, ed. Jean Meuvret and Micheline Baulant, 2 vols. (Paris, 1960).

Bibliography

'Projet de dépôt de mendicité sous Louis XIII', *Revue retrospective* series 8, 2 (1835), 207–86.

Ramelli, Agostino, *Le diverse e artificiose machine* (Paris, 1588).

The various and ingenious machines of Agostino Ramelli, tr. Martha Teach Gnudi (Baltimore, 1976).

Rebuffi, Pierre, *Les édicts et ordonnances des roys de France depuis l'an 1226 jusques à present* (Lyons, 1573).

Recueil des monuments inédits de l'histoire du tiers état, ed. Augustin Thierry, 4 vols. (Paris, 1850–70).

Recueil de poésies françoises des XVe et XVIe siècles, ed. Anatole de Montaiglon, 13 vols. (Paris, 1872–90).

Recueil des privileges, concessions et reglemens de commissaires, enquesteurs et examinateurs des Chastellet de Paris (Paris, 1509).

Roaldès, François, *Discours de la vigne*, ed. Philippe Tamizey de Larroque (Bordeaux, 1886).

Ronsard, Pierre de, *Le tombeau de feu Roy très-chretien Charles IX* (Paris, 1574).

Sanches, Francisco, *That Nothing Is Known*, ed. Elaine Limbrick and Douglas F.S. Thomson (Cambridge, 1988).

Sauval, Henri, *Histoire et recherches des antiquites de la ville de Paris*, 3 vols. (Paris; 1724, Farnborough, 1969).

Scaliger, Joseph Juste, *Opuscula Varia antehac non edita* (Paris, 1610).

Scriptores rei rusticae veteres latini Cato, Varro, Columella, Palladius, ed. Johann Matthias Gesner, 2 vols. (Leipzig, 1725).

Serres, Olivier de, *La cueillette de la soye par la nourriture des vers qui la font* (Paris, 1599).

Le théâtre d'agriculture (Paris, 1600).

La seconde richesse du meurier-blanc qui se trouve en son escorce, pour en faire des toiles de toutes sources (Paris, 1603).

Sorbin, Arnaud, *Histoire véritable des choses memorables advenues tant durant la règne de trepas du très haut et très puissant roy très chretien Charles IX*, Archives curieuses de l'histoire de France, VIII, 273–331.

Spifame, Raoul, *Dicaearchie Henrici, regis christianissimi, Progymnasta* (n.p., 1556).

Vues d'un politique du XVIe siecle sur la législation de son temps, ed. Jean Auffrey (Amsterdam, 1775).

'Statuts pour les hospitaux des pauvres enfermez' (Paris, 1611), *Archives curieuses de l'histoire de France*, XV, 271–84.

Suberville, Henry de, *L'Henrymètre* (Paris, 1598).

Sully, Maximilien de Bèthune, duc de, *Mémoires*, ed. Louis-Raymond Lefèvre (Paris, 1942).

Les œconomies royales, ed. David Buisseret and Bernard Barbiche, 2 vols. (Paris, 1970–88).

Tarde, Jean, *A la recontre de Galilée: deux voyages en Italie*, ed. Francois and Marcel Tetel (Geneva, 1984).

Tiraqueau, André, *De nobilitate* (Paris, 1549).

Turquet de Mayerne, Louis, *Traicté des négoces et traffiques ou contracts qui se font en choses meubles, reiglement et administration du bureau ou chambre politique des marchans ...* (Paris, 1599).

Bibliography

Veron de Forbonnais, François, *Recherches et considerations sur les finances de France depuis l'année 1595 jusqu'à l'année 1721*, 2 vols. (Basle, 1758).

Viète, François, *Introduction to the analytical art*, tr. J. Winfree Smith in Klein, Joseph, *Greek Mathematical Thought and the Origin of Algebra*, tr. Eva Braun (Cambridge, Mass., 1968), pp. 315–53.

Vinet, Elie, *Le safran de Roche-Foucaut. Discours du cultivement de safran, des vertus, proprietes et profit d'icelui* (Poitiers, 1568).

    L'arpenterie ... livre de geometrie enseignant à mezurer les champs et plusieurs autres chozes, (Bordeaux, 1577).

    L'arpenterie et la maniere de fere les solaires que communement on apele quadrans (Bordeaux, 1583).

The Work of Jacques Le Moyne de Morgues: A Huguenot Artist in France, Florida and England, ed. Paul Hutton, 2 vols. (London, 1977).

SECONDARY WORKS

Aclocque, Geneviève, *Les corporations, l'industrie et le commerce à Chartres du XIe siècle à la Revolution* (Paris, 1917).

Ambrosoli, Mauro, *Scienzati, contadini e proprietari: botanica e agricoltura nell'Europa occidentale 1350–1850* (Turin, 1992).

Alibeux, Henri, *Les premières papeteries françaises* (Paris, 1926).

Anderson, Perry, 'Nation-States and National Identity', review of Fernand Braudel, *The Identity of France*, vol. II: *People and Production*, tr. Sian Reynolds (London, 1990), *London Review of Books* 13, no. 9, 9 May 1991, pp. 3–8.

Arpin, Marcel, *Histoire de la meunerie et de la boulangerie depuis les temps pré-historiques jusqu'à l'année 1914*, 2 vols. (Paris, 1948).

Atkinson, Geoffrey, *Les nouveaux horizons de la renaissance française* (Geneva, 1935, 1969).

Audin, M., 'Les grèves de l'imprimerie à Lyon au seizième siècle', *Gutenberg Jahrbuch* 1938, pp. 172–89.

Auvray, Louis, *Dictionnaire générale des artistes de l'école française* (Paris, 1895; New York, 1976).

Baader, Gerhard, 'Jacques Dubois as a Practitioner' in *The Medical Renaissance of the Sixteenth Century*, ed. A. Wear, R.K. French and I.M. Lonie (Cambridge, 1986), pp. 146–54.

Babelon, J.P., *Henri IV* (Paris, 1982).

    Nouvelle histoire de Paris. Le XVIe siècle (Paris, 1986).

Bailly, Robert, 'L'assèchement des étangs de Rochefort-Pujaut: XVI–XVII siècles', *Rhodanie* 6 (1989), 36–43.

Ballon, Hilary, *The Paris of Henri IV: Architecture and Urbanism* (Cambridge, Mass. and London, 1991).

Balmas, Enea, 'Jacques Gohory, traduttore del Machievelli' in *Saggi e studi sul rinascimento francese* (Padua, 1982), pp. 23–73.

Barbiche, Bernard, *Sully* (Paris, 1978).

Bardon, Achille, 'L'exploitation du bassin houillier d'Alais sous l'ancien régime,' *Mémoires de l'Académie de Nîmes* 20 (1897), 133–516.

Bibliography

Baret, H., *Histoire du travail dans l'ancienne généralité de Lyon: Lyonnais, Forez, Beaujolais* (Saint-Etienne, 1939).

Barnes, Barry, 'Sociological Theories of Scientific Knowledge' in *Companion to the History of Science*, ed. R.C. Olby *et al.* (London, 1990), pp. 60–77.

Baron, Hans, 'The *Querelle* of the Ancients and the Moderns as a Problem for Renaissance Scholarship' in *Renaissance Essays*, ed. Paul Oscar Kristeller and Philip P. Wiener (New York, 1968), pp. 95–114.

Basalla, George, *The Evolution of Technology* (Cambridge, 1988).

Baulant, Micheline and Beutler, Corinne, 'Les droits de la communauté villageoise sur les cultures: glanage et chaume en France, XVIIe siècle' in *Agricultura e transformazione dell'ambiente secoli XIII–XVIII*, ed. Annalisa Garducci, *Atti delle Undicesimo Settimana di Studio (25–30 aprille 1979) Istituto Internazionale di Storia Economica 'Francesco Datini'* (Florence, 1984), pp. 69–85.

Baumgartner, F.J., 'Sunspots or Sun's Planets: Jean Tarde and the Sunspot Controversy of the Early Seventeenth Century', *Journal of the History of Astronomy* 18 (1987), 44–54.

'Galileo's French Correspondents', *Annals of Science* 45 (1988), 169–82.

'The Origins of the Provençal School of Astronomy', *Physis* 28 (1991), 291–304.

Beaulieu, A., 'Mersenne, rival de Pieresc', *Peiresc ou la passion de connaître: actes du colloque de Carpentras 5–7 novembre, 1987* (Paris, 1990), pp. 23–46.

Becker, Abraham Henri, *Un humaniste au XVIe siècle: Louis Le Roy* (Paris, 1896).

Beckmann, Johann, *History of Inventions, Discoveries and Origins*, tr. William Johnston, 3 vols. (London, 1797).

Belhoste, J.F., 'Une silviculture pour les forges: XVIe–XIXe siècles' in *Forges et forêts: recherches sur la consommation proto-industrielle de bois*, ed. Denis Woronoff (Paris, 1990), pp. 222–31.

'La maison, la fabrique et la ville: l'industrie du drap fin en France: XV–XVIIIe siècles', *Histoire, économie, société* 13 (1994), 457–71.

Belhoste, J.F. *et al.*, *La métallurgie normande: XII–XVIIe siècles–la révolution du haut fourneau* (Caen, 1991).

Benedict, Philip, 'Rouen's Trade during the Era of the Religious Wars (1560–1600)', *Journal of European Economic History* 13 (1984), 29–73.

'Civil Wars and Natural Disasters in Northern France' in *The European Crisis of the 1590s: Essays in Comparative History*, ed. Peter Clark (London, 1985), pp. 84–106.

'French Cities from the Sixteenth Century to the Revolution' in *Cities and Social Change in Early Modern France*, ed. Benedict (London, 1989), pp. 7–68.

Benoist, Luc, *Le compagnonnage et les métiers* (Paris, 1980).

Benoit, Serge, 'Les Hospitaliers et les débuts de le sidérurgie indirecte dans le Grand Prieuré de Champagne' in *Colloque: moines et metallurgie dans la France médiévale*, ed. Benoit and Denis Cailleaux (Paris, 1991), pp. 213–67.

Benoît, Paul, 'Les techniques minières en France et dans l'Europe aux XVe et XVIe siècles', *Journal des Savants* (1988), 75–119.

'Calcul, algèbre et marchandise' in *Eléments d'histoire des sciences*, ed. Michel Serres (Paris, 1989), pp. 197–222.

Bénouls, Mustapha Kemal, *Le dialogue philosophique dans la littérature française du seizième siècle* (Paris, La Haye, 1976).

Bibliography

Berg, Maxine, 'Markets, Trade and European Manufacture' in *Markets and Manufactures in Early Industrial Europe* (London, 1991), pp. 3–26.

Bernard, Jacques, *Navires et gens de mer à Bordeaux (vers 1400–vers 1550)*, 2 vols. (Paris, 1968).

Bernhardt, Jean, 'Les activités scientifiques de Nicolas Claude Fabri de Peiresc', *Nouvelles de la Republique des lettres* 11 (1981), 165–84.

Berriot-Salvadore, Evelyne, *Les femmes dans la société française de la Renaissance* (Geneva, 1990).

Beutler, Corinne, 'Un chapitre de la sensibilité collective: la littérature agricole en Europe continentale au XVIe siècle', *Annales: ESC* 28 (1973), 1280–1301.

Bezard, Yvonne, *La vie rurale dans le sud de la région parisienne de 1450 à 1660* (Paris, 1929).

Biéler, André, *La pensée économique et sociale de Calvin* (Geneva, 1959).

Biraben, Jean-Noel, *Les hommes et la peste en France et dans les pays européens et méditerranéens*, 2 vols. (Paris, La Haye, 1975).

Blunt, Anthony, *Philibert de l'Orme* (London, 1958).

Bois, Guy, *The Crisis of Feudalism: Economy and Society in Eastern Normandy* (Cambridge, Paris, 1984).

Boissière, Jean, 'La consummation parisienne de bois et les sidérurgies périphériques: essai de mise en parallèle (milieu XVe–milieu XIXe siècles)' in *Forges et forêts*, ed. Woronoff (Paris, 1990), pp. 29–56.

Boissonade, Prosper, 'Les voies de communications terrestres et fluviales en Poitou sous le règne de Henri IV', *Revue Henri IV* 2 (1907–8), 193–228, 295–311; 3 (1909), 64–102.

Le socialisme d'état (Paris, 1927; Geneva, 1977).

'Le mouvement commerciale entre la France et les Iles Britanniques au XVIe siècle', *Revue historique* 134 (1920), 193–225; 135 (1920), 1–27.

Histoire de Poitou (Paris, 1925).

Bondois, Paul M., 'Le développement de l'industrie verrière dans la régionne parisienne de 1515 à 1665', *Revue d'histoire économique et sociale* 23 (1936–7), 49–72.

Bosseboeuf, L.A., 'La fabrique des soiries de Tours', *Mémoires de la société archéologique de Tours*, 41 (1900), 193–526.

Bottin, Jacques, 'Structures et mutations d'un espace proto-industriel à la fin du XVIe siècle', *Annales: ESC* 43 (1988), 975–95.

'Grand commerce et produit textile à Rouen, 1550–1620', *Bulletin du centre d'histoire des espaces atlantiques*, NS 15 (1990), 265–79.

'Les jeux de l'échange et de la production en Normandie à la fin du XVIe siècle', *Histoire, économie et société* 9 (1990), 373–7.

Bourde, André J., *Agronomie et agronomes en France au XVIIIe siècle*, 2 vols. (Paris, 1967).

Bourgeon, J.L., 'La fronde parlementaire à la veille de la Saint-Barthélemy', *Bibliothèque de l'école des Chartes* 148 (1990), 17–89.

Boutiller, François, *La verrerie et les gentilshommes verriers de Nevers* (Nevers, 1885).

Bouvier-Ajam, Maurice Jean, *Histoire du travail*, 2 vols. (Paris, 1957–69).

Bouwsma, William J., *John Calvin: A Sixteenth Century Portrait* (New York, 1988).

Boyer, Hippolyte, *L'ancien compagnonnage à Bourges* (Bourges, 1891).

Braudel, Fernand, *Civilisation materielle et capitalisme XV–XVIIIe siècles*, 3 vols. (Paris, 1967–79), tr. Miriam Kochan, 3 vols. (London, 1981–4).

Bibliography

La Méditerranée et le monde méditerranéen à l'époque de Philippe II (Paris, 1949); 2nd edn, 2 vols. (Paris, 1966); tr. Sian Reynolds, 2 vols. (New York, 1972–3).

L'identité de la France, 3 vols. (Paris, 1986).

Brazza, Francesco Savorgnandi, *Technici e artigiani italiani in Francia* (Rome, 1942).

Brazzini, Gianfranco, *Dall'economica aristotelica all'economica politica. Saggio sul 'Traicte' di Monchretien* (Pisa, 1988).

Brenner, Robert, 'Against the Neo-Malthusian Orthodoxy' in *The Brenner Debate: Agrarian Class Structure and Economic Development in Pre-Industrial Europe*, ed. T.H. Aston and C.H.E. Philpin (Cambridge, 1985), pp.10–63.

Brown, Harcourt, 'Nicolas Claude Fabri de Peiresc', *DSB* x, 488–92.

Brunelle, Gayle K., *The New World Merchants of Rouen: 1559–1630* (Kirksville, Mo., 1991).

Brutails J.A., 'Deux chantiers bordelais (1486–1521)', *Le moyen âge* 13 (1900), 437–51.

Buisseret, David, 'Les ingénieurs du roy Henri IV', *Bulletin de géographie* 77 (1964), 13–84.

'The Communications of France during the Reconstruction of Henri IV', *Economic History Review* 2nd series, 19 (1965), 43–53.

Sully and the Growth of Centralized Government in France 1598–1610 (London, 1968).

Bulard, Marcel, 'L'industrie de fer dans la Haut-Marne', *Annales de géographie* 13 (1904), 223–42.

Cambridge History of Renaissance Philosophy, ed. Charles Schmitt *et al.* (Cambridge, 1988).

Capitan, Jean, 'Notules sur la Bièvre', *Bulletin de la Montagne Sainte-Geneviève et ses abords* 5 (1905–8), 245–61.

Capul, Maurice, *Abandon et marginalité: les enfants placés sous l'ancien régime* (Toulouse, 1989).

Carsalade Du Pont, Henri de, *La municipalité parisienne à l'époque d'Henri IV* (Paris, 1971).

Catalogue des livres imprimés de la Bibliothèque du Roy. Jurisprudence, vol. II (Paris, 1753).

Céard, Jean, *La nature et les prodiges: l'insolite au XVIᵉ siècle en France* (Geneva, 1977).

'Relire Bernard Palissy', *Revue de l'art* 78 (1987), 77–83.

'Bernard Palissy et l'alchimie' in *Actes du colloque Bernard Palissy (1510–1590): l'écrivain, le réformé, le céramiste. Journées d'études 29 et 30 juin 1990. Saintes–Abbaye-aux-Dames*, ed. Frank Lestringant (Saintes,1992), pp. 155–66.

Chapin, Seymour L., 'Astronomical Activities of Nicholas Claude Fabri de Peiresc', *Isis* 48 (1957), 13–29.

Charmasse, Anatole de, 'Note sur l'exploitation de la houille au Creusot au XVIᵉ siècle: 1510–11', *Mémoires de la société éduenne* NS 12 (1883), 387–402.

Chauvet, Paul, *Les ouvriers du livre en France des origines à la revolution française de 1789* (Paris, 1942).

Chermette, Alexis, 'Martine de Bertereau 1590–1643: une femme ingénieur des mines au XVIIᵉ siècle', *Mémoires de l'academie des sciences, belles-lettres et arts de Lyon*, 3rd series, 40 (1986), 46–57.

Chevalier, A.G., 'The Antimony War – A Dispute Between Montpellier and Paris', *CIBA Symposium* 2 (1940), 418–23.

Chevalier, Louis, *Labouring Classes and Dangerous Classes in Paris During the First Half of the Nineteenth Century*, tr. Frank Jellinek (New York, 1973).

Cifoletti, Giovanna Cleon, 'Mathematics and Rhetoric : Peletier and Gosselin and the Making of the French Algebraic Tradition' (Ph.D. Dissertation, Princeton University, 1992).

Bibliography

Ciriacono, Salvatore, 'Silk Manufacturing in France and Italy in the Seventeenth Century: Two Models Compared', *Journal of European Economic History* 10 (1982), 167–200.

Clark, Stuart, 'French Historians and Early Modern Popular Culture', *Past and Present* 100 (1983), 62–99.

Cohn, Bernard S., 'Anthropology and History in the 1980s', *Journal of Inter-Disciplinary History* 12 (1981), 227–52.

Colart-Bodet, Suzanne, 'Un distillateur français, médecin et fabricant de remèdes, précurseur de Galilée? ou du rôle méconnu des distillateurs dans la transition entre la scolastique et la science moderne', *Vorträge der Hauptversammlung der Internationalen Gesellschaft für Geschichte der Pharmacie* (Stuttgart, 1975), pp. 11–20.

Le code alchimique dévoilé: distillateurs, alchimistes et symbolistes (Paris, 1989).

Cole, Charles Woolsey, *French Mercantilist Doctrines before Colbert* (New York, 1931, 1969).

Collins, James B., *Fiscal Limits of Absolutism: Direct Taxation in Early Seventeenth Century France* (Berkeley, 1987).

Classes, Estates and Order in Early Modern Brittany (Cambridge, 1994).

Coornaert, Emile, 'Anvers et le commerce parisien au XVIᵉ siècle', *Mededelingen van De Koninklijke Vlamse Academie voor Wetenschappen, Letteren en Schone Kunsten van Belgie* (Brussels,1950).

Les corporations en France avant 1789 (Paris, 1968).

Costabel, P., 'Les satellites de Jupiter de Galilée à Newton', *Peiresc ou la passion de connaître* (Paris, 1990), pp. 91–108.

Coudouin, André, 'Recherches sur les métiers de la soierie à Tours dans la première moitié du seizième siècle' (University of Tours, Ph.D. Thesis, 1976).

Couturier, Marcel, 'Investissement culturelle à Chartres: 1480–1600', *Bulletin des sociétés archéologiques d'Eure-et-Loir* 122 (1978), 1–32.

Coyecque, Emile, 'L'assistance publique à Paris au milieu du XVIᵉ siècle', *Bull. soc. hist. Paris* 15 (1888), 105–18.

Croix, Alain, *La Bretagne aux 16ᵉ et 17ᵉ siècles: la vie, la mort, la foi*, 2 vols. (Paris, 1981).

Crouzet, Denis, *Les guerriers de Dieu: la violence au temps des troubles de religion, vers 1525– vers 1610*, 2 vols. (Seyssel, 1990).

Darnton, Robert, 'The History of *Mentalités*: Recent Writings on Revolution, Criminality and Death in France' in *Structure, Consciousness and History*, ed. Richard Harney and Stanford M. Laymon (Cambridge, 1978), pp.106–36.

D'Avenel, Georges, *Paysans et ouvriers depuis sept cent ans* (Paris, 1899).

Davis, Natalie Zemon, 'A Trade Union in Sixteenth Century France', *Economic History Review* series 2, 19 (1966), 48–69.

'René Choppin on More's Utopia', *Moreana* 19–20 (1968), 91–5.

'Strikes and Salvation in Lyons' in *Society and Culture in Early Modern France* (Stanford, 1975), pp. 1–16.

'Les femmes dans les arts mécaniques au XVIᵉ siècle' in *Mélanges en hommage de Richard Gascon* (Lyons, 1980), I, 139–67.

The Return of Martin Guerre (Cambridge, 1983).

Debeir, Jean-Claude, Deléage, Jean-Paul, Hémery, Daniel, *Les servitudes de la puissance: une histoire de l'énergie* (Paris, 1986).

Bibliography

Debus, Allen G., *The Chemical Philosophy: Paracelsian Science and Medicine in the Sixteenth and Seventeenth Centuries*, 2 vols. (New York, 1977), pp. 67–88.

Man and Nature in the Renaissance (Cambridge, 1978).

'Palissy, Plat and English Agricultural Chemistry in the Sixteenth and Seventeenth Centuries' in Debus, *Chemistry, Alchemy and the New Philosophy, 1550–1700* (London, 1987), pp. 66–88.

The French Paracelsians: the chemical challenge to medical and scientific tradition in early modern France (New York, 1991).

Degaast, Georges and Rigaud, Germain, *Les supports de la pensée* (Paris, 1942).

Delarue, Henri, 'Olivetan et Pierre de Vingle à Genève, 1532–1533', *BHR* 8 (1946), 105–18.

Delumeau, Jean, *L'alun de Rome, XVe–XIXe siècle* (Paris, 1962).

Le péché et la peur. La culpabilisation en Occident: XIIIe–XVIIIe siècles (Paris, 1983).

Denis, Frédéric-August, *Lectures sur l'histoire de l'agriculture dans le département de Seine-et-Marne* (Meaux, 1881).

Depauw, Jacques, 'L'assistance à Paris à la fin du XVIe siècle', *Societé francaise des hôpitaux* no. 59 (1989), 10–21.

Derouet, Bernard, 'Une démographie differentielle: clés pour un système auto-régulateur des populations rurales d'ancien régime', *Annales: ESC* 35 (1980), 3–37.

Descimon, Robert, 'Paris on the Eve of Saint Bartholomew: Taxation, Privilege and Social Geography' in *Cities and Social Change in Early Modern France*, ed. Benedict (London, 1989), pp. 63–104.

Descimon, Robert, Guery, Alain and Le Goff, Jacques, *L'état et les pouvoirs* (Paris, 1989).

Dessaix, Paul, *Montchrétien et l'économie politique nationale* (Paris, 1901; Geneva, 1970).

Destray, Paul, 'Les houillières de La Machine au XVIe siècle', *Revue internationale du commerce et de l'industrie et de la banque* 15 (1914), 361–92.

Devèze, Michel, *La vie de la forêt française au XVIe siècle*, 2 vols. (Paris, 1961).

Dewald, Jonathan, *Pont-St-Pierre, 1398–1798: Lordship, Community and Capitalism in Early Modern France* (Berkeley, 1987).

Deyon, Pierre, 'Variations de la production textile aux XVIe et XVIIe siècles: sources et premiers resultats', *Annales: ESC* 18 (1963), 921–55.

'La concurrence internationale des manufacturers lainières', *Annales: ESC* 27 (1972), 20–32.

Les temps des prisons (Paris, 1975).

'L'enjeu des discussions autour du concept de proto-industrialisation', *Revue du Nord* 61 (1979), 9–15.

Dictionnaire des lettres françaises, ed. Monseigneur Georges Grenté, *Le seizième siècle*, ed. A. Pauphilet *et al.* (Paris, 1951).

Diefendorf, Barbara B., *Beneath the Cross: Catholics and Huguenots in Sixteenth Century Paris* (New York, 1991).

Dienne, Edouard de, *Histoire du dessèchement des lacs et marais en France avant 1789* (Paris, 1891).

Dinges, Martin, 'Materielle Kultur und Alltag. Die Unterschichten in Bordeaux im 16/17 Jahrhunderts', *Francia* 15 (1987), 257–79.

Stadtarmut in Bordeaux 1525–1675: Alltag Politik, Mentalitäten, (Bonn, 1988).

Doe, Janet, *A Bibliography of the Works of Ambroise Paré, 1545–1940* (Amsterdam, 1976).

Bibliography

Dosse, Francois, *L'histoire en miettes. Des Annales à la 'nouvelle histoire'* (Paris, 1987).

New History in France: The Triumph of the Annales, tr. Peter V. Conroy, Jr (Urbana, Chicago, 1994).

Dow, James, 'The Image of Limited Production in Peasant Society', *Human Organization* 40 (1982), 361–3.

Droz, Eugénie, *Chemins de l'hérésie. Textes et documents*, 4 vols. (Geneva, 1976).

Dufay, Bernard *et al.*, 'L'atelier parisien de Bernard Palissy', *Revue de l'art* 78 (1987), 33–60.

Dulieu, Louis, 'Pierre Richer de Belleval', *Monspeliensis Hippocrates*, 1968, pp. 1–8.

'Laurent Joubert, chancelier de Montpellier', *BHR* 31 (1969), 139–67.

La pharmacie à Montpellier de ses origines à nos jours (Lamalou-les-Bains (Herault), 1973).

Dumas, Georges, 'Les tailleurs d'habits et les bonnetiers de Paris du XIIIe au XVIe siècle', *Ecole des Chartes, Position des thèses*, 1951, pp. 5–6.

Dupèbe, Jean, 'L'alimentation des pauvres selon Sylvius' in *Pratique et discours alimentaires à la renaissance: colloque de Tours, 1979* (Paris, 1982), pp. 41–56.

Duval, Jules, *Mémoire sur Antoine de Montchrétien sire de Vatville* (Paris, 1868; Geneva, 1971).

Early Modern Witchcraft: Centres and Peripheries, ed. Bengt Ankarloo and Gustav Henningsen (Oxford, 1990).

Eisler, Colin T., *The Master of the Unicorn: The Life and Work of Jean Duvet* (New York, 1979).

Ellenberger, François, *Histoire de la géologie* (Paris, 1988).

Ellerbroek, G.G., 'Montaigne et les applications de la technique', *Neophilologus* 28 (1943), 1–6.

Elmore, Richard Francis, 'The Origins of the Hôpital-Général of Paris' (University of Notre Dame, Ph.D. Dissertation, 1975).

Enjalbert, Henri, 'Le commerce de Bordeaux et la vie économique dans le Bassin Aquitaine au XVIIe siècle', *Annales du Midi* 62 (1950), 21–35.

Fagniez, Gustav, *L'économie rurale de la France sous Henri IV: 1589–1610* (Paris, 1894).

L'économie sociale de la France sous Henri IV: 1589–1610 (Paris, 1897; Geneva, 1975).

Farr, James Richard, *Hands of Honour: Artisans and their World in Dijon, 1556–1650* (Ithaca, 1988).

Fauquex, Charles, *L'industrie textile à Beauvais* (Beauvais, 1974).

Favaro, Antonio, 'Di Giovanni Tarde e di una sua visita a Galileo dal 12 al 15 novembre 1614', *Bulletino di bibliografia e storia delle scienze matematiche e fisiche* 20 (1987), 345–71.

Favier, Jean, *Paris au XVe siècle, 1380–1500* (Paris, 1974).

Favreau, Robert, *La ville de Poitiers à la fin du moyen âge*, 2 vols. (Poitiers, 1978).

Fels, Marthe de, *Olivier de Serres* (Paris, 1983).

Fenoaltea, Stefano, 'Transaction Costs, Whig History and the Common Fields', *Politics and Society* 16 (1988), 171–240.

Ferrie, Richard, 'Two Exegetical Treatises of François Viète' (Indiana University, Ph.D Dissertation, 1980).

Fleury, Ernest-Jules-Fréderic Lamé, *De la législation minérale sous l'ancienne monarchie* (Paris, 1857).

Foisil, Madeleine, *Le sire de Gouberville: un gentilhomme normand au XVIe siècle* (Paris, 1985).

Foley, Vernard *et al.*, 'Besson, Da Vinci and the Evolution of the Pendulum: Some Findings and Observations', *History and Technology* 6 (1988), 1–43.

Bibliography

Forbes, R.J., *Pierre Belon and Petroleum* (Leiden, 1958).

Fosseyeux, Marcel, 'L'assistance parisienne au milieu du XVIe siècle', *MSHP* 43 (1916), 83–128.

Fourest, Henri-Pierre, *L'œuvre des faïenciers français du XVIe à la fin du XVIIIe siècles* (Paris, 1966).

Fournier, Edouard, *Le vieux-neuf, histoire des inventions et decouverts modernes*, 2 vols. (Paris, 1859).

Fourquin, Guy, *Les campagnes de la région parisienne à la fin du moyen âge* (Paris, 1964).

Franklin, Alfred, *Extrait des notices historiques et topographiques sur les anciens plans de Paris. Notice extraite des études archéologiques sur les anciens plans de Paris* (Paris, 1851).

Dictionnaire historique des arts, métiers et professions exercés dans Paris depuis le treizième siècle (Paris, 1906, New York, 1968).

Furet, François, 'Beyond the Annales', *Journal of Modern History* 55 (1983), 389–410.

Garnier, Bernard, 'Pays herberger et pays "ouvert" en Normandie, XVIe – début du XIXe siècle', *Revue d'histoire économique et sociale* 53 (1975), 493–525.

Gascon, Richard, *Grand commerce et vie urbaine au XVIe siècle: Lyon et ses marchands*, 2 vols. (Paris, 1971).

Gennep, Arnold van, *Manuel de folklore français contemporain*, 4 vols. (Paris, 1947).

Gérard, Pierre, Sicard, Germain and Saulais, Brigitte, 'Les moulins de Toulouse' in *Technologies et cultures traditionelles. Mission d'action culturelle en milieu scolaire* (Toulouse, 1980), pp. 49–60.

Geremek, Bronislaw, 'La populazione marginale tra il medioevo e l'era moderna', *Studi storici* 9 (1968), 23–40.

La salariat dans l'artisanat Parisien aux XIIIe–XVe siècles (Paris, La Haye, 1968).

'Criminalité, vagabondage, pauperisme: la marginalité à l'aube des temps modernes', *Revue d'histoire moderne et contemporaine* 21 (1974), 337–75.

Giacomotti, Jeanne, *French Faience* (New York, 1963).

Gille, Bertrand, *Les origines de la grande métallurgie en France* (Paris, 1947).

'Fonctions économiques de Paris' in *Paris, fonctions d'une capitale*, ed. Guy Michaud (Paris, 1962), pp. 115–49.

Gillot, Hubert, *La querelle des anciens et modernes* (Paris, 1914, Geneva, 1968).

Ginzburg, Carlo, 'Deciphering the Sabbath' in *Early Modern Witchcraft*, ed. Ankarloo and Henningsen, pp. 121–37.

Ecstasies: Deciphering the Witches' Sabbath (London, 1991).

Girard, Luse, 'La production logique de l'Angleterre au XVIe siècle', *Etudes philosophiques* 59 (1985), 303–24.

Giraud, Louis, *Le premier jardin des plantes de France: étude historique et documents* (Montpellier, 1911).

Godart, Justin, *L'ouvrier en soie. Monographie du tisseur lyonnais, étude historique, économique et sociale* (Lyons, 1879; Geneva, 1976).

Goldstone, Jack A., 'Regional Ecology and Agrarian Development in England and France', *Politics and Society* 16 (1988), 287–334.

Gonnet, Giovanni, 'Le premier synode de Chanforan de 1532', *BSHPF* 99 (1953), 203–21.

Goodman, David C., *Power and Penury: Government, Science and Technology in Philip II's Spain* (Cambridge, 1988).

Bibliography

Goodman, Jordan and Honeyman, Katrina, *Gainful Pursuits: The Making of Industrial Europe: 1600–1914* (London, 1988).

Gosselin, Edward A., 'Bruno's French Connection: A Historiographical Debate' in *Hermeticism and the Renaissance: Intellectual History and the Occult in Early Modern Europe*, ed. Ingrid Merkel and Allen G. Debus (Washington, 1988), pp. 166–81.

Goubert, Pierre, *Beauvais et le Beauvaisis de 1600 à 1730: contribution à l'histoire sociale de la France du XVIIe siècle* (Paris, 1966).

Goubert, Pierre and Roche, Daniel, *Les Français et l'ancien régime*, 2 vols. (Paris, 1984).

Goulauen, J.P. and Perradeau, Y., *Economie, croissance, cycles économiques* (Paris, 1987).

Gourmelon, Roger, 'L'industrie et le commerce des draps à Paris du XIIIe au XVIe siècles', *Ecole des Chartes, Position des thèses*, 1950, pp. 61–3.

'Etude sur le rayonnement commercial des marchands drapiers au XVIe siècle', *Bulletin philologique et historique (jusqu'à 1610) du comité des travaux historiques et scientifiques*, 1961, pp. 265–75.

Grass, Milton and Grass, Ann, *Stockings for a Queen: The Life of the Rev. William Lee, the Elizabethan Inventor* (London, 1967).

Greengrass, Mark, *France in the Age of Henri IV: The Struggle for Stability* (London, 1984).

'The Later Wars of Religion in the French Midi' in *The European Crisis of the 1590s: Essays in Comparative History*, ed. Clark (London, 1985), pp. 106–35.

Grendler, Paul F., 'Schools in Western Europe', *Renaissance Quarterly* 43 (1990), 775–87.

Gueneau, Louis, *L'organisation du travail à Nevers aux XVIIe et XVIIIe siècles* (Paris, 1919).

Guerlac, Henry, 'Guy de la Brosse and the French Paracelsians' in *Science, Medicine and Society in the Renaissance: Essays to Honor Walter Pagel*, ed. Debus (New York, 1972), I, 177–99.

Guiffrey, Jules, 'Les Gobelins, teinturiers en ecarlate au faubourg Saint Marcel', *MSHP* 31 (1904), 1–92.

Guillerme, André, *The Age of Water: The Urban Environment in the North of France, A.D. 300–1800* (College Station, Texas, 1988).

Gundersheimer, Werner L., *The Life and Work of Louis Le Roy* (Geneva, 1966).

Gutton, Jean-Pierre, 'A l'aube du XVIIe siècle: idées nouvelles sur les pauvres', *Cahiers d'histoire* 10 (1965), 87–97.

La société et les pauvres: l'exemple de la généralité de Lyon, 1534–1789 (Paris, 1971).

Domestiques et serviteurs dans la France de l'ancien régime (Paris, 1981).

Guyot, Joseph, *Chronique d'une ancienne ville royale Dourdon, capitale de Hurepoix* (Paris, 1864).

Gwynn, Robin D., *Huguenot Heritage: The History and Contribution of the Huguenots in England* (London, 1985).

Haag, Eugène and Haag, Emile, *La France protestante*, 10 vols. (Paris, 1846–59; Geneva, 1966).

Hagen, William, 'Capitalism and the Countryside in Early Modern Europe: Interpretations, Models, Debates', *Agricultural History* 62 (1988), 13–45.

Hall, A.R., *The Scientific Revolution: 1500–1800* (London, New York, 1954).

Hamby, W.B., *Ambroise Paré: Surgeon of the Renaissance* (Saint Louis, Mo., 1967).

Bibliography

Hamy, E.T., 'Un précurseur de Guy de la Brosse, Jacques Gohory et le Lyceum Philosophal de Saint-Marceau-les-Paris, 1571–1576', *Nouvelles archives du Musée*, 4th series, 1 (1899), 1–26.

Harrie, Jean Ellen, 'François Foix de Candale and the Hermetic Tradition in Sixteenth Century France' (Ph.D. Dissertation, University of California, Riverside, 1975).

Harsin, Paul, *Crédit public et banque d'état en France du XVIe au XVIIIe siècle* (Paris, 1933).

Harvard College Library Catalogue of Books and Manuscripts: French Sixteenth Century Books, 2 vols., ed. Ruth Mortimer (Cambridge, 1964).

Harvey, David, *The Condition of Post-Modernity* (Oxford, 1989).

Hauser, Henri, *Ouvriers du temps passé: XVe–XVIe siècles* (Paris, 1899; Geneva, 1982).

  Les compagnonnages d'arts et métiers à Dijon aux XVIIe et XVIIIe siècles (Dijon, 1907; Marseilles, 1979).

  'Le système social de Barthélemy de Laffemas', *Revue bourguignonne* 19 (1908), 113–31.

  Les débuts du capitalisme (Paris, 1931).

  La modernité du XVIe siècle (Paris, 1963).

Heller, Henry, *The Conquest of Poverty: The Calvinist Revolt in Sixteenth Century France* (Leiden, 1986).

  Iron and Blood: Civil Wars in Sixteenth Century France (Montreal, 1991).

Hennezel, Henri, *Claude Dangon. Essai sur l'introduction des soieries façonnées en France d'après des documents inédits, 1605–13* (Lyons, 1926).

Henson, Gravenor, *History of the Framework Knitters*, introd. Stanley D. Chapman (Nottingham, 1831; New York, 1970).

Hesse, Philippe-Jean, *La mine et les mineurs en France de 1300 à 1550* (Paris, 1973).

Hickey, Daniel, 'The Socio-Economic Context of the French Wars of Religion. A Case Study: Valentinois-Diois' (McGill University, Ph.D. Dissertation, 1973).

  'Innovations and Obstacles to Growth in the Agriculture of Early Modern France: The Example of Dauphiné', *French Historical Studies* 15 (1987), 208–40.

Hill, Bert S., 'A Revolving Bookcase by Agostino Ramelli', *Technology and Culture* 11 (1970), 389–400.

Hill, Christopher, 'Pottage for Freeborn Englishmen: Attitudes towards Wage Labour in Sixteenth and Seventeenth Century England' in *Socialism, Capitalism and Economic Growth: Essays Presented to Maurice Dobb*, ed. C. Feinstein (London, 1967), pp. 338–50.

Hilliard, Denise, 'Jacques Besson et son Théâtre des instruments mathématiques', *Revue français d'histoire du livre* NS 48 (1979), 5–38.

  'Jacques Besson et son Théâtre des instruments mathématiques, recherches complémentaires', *Revue français d'histoire du livre* NS 50 (1981), 47–77.

Hilliard, Denise and Poole, Emmanuel, 'Oronce Finé et l'horloge planétaire de la Bibliothèque Sainte-Geneviève', *BHR* 33 (1971), 311–51.

Histoire de l'Ile-de-France et de Paris, ed. M. Mollat (Toulouse, 1971).

Histoire de la France rurale, ed. Georges Duby and Armand Wallon, vol. II: *L'âge classique: 1340–1740*, ed. Hughes Neveux, Jean Jacquart, Emmanuel Le Roy Ladurie (Paris, 1975).

Histoire de la France urbaine, ed. Duby, vol. II:, *La ville classique*, ed. Roger Chartier et al. (Paris, 1981).

Bibliography

Histoire de Languedoc, ed. Philippe Wolf (Toulouse, 1988).

Histoire de Marseille, ed. Edouard Baratier (Toulouse, 1989).

Histoire de Rouen, ed. M. Mollat (Toulouse, 1979).

Histoire du commerce de Marseille, ed. Gaston Rambert, vol. III: *De 1480 à 1599* by Raymond Collier and Joseph Billioud (Paris, 1951).

Histoire du Havre et de l'estuaire de la Seine, ed. André Corvisier (Toulouse, 1983).

Histoire économique et sociale de la France, ed. Fernand Braudel and Ernest Labrousse, part I: *De 1450 à 1660*: vol. I: *L'état et la ville*, ed. Pierre Chaunu and Richard Gascon (Paris, 1970).

Hoffman, Philip T., 'Land Rents and Agricultural Productivity: The Paris Basin, 1450–1789', *Journal of Economic History* 52 (1991), 771–805.

Holmes, Douglas R., *Cultural Disenchantments: Worker Peasantries in Northeast Italy* (Princeton, 1989).

Hoock, Jochen and Jeannin, Pierre, 'La contribution de l'imprimerie à la diffusion du savoir commercial en Europe au 16ᵉ siècle' in *La ville et l'innovation en Europe: 14ᵉ–19ᵉ siècle*, ed. B. Lepetit and J. Hoock (Paris, 1987), pp. 45–58.

Hooykaas, Reijer, *Humanisme, science et réforme, Pierre de la Ramée: 1515–1572* (Leiden, 1958).

Howard, Rio, 'Guy de la Brosse: The Founder of the *Jardin des Plantes*' (Cornell University, Ph.D. Dissertation, 1974).

'Guy de la Brosse and the *Jardin des Plantes* in Paris' in *The Analytic Spirit: Essays in the History of Science*, ed. Harry Woolf (Ithaca, 1981), pp. 195–224.

La bibliothèque et la laboratoire de Guy de la Brosse au Jardin des Plantes à Paris (Geneva, 1983).

Howell, W.S., *Logic and Rhetoric in England* (Princeton, 1956).

Hunt Lynn, *Politics, Culture and Class in the French Revolution* (Berkeley, 1984).

'French History in the Last Twenty Years: The Rise and Fall of the *Annales* Paradigm', *Journal of Contemporary History* 21 (1986), 209–24.

Huppert, George, *Public Schools in Renaissance France* (Chicago, Urbana, 1984).

Inventaire des arrêts du Conseil d'Etat (règne de Henri IV), ed. Noel Valois, 2 vols. (Paris, 1886–93).

Israel, Jonathon I., *Dutch Primacy in World Trade 1580–1740* (Oxford, 1989).

Empires and Entrepôts: The Dutch, the Spanish Monarchy and the Jews, 1585–1713 (London, 1990).

Jacob, Margaret C., *The Cultural Meaning of the Scientific Revolution* (Philadelphia, 1988).

Jacquart, Jean, *La crise rurale en Ile-de-France, 1550–1670* (Paris, 1974).

Paris et Ile-de-France au temps des paysans (Paris, 1990).

'Les problèmes de la paysannerie française au temps de Henri III' in *Henri III et son temps*, ed. Robert Sauzet (Paris, 1992), pp. 277–84.

Jacquart, Jean, Neveux, Hugues and Le Roy Ladurie, Emmanuel, *Histoire de la France rurale*, ed. Georges Duby and Armand Wallon, vol. II: *L'âge classique: 1340–1789* (Paris, 1975).

Jeanclos, Yves, *Les projets de réforme judiciare de Raoul Spifame au XVIᵉ siècle* (Geneva, 1977).

Bibliography

Jeannin, Pierre, 'Conjoncture et production du cuivre dans les Vosges méridionales à la fin du XVIe et au début du XVIIe siècle' in *Conjoncture économique, structures sociales. Hommage à Ernest Labrousse* (Paris, 1974), pp. 121–38.

'La proto-industrialisation: développement ou impasse?' *Annales: ESC* 35 (1980), 52–65.

Jones, Eric Lionel, *Growth Recurring: Economic Change in World History* (Oxford, 1988).

Julien, Jacques, *et al.*, *L'état et les conflits* (Paris, 1990).

Jürgens, Madeleine, *Documents du Minutier Centrale des notaires de Paris. Inventaires après décès*, vol. I: *1483–1547* (Paris, 1985).

Kaplan, Steven Laurence, *Provisioning Paris: Merchants and Millers in the Grain and Flour Trade during the Eighteenth Century* (Ithaca, 1984).

Karcher, Aline, 'L'assemblé des notables de Saint-Germain-en-Laye, 1583,' *Bibliothèque de l'école des chartes* 114 (1956), 115–62.

Kellenbenz, Herman, 'Industries rurales en Occident à la fin du moyen âge au XVIe siècle', *Annales: ESC* 18 (1963), 833–82.

Keller, Alexander, 'The Idea of Progress in Rabelais', *Publications of the Modern Language Association* 66 (1951), 235–43.

'Mathematical Technologies and the Growth of the Idea of Technical Progress in the Sixteenth Century' in *Science, Medicine and Society in the Renaissance: Essays to Honour Walter Pagel*, ed. Allen Debus, vol. I (New York, 1972), pp. 11–27.

'The Missing Years of Jacques Besson, Inventor of Machines, Teacher of Mathematics, Distiller of Oils and Huguenot Pastor', *Technology and Culture* 14 (1973), 28–39.

'A Manuscript Version of Jacques Besson's Book of Machines' in *On Pre-Modern Technology and Science: A Volume of Studies in Honor of Lynn White Jr.*, ed. Bert S. Hall and Delno C. West (Malibu, Calif., 1976), pp. 75–103.

Kerridge, Eric, *The Agricultural Revolution* (New York, 1968).

Kinser, Samuel, 'Temporal Change and Cultural Process in France' in *Renaissance Studies in Honour of Hans Baron*, ed. Anthony Molho and John A. Tedeschi (De Kalb, Ill., 1971), pp. 703–55.

'*Annaliste* Paradigm? The Geological Structuralism of Fernand Braudel', *American Historical Review* 86 (1981), 63–105.

Kirsop, W., 'The Legend of Bernard Palissy', *Ambix* 12 (1961), 136–54.

Klein, Jacob, *Greek Mathematical Thought and the Origin of Algebra*, tr. Eva Braun (Cambridge, Mass., 1968).

Kleinclausz, Arthur Jean, *Histoire de Lyon*, 3 vols. (Lyons, 1939–52).

Korner, Martin H., *Solidarités financières suisses au XVIe siècle* (Paris, Lucerne, 1980).

Kuhn, Thomas S., 'Mathematical versus Experimental Traditions in the Development of Physical Science', *Journal of Inter-Disciplinary History* 7 (1976), 1–31.

Langé, Christine, 'L'émigration française en Aragon, XVIe siècle et première moitié du XVIIe siècle', in *Les Français en Espagne à l'époque moderne (XVIe–XVIIe siècles). Colloque Toulouse, 7–9 Octobre 1987* (Paris, 1990), pp. 26–44.

Larivière, F. Soulez, *Les ardoisières d'Angers* (Angers, 1979).

Larmour, Ronda, 'The Grocers of Paris in the Sixteenth Century' (Columbia University, Ph.D. Dissertation, 1963).

La Roncière, Charles de, *Histoire de la marine française*, 6 vols. (Paris, 1900–32).

Lavastre, Louis, *Dentellières et dentelles du Puy* (Le Puy, 1911).

Bibliography

Lavisse, Ernest, *Histoire de la France depuis les origines jusqu'à la Revolution*, vol. IV, pt. II: *Henri IV–Louis XIII (1598–1643)*, ed. H. Mariéjol (Paris, 1911).

Legré, Louis, *La botanique en Provence au XVIe siècle. Pierre Pena et Mathieu de Lobel* (Marseilles, 1899).

La botanique en Provence du XVIe siècle: Louis Anguillara, Pierre Belon, Charles de l'Ecluse, Antoine Constantin (Marseilles, 1901).

Lemarchand, Guy, 'Les grands tendances de l'historiographie française', *Cahiers d'histoire de l'institut de recherches marxistes* 31 (1987), 14–88.

Léon, Pierre, 'Réflexions sur la siderurgie française à l'époque ante-colbertienne (1500–1650)' in *Schwerpunkte der Eisengewinnung und Eisenverarbeitung in Europa: 1500–1650*, ed. Hermann Kellenbenz (Cologne, 1974), pp. 106–25.

Lepage, Henri, *Nicolas Briot, graveur de monnaies du duc de Lorraine Henri II* (Nancy, 1858).

Lequenne, Fernand, *Olivier de Serres, agronome et soldat de Dieu* (Paris, 1983).

Le Roque, Aurèle, 'Bernard Palissy' in *Toward a History of Geology*, ed. Cecil J. Schneer (Cambridge, Mass., 1969), pp. 226–41.

Leroux, Désirée, *La vie de Bernard Palissy* (Paris, 1927).

Le Roy Ladurie, Emmanuel, *Les paysans de Languedoc*, 2 vols. (Paris, 1966).

Histoire du climat depuis l'an mil (Paris, 1967), tr. Barbara Bray (London, 1972).

Montaillou: village occitan de 1294 à 1324 (Paris, 1975), tr. Bray (New York, 1978).

'L'histoire immobile,' *Annales: ECS* 29 (1974), 673–93, republished in *Le territoire de l'historien* (Paris, 1978), II, 7–34; *The Mind and the Method of the Historian*, tr. Sian and Ben Reynolds (Chicago, 1981), pp. 1–27.

Le carnaval de Romans: de la chandeleur au mercredi des cendres, 1579–80 (Paris, 1979), tr. Mary Feeney (New York, 1989).

L'argent, l'amour et la mort en pays d'oc (Paris, 1980); *Love, Death and Money in the Pays d'Oc*, tr. Alan Sheridan (New York, 1982).

Jasmin's Witch, tr. Brian Pearce, (London, 1987).

The French Peasantry, 1450–1660, tr. Alan Sheridan (Berkeley, 1987).

'Demographie et histoire rural en pespective' in *Histoire de la population française*, ed. Jacques Dupâquier *et al.* (Paris, 1988), I, 513–24.

'L'historiographie rurale en France: XIV–XVIIIe siècles: essai d'histoire agraire systématique ou "eco-systématique" in *Marc Bloch aujoud'hui: histoire comparée et sciences sociales*, ed. Hartmut Atsma and André Burguière (Paris, 1990), pp. 223–52.

Le Roy Ladurie, Emmanuel and Goy, Joseph (eds.), *Prestations paysannes, dîmes, rente foncière preindustrielle*, 2 vols. (Paris, 1982), tr. Susan Burke (New York, Paris, 1982).

Les travaux et les jours dans l'ancienne France, exposition organisée sous les auspices des chambres d'agriculture avec le concours du Musée nationale des arts et traditions populaires par le comité nationale constitué pour commemorer le IVe centenaire d'Olivier de Serres, ed. Marc Bloch *et al.* (Paris, June–September, 1939).

Lestringant, Frank., 'Le prince et le potier: introduction à la "Recepte veritable" de Bernard Palissy (1563)', *Nouvelle revue du XVIe siècle* 3 (1985), 5–24.

Le Huguenot et le sauvage (Paris, 1990).

L'histoire en France, ed. Thierry Paquot (Paris, 1990).

Linge, Alison K., 'Empirics and Charlatans in Early Modern France: The Genesis of the

Classification of "Other" in Medical Practice', *Journal of Social History* 19 (1985–6), 583–604.

Longeon, Claude, *Hommes et livres de la renaissance* (Saint-Etienne, 1990)

Louis, Armand, *Mathieu de l'Obel (1538–1616): épisode de l'histoire de la botanique* (Ghent-Louvain, 1980).

Mahoney, Michael Sean, *The Mathematical Career of Pierre de Fermat: 1601–1665* (Princeton, 1973).

Malgaigne, Joseph Francois, *Surgery and Ambroise Paré*, tr. Wallace B. Hamby (Norman, Okla., 1965).

Margolin, Jean-Claude, 'L'enseignement de mathématiques en France (1540–70), Charles de Bovelles, Finé, Peletier, Ramus' in *French Renaissance Studies*, ed. Peter Sharrat (Edinburgh, 1976), pp. 109–55.

Martin, Felix, *Adam de Crappone et son œuvre* (Paris, 1874).

Martin, Germain, *L'industrie et le commerce du Velay aux XVIIe et XVIIIe siècles* (Le Puy, 1900).

Le tissage du ruban à domicile dans les campagnes de Velay (Paris, 1913).

Martin, Saint-Léon Etienne, *Le compagnonnage* (Paris, 1901).

Marx, Karl, *Capital*, ed. and tr. Ben Fowkes (New York, 1977).

Mathorez, J., 'Un radical-socialiste sous Henri II. Raoul Spifame', *Revue politique et parlementaire* (1914), 538–59.

Mazerolle, Fernand, *Nicolas Briot, medailleur et mecanicien (1580–1646)* (Brussels, 1891).

Les médailleurs français du XVe siècle au milieu du XVIIIe siècle, 2 vols. (Paris, 1902).

Mazlish, Bruce, *The Co-evolution of Humans and Machines* (New Haven, 1993).

Mazzaoui, Maureen Fennell, *The Italian Cotton Industry in the Later Middle Ages: 1100–1600* (Cambridge, 1991).

Ménard, Léon, *Histoire civile, ecclésiastique et littéraire de la ville de Nîmes*, 7 vols. (Paris, 1744–58).

Merle, Léon, *La métairie et l'évolution agraire de la Gâtine poitevine de la fin du moyen âge à la Révolution* (Paris, 1958).

Metzger, Hélène, *Les doctrines chimiques en France de début du XVIIe siècle à la fin du XVIIIe siècle* (Paris, 1969).

Meuvret, Jean, 'Agronomie et jardinage au XVIe siècle' in *Etudes d'histoire économique* (Paris, 1971), pp. 153–61.

Michaud, Louis-Gabriel *et al.*, *Nouvelle biographie universelle*, 45 vols. (Paris, 1854–65).

Mireaux, Emile, *Une province française au temps du grand roi. La Brie* (Paris, 1958).

Miron de l'Espinay, A., *François Miron et l'administration municipale de Paris … de 1604 à 1606* (Paris, 1885).

Mollat, Michel, 'Rouen avant port de Paris à la fin du moyen âge,' *Bulletin de la société historique, géographique et scientifique de la région parisienne* 71 (1951), 1–8.

Le commerce maritime normand à la fin du moyen âge: étude d'histoire économique et sociale (Paris, 1952).

Monter, William, 'Historical Geography and Religious History in Sixteenth Century Geneva', *Journal of Interdisciplinary History* 9 (1979), 399–437.

Moriceau, Jean-Marc, 'Le laboureur et ses enfants. Formation professionnelle et mobilité sociale en Ile-de-France (second moitié du XVIe siècle)', *Revue d'histoire moderne et contemporaine* 40 (1993), 353–86.

Les fermiers de l'Ile-de-France XV–XVIIIe siècle (Paris, 1994).

Morse, John S., 'The Reception of Diophantus's Arithmetic in the Renaissance' (Princeton University, Ph.D. Dissertation, 1981).

Mousnier, Roland, 'L'opposition politique bourgeois à la fin du XVIe siècle et au début du XVIIe siècle', *Revue historique* 213 (1955), 1–20.

Les institutions de la France sous la monarchie absolue: 1598–1789, 2 vols. (Paris, 1974–80), tr. Brian Pearce (Chicago, 1979–84).

Muchembled, Robert, *La sorcière au village* (Paris, 1991).

Nadal, Jorge and Giralt, Emile, *La population catalane de 1553 à 1717: l'immigration française* (Paris, 1960).

Nakam, Géralde, *Les Essais de Montaigne, miroir et procès de leurs temps: témoignage historique et création littéraire* (Paris, 1984).

Nef, John U., 'A Comparison of Industrial Growth in France and England from 1540 to 1640', *Journal of Political Economy* 44 (1936), 505–33.

Industry and Government in France and England, 1540–1640 (Philadelphia, 1940).

The New Cultural History: Essays, ed. and introd. Lynn Hunt (Berkeley, 1989).

Pala, Alberto, *Descartes e lo sperimentalismo francese: 1600–1650* (Rome, 1990).

Pallier, Denis, *Recherches sur l'imprimerie à Paris pendant la Ligue, 1585–1594* (Geneva, 1975).

Palmer, Bryan D., *Descent into Discourse* (Philadelphia, 1990).

Panichi, Nicola, *Antoine de Montchrétien. Il circolo dello stato* (Milan, 1989).

Papy, Louis, *L'homme et la mer sur la côte de la Loire à la Gironde, étude de géographie humaine* (Bordeaux, 1941).

Parent, Annie, *Les métiers du livre à Paris au XVIe siècle* (Geneva, 1974).

Parinetto, Luciano, *Streghe e politica: dal Rinascimento italiano a Montaigne, da Bodin a Naude* (Milan, 1983).

Pariset, Ernest, *Histoire de la fabrique lyonnaise, étude sur le régime social et économique de l'industrie de la soie à Lyon depuis le XVIe siècle* (Paris, 1901).

Parsons, William Barclay, *Engineers and Engineering in the Renaissance* (Cambridge, Mass., 1968).

Partington, James Riddick, *A History of Chemistry*, 4 vols. (London, 1962).

Pasquier, Emile, *Un curé de Paris pendant les guerres de religion René Benoist, le pape des Halles: 1521–1608* (Angers, 1913; Geneva, 1970).

Patterson, T.S., 'Jean Beguin and his *Tyrocinium Chymicum*', *Annals of Science* 2 (1937), 243–98.

Pavard, J.M., 'Production et rendement ceréalières à Cheux au début du dix-septième siècle', *Annales de Normandie* 26 (1976), 41–65.

Pearl, Jonathan L., 'Pieresc and the Search for Criteria of Scientific Knowledge', *Proceedings of the Sixth Annual Meeting of the Western Society for French History* VI (1978), 110–19.

'The Role of Personal Correspondence in the Exchange of Scientific Information in Early Modern France', *Renaissance and Reformation* 9 (1984), 106–13.

Perelman, Michael, *Classical Political Economy: Primitive Accumulation and the Social Division of Labour* (London, 1983).

Bibliography

Péréz-Ramos, Antonio, *Francis Bacon's Idea of Science and the Master's Knowledge Tradition* (Oxford, 1988).

Pertile, Line, 'Montaigne in Italia: arte, technica e scienza dal *journal agli Essais*', *Saggi e richerche di letteratura* 13 (1973), 49–92.

Philippe, Robert, 'Les premiers moulins à vent', *Annales de Bretagne* 32 (1982), 99–120.

Picot, Emile, *Les Français italianisants au XVIe siècle* 2 vols. (Paris, 1908; New York, 1968).

Pillorget, René, *Nouvelle histoire de Paris. Les premiers bourbons* (Paris, 1988).

Poitrineau, Abel, *Remues d'hommes: essai sur les migrations montagnards en France aux XVIIe et XVIIIe siècles* (Paris, 1982).

Poussou, Jean Pierre, 'Le dynamisme de l'économie française sous Louis XVIe', *Revue économique* 40 (1989), 965–84.

'Manufactures' in *Dictionnaire du grand siècle*, ed. François Bluche (Paris, 1990), pp. 359–60.

Ramsay, G.D., *The English Wool Industry* (London, 1982).

Rapp, Richard, 'The Unmaking of the Mediterranean Trade: International Trade Rivalry and the Commercial Revolution', *Journal of Economic History* 35 (1975), 499–525.

Reeds, Karen M., *Botany in Medieval and Renaissance Universities* (New York, 1991).

Rethoré, Gombert-Alexandre, *Recherches historiques sur Jouarre et ses environs. La Commanderie de Bibartaut et ses environs* (Meaux, 1877).

Recherches historiques sur Jouarre et ses environs. Territoire de Jouarre (Meaux, 1895).

Histoire de Saint-Cyr-sur-Morin et des hameaux environnants compris dans la censive de l'abbaye de Jouarre (Paris, 1896).

Reynolds, Terry S., *Stronger than a Hundred Men: A History of the Vertical Water Wheel* (Baltimore, 1983).

Richet, Denis, 'Croissance et blocages en France du XVe au XVIIIe siècle', *Annales: ESC* 23 (1968), 759–87.

'Aspects socio-culturels des conflits religieux à Paris dans la seconde moitié du XVIe siècle', *Annales: ESC* 32 (1977), 764–89.

Rivals, Claude, *Le moulin à vent et le meunier dans la société traditionelle française* (Paris, 1987).

Roche, Daniel, *The People of Paris: An Essay in Popular Culture in the 18th Century*, tr. Marie Evans and Gwynne Lewis (Berkeley, 1987).

Roseberry, William, *Anthropologies and Histories: Essays in Culture, History and Political Economy* (New Brunswick and London, 1989).

Ross, George, 'Intellectuals against the Left: The Case of France', *Socialist Register*, 1990, pp. 201–29.

Rossi, Paolo, *Philosophy, Technology and the Arts in the Early Modern Era* (New York, 1970).

Rostaing, Léon, *La famille de Montgolfier, ses alliances, ses descendants* (Lyons, 1933).

Sanabria, Sergio Luis, 'From Gothic to Renaissance Stereotomy: The Design Methods of Philibert de l'Orme and Alonso de Vandelvira', *Technology and Culture* 30 (1989), 266–99.

Sébillot, Paul, *Les travaux publics et les mines dans les traditions et les superstitions de tous les pays* (Paris, 1894).

Le folk-lore de la France, 4 vols. (Paris, 1907, 1968).

Bibliography

Ségal, Alain, 'L'instrumentation chirurgicale à l'époque d'Ambroise Paré', *Histoire des sciences médicales* 25 (1991), 109–26.

Sewell, William H., *Work and Revolution in France: The Language of Labour from the Old Regime to 1848* (Cambridge, 1980).

Sharrat, Peter, 'Peter Ramus and the Reform of the University: The Divorce of Philosophy and Eloquence' in *French Renaissance Studies: 1540–70, Humanism and the Encyclopedia*, ed. Sharrat (Edinburgh, 1976), pp. 4–20.

Shuster, John A., 'The Scientific Revolution' in *Companion to the History of Modern Science*, ed. R.C. Olby *et al.* (London, 1990), pp. 217–22.

Simon, Julian L., 'Demographic Causes and Consequences of the Industrial Revolution' in *Population and Development in Poor Countries*, ed. Simon (Princeton, 1992), pp. 24–40.

Skalnik, James Veazie, 'Ramus and Reform: The End of the Renaissance and the Origin of the Old Regime in France' (University of Virginia, Ph.D. Thesis, 1990).

Sol, Eugène, 'La propriété en Quercy avant le XVIIe siècle', *Revue d'histoire économique et sociale* 23 (1936–7), 873–81.

Soman, Alfred, 'Le procès de sorcellerie au Parlement de Paris (1565–1640)' in *Sorcellerie et justice criminelle: le Parlement de Paris (16e–18e siècles)* (London, 1992), pp. 790–814.

'The Parlement of Paris and the Great Witch Hunt' in ibid., pp. 31–44.

Spooner, Frank, *The International Economy and Monetary Movements in France, 1493–1725* (Cambridge, Mass., 1972).

Steinfeld, Robert J., *The Invention of Free Labor: The Employment Relation in English and American Law and Culture, 1350–1870* (Chapel Hill, 1991).

Tanguy, Jean, *Le commerce du port de Nantes au milieu du XVIe siècle* (Paris, 1956).

Tarde, Gabriel, 'Observations au sujet des astres de Bourbon du Chanoine Tarde', *Bulletin de la société d'histoire et d'archéologie du Périgord* 4 (1877), 169–73.

Taussig, Michael T., *The Devil and Commodity Fetishism in South America* (Chapel Hill, 1980).

Teisseyre, Line, 'L'industrie lainière à Nîmes au XVIIe siècle: crise conjoncturelle ou crise structurelle?' *Annales du Midi* 88 (1976), 383–400.

Thirsk, Joan, 'The Fantastical Folly of Fashion: The English Stocking Knitting Industry, 1500–1700' in *Textile History and Economic History*, ed. N.B. Harte and K.G. Ponting (Manchester, 1973), pp. 50–73.

Economic Policy and Projects: The Development of a Consumer Society in Early Modern England (Oxford, 1978).

Thomson, J.K.J., *Clermont-de-Lodève, 1633–1789: Fluctuations in the Prosperity of a Languedocian Cloth-Making Town* (Cambridge, New York, 1982).

'Variations in Industrial Structure in Pre-Industrial Languedoc' in *Manufacture in Town and Country before the Factory*, ed. Maxine Berg, Pat Hudson and Michael Sonenscher (Cambridge, 1983), pp. 61–91.

Thomson, Ross, 'Primitive Capitalist Accumulation,' *The New Palgrave: A Dictionary of Economics*, ed. John Eatwell, Murray Milgate and Peter Newman (London, 1987), III, 963–6.

Thullier, Guy, 'Forges et fourneaux en Nivernais vers 1600', *Bulletin philologique et historique (jusqu'à 1715) du comité des travaux historiques* (1957), 463–70.

Bibliography

Georges Dufaud et les débuts du grand capitalisme dans la métallurgie en Nivernais du XIXe siècle (Paris, 1959).

Tilly, Charles, 'How One Kind of Struggle–War–Reshaped All Other Kinds of Struggle in Seventeenth Century France', Ann Arbor, CRSO Working Paper no. 241 (1981).

'Demographic Origins of the European Proletariat' in *Proletarianization and Family History*, ed. David Levine (Orlando, Fla., 1984), pp. 1–85.

Trénard, Louis, 'Le charbon avant l'ère industrielle' in *Charbon et sciences humaines: actes du colloque organisé par la faculté des lettres de l'université de Lille en mai 1963*, ed. Trénard (Paris, 1963), pp. 53–101.

Trocmé, Etienne and Delafosse, Marcel, *Le commerce rochelais de la fin du XVe siècle au debut du XVIIe* (Paris, 1952).

Truant, Cynthia, 'The Guildswomen of Paris: Gender, Power and Sociability in the Old Regime', *Proceedings of the Annual Meeting of the Western Society for French History* 15 (1988), 130–38.

Tuetey, Alexandre, *Inventaire analytique des livres de couleurs et bannières du Châtelet de Paris*, 2 vols. (Paris, 1899).

Tulippe, Omer, *L'habitat rurale dans l'ouest du département de Oise: essai de géographie du peuplement* (Liège, 1934).

Turgeon, L., 'Les idées économiques de Sully,' *Revue d'histoire économique et sociale* 11 (1923), 249–69.

Ultee, J. Martin, 'The Suppression of Fetes in France (1666)', *Catholic Historical Review* 52 (1976), 181–99.

Usher, Abbot Payson, *The History of the Grain Trade in France 1400–1710* (Cambridge, Mass., 1913; New York, 1973).

A History of Mechanical Inventions, rev. edn (Cambridge, Mass., 1954).

Vardi, Liana, 'Construing the Harvest: Gleaners, Farmers and Officials in Early Modern France', *American Historical Review* 98 (1993), 1424–47.

Vaschalde, Henry, *Olivier de Serres, seigneur de Pradel, sa vie et ses travaux, documents inédits* (Paris, 1886).

Viazzo, Pior Paolo, *Upland Communities: Environment, Population and Social Structure in the Alps since the Sixteenth Century* (Cambridge, 1989).

Vidalenc, Jean, *La petite métallurgie rurale en Haut-Normandie sous l'ancien régime* (Paris, 1946).

Walker, Donald P., *Unclean Spirits: Possession and Exorcism in France and England in the Late Sixteenth and Early Seventeenth Centuries* (Philadelphia, 1981).

Wallerstein, Immanuel, 'Beyond Annales', *Radical History Review* 49 (1991), 7–15.

'Braudel on Capitalism or Everything Upside Down,' *Journal of Modern History* 63 (1991), 354–61.

Walton, Craig, 'Ramus and Bacon on Method', *Journal of the History of Philosophy* 9 (1971), 289–302.

Warner, Marina, *Joan of Arc: The Image of Female Heroism* (London, 1981).

Weber, Henri, 'L'exorcisme à la fin du XVIe siècle, instrument de la contre-Réforme et spectacle baroque', *Nouvelle revue du XVIe siècle* 1(1983), 79–101.

Webster, Charles, *The Great Instauration: Science, Medicine and Reform: 1626–1640* (London, 1975).

Bibliography

From Paracelsus to Newton: Magic and the Making of Modern Science (Cambridge, 1982).

Whyte, Lynn, Jr., 'Technology, Western' in *Dictionary of the Middle Ages*, ed. Joseph R. Strayer (New York, 1988), XI, 654.

Wilson, D.B., 'The Discovery of Nature in the Work of Jacques Peletier du Mans', *BHR* 16 (1954), 298–311.

Wolf, Eric and Cole, John W., *The Hidden Frontier: Ecology and Ethnicity in an Alpine Valley* (New York, 1974).

Wrightson, Keith, 'Alehouses, Order and Reformation in Rural England, 1590–1660' in *Popular Culture and Class Conflict 1590–1914: Explorations in the History of Labour and Leisure*, ed. Eileen and Stephen Yeo (Sussex, 1981), pp. 1–27.

Wroth, Warwick, 'Nicholas Briot', *DNB* II, 1259–60.

Zeller, Gaston, 'Aux origines de notre système douanier' in *Aspects de la politique française sous l'ancien régime* (Paris, 1964), pp. 245–318.

'L'industrie en France avant Colbert' in ibid., pp. 319–35.

Index

Index

CAMBRIDGE STUDIES IN EARLY MODERN HISTORY

256

Chapter Head